Justi, Ferdinand; Stevenson, Sara Yorke; Jastrow, Morris

Egypt and Western Asia in Antiquity

A History of all Nations

Justi, Ferdinand; Stevenson, Sara Yorke; Jastrow, Morris

Egypt and Western Asia in Antiquity

A History of all Nations

Inktank publishing, 2018

www.inktank-publishing.com

ISBN/EAN: 9783747748077

EGYPT AND WESTERN ASIA IN ANTIQUITY

BY

FERDINAND JUSTI, PH. D.
PROFESSOR OF COMPARATIVE PHILOLOGY IN THE UNIVERSITY OF MARBURG,
AUTHOR OF A "HISTORY OF ANCIENT PERSIA," "HISTORY OF IRAN," ETC.

SARA YORKE STEVENSON, SC. D.
PRESIDENT OF THE DEPARTMENT OF ARCHÆOLOGY OF THE UNIVERSITY OF PENNSYLVANIA, CURATOR OF THE EGYPTIAN AND MEDITERRANEAN SECTION OF THE MUSEUM OF SCIENCE AND ART, UNIVERSITY OF PENNSYLVANIA

AND

MORRIS JASTROW, JR., PH. D. (LEIPZIG)
PROFESSOR OF SEMITIC LANGUAGES IN THE UNIVERSITY OF PENNSYLVANIA

IN PART TRANSLATED UNDER THE SUPERVISION OF

JOHN HENRY WRIGHT, LL. D.
PROFESSOR OF GREEK IN HARVARD UNIVERSITY AND DEAN OF THE GRADUATE SCHOOL, EDITOR-IN-CHIEF OF THE "AMERICAN JOURNAL OF ARCHÆOLOGY, SECOND SERIES"

VOLUME I

OF

A HISTORY OF ALL NATIONS

LEA BROTHERS & COMPANY
PHILADELPHIA AND NEW YORK

GENERAL PREFACE.

IN the wonderful intellectual movement of the past half-century historical science has shared in the advance made by all departments of human knowledge. New sources of information have been opened in every part of the world, which have thrown fresh light on the development of the race in all ages, from the prehistoric period down to the present day. Excavations of buried cities have revealed ancient and forgotten civilizations; the study of the languages of the East has given us a fairly accurate knowledge of the empires and religions of Asia; the enormous accumulation of inscriptions and the discovery of manuscripts have furnished new insight into the history and institutions of Greece and Rome; the wealth of documentary material respecting the Middle Ages has enabled students to reconstruct the political and social history of the European commonwealths; while for modern times the throwing open of the archives of nearly all nations has laid bare the secret springs of action which have influenced the present and will mould the future. Everywhere there has been untiring zeal of investigation, which has accumulated an enormous mass of materials unknown to the past generation. These have been analyzed and the results co-ordinated in thousands of monographs.

This accumulation has led to a complete change in the manner of treatment. History is no longer a merely superficial account of events which are conspicuous on the surface,—battles and sieges and dynastic changes. It seeks to trace the causes of events; it concerns itself not only with political but also with social phenomena; it reconstructs society, and explains the development of civilization as this follows the changing fortunes of nations. It is no longer a more or less illusory romance, but a science which deals with the highest interests of mankind, and teaches wisdom from the lessons of the past.

Such being the modern aims of history, and such the vast mass of materials from which it is constructed, it follows self-evidently that no single mind can grasp it in its entirety. Like all other sciences, it has become specialized, and only specialists are competent to treat of its various sections. To write a general history of mankind, therefore, requires the collaboration of scholars, each of whom has made a particular era the subject of his life-work. But not only has history become specialized: with the widening of knowledge its broader relations and aspects have become more clearly discerned, and in particular the interaction of diverse nations, with their dissimilar civilizations, is understood as never before. In place of the earlier special and detailed histories of individual nations, each necessarily recounted with slight reference to the others, there is now for the first time rendered possible a general and comprehensive history of all nations, in which the progress of human civilization is treated period by period, more like one mighty river than as a multitude of separate streams. Such a history is far more significant and instructive than the works of the earlier type could ever be. These are the conceptions that inspired the preparation of the *Allgemeine Weltgeschichte*, of which the first nineteen volumes of the present work are a carefully edited translation, slightly condensed, with additions. The remote antiquity of Egypt and the East has been entrusted to the well-known Orientalist, Professor Ferdinand Justi of Marburg; Greece and Rome to the eminent historian of classical antiquity, Professor G. F. Hertzberg of Halle; the early Middle Ages to Dr. Julius von Pflugk-Harttung of Berlin, and the later mediaeval period to Professor Hans Prutz of Königsberg, both of whom are recognized as leading authorities in these fields; the period between the Reformation and the French Revolution to Professor Martin Philippson, now of Berlin, whose published works have manifested an absolute command of his materials and practised skill in their use; while Professor Theodor Flathe of St. Afra, in Meissen, has contributed the history of the agitated period which stretches from the French Revolution to the close of the Franco-Prussian War (1871). Thus the history of the Old World as here presented is a concentration within moderate space of the best German learning and research on the subject.

Yet, in view of the daily additions to our knowledge of the past, it has been felt that, to render the work fully representative of the existing state of historical research, some additions to the original were requisite. For the somewhat scattered references to Biblical history and literature by Professor Justi, it has been thought desirable to substitute a more complete and connected account, which has been supplied by the well-known specialist in Hebrew, the Rev. Dr. P. H. Steenstra, Professor in the Episcopal Theological School of Cambridge; this account appears in the second volume, in which also will be found an account of the most recent developments concerning the ancient civilizations of Babylonia and Assyria, and their connection with the history of Israel by Morris Jastrow, Jr., Professor of Semitic languages in the University of Pennsylvania, as well as a review of the Empire of the Persians and India by Dr. A. V. Williams Jackson, Professor of Indo-Iranian languages in Columbia University. Similarly the omission from the original work of an account of China and Japan in antiquity—an antiquity which in these belated nations extends well into the nineteenth century—has been made good by the addition, in the same volume, of three interesting chapters on Chinese and Japanese history, which have been contributed by F. Wells Williams, Professor of Modern Oriental History in Yale University. The recent remarkable discoveries, illustrating the most ancient history of Egypt, have required the rewriting of the section on that country in Volume I., which has been performed by Mrs. Sara Yorke Stevenson, Curator of the Egyptian Section of the Museum of Science and Art of the University of Pennsylvania, and similarly the investigations in Crete and elsewhere which have revolutionized early Greek history have been treated in Volume III. by William Nickerson Bates, Assistant Professor of Greek in the University of Pennsylvania. To the fifth volume has been appended a new chapter on late Roman literature and education by George W. Robinson, A.B., of Cambridge, Massachusetts. Throughout the whole, but more especially in the earlier volumes, the Editor has added paragraphs and notes wherever they seemed to be called for.

To adapt the work more thoroughly to the wants of the American reader the sections concerning the New World have been replaced with three additional volumes, written by the late distinguished Professor John Fiske, of Cambridge, Massachusetts, who has presented in them a brilliant survey of the history of the Two Americas from their discovery up to the time of his death, since when it has been continued by Professor Henry Morse Stephens, of the University of California. A separate volume has also been prepared, which brings the history of the three Continents of the Old World down to the present century, embracing the events which are destined to influence it greatly in the future, in the rise of the Japanese Empire, and the expansion of the white races over the earth. This volume has been contributed by Professor Charles M. Andrews, of Bryn Mawr College, Pennsylvania, and by William E. Lingelbach, Assistant Professor of Modern European History in the University of Pennsylvania, gentlemen whose special qualifications for the task have been amply demonstrated. All this additional matter has, of course, been designated as such, and it is confidently hoped that the combined labor of so many eminent specialists will be found to have brought before the reader the results of the most recent research into the history of mankind in all ages and in all lands.

This general "History of All Nations" consists, accordingly, of twenty-four volumes: five on Antiquity, five on the Middle Ages, ten on the Modern History of the Old World, and three on the Two Americas, with a comprehensive Index volume to the whole.

In the effort to unite completeness with due condensation the aid of illustrations has been lavishly invoked. Maps have been introduced wherever necessary to aid in the comprehension of the text; and sources of all kinds have been freely laid under contribution wherever they can supplement description or convey more definite impressions to the understanding through the eye. In the selection of illustrative material especial care has been exercised to give that which is authentic, whether in the representation of persons and places, of monuments and works of art, of documents and events, or of coins and inscriptions.

To facilitate the use of the History as a work of reference very full analytical Tables of Contents have been furnished for each volume. Chronological Tables seemed to be necessary for the History of Antiquity only, owing to the vastness of the periods of time passed in review in the first five volumes. These Tables have been expanded and otherwise modified in the light of most recent research, and are affixed to the fifth volume. The Editor believes that the devotion of the whole final volume to a General Index of the entire world's history in a single alphabet is not only a fitting conclusion of this monumental series, but also a unique feature which cannot fail to be of practical value to every reader. This index includes not only proper names, but also important topics.

Many American scholars have, as translators, revisers, and makers of indexes, assisted the Editor in the preparation of this History for American and English readers. James Hunter, A.M., of Philadelphia, translated ten volumes wholly or in part; Rev. Joseph H. Myers, D.D., of Washington, two volumes entire and parts of two others; John K. Lord, Ph.D., Professor of Latin in Dartmouth College, translated the two volumes on Ancient Rome, and Charles Forster Smith, Ph.D., Professor of Greek in the University of Wisconsin, translated the volume on Ancient Greece. Louis Pollens, Ph.D., lately Professor of French at Dartmouth College, prepared the translation not only of the volume that treats of the Reformation, but also of a part of the following volume (on the Counter-Reformation). Frank E. Zinkeisen, Ph.D., for a time Professor of History in the University of Illinois, translated the volumes on the Age of Feudalism and Theocracy and the Age of the Renaissance, besides assisting in other ways on other volumes. Herman W. Hayley, Ph.D., formerly Instructor at both Harvard and Wesleyan Universities, was the translator of the volume on the Age of Charlemagne. Professor William Wells Eaton, of Middlebury College, co-operated in the translation of the first volume, and Nathan Haskell Dole, A.B., of Boston, in that of the second volume. The following scholars, who have been or now are teachers of History at Harvard University, assisted the Editor here and there in the revision of the translations and in part in the preparation of the manuscripts for the press: George Bendelari, A.B., Professor Charles Gross, Ph.D., Sidney Bradshaw Fay, Ph.D., Henry E. Scott, A.M., and James Sullivan, Ph.D. Aid in the indexing was rendered by Dr. Fay, Mr. Scott, Maurice W. Mather, Ph.D., and the Rev. Charles F. Robinson. The Editor has read and revised both manuscript and proofs of all the translated volumes, and has prepared the analytical Tables of Contents that accompany these volumes and the volumes on American history. In all parts of his work he has had the able assistance of Mr. George W. Robinson.

The Editor entertains the hope that the result of this united labor, to which some of the foremost historical writers of the Old and New Worlds have contributed, will furnish what has hitherto been lacking in English, a trustworthy account, at once comprehensive and detailed, of the history of mankind from the earliest times to the present day, reflecting the latest investigations and presented in a form to excite the interest of all intelligent readers.

GENERAL CONTENTS.

(For Analytical Contents, see Page 347.)

BOOK I.

EGYPT, FROM THE EARLIEST TIMES TO THE SHEPHERD KINGS (ABOUT 1800 B. C.).

BOOK II.

ASIA: THE BEGINNINGS OF HISTORY IN WESTERN ASIA,—BABYLONIA, SYRIA, AND ASIA MINOR.

BOOK III.

EGYPT AND WESTERN ASIA: THE NEW EMPIRE IN EGYPT AND THE RISE OF ASSYRIA.

CHAPTER VI.

CHAPTER VII.

CHAPTER VIII.

LIST OF ILLUSTRATIONS.

LIST OF PLATES.

BOOK I.

EGYPT.

EGYPT.

FROM THE EARLIEST TIMES TO THE SHEPHERD KINGS (ABOUT 1800 B.C.).

INTRODUCTION.

PREHISTORIC EGYPT.

WITHIN the last few years remarkable discoveries in the valley of the Nile have furnished material for a new chapter of Egyptian history. Not only have the first dynasties of Manetho—of which little was known beyond hypothetical names—taken their places at the head of the monumental record, but beyond them, through the penumbra of proto-historic times, a large amount of material takes us back to the pre-historic period.

The word 'prehistoric' is relative and conveys no definite idea of time. Its value varies according to the development of the country or of the men to whom it is applied. In America, for instance, 'prehistoric' may mean pre-Columbian; in Egypt it must mean at least six thousand years ago.

The above remarks apply with even more force to the word 'stone-age.' In some parts of the world the stone-age has continued to the present time. It has notably survived through countless ages in Egypt, where Mr. Maspero states that he saw a man who still shaved his head with flint blades. When questioned, he said that flint razors were good enough for his fathers, and surely must be good enough for him. The man was eighty years old. He stated that in the days of his youth the custom was still common in Egypt. He therefore covered his sore head with fresh leaves to allay the irritation caused by the operation; but continued the process to the end of his life. Indeed, to this extra-ordinary conservatism among the Egyptians are due many interesting survivals from primitive times which are of great assistance in an attempt at understanding many ideas and customs which have been handed down from generation to generation since the dawn of civilization.

However this may be, and notwithstanding the evidence implied in so tenacious a survival, only a few years ago the existence of a stone-age in the Nile valley was regarded by many as a problematic possibility which could not be dealt with as a fact. The earliest remains found at Gizeh revealed a high civilization already fully developed. A few monuments, because of their archaism, often on their own merits, were assigned to the Second or Third dynasty of Manetho, which seemed hardly less legendary than his Divine Dynasties. History proper opened with the monuments of Medum and of Gizeh—i.e., with the Fourth Dynasty and King Seneferu. The beginnings of the civilization which bequeathed to the world the great pyramids and the granite temple were unknown, and its origins were a mystery.

The use of flint implements throughout the long period of Egyptian history was calculated to cast a doubt upon the age of the specimens offered to the scrutiny of scholars, none of which was found in undisturbed strata of an age determined by the presence of extinct fauna. This uncertainty long seemed to make the hope of reaching any definite conclusion upon the subject a remote one. The general physical conditions of Egypt were such as to preclude any reasonable expectation of finding vestiges of paleolithic man under such convincing geological conditions as have conclusively established his presence in western Europe and in other parts of the quaternary world. Nevertheless, many distinguished scholars—Hamy, Arcelin, Lubbock, Pitt-Rivers, and others too numerous to mention—labored to solve the problem, and accumulated sufficient evidence to warrant a belief in his existence.

Among the most important of the earlier contributions to the subject was that of General Pitt-Rivers, who, in 1881, found worked flints of the paleolithic type imbedded in the indurated stratified gravel between Biban-el-Moluk and Gurnah (Thebes), in which tombs of the Eighteenth Dynasty had been cut. The locality lay along the bed of an ancient stream, which once drained a side valley into the river, forming as it reached it an estuary in the shape of a small delta. The gravel is sixty yards away from the highest mark of the Nile flood; and the tombs are cut quite to the end of the gravel in parts facing the Nile. At the mouth of the Wadi, between it and the line of the inundation, is a cemetery which, of course, must have been buried beneath the gravel had any been deposited since the graves were made.[1] Since then, considerable corroborative evidence has been added, notably by Mr. Petrie; and while it is impossible to tell at what geological period paleolithic man entered the Nile valley, there can be no reasonable doubt of his presence there.

The rocky formation of Egypt for some five hundred miles from the coast is of eocene limestone. It belongs to the same formation as the great masses of tertiary limestone found at Gibraltar, Malta, Southern France, Athens, and Syria. In the neighborhood of Gebel-Silsileh this formation gives place to Nubian sandstone, and at Assuan this is again broken into by the great granite hills and rocks which—before the construction of the dam recently thrown across the river at this point—formed so picturesque a setting to the lovely island and temples of Philae (see p. 34, Fig. 8). Here were the famous quarries whence the materials were obtained by the Pharaohs for the obelisks and noble monoliths which lent such imposing dignity to the art and to the architecture of Thebes, Memphis, and other great Egyptian capitals.

At the close of the eocene period it would seem that the limestone deposit was raised in a wide tableland, over which swept the drainage of northeastern Africa. To the east this was, as it is now, bounded by the high mountains of the eastern desert. Amid the masses of granite and other crystalline rocks, some of which rise to a height of some six thousand feet, were other important quarries, also used in historic times. These mountain ranges barred any outlet to the Red Sea. In the miocene period a further elevation of the eastern desert must have taken place, causing a cleft from the old coast-line to Asiût. The river fell into this break, and it is regarded as probable that the surface basalts of Khankah, north of Cairo, are the result of the water reaching the heated strata below, thus causing a volcanic disturbance, resulting in the hot springs which silicified the sandstone of Gebel-Ahmar, and the trees of the petrified forest near Helawan.

It would also appear that in these ancient days a gulf—the outline of which may roughly be followed eastwardly along the foot of the Libyan hills, the Gebel Mokattam, and the Gebel Geneffe, to the present Suez Canal—stretched from the great inland sea at least as far up as the sandy plateau above which to-day tower the pyramids

[1] Journal of the Anthropological Institute, vol. xi., 'On the Discovery of Chert Implements in Stratified Gravel in the Nile Valley,' p. 389, 1882.

of Gizeh. To the east shallow straits united the Mediterranean with the Red Sea, separating the African continent from Asia.[1] This gulf was gradually filled up by the alluvial deposits, which already at the opening of the historic period formed the wide plains of the delta, until they reached a point where a strong eastward coast-current seized upon them and swept them toward the frontier of Syria.[2]

Since then, many thousand years have elapsed, but the coast-line of the delta has remained practically unchanged. The interior, however, is gradually rising and drying. The latest observations taken show that the coast is by degrees lowering and diminishing near Alexandria, while it is steadily rising in the neighborhood of Port-Said.

Herodotos avers that, according to Egyptian tradition, Mena, the founder of the United Empire, found the lower part of the valley under water; the sea reaching to the Fayum; and that in his day the country north of Thebes was an unhealthful swamp.[3] But while in early historic times the delta must have been more swampy than it is at present—a fact which may account for its later development and for the small part which it appears to have played in earliest history[4]—the general conditions and outline of the country have probably not materially altered in the historic period, and the tradition preserved by the Greek historian could be but an echo of prehistoric memories.

During those remote ages the climate was moist and the rainfall abundant. This is shown by the deep cuts, and by the denudation of the cliffs and the wadis, in the now arid regions beyond the flood-line. The country was wooded and probably resembled the present valley of the Nile in the interior of Africa. Primeval forests covered its banks; luxurious weeds and rushes formed a thick undergrowth over swamps

[1] Aristotle (Meteor. I. xiv.) states that the Red Sea, the Mediterranean, and the space now occupied by the delta, once formed but one sea.

[2] Schweinfurth (Bulletin de l'Institut Égyptien, 1ère Série, xii., p. 206) says: "Il a fallu environ deux cents siècles pour que le sol de l'Égypte ait acquis la puissance que nous constatons aujourd'hui." Others reckon that it took some seventy-five thousand years for the Nile to form its estuary.

[3] Herod. II., iv., v., and xcix.

[4] At the court of the pyramid builders, for instance, the 'great men of the South' hold an important place; but there is no mention of any great men of the North. M. Erman has also pointed out that the South is always mentioned first. The delta is called the 'North Country,' while the South is simply 'the South.' Under the Middle Empire we meet with a 'Governor of the North Country,' and under the Old Empire there was but one province in the delta. (Erman, 'Life in Ancient Egypt,' pp. 80-83.)

inhabited by the crocodile; and the hippopotamus, which has now retreated to southern Nubia, was still hunted by the sportsmen of Memphis as late as the days of Herodotos. The papyrus plant also, now only met with under the ninth parallel, was then still abundant.

The old surfaces of the desert plateau of Upper Egypt have weathered dark brown from long exposure. And so have the flints and waste flakes (rejects) of the paleolithic type found there. Flints which, according to Mr. Petrie, are known to be seven thousand years old, and are found under the same conditions of exposure, have hardly become discolored. This may serve to gauge, in a general way, the antiquity of these vestiges of man.[1]

At that time there was a far higher river-bed than at present. The heavy rainfall found its way to the river by the deep channelled cliffs. The land also was lower and estuaries were formed. This may be gathered from the large rolled gravels associated with mud deposits, such as have been referred to as existing at Thebes, and which are found at fifty feet or more above the present water-level. Water-worn flints of the paleolithic type are found high up on the hills, and in the beds of stream courses that once flowed from the high plateau. From the time when the paleolithic Egyptian chipped his primitive implements on the elevated tableland of the present desert—then possibly a fertile moist region where he could find sustenance and minister to his simple needs—to his next appearance on the misty horizon of prehistoric investigation, an enormous lapse of time must have run its course. Many geologic and climatic changes must have taken place. Who can tell how many different tribes may have wandered into the fertile valley and left their unrecognized impress upon its population? It is probable that, among the innumerable deposits left by the primeval flint-workers, are the unidentifiable remains of intervening ages.[2] Be this as it may, the next glimpse we get of human existence on the banks of the Nile shows us a large population, dwelling in settlements in Upper Egypt, under much the same conditions as prevail at the present day. Their

[1] For the entire subject of geological changes and climatic conditions, compare Flinders-Petrie, 'History of Egypt,' vol. i., ch. i.; Maspero, 'Hist. Anc. des Peup. de l'Orient Classiq.,' vol. i. (Les Origines), ch. i.; Erman, 'Aegypt und Aegypt. Leben,' vol. i., ch. i.; Élie de Beaumont, 'Leçons de Géologie,' vol. i., pp. 405–492; Oscar Fraas, 'Aus dem Orient,' vol. i., pp. 175, 176; Prof. Hull, 'Journal of the Victoria Institute,' 1890.

[2] Maspero suggests ten thousand years as a possible period for the development of Egyptian civilization.

remains have been found in the last seven years by MM. de Morgan, Petrie, Quibell, Reisner, and others, in the course of excavations conducted among the débris of their villages and in many nekropoles stretching over a territory of some one hundred miles or more, on both sides of the river, from Silsileh to Sohag. Their skulls and skeletons have been subjected to accurate measurement, and submitted to competent study at the College of Surgeons at Oxford,[1] and at the Medical School at Cairo, as well as by individual anatomists.[2] But while the field of investigation has been widely extended, the question of ultimate origin remains unsettled. The most recent conclusion based upon the careful expert examination of the material lately collected, is that the men to whom it belonged already were in the main fellahin.[3] There is, however, no doubt that before the dawn of the historic period a dominant Libyan element dwelt in the Nile valley. This is shown by the results of the examination of the remains at Oxford. Moreover, the evidence of the rudely carved figures found in 1887 at Ballas and Nagadah by Mr. Petrie and M. Quibell, as well as that of the interesting heads and fine ivory statuettes of early dynastic times obtained at Hierakonpolis by the latter scholar (see 'Hierakonpolis,' PLATE VI., i.–v.), and especially that of the remarkable portrait of a predynastic king of Upper Egypt, discovered at Abydos in 1902 by Mr. Petrie (Abydos II., p. 38, Fig. 5), requires little comment. All these introduce us to an orthognathous human type whose aquiline nose, dome-shaped skull, and pointed beard show an affinity with the type known and represented by the historic Egyptians themselves as the Tehennu,—i.e., the western people of Libya,[4]—an affinity which is further confirmed by important cultural similarities.[5] We may therefore rea-

[1] The College of Surgeons at Oxford have pronounced the Nagadah men to be allied to the white race which inhabited the Libyan region in earliest times.

[2] Dr. Fouquet, who examined the material discovered by MM. de Morgan and Amélineau, also identified their remains with those of the men of Cro-Magnon (dolichocephalic, with smooth hair, not infrequently light in color, and belonging in their general character to the so-called Caucasian or white race). (Comp. de Morgan, 'Recherches,' etc., vol. ii., p. 50.)

[3] I am indebted to M. Quibell for this information with regard to the result of the study of the material at the Medical School of Cairo.

[4] Petrie, 'The Races of Early Egypt,' Journal of the Anthropological Institute of Great Britain and Ireland, vol. xxxi., p. 248, etc., 1901.

[5] Naville, 'Figurines Égyptiennes de l'Époque Archaique,' Recueil de Travaux Relatifs à la Philologie et à l'Archéologie Égyptiennes et Assyriennes, vol. xxi., p. 212, 1899, and xxii., p. 65, 1900.

sonably conjecture that this so-called Caucasian or, properly speaking, European type, extended along the littoral of the Mediterranean basin, as far east as Syria, where it is said to be represented by the Amorites.

Indeed the early population of northwestern Africa itself was mixed. The geographical isolation which, in the historic period, has tended to produce an amalgamation of the various ethnographic elements into one main type, was possibly much less great in prehistoric times. The Sahara was probably not then the arid region which it has become; and it apparently sustained a considerable population. This may be gathered from the numerous stone implements found over the region, in parts of the desert now quite uninhabitable. In prehistoric days fair-haired men, classified by anthropologists with the widespread race of Cro-Magnon, lived in North Africa, which some authorities are inclined to regard as the home of the race. The megalithic monuments which they built seem older than those of Western Europe. Another light-skinned but dark-haired and short-headed race also lived in North Africa and in the Canary Islands when the fair-haired Europeans came there. Their remains have been compared to those of the pre-Aryan Armenians, and also display similarities with the pre-Aryans of Southern Europe. Like the fair-haired Libyans, they probably sprang from some point in the vicinity of the Mediterranean region. Out of the somewhat complicated evidence one fact stands out clearly: that is, that the destiny of the Northern Africans in the stone-age of their industrial development was quite as closely linked with that of the other inhabitants of the Mediterranean basin as it was in later times. This inference is strengthened by the affinity existing between the Nagadah culture and that of the Mediterranean stations of the late neolithic age. In the early Egyptian sepulchral deposits pottery has been found of a type commonly met with in the transition, or aeneolithic stations of Spain, Bosnia, Istria, Crete, the Aegaean Islands, and other points of the Mediterranean area. On the other hand, it is worthy of remark that a bowl of the black and red polished ware typical of the Egyptian predynastic pottery—now in the museum of the University of Pennsylvania—was found by Dr. M. O. Richter in Cyprus, at the lowest stratum of his copper-bronze age, to which—prior to the discoveries at Nagadah—he independently assigned the approximate date 4000 B.C.[1]

[1] Other similar specimens are said to have been found—notably very recently at Vasiliki, near Gournia (Crete), by the Philadelphia Expedition.

Mr. Petrie, as a result of his most recent researches, feels justified in dividing the newly discovered prehistoric remains into sequences covering in the aggregate a period of two thousand years—beginning with a population wearing goat skins and manufacturing the simplest pottery—and running through the gradual stages of an elaborate and wealthy civilization. This he regards as having reached a decadent stage when it was overthrown and vitalized by the dynastic Egyptians. According to his latest view, four racial types preceded the Libyan in Egypt; and the latter was the dominant race when the power of the dynastic Egyptians asserted itself over the land.

Without going into the interesting problems suggested by the above, or even attempting here to follow Mr. Petrie in his effort to trace the evolution of the primitive men of Nagadah, certain broad outlines of their culture are sufficient for our present purpose.

They skilfully polished their maces and stone vessels, and the regularity with which they flaked their flint blades, and obtained an exquisitely fine serrated edge on their peculiar flint forked lance-heads, was unsurpassed by any known people in the same stage of industry. (See Fig. 2, p. 23.) Their flint bangles, cut out of a single stone and worked down to a circlet one-eighth of an inch in thickness, are marvels of stone-workmanship (ibid.). They buried their dead in square pits dug out of gravel beds, roofed over with beams and brush. The better tombs were faced inside with mud or mud brick-work and matting. The preserved body, often wrapped in a hide or in a mat, lay on its left side. The knees were drawn up, the hands were raised to the head, which was placed to the south, facing the west. Green paint, on a slate palette, was near the head and hands; and this recalls the curious practice of painting a band of green across the face and eyes, which is observed on the statues of the early historic period.[1] They surrounded their dead with food and other necessities of their simple life, which they evidently believed was to continue in the grave; and a mass of fine hand-made pottery of various sizes and forms surrounded the body. (See Fig. 1.) Pear-shaped maces, sharp-edged disks, flint forked lances, and knives were their principal weapons. Bone spoons and ornamented

[1] The tradition attached to the painting of the eyes survived throughout Egyptian history. 'Uatit' or the 'green painted eye' was the 'good' eye, the 'well' eye, a belief which gave rise to the superstitious reverence for the amulet, the 'sacred eye'; the process of painting the eyes with 'mesd'emt' being regarded as a cure for ophthalmia.

hair-combs are found. Exquisitely made vessels of granite, basalt, porphyry, as well as the softer alabaster, were skilfully polished with emery, blocks of which attest the fact. Carnelian and blue-glazed quartz-rock beads and shells were among their ornaments. Mud brick was used; and bucrania—i.e., the skulls of horned animals—probably furnished decoration for their buildings. At least, an ivory tusk of the early historic period, found by M. Quibell at Hierakonpolis, gives the façade of a low building over the four doors of which hang bucrania; and horned skulls, evidently prepared for the purpose of hanging to a wall, have been found in later Libyan deposits. (Fig. 2.) From this style of decoration evidently originated the Hathor heads which formed so conspicuous and odd an architectural feature of many of the later temples, and which already appear on the palettes of King Narmer, whose archaic remains Mr. Petrie regards as pre-Menite. (PLATE V. *b*.)

The Nagadah culture seems to put us in the presence of a very archaic stage of Egyptian life and faith—humble, yet developing along the lines of the later peculiar culture so familiar to us. On some of the pottery found by Mr. Petrie in the prehistoric and early dynastic interments, as well as through the entire course of Egyptian history, are written characters or marks which have excited considerable interest. According to Mr. Petrie and Arthur J. Evans, many of these marks are identical with others found at various points of the Mediterranean region, from the Spanish peninsula to Crete and to Asia Minor.[1] The conclusion is drawn by these eminent scholars that from a very remote time a signary was in use among those widely separated peoples. But the whole subject is new and requires careful study.

Were these prehistoric Egyptians immigrants in the Nile valley? If so, who preceded them, and whence did they come? Did they develop their own culture, gradually forming the petty states of Upper Egypt which eventually overcame the region of the delta and became united into one empire? Or were they the victims of a conquest or of conquests from the east? Confident answers have been given to all these questions by more or less ingenious scholars; but they nevertheless must for the time remain matters of speculation. The discovery

[1] For a comparative study of the characters of the signaries found in Egypt, Karia, Spain, Crete, Cyprus, see Petrie, 'Royal Tombs,' i., p. 32; also Arthur J. Evans's 'Cretan Pictographs and Pre-Phœnician Script,' Tables I. and III.

of dwarfs among them has led to the suggestion that pigmies once occupied the lower Nile valley; and steatopygous statuettes found with their remains, taken in connection with the measurements of certain skulls which approach the Hottentot type, have also given rise to speculation with regard to a possible connection with those now distant African tribes.

Many scholars have looked to Asia for the source of Egyptian culture, if not for that of Egyptian origin.[1] Some of them have brought the Egyptians over the Isthmus;[2] others, by the more circuitous route of the straits of Bab-el-Mandeb.[3] But so long as similar material, in as complete a sequence and revealing identity of culture at the same time or earlier, is not found in Asia, it must seem fruitless, interesting as the subject may be, to step from the domain of fact to that of simple hypothesis. Unlike most nations, the Egyptians themselves preserved no traditional recollection of a migration, of a foreign conquest, or even of the advent of a culture hero. There is nothing in their annals, their legends, or their religious myths to indicate such events. Their legendary wars were, as it were, local wars, in the course of which brother was arrayed against brother; the North against the South; Osiris and Horos against Set. Their hieroglyphs—as far as their exact nature can be ascertained—all reproduce the fauna, the flora, and other objects falling under the observation and the experience of the dwellers in the Nile valley. The importation of a foreign animal or object from time to time may be approximately dated by its use among the hieroglyphs. The ideogram for 'land' was a flat plain; while the sign for 'foreign land' was a mountain chain. Their beliefs regarding life after death, and their consequent burial customs, link them with the men of the dolmens rather than with those of Babylonia, where the ancient structures are temples and palaces, not tombs; and where the latter play no conspicuous part. So far, no fact that cannot otherwise be

[1] De Rougé, Brugsch, Ebers, Lauth, Lieblein, and others, seek the cradle of the Egyptians in Asia. Hommel goes to the extreme of deriving their entire culture from that of the Babylonians. (See 'Geschichte Babyloniens und Assyriens,' p. 12, etc.; and especially 'Der Babyl. Ursprung der Eg. Kultur,' 1892, where he seeks to show that the Heliopolitan myths and the Egyptian religion are derived from those of Eridu.)

[2] De Rougé, 'Recherches,' etc.; Brugsch, 'Geschichte Egyptens,' p. 8; Wiedemann, 'Aeg. Geschichte,' p. 21.

[3] Ebers, 'Aeg. und die Bücher Moses,' p. 48; Dümichen, 'Geschichte des alten Aegyptens,' pp. 118, 119; Brugsch, 'Aeg. Beiträge zur Volkerkunde der altesten Welt,' Deutsche Revue, 1881, p. 48.

explained has been brought forward to show that Egyptian civilization was derived from Asia; and important cultural differences exist between the two oldest civilized nations of the ancient world, which are best accounted for by the theory of an independent development.

At least such seems to be the view held by the two highest authorities in France and Germany, whose general scholarship, as well as long-established reputation as Egyptologists, makes their opinion of singular value. M. Maspero, in his monumental work,[1] says that if one examines closely into the matter the theory of an Asiatic origin, although attractive, is difficult to maintain. The mass of the Egyptian population presents the characteristics of the peoples which at all times have settled in the Libyan continent bordering on the Mediterranean. They belong to North Africa, and came into Egypt from the west. Such is also the view of the naturalists and of the ethnologists. On the other hand, many of the word-roots of the Egyptian language seem to belong to the Semitic group. Personal pronouns are constructed with suffixes; and the most simple and archaic tense of the conjugation is formed with an affix; indeed it may be said that most of the grammatical processes of the Semitic languages are found in a rudimentary form in Egyptian. One might conclude therefrom that the Egyptians and the Semites, after having belonged to one group, had early separated at a time preceding that when their language became fixed, and that under different surroundings the two families had independently developed what they possessed in common. The Egyptian first cultivated, became first crystallized, the Semitic languages continued to develop.

This view seems to be shared by Dr. Erman,[2] who, moreover, suggests, as an hypothesis in accordance with all the facts brought to bear upon the question by ethnologists as well as by philologists, that a Libyan invasion of the Nile valley gave its inhabitants its language; that a similar invasion of Syria and Arabia produced the Semitic language; and that the latter regions later gave the same to East Africa. He concludes, however, that these movements took place at so remote a period "that we may conscientiously believe the Egyptians to be natives

[1] Maspero, 'Histoire ancienne des Peuples de l'Orient classique,' i., pp. 45, 46.

[2] Erman, 'Aegyptens und Aeg. Leben,' 54, 55. Also compare Erman, 'Verhältniss des Aegyptischen zu den Semitischen Sprachen,' in the Zeitschrift der Morgenlandischen Gesellschaft, xlvi., 85–129.

of their own country, children of their own soil, even if it should be proved that their old language, like their modern one, was imported from other countries."

M. Naville,[1] in a study of certain important cultural relations existing between the Libyan populations and the Egyptians, as revealed in the earliest known monuments, regards the North African character of the Egyptian civilization as 'established.' And after going over the question of the Semitic linguistic elements present in the Egyptian tongue, he says: "No doubt there are in Egyptian Semitic elements; but there are also other elements; and the more we penetrate into those distant ages—of which we are beginning to perceive the length and the remoteness—the fainter become the traces of the Semites, and of their influence upon the culture and the language of Egypt."

That a mixture of races already existed at an early date is abundantly proved. But in all ages Egypt has revenged itself upon intruders and foreign invaders by absorbing them; and it would seem as though this capacity for assimilation had existed from the earliest time to which we have access. The vicissitudes of the prehistoric Egyptians were numerous and varied. This is revealed in the art of the Thinite kings at the very dawn of history. At Hierakonpolis, at Abydos, and other sites; on the palettes of King Narmer, on the archaic fragments in the Louvre and in the British Museum—such as those published by Steindorff—as well as among the recent 'finds' at Abydos, are representations which show at least two or perhaps more human types, other than the Libyan to which we have already referred.[2] They appear as warriors, some as conquering, some as conquered foes. One brandishes a double battle-axe. And whatever their history, whether they came

[1] Naville, 'Figurines de l'Époque Archaique.' 'Recueil de Travaux,' etc., 1900, p. 78, Pl. I.–III. M. Naville regards the population as indigenous in Africa, with a conquering element, such as the Turks appear to be among the Arabs, or as the Normans are among the British. The indigenous inhabitants are the 'Anuu'—the bearded archers of the slates. The conquerors, according to his view, came from Bab-el-Mandeb and Punt, and spoke a Semitic language, although they may not have been Semites. ('Recueil,' etc., vol. xxiv., p. 120.) M. Petrie also brings the dynastic Egyptians into Egypt over the straits of Bab-el-Mandeb.

[2] Mr. Petrie thinks that he can detect seven. But, as he himself remarks ('Races of Early Egypt,' in Journal of the Anthropological Institute, vol. xxxi., 1901, p. 250), some of them may well be the result of a mixture of the main types. In a lecture recently delivered in London he claims that five types of men preceded the dynasties, the fifth of which is the Libyan.

from the Mediterranean, the Red Sea, or the Libyan desert, each probably contributed something to the population or to the culture of the petty states which composed the United Empire of King Mena.

It may be gathered from the above that the glimpse now obtained of the inhabitants of the Nile valley at this remote period, if fragmentary and incomplete, is fairly clear. We see them living in a transition stage of culture, acquainted with copper, but commonly using stone tools; navigating in their long river boats, and more or less in touch with contemporary peoples in the same stage of industry. As far back as modern research can reach, Egypt is already playing its part among nations in conformity with its general surroundings, and working out its destiny under conditions most favorable to the development of civilization.

This civilization had already acquired most of its distinctive features, and was far away from its early beginnings, when the historic period opens under King Mena. In the last few years the once legendary founder of the Egyptian United Empire, whose greater exploits had been handed down by tradition through the Greek historians, has passed from the realm of myth to that of practical fact. In 1896, M. de Morgan, then Director of the Service of Antiquities under the Egyptian government—and to whom belongs the credit of having been the first to recognize the true nature of the Nagadah material—made the discovery, in that locality, of a large panelled brick tomb (190 × 50 cubits) of very archaic character. In this tomb, among other sepulchral deposits, was found an ivory tablet bearing the standard name 'Aha,' and also another name which he originally read Hesepti (see p. 18), and therefore attributed to the fifth king of the First Dynasty; but which, subsequently, Dr. Borchardt identified with that of Mena. While the reading of the name, and its consequent identification, at first led to considerable discussion, and were resisted by some scholars, subsequent researches based upon additional material discovered at Abydos greatly strengthened its probability, and the identification is generally accepted. A doubt, however, now exists as to the ownership of the tomb itself. Another archaic tomb, forming one of the group of royal tombs of the first dynasty found at Abydos, and surrounded by thirty-four minor burials of contemporary retainers, in which were found many objects bearing King Aha's name, was opened in 1902 by Mr. Petrie. The presumption is, therefore, that the latter is the Thinite founder's tomb; and that the isolated royal monument in the nekropolis of Nagadah may be that of some other personage connected with him—perhaps that of his queen, Neit-Hotep, whose name is inscribed, not only upon several ivory labels found in it, but also on objects found at Abydos. However this may be, the abundant material contemporary with Mena and his early successors shows us at the opening of history an advanced civilization. In addition to the fine stonework of preceding generations—the progress of which is here represented by superb vases of every obtainable kind of hard stone—other arts and industries had been developed. Numerous ivory and ebony inlays tell of artistic furniture. Copper and gold were used,[1] and the hieroglyphic system of writing had been evolved, and appears in short sentences and in archaic forms.

From 1896 to 1899 the nekropolis of Abydos was excavated by M. Amélineau; and the scientific significance of the site burst upon the learned world with dramatic effect, when among the many inscribed fragments brought to Paris by the fortunate explorer after his two first campaigns, Dr. Erman and Dr. Sethe recognized the names of some of the kings of the first dynasty of Manetho.

In 1899 M. Amélineau retired, looking upon the nekropolis of Abydos as exhausted (complètement épuisée). Mr. Petrie then obtained from the authorities the right to excavate there. This experienced field archeologist, working from 1899 to 1902, was able to bring to light a large amount of inscribed material, from which the attempt may be made partly to reconstruct the two first dynasties of Manetho. Among the royal names found, there are some the archaism of whose surroundings have led Mr. Petrie to regard as representing the Thinite dynasty of ten kings, who, according to the Ptolemaic historian, were the immediate predecessors of Menes. The practice of the Egyptian kings of adopting a standard, or Horos name, upon their accession to the throne, in addition to their personal and other titular names, makes the identification of monumental names with those of the later official

[1] Analysis by Dr. Gladstone, F.R.S., shows practically pure copper, with 1 per cent. of manganese, and no tin. The gold is under King Zer (Mena's successor), 79.7 to 13.4 of silver; under King Merseklm = 84.82 to 13.5 of silver; under King Qa (the seventh king of the First Dynasty), 84 to 12.95, with no iron or copper.

lists of extreme difficulty; save in such cases as, for instance, when both names are found on the same object. It may well be that Mr. Petrie's preliminary study may have to be revised as additional material bearing upon the question comes to light; meanwhile his identifications may be regarded as practically established for the First Dynasty.

Pre-Menite Kings. Ka, Zeser, Narmer, Sma.

First Dynasty.

Manetho.	Seti's List.	Tombs.
1. Menes.	Mena.	Aha-Men.
2. Athothis.	Teta.	Zer-Ta.
3. Kenkenes.	Ateth.	Zet-Ath.
4. Uenephes.	Ata.	Den-Merneit.
5. Usafais.	Hesepti.	Den-Setui.
6. Miebis.	Merbap.	Azab-Merpaba.
7. Semempses.	Semenptah.	Mersekha-Shemsu.
8. Bienekhes.	Qebh.	Ka-Sen.

Second Dynasty.

1. Bokhos.	Bazau.	Hotep-Ahaui.
2. Kaiekhos.	Kakau.	Raneb.
3. Binothris.	Beneteren.	Neheren.
4. Tlas.	Uaznes.	Sekhemab-Perabsen.
5. Sethenes.	Senda.	Kha-Sekhem.
5. Khaires.	. .	Ka-Ra.
7. Neferkheres.	Zaza.	Kha-Sekhemui.

It is deeply to be regretted that these important tombs should have been often and ruthlessly ransacked in ancient, and especially in modern times. Only the refuse of this rich mine of precious information remained to be collected. But even that refuse has furnished data for the study of the earliest organized community of which we possess any knowledge, and has set back the beginnings of authentic history some five hundred years. Moreover, the connection between the close of the prehistoric period and the rise of the dynastic power is established through the means of the pottery; and its history may be followed in the stratified ruins of the old town of Abydos. The prehistoric is thus linked with reigns of the historic kings. On the other hand, through the temple offerings, among which are some admirable ivory carvings, the development of art can be traced. In Mr. Petrie's opinion there is a difference between the art of the dynastic and that of the prehistoric peoples, and he argues that the former were a conquering race, whom he credits with the hieroglyphic system of writing. These, according to his view, were endowed with an artistic sense, while the prehistoric people were a mechanical race, from whose culture the conquerors adopted some of the elements which became united with their own. However this may be, the early historic material consists of stone fragments—of stelae and of vases—of jar sealings, inscribed with royal names, of ivory, bone, and ebony tablets and labels giving in brief inscriptions some all too scanty information concerning these monarchs; stone and alabaster vases—some of which are of huge proportions—bearing royal names and titles; others small, of rock crystal, or of polished marble capped with gold and fastened with a twisted gold wire the delicacy of which could not be surpassed to-day; games, ornaments, feet of furniture admirably carved in the shape of those of hoofed animals; fluted columns of ivory or of ebony, which once formed parts of elegant caskets or of other articles of furniture; the great stelae of the kings, and the humble limestone epitaphs of their servants—all these relics of the highest civilization reached by man six or seven thousand years ago, teem with historic suggestion; but they are surpassed in human interest by the crowning discovery, in 1902, of the mummied arm of the queen of King Zer—the Teta of the official lists, and the immediate successor of Mena. This arm had been torn off from the body of the queen by early grave robbers, and had been concealed in a hole in the wall of the tomb. The object of this desecration of the queen's mummy became manifest as soon as the prize was examined. On the arm were three bracelets of gold and precious stones—turquoise, amethyst, and lapis-lazuli. These are now in the museum at Cairo. (See PLATE V.)

The most important result of the discoveries of the last few years is the tying together of many hitherto loose and disconnected threads in Egyptian culture. The day is forever past when serious scholars could exclaim, with more eloquence than accuracy, that Egyptian civilization, "like Pallas-Athênê, had burst upon the world armed cap à pie at the foot of the pyramids." From the prehistoric interments of Nagadah to the reign of Aha-Mena; from the latter to the pyramids of Gizeh, a natural sequence may be traced through the upward stages of a laborious evolution. Even in the prehistoric age the original pit dug out of the ground had been improved into a large sepulchral chamber, lined with mats, roofed with timber and brush wood, and fitted with vases and other furniture. The early dynastic tombs were much the same, only they were lined and floored with timber. The offerings at first were dropped between the timber lining and the side of the pit. Later regular cells were built for the offerings; and, lastly, an elaborate series of store-rooms was added. The tomb originally had an entrance. Later a sloping hole led to it; in time a stairway was made; and at last a long passage appears, such as is seen in the pyramids. A similar evolution can be traced in the outer form of the tomb. At first the sand was heaped over the pit or the chamber in a slightly raised mound. Next, this heap was walled in for the purpose of keeping in the sand. Then the wall was gradually raised and became a brick block (mastaba). At last this expanded and rose upward in a mass of concentric coatings, which eventually reached the pyramidal shape, as at Medum, and culminated in the pyramids of Gizeh. The wood and mud-brick styles of architecture furnish a clue to the peculiar technique of the later stone work. The hard stone beads of the Nagadah stone-workers, lead to the rich though bead-like jewelry of Teta's queen, which precedes the elaborate goldsmithery of Dashur; while their blue-glazed quartz beads prepare us for the glazed vases of King Mena and the large tiles which were used for wall decoration under the first dynasties, as well as for the fine and varied glazes of later times. The concisely inscribed tablets and labelled offerings of Mena's age foreshadow the gradually increasing use of writing, which grows on the walls of the mastabas of Medum and of Gizeh, until under the sixth dynasty the walls of the entire sepulchral chamber in the royal pyramids of Sakkara are covered with long religious texts. Under Mena we already see the king's earliest emblem, the mighty bull, as he charges into nets, with a freedom which recalls the art of the pre-hellenic Aegaean world. Neit, the Libyan goddess, is a prominent object of worship among the first dynastic kings; and Up-Uatu—a form of the jackal-headed god Anubis, the guardian of the nekropolis and the 'opener of the ways' (to the other world)—after Horos, is the special protector of the king. On the tablet of Mena, in the Museum of the University of Pennsylvania, the monarch is termed: 'The Horos Aha, born of Up-Uatu,' and he is represented worshipping at the shrine of Neit. (See Fig. 5.) From first to last the early Egyptians seem to have steadily pursued a consistent course of development; and we may well hold, with MM. Erman and Maspero, that wheresoever may have been the primeval home of their ancestors, and whatever contingent the original North-Africans may have received at various times from Asia, whenever these settled in the Nile valley, the country conquered and assimilated them; and when the monumental record opens, the stamp of Egypt's peculiar civilization is already set upon the Egyptian people.

S. Y. S.

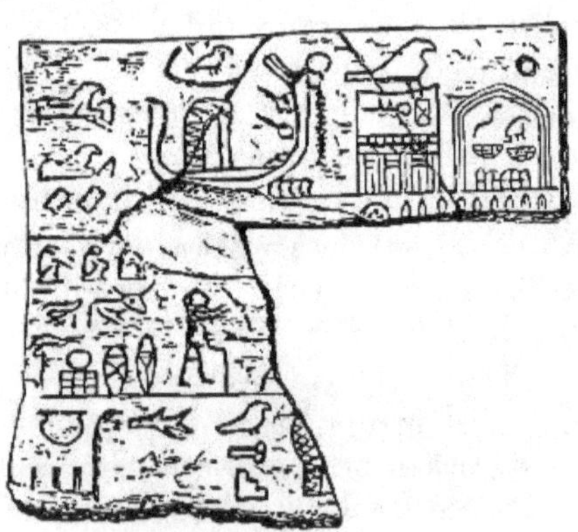

Ivory Tablet of Aha-Mena. (From de Morgan 'Recherches,' etc.—Le grand tombeau de Nagadah.)

CHAPTER I.

EARLIEST EGYPTIAN HISTORY.

THE historical development of Africa has been controlled by its physical geography. In the infancy of navigation the greater part of the continent was cut off from intercourse with the outer world by the ocean and by virtually impassable deserts. That portion of its vast area was therefore limited to such civilization as could be originated among its own populations, and was deprived of the intercourse with other races which stimulates internal development. The indigenous Africans are doubtless capable of organizing great political communities: yet history can afford to be content with the barest allusion, for example, to the empire of Ghana, destroyed by the Mandingos in 1213 A.D., and to that of the Mandingos themselves, which was broken up by the attacks of the Tuariks, and by the discordant ambitions of its provincial governors. It was otherwise with the Mediterranean littoral and the Nile valley. Their accessibility to foreign influences led to an early development. Some four millenniums before Homer sang of "Royal Thebes—

"Egyptian treasure-house of countless wealth,
"Who boasts her hundred gates, through each of which
"With horse and car two hundred warriors march"—

the inhabitants of the Nile Valley had laboriously built up a mighty civilization. For many centuries Egypt remained a leading factor in the world's history, and was the great school of the civilized world. On the other hand, during the Punic wars the balance of universal empire for a time wavered between African Carthage and Rome.

These civilized portions of Africa were occupied by non-African races belonging to the Mediterranean or Caucasian family, which by many are regarded as immigrants; they were the Libyans, the Egyptians, and the Cushites.[1]

[1] Among the Libyans or Berbers are to be reckoned the Amazerks and the Shellooks, descendants of the Mauritanians, the most ancient inhabitants of Morocco;

The Egyptians regarded themselves as autochthones, the remembrance of an immigration, if one had taken place, having vanished from their minds.[1] The name which they gave themselves was Romet 'men.' Others might be Asiatics, Libyans, Negroes—they were 'men' par excellence; and they maintained that the God Horus had created them in the valley of the Nile. The physiognomy of the dynastic Egyptians is discernible in their sculptures, particularly in those of the Old Empire; in these, more than in those of later times, the artists aimed at realistic reproduction. The face bears a mild, often melancholy, expression. The forehead is low, the nose of moderate length, the lips full, the shoulders are remarkably broad; the legs are not powerful; the feet are long.

The physical type of the ancient Egyptians bears a resemblance to that of the Berbers. An inference has been drawn that the Berbers or Libyans are immigrants from Europe. This inference is by no means made improbable by the affinity which clearly exists between the languages of the Egyptians, Berbers, and Cushites,—an affinity which, though not so pronounced as that connecting the Sanskrit and the Greek, is still indisputable, showing itself most evidently in the structure of the language, and particularly in the pronoun. The Semitic tribes who live adjacent to the Cushites, i. e., the Abys-

furthermore, the Kabyles, descendants of the Numidians, and other tribes in Algeria; a few remains in Tunis and Tripoli, and also the dwellers in the oases at the foot of the Atlas Mountains, in the oasis of Awdjila, south of Barca, and in Siwah (the oasis of Ammon); moreover, the Imosharghs (in Arabic Tuariks, 'night-robbers'); probably the ancient Gaetulians; and finally the Guanches, upon the Canary Islands, by whom one hundred years ago the Berber language was still spoken. To the Cushites belong the Bedja, descendants of the Blemyes and of the Ethiopians of Meroë, with the nearly related branches of the Bisharin in the desert east of the Nile; the Ababdeh, dwelling to the north of them, the Zabadaeans of Ptolemy; the Shukurieh, east of Khartum; the Hamran upon the Setit, an affluent of the Atbara; and the Hadendoa, east of the lower Atbara. After the Bedja follow the Dankali, on the eastern margin of the region extending from the fifteenth degree of latitude to the straits of Bab-el-Mandeb; the Agau in western Abyssinia, with the Bogos, Falasha, and Jewaressa; the Somali, inhabitants of the only peninsula in Africa; the Galla or Oromo, with the Shoa and numerous subdivisions; and the Saho, northeast from Axum, perhaps a severed branch of the Galla tribe.

[1] In 1894 Mr. Flinders-Petrie made excavations at Koptos, near Thebes, under the belief that the dynastic Egyptians entered the Nile Valley by the Kosseir-Koptos road from the Red Sea and its southern shores. His discoveries at this point were the first of the recent prehistoric 'finds.' At the lowest of several strata containing remains of 35 reigns ranging from pre-dynastic times to the third century A. D., he found crude statues of the God of Koptos—Min—roughly carved with shells and fish. These establish an early connection with the Red Sea; but their makers obviously had little to contribute to Egypt's artistic or industrial life.

sinians, do not appear on the page of history before the Christian era, though they seem to have immigrated from southern Arabia at an earlier date; they once spoke the now extinct language of the Geez, of which the living representatives are the Tigre and Tigriña; the Amharic dialect, now the chief speech of Abyssinia, though related to that of the Geez, is not in the line of direct descent.

Egypt, *Qêmet*, "the black," the land of the dark soil,[1] is, as Herodotus characterizes it, a gift of the Nile,[2] whose waters, fraught with blessing, have not only created the diluvium of the Delta, but also the fruitfulness of the rainless valley, which is immediately contiguous to the rocky wilderness.

The regular recurrence of the Nile floods had its distinct influence on the nature of the civilization of the people that inhabited these regions. These people, from remotest times, were obliged to devise manifold mechanical and useful arts by which to preserve the blessings bestowed by the river.

Regulations relating to boundaries of property, and the maintenance of all measures securing the profitable use of the water, issued from the rulers and the cultivated classes; thus was developed the sense of justice and order in the life of the state. The ease with which it was possible to transport great burdens, as blocks of stone, upon the water, gave occasion for navigation at an early day, and caused it to be eagerly pursued. In order to form a conception of the difficulties attending culture of the soil in Egypt, we must bear in mind that the valley of the Nile was originally covered with masses of reeds emitting noxious vapors, and lying between sandy hillocks; that the river often changed its course; and that the inundations left a large part of the valley untouched, while in other places the water excavated the soil and formed standing lakes. The Delta was a vast lagoon of islands of sand, upon which grew reeds, papyrus, and lotus. The inhabitants were obliged to regulate the course of the stream by dikes, and to construct canals to the remote parts of the valley, in order to render the sand-flats also fertile.

[1] In Hebrew, Assyrian, and Persian, *Mizraim*, *Muçur*, *Mudrayo*, from which is derived the Arabic *Miçr* now used, 'the land of fortresses' (originally the appellation of a district east of the Delta).

[2] In Egyptian the Nile had the sacred name *Hapi*, the profane, *Aur*; in Assyrian, *Jaru*; in Persian, *Pirac* — from the Egyptian *pi* (article) and *aur* — and in Hebrew *Jeor*.

As Egypt is composed wholly of the broad openings in the valley which are watered by the Nile, its population was necessarily homogeneous. There was no distinction between nomads and permanent settlers, between robber mountaineers and industrious lowlanders. Cultivating a soil of amazing fertility, the people obtained an opulence which even in the early ages secured a luxury that was refined by the arts and sciences which they had acquired. At the same time the soldiery who guarded and protected the provinces of Lower Egypt, which enjoyed but a slight natural defence against Libya and Asia, were not

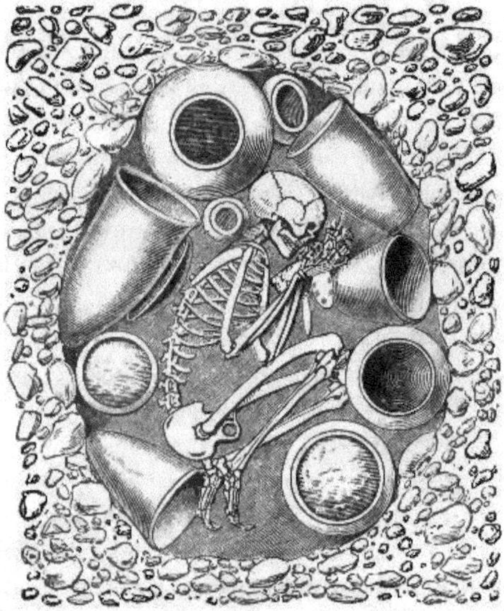

FIG. 1. — Prehistoric interment of Nagadah type (from El Amrah), after de Morgan.

without occupation, and hence when the era of conquests began, they were able to appear in the field endowed with surpassing military science.

The Nile is formed by two large streams, — the White and the Blue Nile.[1] The former, which according to the geographer Ptolemy comes from the Mountains of the Moon, or from the slopes of the mountain-range whose highest peak is Kilimanjaro, under the equator, flows out of Lake Ukerewe or Victoria Nyanza (which receives tributaries from the same mountains), and descending the great Murchison

[1] In Arabic, *Bahr-el-Abiad* and *Bahr-el-Azrak*.

The Murchison Falls.

(From a sketch by Sir Samuel Baker.)

History of All Nations, Vol. I., page 23.

The Nile in the Tropics.

(From a sketch by G. Schweinfurth.)

Falls (Plate I.), after a short distance empties into the northern bay of Albert Nyanza; it then emerges from this lake, and dashes down in the cataract of Gondokoro. Augmented by many affluents, and especially by the waters of the Bahr-el-Ghazal, it reaches the Egyptian Soudan after passing through boundless stretches of forest and swamp (Plate II.), and at Khartum unites with the Blue Nile, which with the Atbara (Astaboras) and other Abyssinian tributaries causes the inundation. The united stream, hereafter receiving no

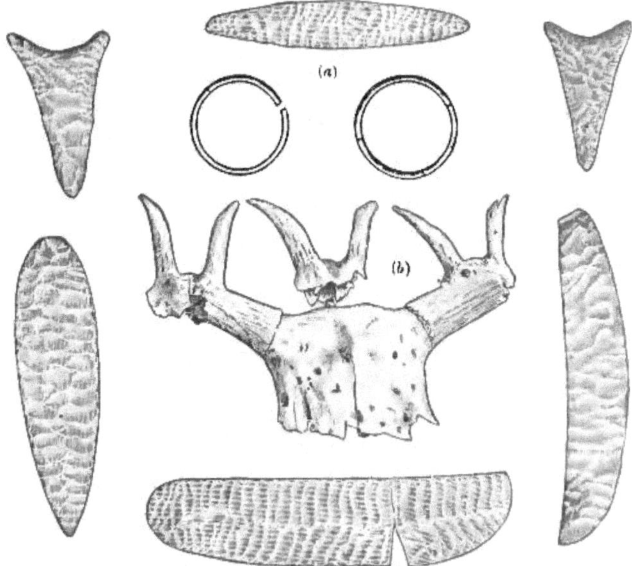

Fig. 2. — (*a*) Prehistoric implements from Nagadah. (Originals in Museum of University of Pennsylvania.) (*b*) Bucrania from Hu.

additional tributaries, separates at Cairo into two main branches, which form the Delta or Lower Egypt (Figs. 1–3). The arable soil of the Delta covers a plain of about 6560 square miles (a little more than Saxony, a little less than Würtemberg or New Jersey), while the remaining territory below Assuan contains a cultivated area of about 5,163 square miles. The mouths of the Nile have changed considerably since ancient times. In antiquity seven mouths or arms were enumerated, namely, from west to east: the Canopic mouth (west from Abukir Bay), the Bolbitine (at Rosetta), the Sebennytic (at the extreme end of the Lake of Burlos), the Phatnitic (at Damietta), the Mendesian and Tanitic (on the borders of Lake Menzaleh), and the Pelusian (southeast of Port Said), the former channel of which is now crossed by the Suez Canal. The first of these, according to the account given by Herodotus, was artificially diverted in its lower section from an older Canopic arm of the Nile; the latter, in the opinion of Aristotle, was the only natural mouth.

At the time before the Nile rises, when it is at the lowest point, the Khamsin, the Egyptian Simoom, begins to blow. It comes from

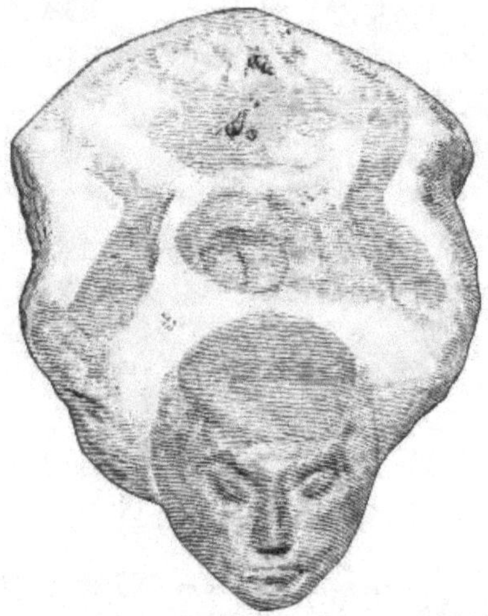

FIG. 3. — Door socket, Hierakonpolis. (From original in Museum of the University of Pennsylvania.)

the southeast; and for fifty days from the end of April it continues, charging the air as it were with electricity by the sand which it carries along; everything is covered with a hot and glowing stratum. Set-Typhon (the god of evil) seems to have won the victory; but soon the Etesian wind rises in the west-north-west, and blows away the dust, and, especially during the dog-days, mitigates the fierce heat of the sun. In early June the rise of the Nile commences, and this, like the preceding drought, is accomplished with such extraordinary and impressive phenomena, that it is not surprising that the awestruck people believed that they observed, in these changes, the immediate intervention of beneficent and of destructive divinities.

The inundation comes from Abyssinia, in whose highlands the rain falls incessantly for three months, and the river rolls an immense mass of mud in upon the lower valley of the Nile. By the end of June the flood reaches Syene or Assuan (Fig. 4), by the beginning of July it strikes the apex of the Delta at Cairo. At the close of September the waters remain for nearly a month at the same elevation, but attain their highest point during the first half of October. In the first months of the following year the water has already retired from the fields and the stream continues to subside until June. In order to be best suited to purposes of cultivation, the waters must have reached a height of twenty-four feet; in our day nearly nine feet additional are necessary. Moreover, the floods cannot be suffered to work as they will; innumerable canals and reservoirs must be contrived, or yet more simple arrangements, as water-wheels, to conduct the water to the

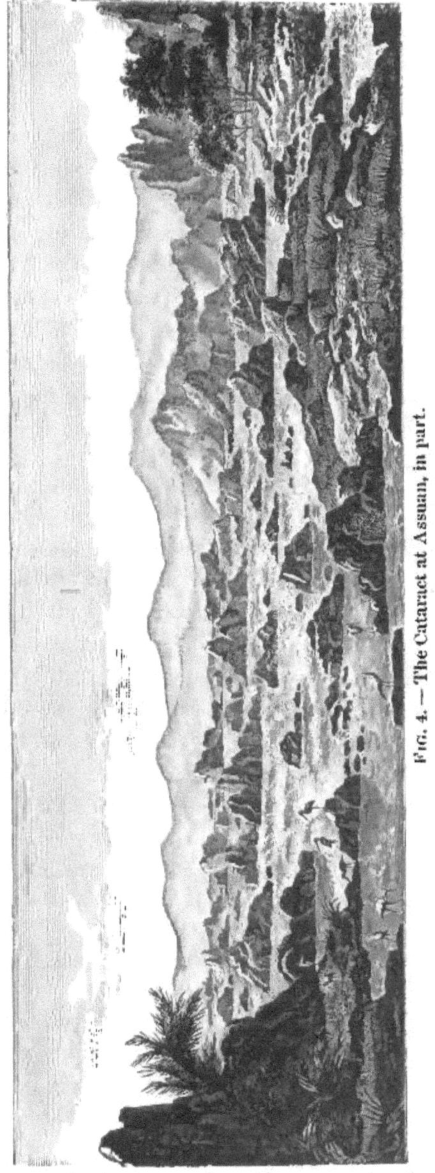

Fig. 4. — The Cataract at Assuan, in part.

more elevated fields in order to cause the necessary deposit of mud and its penetration by the moisture.

All appearances of nature and of human life, which with unvarying uniformity begin and pass away, fulfilling their ends unerringly, with a regularity denied to man, were conceived of by mankind in the childhood of the race as divine acts. Even in the brutes, as it seemed to the Egyptians, the certainty with which they effected their objects, the unchanging nature of their existence, the incomprehensible intuitive skill which without any instruction constantly recurs in each individual, are a revelation of an immediate exercise of divine power. Thus the Nile, which regulated the increase and the fall of its waters in a true dependence upon heavenly manifestations, was a god named Hapi, to whom offerings were poured out, and psalms were sung, as in a hymn composed by Enna in the time of Merenptah, the son of Rameses II.:

"O overflowing of the Nile, to thee will offerings be brought: oxen will for thee be slain; in thine honor shall there be festivals; winged things to thee shall be offered; wild beasts of the fields rejoice: pure flames shall be kindled to thee; gifts such as men bring to the gods shall they bring to the Nile; incense rises up to heaven; oxen, bulls, and fowls shall be roasted; the Nile makes two cavities in Thebais.[1] Full of mystery is his name in heaven; he reveals not his form; vain are all images of him. No temple can contain him, no counsellor can penetrate to his heart; youth delights in thee, thy children thou guidest as their king. Thy law prevails throughout the land, in the presence of thy servants in the Northland; he drinks (wipes away) the tears from every eye, he provides for the fulness of his blessings."

At Gebel-Selseleh (in Egyptian, Khenu), where the Nile bursts through the mountains with impetuous rush, the Pharaoh is portrayed as he is presenting offerings to the divine triad, Amen, Mut, and Khuns. The inscription mentions the two festivals in honor of the issuing forth of the stream out of its two cavities (by Herodotus, the mountains in which these cavities lie are called Crophi and Mophi), and in honor of the arrival of the water at

[1] According to the Egyptian legend, the Nile issues from two caves in the south.

this place. In the first festival (among the Greeks called Neiloa), at the beginning of the rise of the Nile, there used to be offered, according to the account given by the Arabians, a maiden, in any event a wax puppet, in order to obtain a full inundation. Even at this day a clay image as a "bride" is placed on the dike, and this is swept away by the flood before it has reached its highest point. The present inhabitants of Egypt celebrate the 'night of the tear-drop' (June 17), on which a drop falling from heaven, according to the ancient Egyptian faith a tear of the goddess Isis, causes the rise of the water. They also celebrate the festival of the 'filling up of the Nile' (August 19), after which there follows the cutting of the embankment.

As early as the first Pharaoh, Menes (Mena), mention is made of an undertaking relative to the Nile. This king,—the most ancient dynastic ruler whose identity has been established by contemporary monumental evidence,—according to tradition altered the course of the river, and founded Memphis. He is also credited with having brought about a serious political change—i. e., the consolidation of the principalities then dividing the Nile Valley into one united Empire of the "two lands" under the rule of the house of This.

This was a theocratic Empire, in so far that no separation was made between the temple and the state. The chief alteration from the former condition consisted in uniting the numerous provinces of Upper and Lower Egypt under one absolute and sole authority. The king was the ruler in the name of God ; he was the son of God, and once established on the throne, became his incarnation. The temple was the domestic chapel of this earthly god, who shared his sanctuary with the priesthood alone. The priesthood, in addition to its spiritual functions, was invested with the most important secular offices, and was composed largely of the dependents and relatives of the royal family. Although it was possible for men, through education, to attain to the highest positions, yet it was customary for sons to succeed their fathers, and daughters their mothers, — the latter, for example, in discharging the duties of priestesses and temple-women. The consideration with which the Egyptian priesthood was treated was enhanced by the elaborate system of rules that regulated the manner of life of the priests. In externals they were distinguished from the laboring classes by their dress of white linen, over which was thrown, while they were performing priestly functions, a panther's skin: their heads were shaven, and they wore elaborate wigs; they were required to abstain from fish, from the flesh of certain wild animals, from beans, and from other food which was considered unclean. The Greeks,—Herodotus, Diodorus, Strabo, Plato (in the Timaeus),—who in the later periods of the monarchy visited the country, differed in their enumeration of the several orders of society. It would seem that the priests (with whom were included the learned men, authors,—the libraries were in the temples,—high officials, and especially architects), the soldiers, the merchants, the members of different trades, and the peasants constituted distinct classes of society, marked off by sharp dividing-lines. In their precepts, however, the Egyptian sages disclaim arrogance, and allow for changes of condition resulting from life's vicissitudes. There are instances of freedmen who advanced to high places through their own efforts and the King's favor. Ti was a parvenu who rose to a high estate and wedded a princess. The ancestors of the great architect Sen-mut "were not found in writing"—and among court officials were foreigners who may even have been slaves. For instance, the First Speaker to his Majesty King Merenptah, whose duty it was to take charge of all intercourse between the King and his attendants, was a Canaanite—Ben Mat'ana, son of Yupa'a—from d'Arbarsana.[1]

Among the government architects are also found the names of princes and of officers who had intermarried with princesses. Brugsch has given a genealogical list of twenty-five head architects,[2] which reaches back from the time of Darius to the reign of Shishak I., whose architect was named Hor-em-bes, and thence farther back to the time of Rameses II. and Seti I., in whose reigns the famous Bek-en-khuns, builder of the Ramesseum and of many other splendid works, flourished; his statue,

[1] Comp. Erman, loc. cit., 106. Also Mariette, Catalog. d'Abydos, No. 1136, and Abydos, III. 90.

[2] Such genealogies are valuable for ascertaining approximately chronological studies. In these lists three generations are reckoned to a century, while the average duration of the reigns of the several kings must be regarded as much shorter. An architect was named Bek, whose father was Men; the father of the latter, Hor-amu, served under Amenhotep III. as the superintendent of the sculptors; the architect of the latter, under whose direction was erected the colossal statue of Memnon, which was brought from the quarry upon eight boats joined together, was Amenhotep, son of Hapi, whose tomb is at Der-el-Bahri.

with an enumeration of the offices which he filled, and an account of his labors as architect, is to be found in the Glyptothek at Munich.

Pharaoh Mena was a native of Tini, the ancient capital of the province of Thinitis; at a later day this place was overshadowed by the neighboring Abydos. Near this spot was found, some years ago, a tomb with two lions resembling those at Mycenae; which according to an inscription belonged to a family sepulchre in existence since the age of Mena. We have seen (Introduction, pp. 13-18) that Mena's tomb, and perhaps that of his Queen Neit-hotep, have been recently discovered; and that, in some thirty-four contemporary burials of retainers, a large number of objects inscribed in his name have been found. There is now, therefore, an abundance of material to prove the identity of the until now semi-legendary personage, who henceforth must stand unchallenged at the threshhold of History. His worship continued throughout the ages; and his priesthood is on record as late as the reign of Psammetichus. According to tradition, he was killed by a hippopotamus—perhaps an allusion to some rebellion of Set-worshippers, to whom that animal was sacred. Mena introduced the pomp and ceremony of royalty, and the laws which he established were revealed to him by the god Thoth. His most important work was the building of Memphis.[1] Herodotus relates that he erected a dike to protect the town from the overflow of the river. The flood had formerly swept close by the Libyan range of mountains; but the king, by means of the dike constructed a hundred stadia higher up, had compelled the stream to flow in the new bed as it is to-day, so that the town came to lie on the west bank; and by excavating a lake, the town was protected also on the west. (This dike was discovered by Linant Bey, about thirteen miles south of Memphis.) The town extended from the present Bedrashen, beyond Mitrahineh and Sakkara ('the temple of Sokar'), as far as Abusir ('the temple of Osiris'). It existed until the end of the kingdom, although at one time it suffered greatly from the Shepherd Kings, after whose expulsion it was rebuilt. It was again much injured by the Persians, and finally lost its importance by the founding of Alexandria (332 B.C.). When in 638 A.D., upon the site of ancient Babylon, on the right bank of the Nile opposite the island Roda, the modern Old Cairo, and, later,

[1] *Men-no-fer*, 'the good dwelling,' or *Na-ptah* (Hebrew *Noph*), 'the town of Hephaestus'; in the lists of the provinces it is styled the 'town of the white wall.'

Cairo itself, were built, the ancient city of Memphis ceased to exist. The stones of the monuments of the temple of Ptah, of the 'white wall' or castle, and of the seat of the princes of the provinces or nomarchs, as well as those of many Grecian edifices, were appropriated and used for new foundations; so that at the time of Abdul-Atif (who died in 1232) there remained only one monolithic apartment or naos of green stone, with figures of beasts (sphinxes) and of men of immense size, together with a mass of wonderful ruins, inhabited by bands of robbers who drove a traffic in the ransacked treasures of antiquity. In our day the heaps of rubbish at Mitrahineh are overgrown with palm-trees; and there remains only a statue of Rameses II., about fifty-three feet in height, formed of a single piece of limestone, which lies on the right side, having fallen to the ground; it was set up by this Pharaoh in front of the pylon of the temple of Ptah, of which a few pieces of the foundation remain.

One might well conceive that the Pharaoh who introduced monarchy also brought about a division of the land into districts or nomes [1] in order to lighten the labor of administration. It is more likely, however, that the petty states brought together to form Mena's Empire were simply turned into its provinces, each retaining its original limits, as well as its nobility, its militia, and its special standard. At least, these standards appear on the earliest monuments, such, for instance, as are found at Abydos and at Hierakonpolis. Furthermore, the forty-two judges of the other world, who, according to the "Book of the Dead," were summoned from the chief cities of the kingdom to form a tribunal, stand in evident agreement with the number of the nomes, and this connection of the nomes with the ancient doctrine of Hades attests their great antiquity. In the division of the country into nomes, use was probably made of pre-existent conditions. The inhabitants were anciently doubtless divided into numerous clans, each with a patriarch as chief, who also served as priest of the deity of the tribe. With the change from the nomadic to a settled manner of life, effected by their new relations to the soil, the bonds of kindred were relaxed as the territorial tie strengthened. The patriarch was transformed into a chieftain or prince, his tent became a temple, and he fell into the possession of the best land and largest herds. Thus arose small

[1] Greek, *nomos*; in sacred Egyptian, *hesp*; in profane, *p-tosh*.

cantons with their several deities, which in later ages were at times in antagonism. When one princely house gained ascendancy over the others, and stood at the head of the united kingdom, it gave the preference to its own district, and sought to exalt its local deity above other gods.

It would seem that Upper Egypt annexed the 'North Country.' The 'two lands' never were quite merged into one. They were *united.* And as the evidence of this union, the Pharaohs wore a double crown; the southern white, the northern red, blended in a single one, the *pshent.* The Government remained twofold. Public lands and state property were divided; and high administrative officials were Treasurers or Supervisors of 'the two houses' of silver, or of grain, etc.

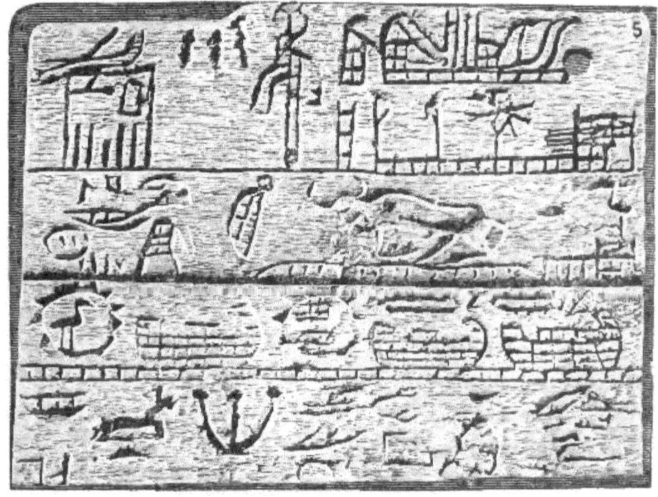

FIG. 5. — Ebony tablet of Aha (Mena). (From original in Museum of the University of Pennsylvania.)

Besides occasional mention of the names of the provinces, we possess, certainly from the date of the New Empire down to the times of the Romans, records of the provinces or nomes, from which it appears that the division remained the same for thousands of years. The apparent differences in the several lists are explained by the existence of subordinate nomes, mentioned perhaps between two principal nomes. Every province had its capital (*nut*) with a local deity, whose worship was performed by chosen or by hereditary priests. This was the seat of the hereditary ruler (*hik*), the head of the administration and of the military department, to whom was also intrusted the collection of the tribute; under him were toparchs

FIG. 6. The first and the second nomes in Upper Egypt. (From a list in the temple of Rameses II. in Abydos, Nineteenth Dynasty, about 1350 B.C.)

or subordinate rulers. In every nome a distinction was made between arable land and land where at high water were formed swamps in which were reared water-fowl, lotus, and papyrus, and which, when dry, was used for pasture. Finally there were the principal canal (*mer*) for purposes of irrigation and navigation, and the side canals. The god of the nome from which the reigning house took its origin, acquired a preferred position. In turn Ptah, Ra, Amen, assumed the highest rank among the gods. The influence of the Sacred Colleges was also an important factor in the religious evolution of the people. Thus Heliopolis and Hermopolis, while in the historic period they furnished no reigning house, made a powerful impression on the religious thought of the people; and their gods and doctrine played an important part in Egyptian intellectual life. A nome might include a number of minor provinces. For instance, the first, south of Assuan, possessed a longer or shorter portion of the Nubian valley of the Nile, according to the

FIG. 7.—Coin of the nome Ombites.

greater or less extent of the power of Egypt. Among ancient non-Egyptian writers, Herodotus first names eighteen nomes up to the two lying together in the Delta occupied as their allotment by the warrior classes, — the Hermotybies and Calasiries (in Egyptian, Kelashes). Diodorus relates that Sesostris established thirty-six nomes; and the same number is given by Strabo, who assigns ten to the Thebais, the same number to the Delta, and sixteen to Middle Egypt. The latter region contained at times only seven nomes, and hence was called Heptanomis; afterwards an eighth was added, the nome of Arsinoë (Fayum; in Coptic, *P'a-iom*, 'lake-land'). Pliny mentions forty-four nomes, and Ptolemy, in the Delta alone, twenty-four. The names that occur are in part borrowed from the popular or demotic Egyptian, as Pathyrites (Egyptian, *Pa-hathor*); in part they are Greek paraphrases, as Apollonopolites (from Apollo, or Hor-hut, whose temple was in the chief town), or Lycopolites, of 'the city of the wolves' (jackals), where the sacred animal of Anubis was worshipped. Brugsch has fully treated of the lists of the nomes in speaking of geographical inscriptions. In these (see Fig. 6) the representation of a nome appears in the form of a human figure, a woman, or a form partaking of the attributes of both sexes bearing in hand the principal products of the locality. Upon the head is the ideogram of the nome, and above this the device for the 'standard'; the latter is also often found alone. Four lists of the times of the Eighteenth, Nineteenth, and Thirtieth Dynasties are preserved, but are so far injured that they show very imperfectly the names of the nomes. Two only, belonging to the age of Seti I. and Rameses, which were found by Brugsch at Abydos, present a larger series of names, and, as a supplement, add a complete list of the towns, which are grouped under their appropriate nomes. Of the period of the Macedonian Ptolemies there are six lists, of which the fullest had its origin at Edfu in the age of Ptolemy IX. (known also as Alexander I.). The king is represented in each nome as offering or presenting the nome to the god Hor-hut. Finally there are five lists of the period of the Roman Empire. The situation of the nomes or provinces we ascertain by comparing together the names on the Egyptian monuments, those given in the lists of Herodotus, Strabo, Pliny, and Ptolemy, modern names of places, and especially the later provincial coins. In this investigation great credit is due to Brugsch, de Rougé, Dümichen, Maspero, Erman, Müller, Griffith, and others, and yet the subject is by no means exhausted, particularly with regard to the nomes of the Delta.

The province of Nubia appears on the lists as the southernmost nome, to which also was assigned all the conquered region south of the limits of Egypt proper. Here lies the island of Philae (Fig. 8), the frontier island; opposite to it the island Senem (Bigeh); and on the northern limit of this province, opposite Sun (Syene; in Arabic, Assuan), the island of Ab (Elephantine), on which were situated the

FIG. 8.—Small Island near Philae, at the upper end of the Cataracts of Assuan.

chief town and the temple of the god Khnum. Here also is found the famous Nilometer, a staircase leading down to the surface of the river, having on it marks to indicate the height of the water; this was disused at an early day, but in the year 1870 was discovered and again put to use. Farther down are situated Ombos (Fig. 7), with the temple of Sebek-Ra, a god with a crocodile's head; and Khenu (in Arabic, Selseleh), where the stream is so narrowed by sandstone rocks that the people say it could be closed in old times by chains (*selse-*

kh). Of the quarries and the monuments existing there, much has been written. The second province is that of Apollinopolis Magna, or Edfu,[1] where, amid the walls of a very ancient sanctuary, stands a completely preserved temple of the age of the Ptolemies, dedicated to Horus, who is recognized by his hawk's head and double crown. The third province is that of Latopolis, or Esneh (Egyptian, Seni), whose inhabitants regarded the fish *latus* as sacred, and did not venture to eat it; in the Old Empire Nekhebt (El-Kab) was the capital. The Governors of its great fortress were equal in rank with the princes of the blood. At this place, Nekhebt (Eileithyia), the patron goddess, represented as a vulture or as an asp, wearing the white crown of Upper Egypt, was worshipped (Fig. 9). The fourth nome is the Pathyritic, or that of western Thebes, called also Diospolites, on account of Amen (Zeus), who was here held in special reverence, or Hermonthites from the town of Hermonthis (Erment). Koptos, the capital of the fifth nome, where the ithyphallic Min,—the Pan, or Priapus, of the Egyptians,—was worshipped, had a temple which goes back to prehistoric times.[2] This town was the place where the valley approached nearest to the Arabian Gulf, and east of it several roads united at Laketa, from which the two lines of traffic branched off to Berenice, and past the famous porphyry quarries of Hamamat to Kosseir (Leucos limēn). The Tentyritic nome possessed at its capital, Denderah, a noble temple of Hathor, built in the times of the Romans, which, like the temple at Edfu, was erected on the site and according to the plan of a more ancient sanctuary. The seventh province, that of Diospolis Parva (Egyptian, Ha), was so called because in the chief town, together with the nome deity Isis-Hathor, the god Amen of Thebes received worship. In the province of Abydos was said to be the tomb of Osiris, a famous resort of pilgrims,

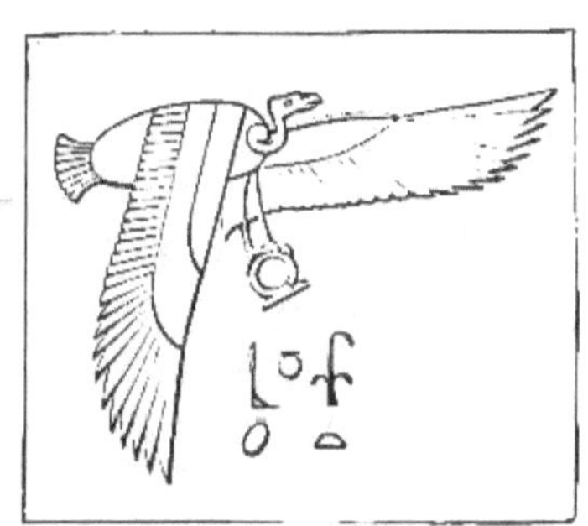

Fig. 9.—Nekhebt.

[1] Edfu, in Egyptian, *Atbu*, 'the place of the stabbing,' namely, of Typhon by Horus, which took place here.

[2] See note to page 20.

where wealthy Egyptians were buried near the God. In 1898 Amélineau discovered at Abydos—in a tomb which turned out to be that of King Zer (Teta) of the First Dynasty—a granite cenotaph of Osiris of late date. Certain peculiarities of the tomb and the presence of votive offerings make it probable that this was the so-called tomb of the God, where, in the New Empire, pilgrimages were made. (See above, p. 62.) The ninth province, Panopolites, with its capital Khemmis (Akhmin), where the God Min was worshipped, was formerly the seat of the wool industry. The tenth province was Aphroditopolites (in Egyptian, Tebu, now called Itfu), where Hathor-Isis was worshipped; and to the east lay the eleventh nome, or Antaeopolites. Here was the town of Tuka (in El-Kebir), the abode of Antaeus, who is identical with the Asiatic-Egyptian war-god Reshpu, and, in the latest Osiris myth, with Horus. At a later day the province of Aphroditopolis disappears from the lists; and in its place is found the province of Shet, in which Aphroditopolis on the west, and Antaeopolis on the eastern shore of the Nile, are included; to them was added, in the time of the Caesars, Hisopis (Egyptian, Shotep). The deity of this province is Khnum. The twelfth nome, Tu-hef, or that of the 'snake mountain' (in Greek, Hypselites) had for its capital Hierakon, 'the town of the hawk.' The ancient temple and nekropolis were excavated in 1898 by Quibell, who found there important remains of the early dynasties (see Introduction, pages 6–12, also PLATE V. and Fig. 3), and among other valuable objects of the Old Empire, a large copper statue of Pepi I Meri-Ra, and a superb golden hawk. The thirteenth and fourteenth provinces are the two Lycopolites, lying south and north of Siût, in which Anubis, having the head of a jackal (the wolf of Egypt), was worshipped. The northern province had Kesi (Cusae) for its capital, and Hathor was its deity. Under Hadrian this province was divided between the thirteenth and fifteenth; and for the fourteenth a new province was created on the west bank, which, after the town Antinoüpolis, built by him in memory of his favorite Antinoüs, was

FIG. 10.—Coins of the nome Hermonthites.

[1] In Egyptian, Timai; the town is so called upon the Berberini obelisk, reared by Hadrian.

named Antinoites; this town, opposite Ashmunen or Hermopolis, was built in Roman style. The fifteenth province or nome is South Hermopolites, and its capital was Ashmunen, where Hermes-Thoth, the ibis-headed god of learning, was worshipped; in it lie the ruins and tombs of Tel-el-Amarna and the rocky grottos of El-Bersheh. The latter were systematically studied (1892–94) by Messrs. F. Ll. Griffith and P. E. Newberry on behalf of the 'Archaeological Survey of Egypt.' At the frontier town of Temta, where duties on imports coming from the south were levied, and where the great canal branched off from the Nile, flowing as far as the Fayum, we reach, with the sixteenth nome, the northern provinces of Upper Egypt; these provinces of Middle Egypt are called the Heptanomis. The metropolis of this nome, also known as North Hermopolites, was Ha-bennu—that is, the 'town of the phoenix,' and Horus was the provincial deity. Several celebrated rock-tombs, especially those of Beni-Hassan, belong to this nome. The province of Cynopolites derives its name from the jackal-headed god Anubis, which here was worshipped. The capital is the modern Kais (Egyptian, Kasa). The eighteenth province is West Oxyrhynchites, or Alabastropolis, on account of the quarry of alabaster found at Shas. Its capital was Ha-Suten, and Anubis-Sep was its deity. The capital of the nineteenth nome was Oxyrynchus (Behnesa), where MM. Grenfell and Hunt recently discovered a mine of valuable Graeco-Roman papyri. These include, among a mass of business and personal documents, important fragments from the classics and the early Christians; and in both classes of MSS. furnish the earliest examples extant. The town was founded by Unas, the last king of the Fifth Dynasty, and it is probable that Herodotus refers to this province in speaking of the nome Anysius. Its inhabitants had the chief part of the commercial intercourse with the oases in the Sahara, Kenem (Khargeh), Testes (Dachel), and Ta-ah (Farafrah), and brought about importations from them to the valley of the Nile; but this connection with the desert appeared as an influence of Typhon, and it is related in the myth of Osiris that here a contest arose whereby he lost a part of a leg; that is, a part of the desert was rent off by the inundation through the canal Bahr-Jusuf. The twentieth province, Herakleopolites Magnus, had as its deity Har-Shefi, who received divine honors in the town of Ha-Khenen-su, the modern Ahnas (in Coptic, Hennes).

The twenty-first province was divided into two parts, the eastern situated on the Nile, the western constituting the Fayum; at a later day the former was added to the twentieth province. The capital was called Pa-Sebek, the habitation of the god Sebek, to whom the crocodile was sacred; hence the place was named in Greek, Crocodilopolis. It was named Arsinoë, after the queen of Ptolemy Philadelphus (284–246 B.C.), and is to-day called Medînet-el-Fayum. The last province of Upper Egypt is Aphroditopolites, so named from Tepahe; that is, the town of the cow-headed Isis-Hathor,—the modern Atfi.

The provinces of Lower Egypt, respecting some of which there still exist many doubts, begin with Memphites, the nome of Memphis, in which is the seat of government again to-day (Cairo) as it was six thousand years ago. The second nome, Letopolites, had as its chief town Sokhem, perhaps on the site of the village of Usîm, which lies on the west bank of the river, a short distance below Cairo. The god of this nome was Horus, and the goddess, Bast, or Leto. The capital of the province of the West was on the southern point of the Lake Mareotis; its ruins are not as yet discovered. Its deity was Hathor, in the form of a cow lying down. The vicinity of the Natron Lakes and the Oasis of Amen (Siwah) were regarded as belonging to this province; and hence it was called by Strabo, Nitriotes, and by Pliny, Hammoniacus. To this province we may also refer the district which is specially called Mareotis by Pliny and Ptolemy, from the town Marea (in Egyptian, Meri), on the south shore of Lake Mareotis. Lying between this and Alexandria was the nome Menelaites, so-called. The more recently constituted nome of Alexandria, which was established in place of Rhacotis, might pass for an adjunct to the third, perhaps also to the fifth province. The fourth nome, Prosopites, had for its capital town Teka, probably modern Tūkh, southwest from Tanta; the Greek appellation is derived from the town of Prosopis, which Dümichen has identified with the town of Pa-ari-shep, situated in the southern part of the western Delta. The fifth province is Saites (now Sa-el-Hugar), with the sanctuary of the goddess Neith, or Net. As a part of the same is to be regarded the nome of Temi-en-hor ('the fortress of Horus'), situated west, and now called Damanhûr. The sixth province, called Xoites, had Khasûû (now Sakha) as its capital, and lay northeast from Sais. The capital of the seventh province was Pa-neha (now Benha), lying on the southern part of the Damietta branch. Pa-tum was the capital of the eighth province, lying to the east. This is Pithom, mentioned in the Bible, its profane name being Succoth. This town was excavated by Naville in 1883. The region is full of interest as the scene of the Exodus. It was situated at the entrance of the Wady-Tūmilāt, originally a desert tract, which Rameses II. converted into a fruitful region by constructing the canal from the Pelusian

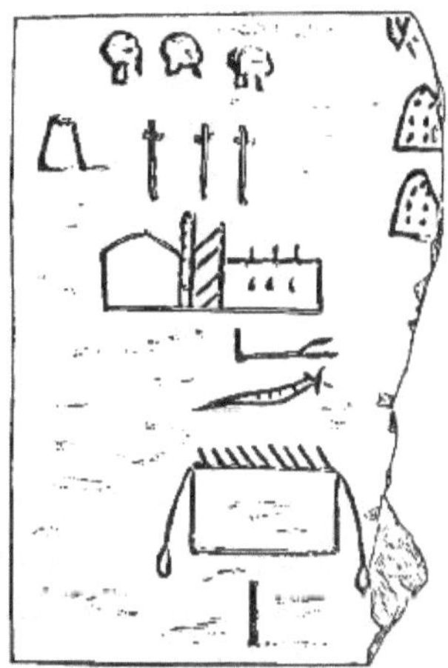

FIG. 11. — Ivory tablet from tomb of King Den-Setui, showing oldest known sectional plan of building. (From original in Museum of the University of Pennsylvania.)

branch of the Nile, in the vicinity of Bubastis (at Zagazīg), as far as Crocodile (Timsāh) Bay. The district near the entrance to the Wady was low, and was fruitful; it was desirable for herdsmen, and was known as the land of Goshen (in Egyptian, Kesem). The ninth province is that of Busiris (in Egyptian, Pa-usiri, 'the home of Osiris'), to-day Abusir, midway on the Damietta branch: the tenth was that of Athribis (in Egyptian, Hat-her-ab, 'the midland dwelling'), whose ruins lie thickly at Benha. Here worship was paid to a Horus. The eleventh province is Lycopolites, at the west of the two former. The name of the capital, Lycopolis, is, on the

Rosetta stone, Pa-mak, 'house of the Evil One,' or Typhon: several lists name Sheten as the capital, which is identified with the modern village of Shenit, north of Horbet, in the neighborhood of Abu-Kebir; but Horbet is the ancient Pharbaethus, mentioned by Herodotus as a separate nome (in Egyptian, Pa-ari-hebi). The twelfth province is Sebennytes (in Egyptian, Teb-nuter, 'the town of the holy calf,' the modern Semennud), on the Damietta branch of the Nile, where in ancient times the Sebennytic Nile flowed. Here also was the scene of a victory of Horus (Anher) over Set, whence he was represented on the coins as a warrior. The thirteenth nome has for its capital the celebrated Heliopolis (An, or On), with the sanctuary of Ra. The capital of the fourteenth province was the city of Zân, from which the hosts of the Pharaohs were accustomed to set forth for Asia. Its site, excavated by Petrie in 1883–4, is strewn with fragments of colossi, obelisks, and other monuments which date from the Old Empire down to later times. Horus was here worshipped in the form of a lion, in which he pursued Typhon amid the forests of the neighboring hills. This is the nome that by the Greeks and Romans was called Tanites; its capital was Tanis (Biblical Zoan, modern San). Many remains of the Hyksos have been found there. The fifteenth or Hermopolitic province had Pa-Tehûti ('the house of Thoth') for its capital, which must have been situated northeast of Bahr-es-Sughaiyir, in the region of the village El-Megnune. The sixteenth was the province of Mendes (in Egyptian, Pa-Ba-neb-ded), where the Sacred Ram—as the soul of Osiris—was worshipped, and whose ruins lie east of El-Mansurah on the Damietta Nile. The seventeenth province extended along the Damietta branch; and its capital was Pachnamunis (Egyptian, Pakhen-en-amen), or Diospolis, situated below Damietta. Bubastis was the eighteenth province. Its capital, where was held the great festival of the cat-headed goddess Bast, was on the site of the modern Tel-Basta. Its temple was excavated by Naville (1889–90). The capital of the nineteenth province was named Am, and its guardian goddess of the north, the snake-headed Uazit or Buto, was revered here. This province is the most eastern of all; for Am is the city which the Hebrews called Sin, and the Greeks Pelusium, the latter thus translating Egyptian *am* ('dirt,' 'mud'), although *am*, the name of the city, is said to mean 'eyebrows,' because the brows of the murdered

Osiris were venerated there as sacred relics. The site of Pelusium is indicated by the modern village of Gerīzet el-Faramah. To this province belonged also Samhut, now Tel-es-semmūt, on the old road to Syria, which is the Magdolus of Hecataeus and of the *Itinerarium Antonini* of the fourth century. The last and twentieth province is the Arabian, with Phacusa as its capital (Kesem, Goshen). Sepd (a form of Horus) was its god. Here was the land of Goshen, in which, according to the Bible, the Hebrews fed their flocks. At the extreme point arose Hat-uar, the fortress of the Hyksos. The boundaries of the nomes in the Delta are to some extent difficult to be ascertained; and their number, originally few, appears to have increased in later times. Herodotus, besides some of those already mentioned, names also the nome Aphthites, which is not known; Onuphites, which is mentioned by Pliny also, and by Ptolemy, and must have extended between Thmuites and Athribites; moreover, Myecphorites, which lay opposite Bubastis upon an island formed by the Tanitic and Pelusian branches of the Nile; the province of Khemmis, by which Herodotus could not have intended Panopolites the ninth nome of Upper Egypt, but rather the region of the island town Khebi, on Lake Burlus, a lagoon in the northernmost part of the Delta; also the nome Papremites, whose capital lay between Damietta and Menzaleh; and the nome Natho, called by Ptolemy Neut, in Egyptian, Na-athu ('the papyrus marshes'), as the water districts of Menzaleh were called, the chief town being Panephysis. The province of Metelites had for its capital Metelis (Egyptian, Senti-nofer, the modern Fua), on the lower part of the Rosetta branch. The province of Phagroriopolis Brugsch places in the Wady-Tūmīlāt. The province Heroöpolites possessed the eastern part of this valley, and was named after Heroöpolis, or Hero, the profane name of the city Rameses, or Ani. Anekhtu ('the strength of the mighty one'). This city was brought to light by Naville in 1883: the name Ero castra of the Romans was according to him derived from the Egyptian *ara*, 'store chamber,' since here were situated the great corn magazines, whose walls, ten feet thick, and doorways are still standing. To-day the place is named Tel-el-Mashūta. Sethroïtes (in Egyptian, Set-rohatu) lay between the nome Tanites and the southeastern part of

Lake Menzaleh; here probably was situated one of the three places which bore the Semitic name Succoth ('tents'), for here lived Semitic nomads. Here were the nome Ptenethu (of Pliny), Phthenotes (of Ptolemy), in which lay the city of Buto, on the lower Sebennytic branch; the nome Menelaites, which is between the provinces of Mareotis and Alexandria, and on its coins presents the image of Harpocrates; here also the nomes Andropolites and Gynaecopolites, according to Brugsch west of Sais, and Cabasites (in Egyptian, Kahebes), east of Metelites; the nome Naucratites, the capital of which was near the modern Nebireh, on the Rosetta branch; and Leontopolites, which Brugsch places south of Mendes.

As we have already shown, division of the land in Egypt was connected with religion in so far that several provinces contributed their local gods to the Egyptian pantheon. The fundamental religious ideas were the same throughout all Egypt; and in general attributes the several deities bore much resemblance one to another. This was natural owing to the common temperament of the Egyptians, and to the similar conditions of life existing in the entire valley of the Nile. The most important source of knowledge with regard to the Egyptian religion is the 'Book of the Dead,' a collection of prayers and formulæ for the use of the deceased in the other world. Copies of selected portions of these forms were deposited with every mummy. Parts of the book were very ancient, but others were of later date. The text of the Turin papyrus was first published by Lepsius. (See PLATE III.) Naville has edited a text based on a comparison of more than eighty copies, and many other scholars have made contributions to the subject. The texts discovered at Sakkarah in 1884 in the Pyramids of Kings of the V. and VI. Dynasties, furnish archaic chapters of similar import, and have proved invaluable for the study of Egyptian beliefs. A large amount of religious literature—hymns, litanies, prayers, myths, magic formulæ, etc.—has also survived.

The oldest form of religion in Egypt was Animism. In this form of primitive religious consciousness the mind sees living entities in all visible objects, and regards that which we style the forces of nature as depending on the free activity of spirits or souls. These spirits, either of their own free motion or under the spell of human incantation, mingle in the affairs of man. They are regarded as taking up their abode either temporarily or permanently in certain objects, and from these entering into intercourse with men. Thus a distinction may be made between a worship of nature,—of hills, streams, trees,—as being physiolatry; a worship of animals, zoölatry; and fetishism, or a superstitious worship of lifeless objects. Idolatry is a more or less artistic development of fetishism. According to the faith of the ordinary believer, the spirit inhabiting the form is so far in man's power that by good or bad treatment he can control it to his advantage; and it is also possible for him to inflict injury on a distant enemy by obtaining possession of his image and piercing or harming it. This aspect of fetishism, or witchcraft, survived through millenniums. In European, as well as in Egyptian history, serious legal proceedings were based upon the official recognition of the power of man thus to vicariously control another, and even to murder him, either by sticking pins into his image, or, if of wax, by melting it before a fire. Totemism,[1] a designation suggested by Lubbock from an Indian word, marks a step in advance of fetishism. A specific individual thing is not now deified, but a sacred character is imparted to all individuals of the same species; thus, by elevating a bear to become a totem, a mysterious relationship of all bears to the men who venerate him is established. These totems are beings to which man feels himself subordinated, and whose favor it is advantageous for him to acquire. At this stage of human development the worship of the sun appears. This is the most conspicuous feature of the religion of Egypt in historic times, and in connection with ancestor worship it constituted the fundamental doctrine of the faith of Heliopolis, which eventually influenced the local worships of the entire land. To this stage also belongs the worship of the animal species; for the reason that the more powerful spirits have taken up their abode in animals on account of their innate superior energies, and in contrast with the more imperfect existence of plants and lifeless objects. Animals noted for their beauty and strength, for their value to man, for the terror which they inspired, or for certain well-defined instincts which seemed to establish a relation between them and some deified aspect of nature, led man to the belief that he must seek by worship for the favor of their indwelling spirits, and must thus avert the evil that might be inflicted by them. The several provinces of

[1] The word in the Algonquin language is *otem*, e. g., *kit-otem*, 'a family mark.'

Egypt had their escutcheons or standards, on which appeared the animal or object sacred to the locality; and we find in the sanctuaries of the temple sacred animals fed by the priests and honored as divine. There is, however, no indication that the Egyptians ever claimed kinship with or attempted to trace their descent from the local 'totem.' Deities were represented with the heads of animals whose conspicuous qualities seemed to present some analogy to the special attributes with which they were credited by their worshippers. To Kaiechos, the second Pharaoh of the Second Dynasty, was anciently ascribed the introduction of the worship of the Memphian Apis, of the Heliopolitan Mnevis, and of the Mendesian ram, from which perhaps is to be understood that official recognition was given by this king to the ancient faith of these localities. It should be remembered that traces of a primitive animal-worship may be found among other nations—notably among the Greeks. It is difficult not to see in the eagle of Zeus, the serpent of Asklepios, the owl of Athênê, for instance, a dim reminiscence of a remote stage of the people's religious evolution, when the Spirit of the Heavenly Power seemed to dwell in the eagle, and when the owl and the serpent were regarded as the embodiments of Athênê and Asklepios. The Egyptian priests maintained, even down to the latest times, a shrewd policy, according to which, while they were advancing toward an esoteric monotheism, they encouraged among the people the exoteric practices of the most unbridled fetishism.

The nome from which the first sovereign came was also the birthplace of the best-known and most important myth respecting the gods. Not far from Thinis lies Abydos, whose priesthood originated the Osiris myths, which rendered their sanctuary one of the most famous. The triumph of life over death lies at the foundation of this myth. Osiris and Isis are the children of Nut ('space') and of Seb ('earth,' which is constantly renewed and yet remains imperishable, and thus is a symbol of time). They in turn engendered in a mysterious way before their birth their child Horus. Next to these stands another pair, a brother and sister, Set (Typhon) and Nephthys, the former originally a god of evil, or of nature's fiercest powers, represented in the form of a fabulous animal with a sharp mouth, erect ears, and a forked tail; also in human form with the head of the same animal. He puts to death Osiris, having induced him by deceit to lie in a coffer, which he then shut and threw into the Nile. The coffer floats down the Nile, and on the third day is found by Isis and concealed. While she is with her son Horus at Buto, Typhon discovers the dead body, cuts it into fourteen pieces, which he casts about in different parts of the country. The severed members are the branches of the Nile in the Delta. The place where the Delta begins is called the 'dividing of Osiris' (Kerk-asar); and on the extreme western and eastern mouths of the Nile lie the towns of the right and of the left leg, Hauar-ament on the Canopic branch, and Hauar (Avaris) on the Pelusian. Isis builds a tomb for each member. Osiris, abiding in the underworld, joins himself after the burial to Horus, in order to aid him in the conflict with Typhon. This conflict followed in different places, since Typhon after every struggle came to life again; but it was finally crowned with victory. Typhon here appears as the serpent Apepi,[1] in the water, as, for example, at Ombos; sometimes also in human form, as on the portico of the great temple at Philae.

The meaning of this myth is obvious. Osiris, originally a God of the Dead, under the influence of the religion of Heliopolis becomes the sun, which every evening dies beneath the power of Typhon, the night. Commiserated by Isis, he wakes every morning as Horus, who, as avenger of his father, vanquishes the darkness. The contest takes place in the twilight hidden from the eyes of men, who behold only the result of the victory,—the rising of the new sun. In like manner the earth wakes by night, and Sirius also, the heavenly warder; and the moon rises up as a substitute for the sun, and as the pledge of its resurrection. Thus also Ra, the sun-god of Heliopolis, is styled the soul of Osiris, since he brings the light to its manifestation. Since the sun and the light are the original source of life, Osiris represents also the humidity out of which light produces all life; this finds in the god Hapi, the Nile, its visible expression. Typhon, with his seventy-two officials, represents the seventy-two days of drought, during which Isis, the fruitful earth, languishes and seeks her spouse, until her son has subdued the demon of drought, and the stream pours forth its waters anew. In this manner Osiris finally becomes life, Typhon death, Isis nature (in which both powers partici-

[1] Darkness, in Coptic, is *hof*, 'serpent:' *aphoph* is 'giant.'

pate), and Horus is the resurrection. Horus the elder is probably the most ancient god of the Egyptians. There is reason to believe that, before he came to personify the rising sun, he was originally a heaven god who—as Maspero has happily put it—became transformed into a god in heaven. His eye was the sun, his embodiment was the hawk; 'a hawk issued out of the sun'—(the heavenly abyssus), says the Book of the Dead (lxxi. l. c.). His name 'Her' means 'the above,' the 'Superior,' the 'Most High.' If we may judge by the coins of the nomes, as studied by Jacques de Rougé ('Monnaies des Nomes'), he was worshipped as local deity in at least half of the nomes. As light-god he is identified with the sun-god Ra. Both are depicted with the head of the hawk. Ra-Harmachis is represented with the sun-disk and a serpent, but Horus with the double royal crown upon the hawk's head. The greatest exploit of Horus is his victory over Set, to whom he was opposed as the winged sun-disk, Hor-Behûdti. In this form he was venerated in the temple of Edfu, for here was one of the chief scenes of conflict with Typhon (Fig. 12). The foes (Titans) were cast down from heaven, and appeared at Edfu as crocodiles and hippopotami, but were overcome by means of iron bars, and bound with chains. Horus in the form of a winged disk enters into the bark of Ra, and calls to his aid the goddesses of Upper and Lower Egypt in the form of the two uraeus-serpents (which also adorn the royal crown), who with their fiery breath consume his foes. In memory of this victory the winged sun-disk is conspicuous over all temple doors as a protection against evil. Still other scenes of conflict are mentioned. The myth is evidently to be understood as relating to the subduing of desert lands through the construction of canals. Plutarch (120 A.D.), who describes the Osiris myth as related in his day, adds several features not found in the earlier conceptions; for instance, he states that the coffer containing the corpse of Osiris was carried through the Tanitic branch as far as Byblos in Phoenicia. The Tanitic branch is mentioned because Tanis under the Shepherd Kings was a centre of Typhon-worship. Byblos is given as the place where the body was found, because the Adonis myth originated there, and was regarded as closely related to the Osiris

Fig. 12.—Horus. (Edfu.)

myth. However this may be, Osiris—'Lord of Abydos,' the 'good being,' 'Lord of life,' 'Lord of Eternity'—becomes the type of perfect humanity. He is the Judge before whom all must appear after death. He is the Lord of Amenti (the West), where Maat, the goddess of Truth, holds a conspicuous place. On his head he wears the white crown of Upper Egypt, adorned with the two 'Feathers of Truth.' He holds in his hands the flail and the crook, insignia of supreme power. Before him the dead are brought and, if not found wanting, they become united in him, they partake of his divinity, and may "go out by day" in the Bark of Ra.

Nephthys, sister and spouse of Typhon, yet not hostile to the light-god Osiris, but the one who brought up young Horus, is only another form of Isis, and is likewise originally a deity of the earth. It was said that Osiris had taken her in the dark for Isis, and had begotten Anubis from her, which signifies, according to the language of myths, that in some places she was worshipped as the wife of Osiris. She weeps for dead Osiris, since she is the earth, the mistress of the house (*nebt-ha*), who compassionately takes the deceased under her protection, and hence is styled the goddess of death. Her son Anubis is the 'ruler,' or 'guide' (of the dead). We have already seen (Introd., p. 17) that, in his form of Up-Uatu, he was worshipped at the very beginning of history. He is the god of mummies and of embalming, the guardian of the tomb, and the one who leads in the supposed path to heaven over which the departed travel. Upon his jackal head he wears the royal crown, *pshent*. Sirius, who in heaven watches over the dead body of Osiris, is his star. As Nephthys is only a form of Isis, so are also many other female deities identifiable with mother-earth and with the receptive and productive forces of nature. These forms are only local variations of the same divine being. They are so nearly related that they are confounded, and the same activity is ascribed now to one and now to another of them. Isis wears the reduced figure of a throne upon her head, and often wears a disk and cow's horns. As Hathor she is represented with the head of a cow. She appears as Hathor ('house of Horus'), as mother of Horus, inasmuch as this god, being the child of the sun, rises out of the womb of the earth, the underworld. As goddess of love and joy, of music and feasts, she appears as a dancer with the tambourine. In the story of the two brothers and of the doomed princes (given on a papyrus belonging to the British Museum and translated by Brugsch and others), there appear seven Hathors as fairies or fates determining the future. Even the cow, Methuer, is the motherly goddess, the spouse of Thoth, on whose horns the young god Ra sits and holds fast. The golden light, which in heaven and on earth with enchanting play of colors accompanies the ascent of the sun-god, as well as his victorious going down, encompasses the goddess, who greets the god in both parts of the heavens. Especially in later times did the worship of Isis and Hathor become very popular. Gorgeous temples at Denderah and Philae are proofs of this which still survive. Even in Rome they had a sanctuary, and among the heaps of its ruins interesting excavations have been made. The chisel of Greek sculptors carved statues of Isis, and the picture of Isis nursing the child Horus became the lovely original of the Madonna with the child. Mut ('mother') is also a child-bearing goddess; her sacred animal is the vulture, of which it was fabled that it occurs only as a female bird. As a vulture she hovers protectingly over the Pharaoh, and on the ceiling of the temple-halls a vulture's crest adorns the heads of the mother-goddesses. She coincides in several respects with Nekhebt, who likewise as a vulture hovers with her wings over Osiris and Pharaoh as well as over the source of the sacred river. As guardian genius of the southern country she is portrayed in the form of a serpent, — the serpent which devours noxious creatures in the garden where she lives in summer. But the maternal goddess also lightens the pains of labor, in which capacity she received divine honors at Eileithyia (El-Kab). Neith (i.e., 'the one who is'), or Nebun, worshipped at Sais, in the western Delta, is a form of Isis. She is regàrded as a Libyan goddess, and her worship goes back at least to the time of Mena, who mentions her shrine, and whose queen's name was Neit-hotep. The feline goddess—as lioness (Sekhet), consort of Ptah and mother of Imhotep or Nefer-Tum; as cat (Bast), the tutelary deity of Bubastis—typifies, in its various aspects, the fierce or beneficent action of the sun. The Greeks identified her with Artemis.

Thoth is the local god of the fifteenth nome of Upper Egypt and of the city of Shmun (Ashmunen), the city of the eight primeval gods, or four pairs of personified elemental forces. He is the moon-god, to whom the white ibis is sacred, and therefore he wears on his ibis-head the moon-disk. As light-god he has a place in the sun's bark; as the god of time he bears in his hand the palm-branch symbolizing the year, and on it he records the most important events, the course of the moon lying at the foundation of the most ancient division of the year. Yet later his province as moon-god disappears; and he now appears only in the capacity of scribe, which constitutes him god of the sciences pertaining to the priests. These begin with the observation of the heavenly bodies, and the regulation of the reckoning of time. He is the author of all sacred writings, the founder of libraries, over which his consort Safekh in especial presides. She is a kind of Clio, who records immortalized names on the fruits and leaves of the sacred persea-tree. He is lawgiver, vindicator of souls before the court of the dead, for which reason that shrewd animal the ape, or cynocephalus, sacred to him, sits on the tongue of the balance in which the heart of the dead is weighed. With the advance of mental cultivation, whose protector he is, there increased also the veneration paid to Thoth. From great, he became 'twice' and 'thrice great,' and, known as *Hermes trismegistus*, was the centre of a kind of theosophy which was not without influence in giving form to Christianity in its earliest days.

A second series of myths, allied to those concerning Osiris, originated at Heliopolis. It symbolized the conflict of light and darkness. Ra is the creator of the world; his eyes enlighten the universe; he is the bearer of light and the awakener of all life, and with numerous hosts under the command of Horus, he wars against the serpent Apepi, or darkness. As young Harmachis (Har-em-khu, 'Horus of the horizon') he moves onward in the sacred bark, and passes over the ocean of heaven in an eternal course, attended by the Shesu-hor or servants of Horus, the souls of men from a sinless golden age, which preceded the existing period of the world. One Horus manages the rudder, another stands before him on the bark and watches for Apepi, in order to pierce him with a lance. He is Ra as the midday sun. At the setting sun he is Tûm, or the god who in the shades of the underworld hovers above the waters, and who, as forerunner of the sun's rising, is a god of the resurrection. At this point Nut, the goddess of the heavens, receives him, and the bark floats in the stream of the underworld (the back of the dragon-snake, Apepi), upon which it is drawn with a rope by spirits, from west to east. Here he rises up every day sitting upon a lotus-flower, new-born from the mistress of the underworld, Hathor, in the form of a cow; at the end of every solar year Apepi is transfixed and cast into the sea; but the conflict is continually renewed. Ra is the same deity with whom, on account of the universal presence of the sun, who goes down into the night of Hades, were connected very ingeniously certain esoteric religious doctrines. This is ascertained from the Hymn to Ra, which was discovered at the entrance of the kings' tombs, and forms a kind of introduction to the sculptured representations of the inner apartments with regard to the course of Ra through the universe. In this hymn, which has been translated by Naville, we find an advanced pantheism.

The hymn to Amen-Ra in the temple at El-Khargeh, of the time of Darius, is also pantheistic. The sacred animal of Ra is the white bull Mnevis; Ra is also represented with a hawk's head, as Harmachis. The bird Bennu, a heron (Ardea garzetta), is the Phoenix of the Greeks. Its name means 'that which revolves' or 'turns back.' It symbolized the morning sun arising out of the fiery glow of dawn, and as such was the bird of Ra. But, as the dead sun was held to have become an Osiris, and as the new sun was regarded as arising from the dead body of the old—the Bennu was also sacred to Osiris. The planet Venus, in a text, is called 'the Bennu of Osiris'—or the 'Star of Osiris.' The Phoenix, as the type of resurrection, belongs to a very early date. Even in texts of the Old Empire the deceased is likened unto a Bennu.

The ram-headed god Khnum (Kneph), who wore a special crown, Atef, was the god of Elephantine (Fig. 13). As time went on, he was combined with Ra. At Abaton, near Philae, the sacred Ram, by a play upon words—'Ba' meaning both 'ram' and 'soul'—was called 'the soul of Ra.' At Heliopolis he corresponded to Osiris and was worshipped as his soul. Moreover, as mediator between drought and fertility, Khnum became the lord of the inundation; and at the first cataract, where the Nile enters Egypt, he was worshipped. As creator, it was he who placed upon the potter's wheel the world-egg prepared for him by Ptah out of primeval matter, and created man. Sebek also (Fig. 14) was venerated at Selseleh, in the region of the cataract, and in the Fayum, as the god of the inundation; in Ombos he was united with Hathor and Khnus in a triad; he is known by his crocodile head. Shu was recognized as the son of Ra, the personification of wind and air; he is the 'upright,' who separates and raises the heaven-goddess Nut, each day, from Keb, the earth god.

Fig. 13. Khnum, the Lord of Elephantine.

Fig. 14.—Sebek-Ra.

Among the local gods who came to occupy a prominent place in the Egyptian Pantheon was Ptah, the god of Memphis. He was a creator god, 'the Opener,' who, as the formative power, was developed out of the primeval water, Nun. In Memphis, where he led the divine Triad, he was hailed as Creator of the World, and also as the first ruler of Egypt. He was the "Creator of his own image. He who created himself, who establishes truth, king of the two lands, lord of Heaven." To him the scarabaeus was sacred.

The sacred scarabaeus (*khepera*) with the sun-disk, the principle of light, and the creative power who gave fire to man, deposits in this original matter the germs of all that should come into existence. This insect, *Ateuchus sacer*, is a great beetle, which, after the subsidence of the inundation, creeps forth and rapidly propagates itself; its habits gave rise to the belief that it came into being without having been begotten; and as its eggs are rolled about in the mud and are hidden in the ball thus produced, it was thought that it kept its progeny securely in the ball, and it thus became an image of the world containing in itself the germ of all living things. Since the creator gives form to the germs deposited by the scarabaeus, breaking the world-egg of which heaven and earth are the shells, and from whose inward part his children, the elements, come forth, the beetle was sacred to Ptah; the pygmy figures of Ptah-Sokari-Osiris are often found represented with a scarabaeus on their heads. The beetle served as a symbol of the sun at its meridian; therefore it was represented in association with the sun-disk; and Hor-behûdti, as Agathodaemon, is figured as a winged disk of the sun, or as a scarabaeus with the disk between his feet.

The beetle, as an embodied manifestation of creative and masculine power, was portrayed on terracotta or stone, and was worn as an amulet or inserted in ornaments. The scarabaeus, inscribed with the necessary formulae from the Book of the Dead, was used to replace the heart of the mummy. It was also placed among the wrappings upon its breast. It is often represented in a bark, with Isis and Nephthys worshipping at its side. On the outer cases of the mummies these beetles appear with winged disks or hawks. On the rough surfaces the scarabaei are polished for the reception of ornaments, images of the gods and inscriptions, commonly with the escutcheon or cartouche of the reigning Pharaoh. At times also one finds the name of a Pharaoh on specimens of different ages.

Ptah, the framer of the world, had seven architects under him, the Kabiri of the Phoenicians, with whose help he prepared for Ra the elements of creation. As lord of the laws of growth, as the unerring, intelligent fashioner of all things, as lord of the Egyptian measure of length, he was the lord of law and justice. As a new-born child or a pygmy, that is, as the god of the creation of the universe, as the god that gives unchanging and eternal life, Ptah is represented as a mummy, having, it is true, his hands free in order to hold the sceptre, the rule, and the ringed cross, the symbol of existence; a cap is on his head, such as is worn by smiths. As embodiment of the fire hidden in the world, he imparts, in his capacity of Ptah-Sokari-Osiris, to the sun-god who has gone below, and to the mummy of the departed, the power of resurrection. Since the mind of the deity works upon matter, and out of this activity a third existence, a cosmos, arises, there is commonly a triad of gods, which appear as father, mother, and son, in the language of men. Thus Ptah, with Sekhet and Imhotep (Asklepios), or Nefer-Tûm, forms a trinity, in which the son is but the father returning again to life, and hence is, in mystic speech, the consort of the mother. These triads spread from Egypt over the ancient world: among the Greeks they appear in the mysteries, which are of Oriental origin; in the Theogony of Hesiod seven triads are found, which, however, at a later day are unknown. Triple deities were recognized in the oldest religious formulas of Italy. There was the Quirinal triad of Jupiter, Juno, and Minerva; among the Umbrians, Poimonus, Vesona, and Tursa, and the god Cerfus Mortius, with Prestita and Tursa. Etruscan temples had three cells lying side by side for designated groups of the gods, and the cells at the sides were to the middle in the ratio of three to four. There was also the triad of the Kabiri, Axierus, Axiocersa, and Axiocersus. The sacred animal of Ptah was the bull Apis (Hapi), the eternally creative power of the deity. The white cow, impregnated by a ray from the moon, gave birth to him; his skin was black; he had a white spot on his forehead; on his back a winged disk or eagle, and under the tongue an excrescence in the shape of the beetle. After his death he became Osiris; and it is in this form of Asar-Hapi that he later became an object of worship to the Greeks. Under the name of Serapis—whom they endowed with some of the attributes of Pluto and Asklepios—he became a semi-Greek deity to the Alexandrians, and his fame spread far and wide in Ptolemaic times.

Among other deities might also be mentioned the god Bes, apparently belonging to the land of Punt.[1] He goes through the world as a pilgrim, dispensing mild manners, peace, and jollity; he appears also on mirrors and objects of the toilet, as the toilet-god. He is always portrayed as a grotesque dwarf in a dancing posture; his hands rest upon his hips, and he bears on his head, which is large and thick, a lofty ornament of feathers. He appears again among the Phoenicians as Baal Markod ('god of the dance').

The death and resurrection of Ra, which took place each day, was a pledge that his creatures should not forever dwell in the shades of death. Faith in immortality, or continued existence after

[1] "The Egyptian Ophir," says Brugsch (Eng. Trans., vol. i., p. 114), "without doubt the coast of the Somali Land in sight of Arabia, but separated from it by the sea."—Tr.

death, was so strong with the Egyptians that the numerous obligations imposed by the dogmas connected therewith were fulfilled with an energy which seems to recognize the inflexible character of natural law. In fact, the careful preservation of dead bodies demanded by religion was for the Egyptians an imperative obligation. The poisoning of the river by casting into it the bodies of dead men and animals would in a short time have rendered the existence of man impossible. The Greeks also, inspired in this respect by the noblest and loftiest thought, taught the continued existence of the soul, and burned the body, which was of no further use. Other nations believe in a resurrection of the body, but leave to God the formation of the heavenly body out of the decayed particles of the corpse; thus the Jews have imagined that the bodies of the dead will be reconstructed by God out of the bone *luz* (*os sacrum*). A higher piety, at least a stronger confirmation of the Egyptian's belief in continued existence, is manifested by the patience and devotion with which for thousands of years he excavated sepulchres, sometimes labyrinths and palaces of rock, adorned with splendid decorations (hidden as in the darkness of the night), as the abode after death of kings and priests and millions of the departed. The belief in immortality was as old in Egypt as the kingdom itself; but it appears in the most ancient times as a mere continuation of earthly life in the grave—a far more simple and harmless form than later, when a complicated system of retribution and other inventions awakening dread were connected with it by a priesthood intent upon increasing its influence.

According to the Egyptian belief, man was composed of different parts which at death became released and must be returned to him in order that he might survive. The 'Kha,' or corpse, written with the hieroglyph of a dead fish—the ideogram for anything putrid—must be preserved and made into a mummy—an Osiris—when it became a Sâhû—i. e., the empty form of himself which having been received from the godhead might return to it. Besides the body, there were moral and intellectual, as well as quasi material parts, which must be restored. The 'Ba,' or soul, was represented as a human-headed bird provided with hands. At death it flew to the gods. While approaching our own conception, the 'Ba' was not immaterial, and its survival depended upon proper sustenance.

There are representations of the Soul-bird fluttering over the mummy holding to its nostrils the cross (Life) or the Sail ('nef' or Breath). For the Breath must be returned to the mummy; also his power—'Sekhem'; his shadow 'Khaib'; and his intelligence—'Khu' the 'luminous'—which suggests 'the divine spark.' The heart 'Ab' was also indispensable to his well-being. But that which plays the most conspicuous part in the tomb is the 'Ka' or double. It was the personality—probably suggested by the image, which is limited neither by time nor space, and which can be evoked in one's dreams and thoughts, or by a likeness. At death, man ceased to be; his 'Ka' received the benefit of the offerings; and when it returned to the mummy and 'lived in its coffin' they together enjoyed the same existence as on earth. All living things had 'Kas,' even the gods. The name 'Ren' was also essential. It was man's supreme desire that his name might live. In early times, however, it would seem that power over a man might be obtained by the knowledge of his name, and means were taken to protect it.

Many of these ideas were, no doubt, developed from a simpler philosophy. The 'Ka,' the 'Osiris,' and the 'Sâhû' may represent different local expressions of the same prehistoric conception, later amalgamated into one doctrine. Contradictory views also existed regarding the after-life: While an elaborate ritual provided for man's comfort in his 'eternal abode' by opening his eyes and mouth, that he might see his possessions and taste the viands provided for him, we find the Osirian dead preparing to till the fields of Aalu; or achieving apotheosis by identification with the gods; or traveling by day in the Solar-Bark. Diversity also existed with regard to the fate of the wicked; but whatever their preliminary ordeals, it seems tolerably certain that they ultimately became annihilated. If there was confusion as to these matters, there was no doubt in the ordinary Egyptian mind as to the possibility of attaining immortality, if proper methods were used: An ancient epicurean might sing: "Follow thy heart's desire so long as thou livest on earth . . . for no one carries away his goods with him and no one returns again"; but nevertheless, he carefully prepared his tomb; supplied his 'Ka' with statues to serve as artificial bodies should his mummy be destroyed; provided for its sustenance, real and artificial, for all ages to come; and courted popularity in order that his fellows might look after his future welfare, feed his 'Ka,' keep his memory green, and help his 'name to flourish.' When the end came and the funeral rites had been performed, the soul appeared before the throne of Osiris in the underworld. (PLATE III.[1]) There, in the Hall of the Two Truths (Truth and Justice), in the presence of forty-two gods, each of whom presided over a mortal sin, the defunct was brought by Anubis to vindicate himself. Maât, the Goddess of Truth, bore witness. His heart was weighed in her scales against the feather of Truth by Horos and Anubis. Thoth, the divine Scribe, recorded the result. If not found wanting, his heart was returned to him; the immortal parts of his being were restored to him; and once more he was made a living man—but now to live eternally. He seems to have been free to assume what divine shapes he might wish.[2] That of the sacred hawk, of the Bennu (phoenix), of the asp, of the swallow—that is, probably, of the gods of which these are the embodiments. This should not, however, be mistaken for the pythagorean doctrine of metempsychosis—or the transmigration of souls—as the animals or objects into which the beatified soul thus passed were sacred to certain gods and represented a process of apotheosis, which apparently could be undertaken at will. The religious views of the Egyptians may be studied, not only in their sepulchral texts, such as the Pyramid texts and the Book of the Dead; but also in minor works: 'The Book of Breathings'; 'the Book of Wandering through Eternity'; 'The Book of what there is in Hades'; 'The Book of Transformations'; the Book of 'That my name may flourish,' and others. Their high ethical standards appear in the 125th

[1] DESCRIPTION OF PLATE III.

Plate III. reproduces, in reduced facsimile, a page from a papyrus containing the so-called "Book of the Dead." The scene selected represents the judgment of the dead before the god Osiris. OSIRIS, the judge of the Lower World, is seen seated upon an altar in a temple supported by columns. Opposite, MA, the goddess of truth and justice, is conducting the dead man into the temple. In the centre stands a balance; in one of the scales rests a handled cup, in the other a feather, the symbols of the heart and of truth, respectively. HORUS and ANUBIS, the sons of Osiris, closely watch for the inclination of the balance. Upon it the dog-headed HAPI sits, as the symbol of measure. Before the balance stands the ibis-headed THOTH, the secretary of the gods, and indicates the result of the weighing on a papyrus. Between him and Osiris is seated a female hippopotamus, AMAM, called the Devourer. She acts as accuser of the dead man. THOTH justifies him, if he has led a righteous life. In the upper section of the hall the dead prays to the forty-two judges of the dead, each of whom bears on his head the feather of truth, and has jurisdiction over some one particular sin, of which in the text the dead man has professed himself guiltless.

[2] 'Le Livre des Transformations,' G. Ledrain, Paris, 1870.

N THE LOWER WORLD.

.)

(See page 56.)

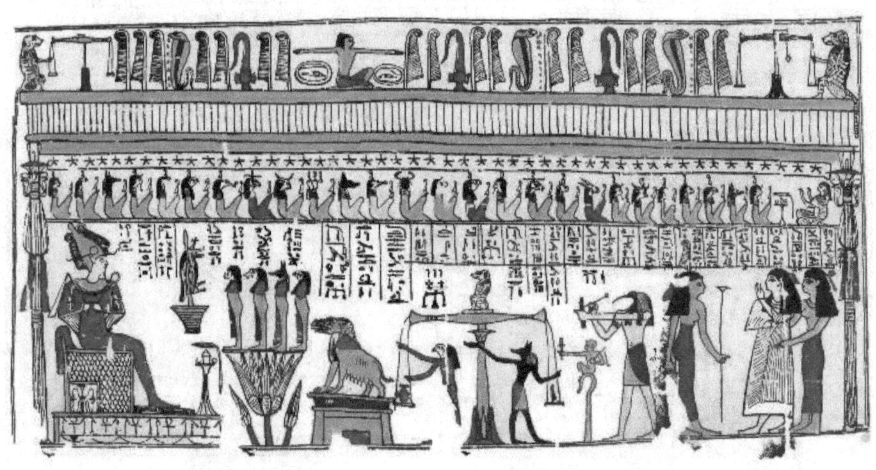

THE JUDGMENT OF THE DEAD BEFORE THE GOD OSIRIS, IN THE HALL OF JUSTICE IN THE LOWER WORLD

(From the Papyrus discovered at Thebes, containing the so-called Book of the Dead.)

Facsimile. Half Original Size.

(See page [illegible])

chapter of the 'Book of the Dead,' which contains the 'Negative Confession' of the defunct before the tribunal of Osiris. The code of morals therein revealed includes, not only the decalogue, but many rules governing good feeling and gentlemanly breeding. The staging of Hades is represented in a similar manner among other nations; and as opinions concerning the underworld are often derived from burial regulations, the ease with which religious ideas are interchanged renders the influence exercised by Egyptian conceptions as natural as it is indisputable. The Greeks borrowed directly from the Egyptians, as they themselves acknowledged. Diodorus, in describing the burial of Apis, draws attention to this matter, and says that the conductor of souls, Hermes (i.e., Thoth), brings the mummy of Apis to a certain place, where it is received by a shape with the mask of Cerberus (probably Anubis); that the ocean over which, according to Homer in the Odyssey, the dead pass, is the Nile; that the Asphodel-meadow is in the vicinity of Memphis on the Acherusian lake (in Egyptian called the "Fields of Aalû" or "Aarû"), which is surrounded by meadows and ponds covered with reeds and lotus flowers. Here the bodies were carried by the Egyptians across the river and lake in a boat called *baris;* the ferryman Charon[1] receives an obolus for the passage, as the Egyptians placed in the mouth of the mummy small pieces of gold; furthermore, here stood the temple of gloomy Hecate (Hathor), and the gate of Cocytus and Lethe with its brazen hinges. In the Iliad (viii. 15) the iron gates and the bronze threshold of Hades are mentioned; likewise in the Old Testament, in "the writing of Hezekiah" (Isaiah xxxviii. 10; Job xvi. 16). The Assyrians, too, imagined that before "the land where man seeth naught" lies a slimy stream, the Acheron; and they held that this land, or rather the vast palace, is encompassed by sevenfold walls, and shut in by gates. Thus also the Egyptian dead, passing through a chasm in the mountain near Abydos on its way to Amenti, went through the brazen gates of twelve pylons, which stood for the twelve hours of the night. These were watched over by serpents—the guardians of the temple and the genii of the earth. The sarcophagi of the New Empire are valuable as showing the manner in which were expressed these beliefs regarding Hades. It is noteworthy that the entire

[1] Horus steers the sun-bark in the underworld.

structure of immortality rested, in Egypt, upon the preservation of the body or the providing of substitutes. The Egyptians never conceived of a soul independent of the body. The doctrine of the resurrection is also foreign to the Egyptian religion; but it readily connects with the Egyptian belief in the possibility of the soul's reunion with the preserved body.

Embalming and interment, as practised by the Egyptians, were most perfectly accomplished. Individuals were so preserved as to be recognizable after thousands of years, and could be destroyed only by the hand of violence. The art reached its highest development under the XVIIIth and XIXth Dynasties—and the mummified head of King Seti I. (see Frontispiece) is a fine example of the degree of perfection attained by the embalmers of Thebes. It still preserves some of the beauty and all the dignity of life. The discovery that dead bodies could be preserved was probably brought about by observing that bodies buried in sand impregnated with natron and other salts remained dry and incorrupt. Herodotus points out that the simplest method of preserving the entire body is to place it in natron after some preceding injections. This process of embalming is described in detail by Herodotus and by Diodorus.

The successors of Mena upon the throne of Egypt are named in the series of kings given by the Sebennytic priest and temple scribe, Manetho. He prepared, by command of Ptolemy II. (284–246 B.C.), a history of Egypt from the historical books preserved in the temples. Of his work only fragments and lists of names are extant. These were preserved partly by Flavius Josephus (born 37 A.D.), who probably did not derive his materials directly from Manetho, but from Alexandrian extracts, and in part by the Byzantine monk, Gregory Syncellus, who at the end of the eighth century composed synchronistic tables. The latter availed himself of extracts made by Julius Africanus and Eusebius, Bishop of Caesarea (who died about 340 A.D.). There has also been preserved from the chronological work of Eratosthenes, librarian in Alexandria, B.C. 276–194, a list of thirty-eight kings. These invaluable catalogues of kings are in part supplemented and in part confirmed by a number of inscriptions and other memorials found at Abydos, Karnak, and Sakkara; by the Turin papyrus, and by genealogical testimonies

PLATE IV.

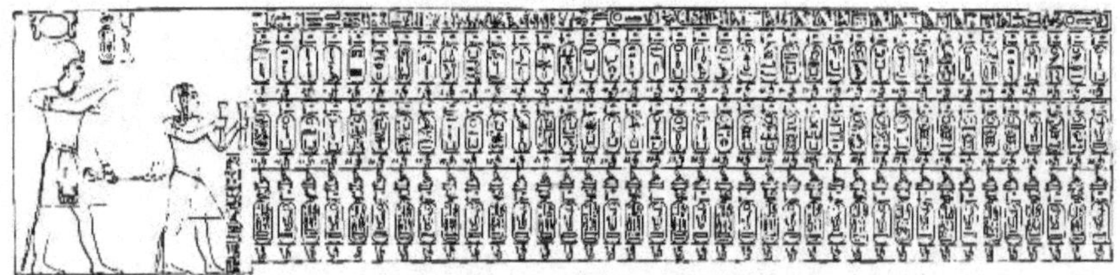

Hieroglyphic Genealogy of the first eighteen Dynasties of the Kings of Egypt.

Bas-relief from Abydos. British Museum. (After Dümichen.)

History of All Nations, Vol. I, page [illegible]

on the monuments. The table of kings known as the Abydos list (PLATE IV.) exhibits Seti I. with his son Rameses venerating their royal ancestors. The reader will find in the subjoined illustration the cartouches or escutcheons of the following kings: 1. Mena. 2. Teta. 3. Atet. 4. Ata. 5. Hesepti. 6. Merbapa. 7. Sem-en-ptah. 8. Kebhu. (Nos. 1–8 of the First Dynasty.) 9. Bezau. 10. Kakau. 11. Ba-en-neter. 12. Uaznes. 13. Senta. (Nos. 9–13 of the Second Dynasty.) 14. Zazai. 15. Nebka. 16. Zeser. 17. Teta. 18. Sezes. 19. Neferka-Ra. (Nos. 14–19 of the Third Dynasty.) 20. Snefru. 21. Khufu. 22. Ratetf. 23. Khafra. 24. Menkaura. 25. Shepseskaf. (Nos. 14–25 of the Fourth Dynasty.) 26. Userkaf. 27. Sahu-Ra. 28. Kaka. 29. Nefer-Ra. 30. Ra-en-user. 31. Menkau-Hor. 32. Tetka-Ra. 33. Unas. (Nos. 26–33 of the Fifth Dynasty.) 34. Teta. 35. Userka-Ra. 36. Meri-Ra. 37. Meren-Ra. 38. Neterka-Ra. 39. Meren-Ra-Mehtiemsaf. (Nos. 34–39 of the Sixth Dynasty.) 40. Neferka-Ra. 41. Menka-Ra. 42. Neferka-Ra. 43. Neferka-Ra Nebi. 44. Tetka-Ra Shema. 45. Neferka-Ra Khentu. 46. Mer-en-Hor. 47. Sneferka. 48. Ra-en-ka. 49. Neferka-Ra-Tererl. 50. Horneferka. 51. Neferka-Ra Pepi Seneb. 52. Neferka-Ra Annu. 53. Menkau-Ra. 54. Neferkau-Ra. 55. Horkau-Ra. 56. Neferarka-Ra. 57. Nebkher-Ra. 58. Sankhka-Ra. (Nos. 40–58 of the Seventh to Eleventh Dynasties.) 59. Sehetepab-Ra (Amenemhat I.). 60. Kheperka-Ra (Usertesen I.). 61. Nubkau-Ra (Amenemhat II.). 62. Khakheper-Ra (Usertesen II.). 63. Khakau-Ra (Usertesen III.). 64. Maāt-en-Ra (Amenemhat III.). 65. Maā-Kheru-Ra (Amenemhat IV.). (Nos. 59–65 of the Twelfth Dynasty.) 66. Nebpehuti-Ra (Aahmes). 67. Zeser-Ka-Ra (Amenhotep I.). 68. Aa-Kheper-Ka-Ra (Thothmes I.). 69. Aa-Kheper-en-Ra (Thothmes II.). 70. Menkheper-Ra (Thothmes III.). 71. Aa-Kheperu-Ra (Amenhotep II.). 72. Menkheperu-Ra (Thothmes IV.). 73. Neb-Maat-Ra (Amenhotep III.). 74. Razerkheperu Setpenra (Horemheb). (Nos. 66–74 of the Eighteenth Dynasty.) 75. Ramenpehuti (Rameses I.). 76. Maamen-Ra (Seti I.). The last row shows nine times repeated the double name of Seti: Maamen-Ra Merenptah Seti.

The table of kings from the tomb of Tunury at Sakkara gives the following names. For comparison with the Abydos list we connect the numbers of the latter with the several names, whence it results that the names of the Twelfth Dynasty stand in an inverted order. The names begin below on the left (see Fig. 15): Merbapen 6, Kebhu 8 (First Dynasty); Neterbau 9, Kakau 10, Baneteren 11, Uaznes 12, Sent 13, Neferkara (wanting in the Abydos list; in Manetho's, Nephercheres) (Second Dynasty); Sekerneferka (wanting in Abydos, Manetho's Necherophes), Zefa (wanting in Abydos, Manetho's Tosorthros), Bebi (Abydos, Zazai 14), Zeser 16, Zeserteta 17, Nebka-Ra (Manetho's Sephuris ?), Huni (the same as 19 on Abydos list) (Third Dynasty); Snefru 20, Khufuf 21, Ratetf 22, Khafra 23, Menkaura 24, four cartouches without names (Fourth Dynasty); Userkaf 26, Sahu-Ra 27, Neferarka-Ra (Abydos, Kaka 28), Shepses-Ka-Ra (wanting in Abydos, in Manetho's Sisires), Khanefer-Ra 29; in the upper row: Menka-Hor 31, Maaka-Ra (Abydos, Tetka-Ra 32), Unas 33 (Fifth Dynasty); Teta 34, Pepi (the same as 36 on Abydos list), Meren-Ra 37, Neferka-Ra 38 (Sixth Dynasty); Sebekka-Ra (a king before the Eleventh Dynasty, but nowhere else named); Makheru-Ra 65, Ma-en-Ra 64, Khaka-Ra 63, Khakheper-Ra 62, Nubkha-Ra 61, Kheper-Ka-Ra 60, Sehetepab-Ra 59 (Twelfth Dynasty); Sankhka-Ra 58, Nebkher-Ra 57 (Seventh to Eleventh Dynasty); Nebpehu-Ra 66, Zeser-Ka-Ra 67, Aa-kheperka-Ra 68, Aa-kheperen-Ra 69, Menkheper-Ra 70, Aa-kheperu-Ra 71, Menkheperu-Ra 72, Maaneb-Ra 73, Zeserkheperu-Ra Setpenra 74 (Eighteenth Dynasty); Menpehuti-Ra 75, Maamen-Ra 76, Usermaa-Ra Setpenra (Rameses II.). The fundamental work devoted to the restoration of these tables was published by Lepsius at Berlin in 1858, with the title of 'Book of the Kings of Ancient Egypt.' Since then, however, considerable new material has been recovered. There is an enormous difference of opinion among competent authorities with regard to the date of the foundation of the United Empire. Many hold that Manetho's dynasties reigned contemporaneously; others, that he only recorded such dynasties as were consecutive. A third group of scholars effect a compromise; and, piecing together the ever-increasing monumental record, regard some dynasties as consecutive and others as contemporaneous. The highest date proposed for Mena is about B.C. 4777. The lowest is about B.C. 3200. The latter is not based upon any chronological fact, but is simply the minimum date at which Mena could have lived.[1] Occasionally, statements are discovered in pre-

[1] Erman Life in Eg., 1894; Ed. Meyer Gesch. des Alten Æg., 1887, giving 2830 B.C. for Fourth Dynasty.

served documents which tempt scholars to use them as fixed points on which to base a chronology. But it is only from the beginning of the New Empire that firmer ground is reached. We may, however, roughly assume as approximate dates—B.C. 4000 for Mena; from B.C. 2500 to 2000 for the Middle Empire; and B.C. 1550 for the New Empire. The now famous Palermo Stone is a valuable guide for the early kings; and Petrie has tentatively restored the First Dynasty, comparing the Egyptian and Manethónian lists with the monumental evidence of Abydos. (See Introduction, p. 15.)

Fig. 15. List of Egyptian Kings from the tomb of Tunury at Sakkarah.

The great archaic tombs of Abydos were marked by two stelae set upright to the east of each. In time these fell. The nekropolis was forgotten. Nothing is found there of the pyramid period or of the Middle Empire. But with the New Empire interest was again awakened in the ancestors. Royal lists were compiled. It is noteworthy that Seti's list at Abydos is the most correct for this early period. Offerings now were made at the royal tombs—ignorantly—as appears from the heaping of offerings at Enzaza's tomb—a mere official of the Sixth Dynasty—while those of Kings Mer-neit and Azab were overlooked. This ignorance accounts for the great tomb of Zer being taken for that of Osiris, whose granite cenotaph was set in it. Priesthoods of Mena and of Teta continued until Ptolemaic times; and, according to tradition, Teta built a palace at Memphis and caused medical works to be written. This is not the only trace of literary activity at this early period. The sixty-fourth chapter of the Book of the Dead is said to have been discovered under the reign of Hesepti—the fifth king of the First Dynasty—King Den-Setui of Abydos—and the medical papyrus of Berlin states that it was

FIG. 16. — Shera and his wife. (Oxford.)

composed under Hesepti and revised under King Sent (Second Dynasty). The tomb of a librarian of Memphis, in the Sixth Dynasty, has been found. This library, according to Galen, still flourished in Roman times, and was consulted by Greek physicians. Several of the early kings appear in popular tales of later times; for instance, in the stories preserved in the Westcar papyri. Tombs and monumental remains of the Second and Third Dynasties have also been found at Abydos, but their identification with the lists is less clear. A tablet in Oxford, of very great antiquity, names a priest Shera as presiding over the worship of Sent (Fig. 16). Tefa also, the second king of the Third Dynasty, is said to have been a physician.

The most ancient medical art consisted of incantations; diseases were attributed to the pernicious influence of demons. Only after centuries had passed were drugs employed in addition to these formulae.

Zeser (Tosorthros of the Third Dynasty) left a record as a great physician. He promoted literature and erected stone buildings. According to Manetho, in the reign of Boethos, the founder of the Second Dynasty, a chasm opened near Bubastis. Petrie regards the statement as probable, as Bubastis is near Abu Zabel, the region of plutonic action.

The third king of the Second (Thinitic) Dynasty, according to Manetho, established female succession to the throne. A number of Horos-names found inscribed on archaic monuments at Abydos and elsewhere, although difficult to identify with their equivalents on the lists, probably belong to these dynasties. Such are 'Mer-sed,' 'Kha-Sekhemui,' 'Per-ab-sen,' whose tombs have been found, and several others which appear on various objects—notably Neter-Kha, who is identified with the Step-Pyramid of Sakkara. The unclassified archaic King Narmer, and the great heiress-queen Ne-maat-hap (Second Dynasty), also stand out with historic distinctness.

The first king of the Fourth (Memphite) Dynasty, Snefru, erected on the frontiers of the Delta fortresses against the Asiatics or Anu. He conquered the peninsula of Sinai, and set men to work the mines of Sarbût-el-khâdem, in the Wady-Sûwik (north-northwest from Serbâl) in search of copper and turquoise. As late as the Twentieth Dynasty these mines were worked; and one may see to-day a great enclosing wall within which are sixteen pillars, or slabs of stone, bearing inscriptions by the overseers of the mines, and making mention of the Pharaohs whom they served, and of their activity and exploits. The same Snefru in Wady-Maghâra, southwest of Sarbût-el-khâdem, not far from the coast, caused men to dig for copper, malachite, and turquoise (which, however, are impure and lose color). Snefru is portrayed on a relief (which unfortunately is nearly ruined) in the act of slaying with a battle-axe a barbarian prostrate upon the ground before him. His pyramid at Medum was excavated by Petrie (1891).

The succeeding Pharaohs, Khufu and Khafra (between whom the tables of Abydos and Sakkara insert Ratetf, probably an elder brother of Khafra), and also Menkaura (Mycerinus), are rendered famous by the pyramids of Gizeh. The accounts of the tyranny and cruelty of

Cheops (Khufu) and Chephren (Khafra) related by Greek authors, proceeded from the reflection that works of those kings, such as the Pyramids, could not have been accomplished without severe enforced service and abuse of human strength. It was not considered that many other rulers who have erected similar stupendous structures have not been godless tyrants. The monuments bear witness that both rulers were venerated as divine as late at least as the Twenty-sixth Dynasty. Of Khufu, an ivory statuette found in 1903 by Petrie has preserved the features. It reveals intelligence and force. Seven diorite and green basalt statues of Khafra were found in a shaft of the granite temple at Gizeh (Figs. 17 and 18). They are now in the Gizeh Museum. The bearing of the head, overshadowed by the wings of the divine hawk (Fig. 18), and the dignity of the pose, convey an impression of majesty.

The son of Menkaura, Hor-tutef, appears to have played an important part in religious history. He is praised as a man of learning, and it is reported that he was sent by his father for the purpose, partly of increasing, and partly of restoring, the temples. Thus it came to pass that he found in Hermopolis the thirtieth and sixty-fourth chapters of the 'Book of the Dead,' inscribed upon an alabaster plate lying at the feet of the deity (Thoth) of that city. This rediscovery of books commonly signifies that the finder was the author, for by their casual discovery in the temple the character of a divine revelation is imparted to them. The successor of Menkaura, Aseskaf (Asychis), erected, according to Herodotus, several structures near the porch of the temple of Ptah. Diodorus attributes to him the origin of astronomy and geometry, as well as the regulation

FIG. 17. — King Khafra.

of the service of the deity, and styles him one of the five great law-givers who ordained rules governing transactions in loans.

A memorial of victory in honor of Sahura, the second king of the Fifth Dynasty, still remains in the Wady-Maghâra, which is so rich

Fig. 18.—King Khafra (bust).

in sculptures. This monarch is portrayed in the act of smiting and killing with a battle-axe the nomadic Mentu (Fig. 19). Sahura founded the town of Pa-Sahura, south of Esneh (the modern Sahera), and built in Memphis the temple of Sekhet. It is not altogether certain in what order his successors are to be arranged, since the monuments give more names than Manetho's list. We may suppose either that we have doublets of some of these names on the monuments, — the Pharaohs being designated not only by their throne names, but also by other names, as Ra-en-user (Rathures) in Manetho is the praenomen of An, — or that Manetho omitted some names which seemed to him unimportant, perhaps because the rulers reigned for a short period.

This An, like his predecessor Sahura, is portrayed in Wady-Maghâra as a conqueror. Of the successor of An, Menkau-hor (the Mencheres of Manetho), a portrait (Fig. 20) is preserved upon a block of stone built into the Serapeum, which probably came from

FIG. 19. — Monument of King Sahura at Wady-Maghára.

the tomb-chapel of his pyramid; the chapel itself has not yet been discovered. The composition of the most ancient book in the world must be referred to the reign of Assa, the last Pharaoh but one of the Fifth Dynasty; it is the papyrus which Prisse acquired at Thebes and presented to the Bibliothèque Nationale, and of which a facsimile was first published by him. The manuscript (Fig. 21) was written at the time of the Twelfth Dynasty, about 2450 B.C., and contains at the opening a moral treatise by a certain Kakemne, who lived under Snefru. The last fifteen pages form a philosophico-moral essay by the nomarch Ptah-hotep, a prince of the blood, contemporary with the Fifth Dynasty.

FIG. 20. — Bas-relief of King Menkau-hor (Mencheres).

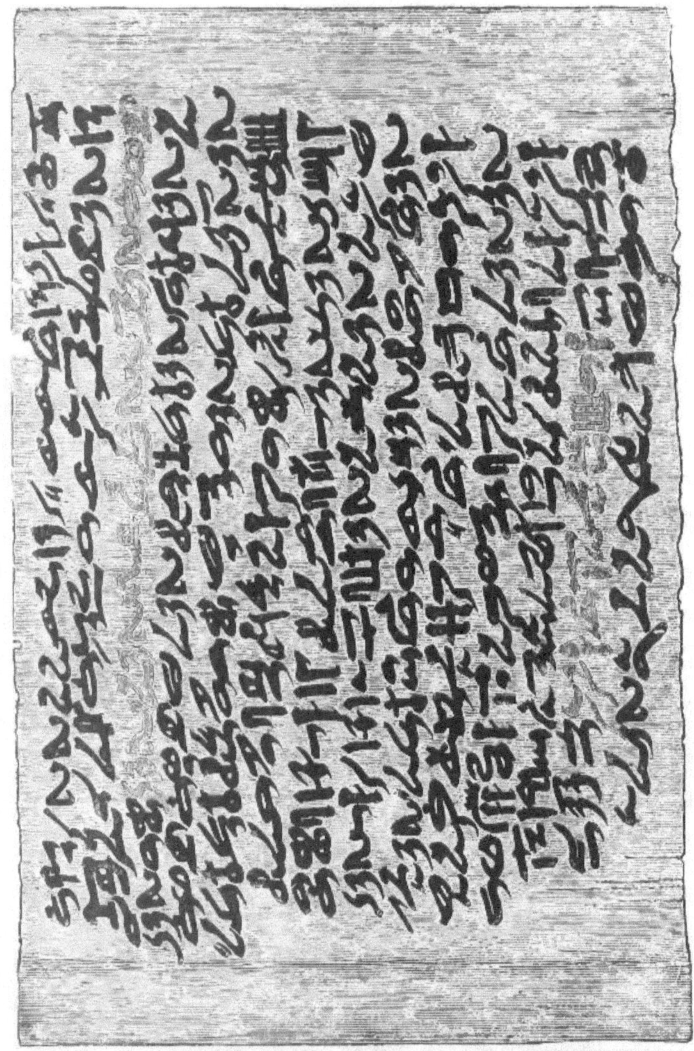

FIG. 21. — Facsimile of the oldest book in hieratic writing, the Prisse papyrus.

It is a collection of moral precepts, many of which might be followed to-day. In substance, style, and even occasional verbal expression, it recalls certain biblical texts, such, for instance, as Ecclesiastes. He was a very old man: Light failed, the ears "had stopped, lips were mute, taste and smell were gone"; but he sought to convey his worldly knowledge for the well-being of men. With his collection of moral sayings he blends profitable rules of life and conduct for most varied circumstances. This work has often been studied and translated.

The last Pharaoh of the Fifth Dynasty erected a temple to Hathor in Memphis, and founded the town Unas, which was named for him. The first king of the Sixth Dynasty, Ati or Teta (in Manetho, Othoes), is supposed to have met with a violent death, being murdered by a servant. Maspero conceives that in the reign of the Teta (by Wiedemann taken to be Othoes) of the monuments, who reigned in Memphis, there arose at Abydos a king, Ati (Othoes); and although this king was murdered, the royal authority of the successors in the Fifth Dynasty, to which Teta belonged, passed over to Ati's son, Meri-Ra Pepi. Pepi—whose pyramid has been identified—like the earlier kings, gained a victory over the Mentu of the Wady-Maghâra, who were constantly renewing their attempts to break up the working of the mines in that region. There is also an inscription concerning Pepi in the stone-quarries of Seiseleh, as well as in those at Hamamât (on the road from Coptos to the Red Sea), where, too, are found inscriptions relating to more ancient rulers. Pepi undertook the erection of buildings at Tanis, and renewed the temple of Denderah according to an old plan found by him,—a plan which was precisely that of Khufu, and of which Thothmes III. subsequently availed himself for his work of restoration. It is said, however, that the plan found by Pepi had existed before the time of Mena. Pepi waged a war against Asiatics with regard to which an inscription in honor of Una, commander of the host, gives more exact information. This inscription, one of the oldest historical documents, and in which for the first time negroes, or Nehesi, are mentioned, has often been translated. For this war large negro forces were raised, among other places, in the country of Wawa, from whence the Egyptians obtained their silver, an indication of the great extent of the kingdom under Pepi. The people attacked by Pepi's army were called Amu and Herusha (that is, 'those living upon the sandy shore'), but their dwelling-place is not clearly described. On the so-called poetic stela of Thothmes III. at Karnak, the Herusha are spoken of next to 'the people at the head of the waters,' that is, the lagoons of the Nile. After five destructive invasions, whereby cultivated lands and vineyards were laid waste, the Herusha retreated to Takhba (Terehbah or Tatepba), whither Una sailed in ships, and there overcame them. As the highest mark of distinction for his services, Una obtained leave not to put off his sandals in the king's palace, and even in the presence of the king. He was also honored with a dignity not previously conferred, that of viceroy of Upper Egypt.

In the thirteenth year of Pepi the end of a period of the star Sirius is reported to have occurred; this sovereign must therefore have begun to reign in the year 2795 B.C. A second Pepi was the son of the first, and a younger brother of Mer-en-Ra. Both of these are noteworthy for the length of their lives. The second Pepi, according to Manetho, reigned one hundred years, and over ninety according to the Turin papyrus (the name is wanting here). From this it appears that his elder brother died a young man after a reign of seven (in the Turin papyrus fourteen) years, and Pepi when a child succeeded him. The elder brother was found in 1881, in the sepulchral chamber of his pyramid at Sakkara, his skin having a natural appearance, the nose sunken, the lower jaw missing (see p. 73); the body has been removed to the Gizeh museum. The last prince of this dynasty was murdered, having reigned but one year. His legendary sister and consort, Net-akerti (Nitocris), caused an extensive apartment to be constructed under ground, and at its consecration invited those who were principally concerned in the murder. She turned in upon them the water of the river and drowned them; thereupon she threw herself, in order to escape revenge, into a room filled with red hot ashes, and thus ended her life. Many tales are related by the Greeks concerning her, since she was confounded to some extent with the wife of Psammetichus III., of the Twenty-sixth Dynasty. One of these stories is important to the student of folk-lore: it presents the oldest version of the story of Cinderella and the glass slipper. Rhodopis ('the rosy-cheeked'), —so was Nitocris called, Manetho giving her flaxen hair and rosy cheeks — was a hetaera; she was bathing in the Nile, when an eagle carried off one of her sandals, which he dropped upon the knee of the king, who was then holding a court of justice in the open air. Enraptured with the beautiful foot to which the sandal must belong, the king sent messengers throughout the land in search of Rhodopis, and made her his queen.

After Nitocris there commences a dark period. The lists of Manetho give only the total number of the rulers in each dynasty with the years during which they reigned. The Seventh (Memphite) Dynasty continued, according to Manetho, for only 66 days; according to another version, it embraced 70 kings. Eusebius (in Syncellus) gives it five rulers and 75 years. The Eighth Dynasty (Memphite) is reported to have had 27 kings, reigning in all 146 years. The Ninth Dynasty (of Herakleopolis), whose founder was the tyrant Achthoes, had 17 kings with 409 years (in Syncellus there were four kings and 100 years). The Tenth Dynasty (of Herakleopolis) numbered 17 kings, whose reigns lasted 185 years. Finally the Eleventh, with which the importance of Thebes arose, had 16 kings, and continued only 43 years. The brief duration of these dynasties and the dearth of monuments encourage the belief in a period of internal strife. While the Memphite power weakened, the princes of Herakleopolis grew in prosperity. Khati I., Meri-ab-Ra (Akhthoes) founded the Ninth Dynasty. His name is found at the first cataract. It is likely that this dynasty was contemporaneous with the early Theban Antefs. These grew in power and rebelled. The kings of the Tenth Herakleopolitan Dynasty endeavored to suppress them—as appears from the tombs of the lords of Siût who fought for them. Eventually the Thebans prevailed and established the Eleventh Dynasty. Several Antefs appear on the lists and the monuments. One of these bequeathed the crown to a younger brother, who built for him a wooden coffin overlaid with gold, which was deposited in Gurnah, the chief necropolis of Thebes, and is now in the Louvre; the tomb of his wife has also been discovered in Gurnah. Of this queen the Berlin Museum possesses a wooden coffer with an arched cover (Fig. 22). In it there is a small box made of the inner bark of reeds, in which is a basket of fine straw upon a stand. This last contains five alabaster flasks, and one of serpentine, containing medicines. Near it lie two spoons and a small dish, and a large number of medicinal roots. A gilded coffin of another Antef is in the British Museum; and his silver diadem, overlaid with gold, is at Leyden. The tomb of a third Antef contains a statue with an inscription made in the fiftieth year of his reign; the coffin of a fourth Antef, also from Gurnah, is preserved at Berlin. At this court a poem was composed, passages of which are also found in the tombs at Thebes. It commands a cheerful manner of life, since with death all joy ceases. It thus illustrates the description given by Herodotus of Egyptian banquets. We read, among other things, in this song: "Lay of the house of king Antef, the departed, which is composed by the harper. Hail to the good prince. The good destiny is fulfilled. The bodies pass away and others remain behind. Since the days of the ancestors, the gods (i.e., the kings) who have been before time, rest in their pyramids. There have they built houses, whose place is no more, thou seest what has become of them. I heard the words of Imhotep and Hardataf, who both spoke thus in their sayings: 'Behold the dwellings of those men, their walls fall down. Their place is no more. They are as though they had never existed.' Who tells us how it goes with them? Who nerves our hearts until you approach the place whither they are gone? With joyful heart, forget not to glorify thyself, and follow thy heart's desire, so long as thou livest. Put myrrh on thy head, clothe thyself in fine linen, anointing thyself with the true marvels of God. Adorn thyself as beautifully as thou canst and let not thy heart be discouraged. Follow thy heart's desire and thy pleasures so long as thou livest on earth. Let not thy heart concern itself until there comes to thee that day of mourning. Yet he whose heart is at

FIG. 22. — Cabinet of Queen Mentu-hotep.

rest hears not their complaint. And he who lies in the tomb, understands not their mourning. With beaming face celebrate a joyful day, and rest not therein, for no one carries his goods with him. Yea, no one returns again who is gone thither."

Three kings of the name of Mentu-hotep are mentioned. One of them lived between two of the five Antefs, and his name is given upon the list at Karnak. Of one of these is an inscription, made in the forty-sixth year of his reign; he is also shown by the monuments to have been sovereign of Upper and Lower Egypt. These kings have left many traces, not only at Thebes, but at Koptos, Assuan, Sakkara, and at other sites. The last king of the Eleventh Dynasty appears to have been Sankh-ka-ra, who led a great expedition to the land of Punt, the coasts in the vicinity of the strait of Bab-el-Mandeb, the region of Yemen and of Somali. An army went with him and many laborers from Koptos and Kosseir; they dug on the way four artesian wells. They finally reached Arabia, and brought to Egypt the products of that country—spices, frankincense, precious stones, and the like; a fact which gives a conception of the power and enterprising spirit manifesting itself in these last-named Pharaohs. Manetho assigns Ammenemes to the Eleventh Dynasty, who, on account of genealogical relation to the Twelfth Dynasty, has been commonly placed at the head of the latter dynasty.

Mummied head of Meren-Ra Mehti-em-sa-f.

CHAPTER II.

ART IN THE ANCIENT EMPIRE.

IF we review the political record of the Old Empire, we are struck with its insignificance. A few raids in the South, some repressive campaigns against the encroachments of Asiatic tribes on the eastern frontier, cover Egypt's military record. If there were great wars, they have left no traces. We find, however, ample compensation for this in the completeness with which the private life and mode of thought of the Egyptians is unfolded in their art and architecture. The oldest of the dated structures in Egypt are the great tomb of Nagadah and the royal tombs of Abydos. These architecturally stand as a link between the pre-dynastic pit-tombs (see Introduction, p. 8) and the mastabas of the nekropolis of Gizeh. Each of these archaic tombs was practically a large square or oblong pit. Some are as large as 100 × 50 cubits. They are lined with brick-work, roofed over and floored with wood, and closely surrounded by rows of small chambers—the tomb of King Kha-Sekhemui (Second Dynasty) has fifty-seven—which, in the earlier examples—as in the tombs of Zer and Zet—open from it, but which, by King Mer-neit, were built separately around the main tomb. By Den-Setui, an entrance passage and a stairway were added, which Qa-Sen turned to the north. Petrie has pointed out that, at this stage —i.e., the end of the First Dynasty—we are within reach of the early mastabas and pyramids. By substituting stone for brick-work and wood, and by removing the tombs of retainers further away, the type of mastaba-pyramid of Snefru is obtained. And the latter is the architectural link with the true pyramid.

The nekropolis of Memphis, in expressive Egyptian language styled the 'Land of Life' (*ānkh-ta*), is a vast cemetery, which stretches from Abu-Roash, opposite Cairo, as far as Dashur, south-west of Memphis, a distance of ten hours. In it are several groups of pyramids, at Abu-Roash, Gizeh, Tsawiyet-el-Aryan, Abusir, Sakkara, and Dashur. The embalmed bodies of millions of Egyptians rest here in the sand and rock of the desert, which at this point borders directly upon the valley of the Nile. In external form private sepulchres are rectangular structures extending from north to south with side-walls somewhat inclined. The Arabs call these sepulchres *mastabah*. They are made of brick, at first yellow, later of a dusky color, or of limestone. The east side, turned toward the Nile, is commonly the façade, decorated by a niche near the north corner; near the south corner is the entrance. The more modest mastabas have sometimes no interior work apart from the mummy-pit, except

Fig. 23. — A Table of Offerings.

only a deep recess with a tablet. When the door is on the north, there is a vestibule in front with two square pillars; this is also the case when the door is placed on the south side, yet here, too, the construction of the east side may occur. In a tomb at Gizeh there is to be seen an actual column with a calyx-shaped capital, and quarter-round moulding below. The entrance is never on the west side. Within there is an apartment or chapel, which, as a rule, is adorned with sculptures and paintings; some sepulchres contain vaulted ceilings of separate blocks. A necessary feature is the tablet built into the western wall, upon which the names and titles of the deceased are engraven, as well as the ritual which secures to him the enjoyment of the objects set apart for him (Fig. 23); here the survivors, on visiting the tomb, read or repeated the ritual. Often before the tablet in the wall stands a sacrificial table of granite. The chapel is also decorated with scenes of funeral festivities accompanied by musical performances. On both sides of the niche are sometimes placed portraits of the deceased, with a front view in high-relief, as, for example, in the tomb of Ur-khun, built during the reign of Neferarkara (third king of the Fifth Dynasty) in Sakkara, and at Gizeh in the tomb of Khafra-ankh (Fourth Dynasty). Another part of the interior is the *serdāb*, a hollow place which for the most part is connected with the chamber only by a hole an hand-breadth wide. Since it was not beyond the bounds of possibility that the mummy might be destroyed or removed, the Egyptians took care, by depositing statues of the dead in these serdabs, to provide a material support for the spirit. These 'Ka' statues might be indefinitely multiplied. With such an object in view, it was natural that attention should be paid to the exact reproduction of the features. Realism, not attractiveness, was aimed at. We also understand why old age was never represented. The portrait upon which the spirit must depend in all ages to come always represented the original in the vigor of life. Through the small opening in the serdab the soul could glide, and the stone image could inhale the sacrificial vapor of the offerings to the dead. In a sepulchre at Gizeh the chamber is of considerable length, and upon a long rear wall one observes under the ceiling four square holes, and below, at half the height of the wall, four other slit-like holes; all these eight holes

FIG. 24. — Granary from the tomb of Ameny, Beni-Hassan. (After Maspero.)

open upon four long serdabs, and in conformity to the interior of the latter the slits become wider. Finally, every mastaba has a pit sometimes forty, often more than sixty feet in depth, which is excavated out of earth, either from the external platform of the mastaba through the wall, — as is most commonly done, — or (as in the richly constructed mastaba of Ti) from the soil of the rock chamber. The pit opens below into a passage which leads to the tomb; in a corner of the latter was placed the stone sarcophagus. This inclosed the painted wooden coffin, in the shape of a mummy with a human countenance; it was often gilded. In this coffin lay the mummy. The entrance of the passage to the tomb, as well as the opening of the pit upon the platform or in the chapel, was walled up after the completion of the offering to the dead; the pit was filled with rubbish, among which in the tombs of the Middle Empire sometimes are found the fragments of a wooden bark in which the deceased journeyed through the underworld. The tomb is always placed in the same axis as the upper room or chapel. The mastaba tombs show as yet no amulets or statuettes of ushabtis, but only two or three pointed vessels for water placed against the wall, and also bones of bulls which had been offered to the deceased as nourishment. The slaying of the bull is often represented pictorially in the upper chamber. In the interior of the sarcophagus may be found furniture, consisting of a foot supporting a crescent-shaped head-rest, such as it was the custom to place under the head when sleeping (instead of our pillows), and a number of vessels made of alabaster. The coffin (Fig. 25) is rectangular, with perpendicular corners; the lid, except a part at the two small ends, is rounded off in the direction of its length: the lid is so arranged that a part of its lower rim fits into a groove in the upper edge of the coffin, and the seam is filled with cement. The decoration of the stone coffin is borrowed from the architecture of the wooden dwelling-house. A beautiful example is the syenite coffin of Khufuankh (Gizeh museum). The tomb is the eternal abode, the dwelling is but the shelter for the brief pilgrimage on the earth. In the vicinity of the pyramids at Gizeh tombs are found which are not built up, but chiselled out of the wall of rock; they consist of several chambers with sculptures, and the pit excavated in the soil, a type richly developed in later times in the Theban nekropolis. We may, therefore, follow step by step the evolution of Egyptian sepulchral architecture from prehistoric times to the New Empire.

With the architecture of the tombs sculpture is very closely connected. We have seen that in consequence of the beliefs with regard to the relation of the soul to the mummy, the Egyptians came to deposit statues of the departed, known as 'Ka'-statues, in the serdab or inner chamber; and that in order to facilitate for the soul the identification of its former abode, the resemblance of the image to the living subject must be rendered as exact as possible. The artist to whom was intrusted the making of these statues was therefore compelled to conform to nature. This is a most salutary restraint for an artist, since it guards him against sinking into mannerism and an unnatural treatment. The works of Egyptian artists are therefore distinguished

FIG. 25. — Stone sarcophagus.

by the highest skill in portraiture, and by realistic representation. The admiration excited by these ancient specimens of statuary has often suggested the inquiry as to the kind of technique adopted by the sculptor. Although traces of iron have been discerned even in the time of the Fourth Dynasty, yet the manufacture of steel at that period has not been demonstrated. It is admitted that by some unknown process a hardness approaching that of iron was imparted to bronze. Had steel been in use, there would have been discovered in the oldest pieces of work very sharp edges and deep cuttings, as in later art which employed steel; but there is no instance of the kind. Flinders-Petrie, after a thorough examination of slabs of stone worked with the saw, has proved that saws of bronze were used, and that these were tipped with hard crystals, probably corundum. The investigations of Émile Soldi, directed to objects of art, as well as scenes upon Egyptian reliefs representing the restoration of statues, have brought to light the methods of the artist. With the punch, struck by long hammers, blocks of hard stone, such as granite, were split, and were engraved with figures cut into the stone; the shaping followed with a pick-hammer and chisel, but the latter came into use late and was seldom employed, as for instance, in order to draw the sharp outlines of the hieroglyphics, as well as their straight and crooked edges. All granite statues are polished, not indeed by file and rasp, but by means of moist sandstone powder, which is spread over them with a kind of brush, and is rubbed over the surface by curved pieces of wood or by flat stones. Emery must have been imported from Naxos at an early day, for without the use of this it is impossible to account for many very smooth surfaces. The danger of dislocation in restoring the more delicate parts, as the neck and the extremities, was obviated by the fact that the artist did not separate these from the general mass; the neck up to the head adheres to the back of the chair, or to the pillar on which the figure leans. For the same reason, the beard on the chin is not separated from the neck. The mediocre character of the granite statues is caused by the material and the technique, as has been explained by G. Semper; whilst wooden figures and bronze vessels, and even many limestone statues, show that the artists understood very well how to fashion the extremities separately, and how to give the impression of physical activity, as in the reliefs and pictures. In order to loosen immense blocks of granite in the quarry from the native rock, the stone-cutters introduced wooded wedges, which expanding on being wet split off the stone, or with pointed crowbars they drew furrows around the block, and finally separated it by many blows applied at the same time. It should be noted that the sculptor of reliefs not only drew lines with red paint, forming squares upon the flat surface in order to outline the figures in their just proportions, but also that statues were copied from models previously prepared.

Herodotus relates that King Mycerinus had set up in a hall of his palace about twenty wooden portrait-statues of his wives, and had also caused a hollow wooden image of a cow to be made, in which he put the body of his deceased only daughter. Though the object of these works of art is here erroneously explained, the artistic development of Egypt in his day cannot be questioned.

FIG. 26. — Portrait heads of early date (Sepa and Nesa). Louvre.

Ancient works of art, which appear to belong to the period of the Second Dynasty, are the somewhat clumsily executed statues of Sepa and his wife Nesa (Fig. 26). They are distinguished by the fact that the lower eyelid is marked by a green stripe; the palettes and green paint found in the burials of the Nagadah period show this practice to have belonged to prehistoric times. It was probably ritualistic. (See Introduction, p. 8, note.) The statues of Ra-hotep and of Nefert (Figs. 27, 28) are famous; they were found at Medum in a tomb of the reign of Snefru. They are so life-like that they startled the superstitious Arabs who first saw them into the belief that they were spirits guarding the tomb. Both figures and a high chair, together with the seat, are worked out from a block of limestone, a little less than four feet in height. The man has a round face, hair cut short, a dark, straight beard, full lips; his clothing consists simply of an apron covering the upper part of the thighs; round his neck hangs a cord with a small round talisman; the left arm rests upon the thigh, the right is somewhat raised, and its closed hand is placed upon the heart; the legs are parallel; it is noticeable that the second toe is longer than the first, and that the small toe has its proper shape. In other civilized nations it usually appears misshapen from wearing a shoe. Nefert has thick hair above the eyes, parted from the top of the head; at the sides of the face artificial hair falls down upon the shoulders: the head is encircled by a diadem. The countenance is full, and preserves in the beautiful eyes that somewhat melancholy expression which frequently at this day one observes

Fig. 27. — Statues of Ra-hotep and Nefert. (Gizeh Museum.)

in the faces of Egyptian women. The thick garment like a tunic, reaching to the feet, clings to the form. The arms, which are hidden by it, are placed one above the other, and the hands lie beneath the breasts. The neck is adorned with jewellery richly wrought, and garnished with bands of gold.

All statues were painted. The naked parts of the body in men are painted a reddish brown, in women a yellow color: the hair is always black. The eyes receive a specially careful treatment. The

Vol. I. 6.

so-called Scribe (Fig. 29), from a tomb of the Sixth or Seventh Dynasty, who, according to Oriental custom, is seated upon the ground clothed only in the gown-like apron (*shenti*), and who seems

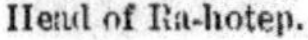

Head of Ra-hotep. FIG. 28. Head of Nefert.

to be writing off words dictated to him by a judge or other official, is indebted for the effect produced — aside from the excellent treatment of the parts of the body — above all else to the eyes. They are bordered by a bronze plate forming the lids and lashes, and consist of a piece of opaque quartz, in which the apple of the eye, made of transparent rock-crystal, is inserted by means of a polished metallic pin. Similar eyes has also the life-like wooden statue of Ra-em-ka in the Gizeh Museum, the so-called Sheikh-el-Beled,[1] or Town-elder (Fig. 30)—which represents this dignitary with a staff in his hand. The head of his wife is perhaps even finer, and both are portrayed in a manner pre-eminently true to nature. These wooden portraits were covered before painting with fine linen glued to them, and which

FIG. 29. — The Scribe (Louvre).

[1] The Arabs who were excavating were struck by his resemblance to their town elder.

was intended to support the stucco; this received the paint, and was at the same time used for a finer kind of modelling. The statue of Ti is yet to be mentioned, one of the most valuable objects in the Gizeh Museum. Ti was a distinguished functionary in the time of An (Fifth Dynasty), by birth one of the people, but married to a daughter of the royal house. The gown-like apron, the only garment of this privy-councillor and high-priest, appears to stand out stiff with starch and ironing, as is often shown in the representation of royal robes. The naturalness of these pieces of statuary is so great that we are ready to believe that in the fellahs of Upper Egypt and their wives in our day we find their very models; the dress of modern Egyptian women consists of the same kind of tunic as that seen in those ancient statues. According to Semper, these Egyptian portrait-statues are not inferior to the Aeginetan in technique, and far excel them in the lifelike expression of countenance. The tomb-statues are made of limestone and wood, and sometimes of bronze, and eyes are inserted also in the bronze statues. The appearance of bronze in the time of the Fifth and Sixth Dynasties is of importance with regard to the history of this metallic composition. The Egyptians called the native bronze 'dark *khomt*,' and this seems to have been impure copper; but for bronze castings, however, only the foreign bronze, *khomt*, could have been used. The most ancient bronze statue in Chaldaea, a canephore,

FIG. 30. Portrait statue of Ra-em-ka.

was found at Affaj on the Euphrates, not far from Bagdad, and furnishes us with the name of a very ancient king, Kudur-mabuk. The Egyptian bronzes, however, are older by far; a bronze handle from the staff of Ratetf (Fourth Dynasty) is in private possession; another of King Pepi is in the British Museum; Flinders-Petrie found pieces of bronze in the pyramid of Abu-Roash. A bronze statue of Pepi, of ancient date (at Paris), bears an inscription with the names upon it of the Shasu, Semitic Bedouins dwelling northeast of Egypt. Inasmuch as the beginnings of civilization coincide with the use of metals, it is noteworthy that copper is as ancient as Egyptian civilization.[1] The tombs of the earliest dynasties and even of prehistoric times yield tools of practically pure copper. (See Introduction, p. 14.) However this may be, the appearance of bronze in Egypt where there was an utter want of tin, of which an alloy of nine per cent. with copper produces bronze, presupposes intercourse with a neighboring people at that time who possessed tin. Since it is highly probably that the Egyptians acquired the prepared bronze by barter, there must have been in that country the necessary buildings for smelting and forging. This unknown people also furnished bronze to the Chaldaeans. Tin is found in but few places on the earth at the utmost, — in the mines of Perak in Malacca; in Banka and Biliton, near Sumatra; also in Britain ('tin islands'), whence, according to Borlase, it was brought as early as the fourteenth or at least the twelfth century B.C., by the enterprise of the Phoenicians, to the emporium of Gades (Cadiz), and to the countries lying upon the Mediterranean. All ancient bronzes, including the Brazen Sea and the oxen in Solomon's temple, contained tin from Cornwall. Tin was found also in Iberia in the Caucasus. According to Diodorus, tin was produced in the island of Panchaea, on the eastern coast of Arabia, but was not exported. Tin for the bronze found in the Troad perhaps came from Crete; it is now found in Mount Sphacia. Whether Egypt obtained her tin from Crete, or whether it was brought to her overland from the Caucasus through the intervention of the Shasu, must, in the present state of our knowledge on the subject, remain a matter of pure speculation. The original method of manipulating bronze was by incrustation or empaestic; that is, a core

[1] Petrie in 1904 found an iron wedge in a Sixth Dynasty deposit (B.C. 3400).

of wood or clay was covered with the metal; in this manner bronze was handled by the Assyrians and Babylonians. Then followed the hollow-hammered work (*sphyrelaton*), such as was practised by the Greeks in very ancient times; the pieces were riveted together, and at a later day soldered. Finally the art of casting was invented. It is remarkable that the oldest Egyptian bronzes show the most recent step in technique,—the hollow casting.

Finely carved ivory statuettes found recently attest Egypt's artistic development under the first dynasties, and the art displayed in reliefs in the mastabas of the Old Empire is of the highest order. The characteristic difference between the execution of the earlier and the later reliefs consists in this: In the first the figures are made to stand out with a moderate elevation from a smooth surface. Theban art, on the other hand, forms hollow reliefs (*en creux*); that is to say, the work is in such a depression that the plane of the whole outside surface is in a line with the relief. The latter, however, gains distinctness through the depressions around the outlines of the figure. Besides stone reliefs, we also find wooden ones, as in the tomb of Hesi at Sakkara. These probably are older than the pyramids of Cheops. They serve to mask four false doors, and represent a scribe who carries his writing implements in his hand, or hanging over his shoulder.

Beside the statues of the occupant of the tomb, there are frequently found figures of servants, who, employed as when alive, are intended to surround the dead with the daily life on earth. There are attractive *genre* pictures,—a naked boy with a sack on his shoulder and a nosegay in his right hand; another is sitting on the ground, and thrusts his right hand into a tall pitcher which he is holding with his left: a girl kneading dough in a vessel placed upon the ground is remarkably realistic; a dwarf by the name of Khnum-hotep, inhabitant of a beautiful tomb at Sakkara, reminds one of the dwarfs of Velasquez.

The reliefs on the tombs, in their varied forms, furnish a glimpse into the life of the Egyptian people, such as is obtained of no other people (see Fig. 24). The art of Telloh, which alone approaches it in age—no sculptures of any serious importance having as yet been recovered at Nippur—is military or hieratic. Even Grecian art, rich and varied as it is, is not so manifold as the Egyptian. This direction of art, as has been shown, received its impulse from the religious conviction that the deceased, as a shade, has sensuous perceptions, especially at those moments when the 'Ba' or the 'Ka' put themselves into communication with him for a time, and that one is bound to enliven the solitude of the tomb by reproductions of the happy earthly life.

It has already been remarked that the human figure is always represented in profile. The eye, however, is not fore-shortened, but represented in its full length, as it appears *de face*, while the arms again are portrayed from the side. The legs are represented in profile, with one stepping out before the other. In stooping figures, only one shoulder is to be seen; and this is so far falsely drawn that it projects in front of the neck, for the artist did not know how to overcome the difficulties of perspective, which are doubled in reliefs. Persian art was the first to achieve complete success in this respect. There are, however, here and there, correct drawings, as in the tomb of Ra-ases at Sakkara. So vast was the amount of work to be done that the laborers were directed merely to follow a fixed rule; and the evident offences against perspective were richly compensated by the invariably skilful treatment, and the vividness and distinctness shown in all movements of the human body. The artist's meaning is clear, aside from the hieroglyphic explanations accompanying the drawings. The representations of country life (Fig. 31) show the plough drawn by oxen, the peasant leaning upon the plough-handle, and the driver with his whip; near by rows of laborers are loosening the soil with hoes, and the sower is scattering seed from a basket, several of which are standing close at hand. The reapers seize their bundles of corn, and cut with the sickle; the grain is winnowed; men take it with a three-pronged fork or pole from the store piled upon a frame, and deliver it to the women, who winnow it and smooth the rising heaps; the threshing of the grain is done by the hoofs of the asses and oxen. Scribes who have reeds in their hands, and others behind the ear, are reckoning up the results of the harvest, sitting before the closed granaries, from which heaps of grain rise up at the top; or they are registering the number of animals in the herds of rams, goats, asses, cattle, gazelles (at that time domestic animals), geese, rabbits (never hens); and they are taking account of that which had been sold, after careful weighing, from the produce received. They also dictate punishments for the idle or evil-doers,

PLATE V

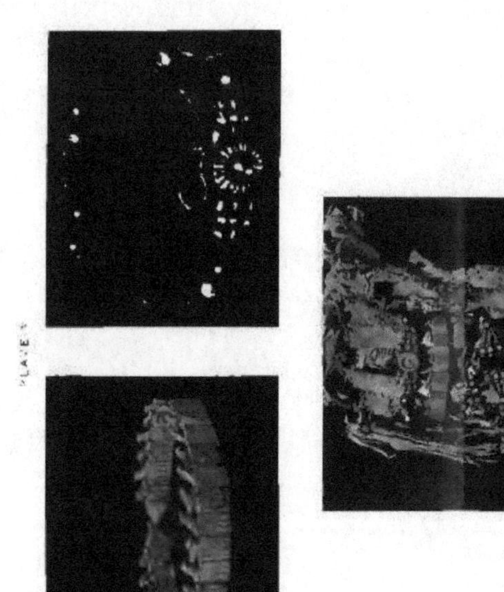

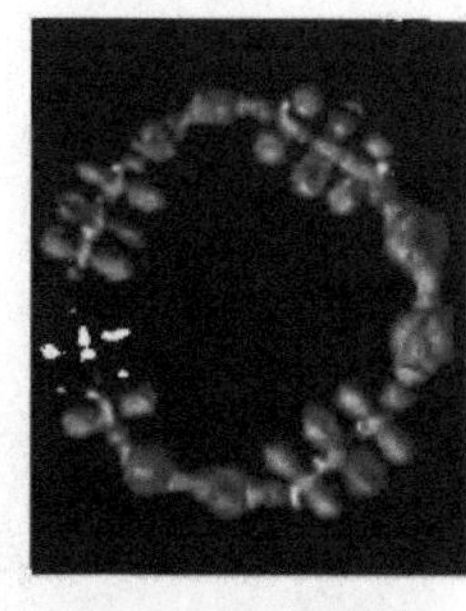

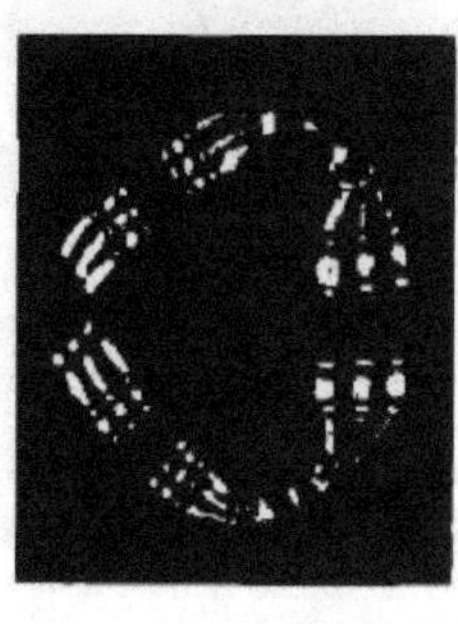

BRACELETS OF QUEEN OF ZER. I DYNASTY. ABYDOS. GIZEH MUSEUM

Palette of King Narmer, Hierakropolis.

who are dragged forward by the overseers. Herds of cattle are driven to the watering-place; the cows are milked, their fore- and hind-feet being chained together, or a person holds the cow by one fore-foot. Here are seen cowherds whose faces show black whiskers and a physiognomy different from the Egyptian type; and there is not wanting a cow which, with the assistance of the veterinary surgeon, is bringing forth a calf. Shepherds are sitting near their sheep-folds, and with them dogs with pointed ears. We see also olive-trees whose fruit men are gathering. Estates personified as male or female servants, whose names are written between the hieroglyphical figures, often recur. They are seen approaching in long rows, bearing their produce on their head,—fruits, liquors, and poultry,—which they are bringing to their lord.[1]

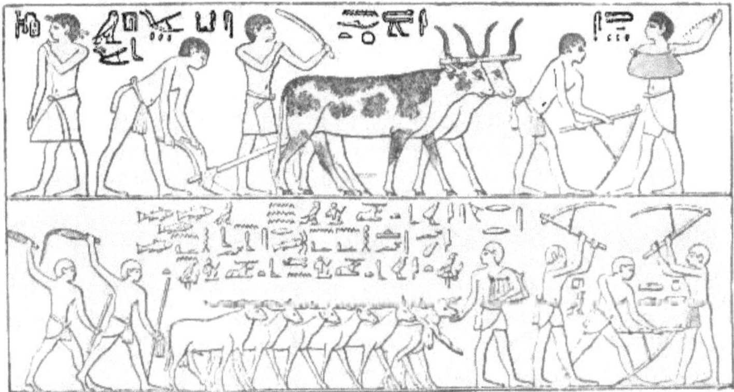

FIG. 31. – Farming scenes. Relief on a wall in the tomb of Ti at Sakkara.

rows, bearing their produce on their heads, — fruits, liquors, and poultry, — which they are bringing to their lord.[1] (PLATE V.)

Among the trades, bakeries appear in which dough is kneaded and bread or cake is made; butchers' establishments are very often represented, in connection with the pictures of offerings of bulls in the chambers of the tombs; the ox is brought in by means of a rope placed over the back in such a manner that one fore-foot is drawn up. From the dead animal, placed on its back, the skin is stripped off with sharp knives, one of which is whetted by a boy standing near; and beside it lie ribs, thighs, and other parts. Antelopes also are

[1] Many of the scenes described in this paragraph are figured on Figs. 24 and 31 and on Plate VI.

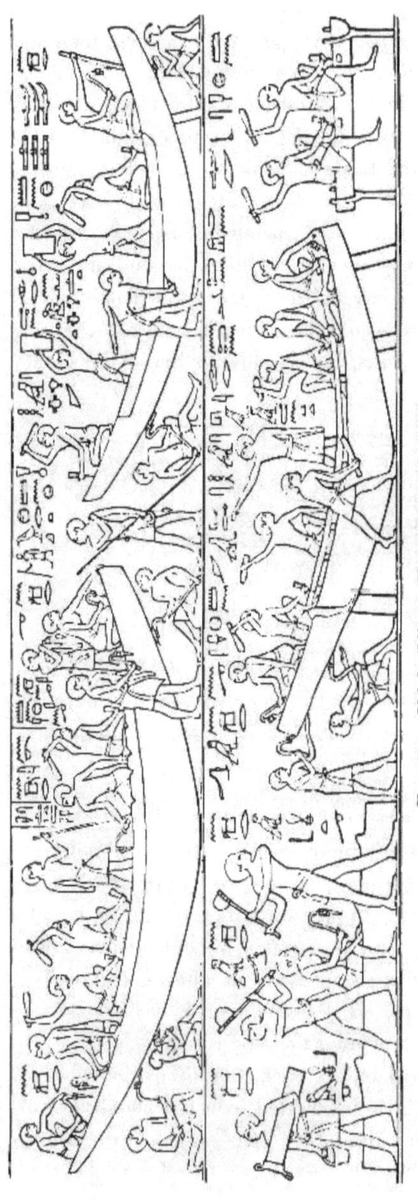

Fig. 32. – Shipbuilding. From the tomb of Ti.

offered in like manner; and the pieces are presented to the dead, together with fowls, vegetables, and roast meats. The process of wine-making appears: the grapes are poured into a sack which is fastened to sticks at both ends; two men turn the sticks in different directions so that the sack is wrung out like wet linen, and the juice falls into a tub. In the same sepulchre are also represented carpenters and joiners with all things fabricated by them, together with their tools, saws, axes, augers, drills, and planes. In the tomb of Ti one can see (Fig. 32) a ship in process of building, a pottery factory with patterns of different vessels, architects, and glassmakers. Among the possessions of the dwellers in the mastaba are to be found skiffs made of papyrus, and large Nile-boats; the last provided with masts, sails, and mats of various styles and colors for protection against the sun, and having twenty to thirty rowers at their seats on each side, while six steersmen with poles stand in the stern. A man is sounding the depth of the water with a pole. The crew, which are to go on board the vessel, carry with them all that is necessary for a fishing-expedition, — harpoons, poles, rudder, anchor; also supplies of food, with small boxes and poultry. The master often causes the men to steer him close to a thicket of bulrushes, which is filled with water-fowl, kept there, and flying about in many spots between the reeds and the lotus-plants, or brooding over their nests; a yellow ichneumon, or a gray, dark-speckled civet, climbs up the swaying cane-brake, and steals from the nest the young birds anxiously fluttering their little wings. The master catches fish, among which are plainly recognized kinds known in natural history; the crew harpoon a hippopotamus (behemoth). Very often fishing with wicker baskets or nets is depicted; and when a great repast is to be prepared, geese are taken with trailing nets from the ponds bordered with beautiful shrubs. The artist follows wholly his observation of nature, and does not forget to interweave pleasing incidents, as when those pulling on the net travel so far forwards that on the slackening of the line they are all thrown one upon another on their backs.

From the paintings in the tombs we may gain an accurate knowledge of the home-life of the Egyptians. The nekropolis in that happy time was not yet darkened and filled with fearful phantasms as it became in the later period of priestly and bureaucratic rule. A delight in life beams upon us from the pleasing picture of elegant tables full of various dishes, — long rows of fat geese suspended on poles; cutlets, hams, pastries, and the like, are shown in the sepulchre of Ti. The survivors gladden the shade of the dead by recalling happy days in painting or in marble; perhaps it was for the marriage of the rich man with the beautiful lady in scarlet apparel that the servants are bringing to the slaughter-bench wild goats and antelopes by the horns, bulls with ropes around the neck, struggling calves with a gripe at the throat and hind-quarter, helping them to a brisker pace, and carrying the fluttering fowls by the neck. The pleasures of the table are heightened by the spectacle of a dance with the accompaniment of the harp and flute. In one picture people are amusing themselves with games at draughts and ball, the latter a kind of roulette, in which balls are rolled to fixed points in the middle through a great number of spiral channels. Funeral offerings on a magnificent scale are represented in the tomb of Ptah-hotep at Sakkara (PLATE VI.).[1]

We have yet to cast a glance at the architectural and many-colored adornments of these ancients tombs, which, although they belong to an early period of human history, excel many later works of ancient art in other countries on account of their coloring, without which a picture is only as it were a skeleton or outline. That the tombs had their origin in the architecture of wooden buildings and carpenter work is a fact which at once strikes the eye. Under the upper sills of the gates and lattice-doors there is a heavy cylindrical beam of stone, in imitation of the wooden roller over which in dwelling-houses a piece of carpet or matting hung, which, when the door was open, was let down as a protection against the rays of the sun. The deep channels separating the door from other parts of the wall are copied above the pins with which the turning of the roller is effected by means of a cord. The bordering of the door, the decoration of the lattices and the walls, so far as these are not occupied by pictures, show board- and lathe-work, which is plastered and painted in very bright colors. In this respect one is reminded of the most ancient style of Chaldaic decoration, palm branches of stone, and high wooden frames of polished tiles placed one within another, cov-

[1] EXPLANATION OF PLATE VI.

The deceased is figured twice, as his name shows; it stands above his right arm. His son holds his father's staff by the right hand, in his left a fowl.

On the left division of the wall, Ptah-hotep is viewing scenes similar to those familiar to him while alive; papyrus plants are gathered at the water's edge; young men are engaged in gymnastic sports; grapes are plucked, trodden in the wine-press, and strained in a bag; gazelles and other game are hunted; a lion, to which a heifer has been offered as bait, is attacked by the hounds; finally fishing-scenes, and scenes where geese are taken from a lake.

The four vertical columns of hieroglyphics inform us that Ptah-hotep had been priest at the pyramids of Kings Assa, Ra-en-user, and Hor-men-ka. On the right division of the wall, servants of the dead priest are represented in a procession bringing animals and cattle, to be used, as the inscription declares, in the cult of the dead. The procession is headed by youths, who by their gymnastic feats lend it life; then follow greyhounds and dogs, smaller animals in baskets, caged lions, ibexes, antelopes, cows with their calves, oxen, swans in number 1225; geese, 11,210, ditto 121,200 (twice); finally young geese 111,020, doves 121,022, small geese 120,000 in number, and storks. The numbers are probably much exaggerated.

PLATE VI.

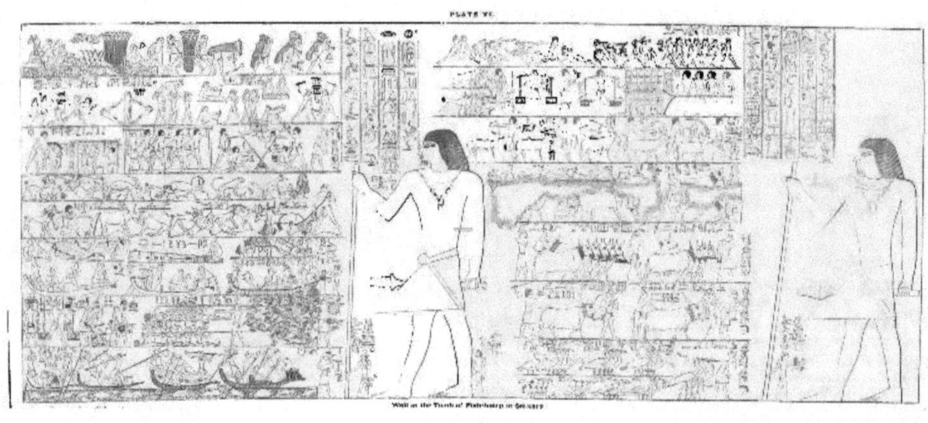

Wall in the Tomb of Ptahhotep in Sakkara

ered with stucco, as in the Wuswas ruins at Warka. In a Theban tomb of a later age this very ancient *motif* is employed as the ornament of a frieze, and it alternates here with figures which remind one vividly of the Grecian frieze with its triglyphs. Sometimes the imitation of woodwork is very simple, as in Tenta's tomb at Gizeh, where narrow depressions are enclosed on both sides by borders which are barred above by two cross-planks, so that the impression is well-nigh made of a small pillar with a square abacus. A diagonal beam, such as we have in our northern wooden houses, is never found. Between the laths of the house-wall, flowers were placed in the interstices, and these appear in the lattice-work of the mastaba as two blended petals of the lotus beneath the calyx, an arrangement that suggested the idea of a peculiar kind of pillar with which we shall become acquainted. The space between the door and the support of the ceiling appears embellished with a matting having a checkered pattern in green and red colors. The astragals are blue, yellow, white, and red, but always painted with a single color, and on the panels are patterns of webbing; for instance, a double row of zigzag lines forming a lozenge-shaped panel; or an embroidery pattern with similar *motif;* a checkered pattern of ribbons interlaced, or plaited straw (mats), in checkered and reticulated form with diversified colors. A row of patterns of five kinds shows gay-colored straw plaiting, as in the wall painted with figures behind the throne of Ra-ases (reign of An, Fifth Dynasty). The upper parts of the wall also show vividly colored cross-stripes of blue, yellow, and green, enclosed by broad dark lines. The borrowing from the embroideries of the dwelling-rooms is so naïve that even the rings are copied, through which are thrust the cords for holding the embroidery frame, as in the tomb of Ptah-hotep at Sakkara. The entire lattice-door is, at the sides and above, bordered by an astragal moulding on which the cords running hither and thither are painted, and which in all periods of Egyptian architecture remained the model for encompassing the angles of the temples and pylons, and was also employed as a welcome aid in joiners' work to cover and hold together the seams of the wooden corners that were cut obliquely. The chain of the basket-maker, executed by the smith, is also imitated in colors upon the small intervening spaces between the side-posts. All these patterns, of an irreproachable taste, which are naturally connected with the arts of embroidery, weaving, and plaiting, appear among many ancient peoples, and we need not maintain that one nation borrows from another. So is it with regard to the Chaldaeans, Assyrians, Etruscans, Greeks, and the rifled tombs of Ancona in Peru. We need only transfer these stone façades of the mastabas into wood, in order to be able to form for ourselves a correct conception of the most ancient wooden dwellings of the Egyptians.

The different parts of the mastaba, and especially the tomb-chamber, the pit, and the place for the coffin, are repeated in the pyramid or royal sepulchre. Here, however, the tumulus, which ancient nations built up to their heroes and kings, suggests the type. The round tumulus of heaped-up earth was exchanged for a four-square pyramid as soon as men undertook to construct it of brick; since not a round but an angular form results from the use of brick, and from the cutting out of stone in blocks for building. Furthermore, the rectilineal shape made it easy to place the structure in conformity with astronomical ideas. The pyramids are oriented according to the quarters of the heavens; and when one considers the importance of the western wall of the mastaba as representing Amenti (Hades), it would seem impossible that the edge of the wall should be made into a curve. This tumulus, as a pyramid, taking its shape from the square foundation stones, gave form also to the sunken pit that leads to the sepulchre. The chamber of the mastaba, together with the chapel, was separated from the pyramid, and the east side of it was placed at some distance. The pyramid, like the pit of the mastaba, was hermetically sealed, and with regard to the bodies contained in it no worship of the dead was possible. These temples of the dead have been demolished, and only in a few pyramids are their foundations still discernible. They were of no great extent. Theban art first removed them from the neighborhood of the royal sepulchres which were dug in the mountain ranges, placed them near the river, and erected them as independent monuments of vast extent and splendor. Neither in the pyramid nor in the ruins of the temple that lay before it have any certain traces of the 'serdab' been found. Perhaps men then believed the mummy of the god-king to be sufficiently safe from violation, partly on account of incessant watchfulness, and partly

Fig. 33.—The Pyramids of Gizeh, from the southwest.

on account of religious fear. The burial chamber of the pyramid lies sometimes in the body of the latter, and sometimes is sunk into the rock on which the building rests; the former occurs in the case of the pyramid of Cheops, where the tomb is placed at one-third of the height above the rock foundation. The latter plan is followed in the third, the pyramid of Mycerinus, where the main chamber lies some thirty feet below the rocky floor. The many passages and apartments of the older Pyramid of Steps at Sakkara are entirely excavated in the rock. The Pyramid of Medum—the next oldest to that of Sakkara—was originally a square mastaba. Its entrance was in the lower part of the north face. To enlarge it, a coating of masonry was added and the original mass was carried upward. This process was repeated seven times until it became a pyramid of steps. A smooth casing was then added at an angle of 11 or 14 degrees. It is the oldest known pyramid, as that of Sakkara never received an outer coating.

The pyramids clearly show that what we regard as the beginning of Egyptian history was only the end of a long previous development. They are not masses of stone roughly heaped up, but the greatest and most enduring structures devised by man. The necropolis of Memphis contains nearly eighty pyramids. The most famous are the three great pyramids situated at Gizeh (Fig. 33). The largest of these occupies a space on which two edifices like St. Peter's at Rome could be placed, and is of such a height that even after the flattening of the top it exceeds the elevation of St. Stephen's at Vienna by about twenty-five feet; it contains 83,000,000 cubic feet of stone, and its outer casing of polished stone, which under Mameluke rule was gradually torn off by the Arabs to furnish building-materials for the neighboring town, represented 7,000,000 cubic feet more. The impression produced by these structures is so powerful that from the remotest times travellers have found no words in which to express their admiration. The scenery surrounding the city of the dead is also unequalled; a sharp line separates the green, fruitful land watered by the Nile and its canals, with its palm-shaded villages and gorgeous Cairo, from the sandstone plateau upon whose rocky surface mighty waves of yellow sand are beating in sublime monotone, and are pitilessly pouring over the works of man's hand.

Like all the others, the entrance to the great pyramid of Khufu

(Cheops) is on its north face. It was named Khufu-khut, 'Khufu's shining throne,' from the polished granite coping which covered it on all four sides, and whose thickness can be estimated by the joints made in the surrounding rocks. Over the opening there lies a block

Fig. 34.—Entrance to the Pyramid of Khufu.

whose weight has been reckoned at 13,000 hundredweight; above it are two blocks placed opposite each other in the position of rafters to relieve the pressure upon it. A gallery descending obliquely, about 100 yards long, terminates in a chamber in the pyramid, the use of which is unknown. Before it enters into the rock, it comes to a spot where an immense block of granite bars further progress. The Arabs, by boring into the mass of stone, built a gallery around this block which mocked their efforts, and through it they reached an obliquely ascending continuation of the first passage. This space suddenly expanded into a hall a little more than six feet wide, twenty-six feet high, and 174 feet in length. This hall is constructed of square blocks of polished limestone from the Mokattam quarries, put together without mortar, and in such a manner that of the five upper layers, out of seven, one always projects above the other, whereby the gradual narrowing of the space above forms a kind of arch. Moreover, since the joints are scarcely visible, the sides of the stones lying upon one another must have been polished. On both sides of the hall there are projecting ridges or panels twenty inches in height; in these holes were cut, in which wooden posts were placed to support the rollers arranged beneath, probably for the purpose of conveying the sarcophagus above. In front of the entrance to the hall a horizontal passage branches off which leads into the so-called "Queen's Chamber," perhaps originally designed for the sepulchral chamber of the Pharaoh. At the upper end of the great hall, 138 feet above the foundation of the pyramid, there follows a horizontal passage which widens into a vestibule; here were placed four portcullises of granite, which with one exception have been demolished by the Arabs. This vestibule is situated directly beneath the apex of the pyramid, whilst the queen's chamber lies north, and the king's south, of the vertical line. The passage terminates in the northeast corner of the sepulchre. The latter extends lengthwise at right angles to the direction of the corridor; it is very roomy, the small east and west walls are seventeen feet long, the two others thirty-four, with a height of nineteen feet. The hall, built entirely of polished granite, has a covering of nine granite slabs, whose length and breadth correspond to the proportions of the walls which they span. In order to relieve the pressure upon this covering, five spaces are contrived above it, of which the highest, by means of blocks set obliquely upon one another in the shape of a roof, diminish the pressure of the superincumbent mass. The lowest of these vacant spaces was discovered in 1763, the others in 1837 and 1838, One can enter only by lying on the ground and crawling into them; they are inhabited by bats, living images of the flitting shades of the dead (Odyssey xxiv. 6). In the two uppermost rooms the name of Khufu and Khnum-Khufu is found, not chiselled into the stone, but as a mark written with red paint by the head architect in the quarry before the blocks were put into position; this finally establishes what was already known through tradition. The sarcophagus in front of the west wall of the chamber was long ago broken open, and is empty. It is to be added that Vyse discovered two small air-passages by which the chambers were ventilated while the laborers were at work in them. By the construction of the outer coping these passages were closed. This coping, according to Philo, in his work on the Seven Wonders of the World, was composed of various stones, — marble (white limestone from Mokattam), black Ethiopian stone (basalt), hematite (perhaps porphyry), and green Arabian stone (*verde antico*); probably these stones formed alternate colored layers of this costly decoration. Flinders-Petrie, who examined the pyramids with the best measuring-instruments, believes that several depressions in the passages and in the chambers must be attributed to the action of an earthquake; and also that two periods in the construction are distinguishable, the later of which, beginning somewhere near the centre of the building, is characterized by greater negligence, and by the use of inferior material.

To the pyramid belongs a second gigantic work of Khufu; viz., the stone causeway which was constructed from the Nile to this spot in order to provide for the conveyance of the blocks of stone from the quarries at Mokattam. Herodotus regards this work, which in his day was still in existence, as a wonder equal to the pyramids. He estimates its length as five stadia (over 3000 feet), and its surface was made of polished stone. It served also to aid in the erection of the second pyramid, while for the third a special road was built, which is yet preserved, and with interruptions reaches to the village of Kum-el-Aswad; it contains blocks twenty-five to thirty feet in length. In front of the east side of the pyramid, and facing the southern half, are three small pyramids, of which the one farthest south is that of Hent-sen, a daughter of Khufu: and near the pyramid, particularly on its west side and north of the second pyramid, are situated many mastabas of the period of the Fourth and Fifth Dynasties.

The second pyramid was built by Khafra (Chephren), and was called Ur ('the great'). It stands near that of Khufu on the south-west; and was attributed to him by ancient writers, such as Herodotus and Diodoros. In the ruins of the temple, near its east side, fragments of a marble mace-head have been discovered inscribed with the name of Khafra. This pyramid appears to be higher than that of Khufu, because the rocky bottom has a greater elevation. But it is thirty feet lower, and is inferior in accuracy, as well as in material. The rock, having an irregular surface, was cut away to level the foundation, and thus a kind of passage was formed on the north and west sides. The stone here used constituted a mass of over 4,300,000 cubic feet. The top of the pyramid still displays a piece of the polished coping of stone which formerly covered the entire surface. The lowest course was of red granite, and the entrance passage was of the same material; though one can with difficulty conceive that it could have utterly disappeared from such structures as the steps of the pyramids, yet such an amount of strength and time was expended on this work of destruction as almost equalled that required for cutting out the stone in the quarries and for transportation of the material. The coping appears to have been the essential thing in the entire enclosure of the tomb, as being especially the bearer of the names and titles of the ruler at rest within. The king's chamber of the second pyramid lies in the rock, but roofed over with slanting limestone slabs. The sarcophagus was of granite. The lid was secured by undercut grooves in which it slid. It was held by bolts which fell into holes and were caught with resin, traces of which still remain. When Belzoni found it, it was sunk into the floor, its lid lay over it. Now the floor is destroyed.

The third pyramid, only 203 feet high and inferior in accuracy, was built by Menkaura (Mycerinus), and was called Her ('the high'). The shelving rock of the foundation was walled up with gigantic blocks. The wall of the pyramid was covered below with polished slabs of granite, farther up with rough stones; yet this royal coping, though not rent off, was so damaged that the shelving ground on which the heart of the building was erected is visible well nigh throughout. On the east side are remains of the tomb-temple. This was built of vast blocks, which were at first supposed to be the rock itself, until the mortar was discovered. The descending gallery in the pyramid is lined with granite; it enters into the rock and shortly becomes almost horizontal. It widens into a room which was whitewashed, and is obstructed by a huge block and three portcullises of stone. Under the apex of the building is situated a large chamber in which a second passage terminates obliquely, and in which was a beautiful sarcophagus of bluish basalt sunk into the floor. A pit with granite projections at the sides is exposed to view; this was concealed by the plaster of the apartment. It terminates in a horizontal gallery which leads to the king's sepulchre. Its sides were composed of granite slabs which were placed as rafters, and so prepared that they formed an arched vault with an even surface. The basalt sarcophagus was about 35 inches in height, 37 in width, and 96 in length. Like the coffins in the mastabas, it was carved in the form of a wooden house with an astragal at the corners under the light cornice. The flat roofing was ornamented like lattice-doors. This sarcophagus was removed by Vyse and sent to England. On its way it was lost with the ship off Cartagena. In the upper chamber of the Pyramid was found a wooden coffin-lid with an inscription of Men-Kau-Ra and part of a skeleton, probably of later date. These are in the British Museum.

The most striking monument in this part of the necropolis is the Sphinx (Fig. 35). Much has been written about its great antiquity. It has even been attributed to prehistoric times. Such a view, however, is not in accordance with the evidence. There is not a single mention or figure of a sphinx, or of its priesthood during the Old Empire. Its probable date is more likely to be the period between the Old and the Middle Empire, to which there is a growing tendency among scholars to assign the sphinxes formerly attributed to the Hyksos period. The sphinx is the image of a god, a lion couchant with the head of a man. It is Harmachis or Har-em-khu, Horus on the horizon, the rising sun-god. He is the symbol of the victorious king, and therefore bears on his head the royal insignia, as do the statues of Khafra; and he lies on the margin of the desert as guardian spirit of the nekropolis. The iconoclastic Arabs have destroyed the nose; but writers who saw it when uninjured extol its beauty. The face was incrusted with stucco painted red. Between the paws of the sphinx Thothmes IV. built a chapel, approached by a stairway. A long inscription relates that Thothmes IV., while upon a hunting-expedition, sleeping beneath its shadow, saw the sphinx in a dream, who obtained from the king the promise to free him from the sand. The inscription is carved on a grand door lintel of red granite, which seems to have been robbed from the neighboring temple of Khafra. Southeast of the sphinx, and entirely buried in the sand, lies the above-mentioned granite temple (Fig. 36) excavated by Mariette, who discovered it. It has been called the Temple of the Sphinx, but in reality had no connection with it. It was probably built under Khafra. In work-

Fig. 35. — The Sphinx. Gizeh. (Before the excavations of Maspero.)

manship it belongs to the Fourth Dynasty. The lower story inside is perfectly preserved, and retains the peculiar recessing decoration attributed to a survival of the original brick- or woodwork used in early times. The massive style of building, which reminds one of the megalithic monuments of prehistoric times, is entirely different from these in regard to the masterly workmanship with which both the granite of the monolithic square pillars and the alabaster of the architrave and the walls are treated is unsurpassed. A long corridor leads from the west to the northwest corner of a hall which extends from north to south, and contains a row of six granite columns sixteen feet in

Fig. 26. — The so-called Temple of the Sphinx at Gizeh.

height. In the southwest corner of the first hall a passage opens into a room, from which six spaces in two rows, one above the other, enter into the wall, the design of which is not clear. In the middle of the east wall of the first hall a passage terminates in a narrow room, with which on both sides small square chambers are connected.

In this long room there is a well or subterranean chamber in which seven statues of Khafra were discovered. The great diorite statue (Fig. 17) is striking. The commanding expression of the king, no less than the technical ability of the artist to overcome so resisting a material, impress one with his power. Another, in which the divine hawk is imparting his life and protection to the king, is even finer in expression.

North of Gizeh lie the pyramids of Abu-Roash, which are greatly damaged, and also those of Abusir. These are the burial places of the kings of the Fifth Dynasty. In 1898–1901, MM. Borchardt and Schäfer, in the course of excavations undertaken under the auspices of the Orient Geselschaft, examined this group and discovered the pyramid of King User-en-Ra (Ne-woser-Rê). The fact that sun-worship acquired special official recognition and popular prominence under the Fifth Dynasty—which claims direct descent from Ra—made these excavations of singular interest. And the most sensational result of the work at Abusir was, accordingly, the bringing to light of one of the monuments peculiar to this time—i.e., a combined pyramid and obelisk dedicated to Ra or Ra-Harmachis—hitherto only known through inscriptions of that epoch, relating to priesthoods attached to their temples. It is a pyramidal platform of brick surmounted by an obelisk. The accompanying temple of the sun-god was also cleared, as well as an older structure designated by Dr. Borchardt as the older palace. Many minor objects were recovered, among which may be mentioned some superb reliefs now at Berlin. The pyramid of King Nefer-Ka-Ra was also examined, as well as many tombs.

The nekropolis of Memphis, situated near the village of Sakkara, is rich in interest. The monument which dominates the entire field of the dead is the Pyramid of Steps (*El-Haram-el-Medarraga*). (PLATE VII.) Manetho says that Uenephes, the fourth king of the First Dynasty, erected pyramids at Kokhome (or 'the black bull'). Mariette, who refers this statement to the Pyramid of Steps, believed that we should recognize in this pyramid the most ancient burial-place of the Apis-bulls. The bones of a bull are reported to have been discovered in it previously, and the words of the inscription on the door, "The great god Ra-nub," also found on a tablet of the Serapeum erected later in the vicinity and first used under Amenhotep III., supports this view. The existence of thirty rock-chambers complicates the problem; but they

The Pyramid of Steps at Sakkara. (After Lepsius.)

may well have served for a row of Apis-mummies. The tradition that Kakau (second king of the Second Dynasty) introduced the worship of Apis, Mnevis, and the ram from Mendes, might be regarded as indicating that the erection of this Apis-mausoleum and of similar buildings at Heliopolis and Mendes had given occasion to this report. Besides, the name Ra-nub is known both as the name of a Pharaoh and also of an Apis. The pyramid consists of six inclined ascending steps, in all nearly 197 feet high, of which each retreats six and one-half feet behind the next; each also decreases in height, so that the lowest step is 38 feet, and the uppermost scarcely 29 feet high. The east and west sides are 42 feet longer than the two others, so that the base forms a rectangle. The layers of stone are not placed, as usual, horizontally, but slope toward the centre of the building. The slabs were brought from the neighboring limestone rocks. In a vertical line an immense pit is open, whose sill lies 131 feet below the surface of the plateau. Around this, and at different elevations, is a complicated system of horizontal galleries, with not less than thirty rock-chambers, which are accessible, not from the pyramid, but from pits that open externally. It is worthy of note that one chamber is incrusted with convex cylindrical sections formed of glazed pumice-stone or of an infusible earth, and in such a manner that the wall seems to be encircled with low pilasters closely joined together. These are covered with a greenish-blue glazing, while strips of another color are drawn over them. The pieces of which these bands consist are bedded in lime, and are made firm by an ear through which passes a metallic wire. Other apartments are inlaid with pieces of clay, Egyptian porcelain, glazed with green, black, red, and purple, forming a sort of tile mosaic. This is regarded by many as later work, although glazing was done in Egypt in prehistoric days. Many indications, however, point to the altering and remodeling of the pyramid in later times, and new passages were made in it probably more than once.[1] On the door, which was removed from the pyramid and is now in Berlin, are panels of limestone, and alternating with these, glazed tiles inscribed with the Horus name 'Neter-Kha.' The name of the same king is found in Sinaï, near a Fourth-Dynasty inscription, and is associated with King Zeser (Third Dynasty) on an inscription at Sehel. A gilded skull and a gilded sole of a foot

[1] See Petrie, 'History,' etc., I., p. 58.

belonging to a mummy, together with other treasures brought from Egypt by Minutoli, were sunk off the mouth of the Elbe.

Numerous remains of pyramids lie together in different groups. Southwest of the Pyramid of Steps lies the Pyramid of Unas (last king of the Fifth Dynasty), examined by Maspero in 1881; this is named Nofer-us ('the very beautiful'). Northwest, but very near the Pyramid of Steps, a pyramid of stone is situated. At a little distance south appears once more a group of three great pyramids, of which that lying farthest to the southwest, Kha-nefer ('the beautiful rising'), belongs to the third king of the Sixth Dynasty, Mer-en-Ra, son of Pepi, whose mummy, as we have already seen, was found there. This is the earliest royal mummy that, so far, has come to light. The chamber contained two sarcophagi. It was broken open by grave-robbers, who had driven a shaft in the stone-work near the

FIG. 37.—Mastaba-el-Faraun.

portcullis. The pyramid in this neighborhood, situated to the northeast, is that of his father, named Men-nefer, 'the beautiful dwelling' (the same word as Memphis). The corridors of this pyramid are covered with inscriptions, hieroglyphics painted green. The chamber of Pepi consists of two divisions; the coping is a pointed roof of huge blocks of limestone, shaped like rafters, placed upon one another; the interior is painted like the mighty heavens, in dark colors and with yellow stars. The sepulchre has been despoiled by robbers. In 1881, before the opening occurred, Brugsch found some fine wrappings of a mummy and one of the hands of Pepi. Furthermore, Brugsch observed that the stones of a more ancient monument, containing inscriptions and pictures, had been used in the construction.

In this vicinity lies the Pyramid of Teta, called Dad-aset, 'the very firm.' The Mastaba-el-Faraun (Fig. 37), 'the mound of Pharaoh,' is the tomb of Nefer-Ka-Ra, brother of Mer-en-Ra, and was styled in the inscriptions Men-ankh, 'House of Life.' This structure is built upon a rectangular foundation of great blocks of freestone, in length 338 feet, in width 236 feet; the sides have an inclination, but this ceases at a height of 65 feet. The granite sarcophagus was in good condition. The lid had not been thrown off, but was pushed on to the ledge of the brickwork, prepared in all these pyramids, between the sarcophagus and the wall, to hold the lid until needed to close. The walls of the sepulchral chamber, like those of the tombs of Unas, Pepi I., and Mer-en-Ra, are covered with religious texts—written, however, in

FIG. 38. — Pyramid of Medum.

smaller characters. Many monuments remain of this reign, which began when Nefer-Ka-Ra was about six years old. At Wadi-Maghara is a fine stela of his second year. His mother is mentioned prominently, with her titles, as though formally regent. Another interesting mention of his second year occurs in the tomb of Herkhuf, at Assuan, who tells of a pigmy dancer, 'Denga,' brought by that officer to the king, on his return from a southern expedition. Nefer-Ka-Ra's monuments are found at Elephantine, at Koptos, where he built in the temple, and at the quarries of Hat-Nub. He is also mentioned in a number of contemporary tombs.

To the nekropolis of Memphis, also, belong the pyramids of Da-hur, beyond which is the boundary of the province of Memphis. These pyramids were the tombs of the kings of the Middle Empire. Opposite to Dashur, to the south of Turah, were the old alabaster quarries of the Wadi Gerrani—discovered in our time by Dr. Schweinfürth—a three or four hours' journey from the valley. Ruins of workmens' huts announce their vicinity. A great stone wall, 30 feet high, 140 feet thick, and 216 feet long, dammed the valley at this point, storing water for the use of men and beasts. The weathering of the stones, which is similar to that of the oldest stone monuments, attests the antiquity of this work.

The Pyramid of Medum (Fig. 38) has already been described (see page 94). It was the tomb of Snefru—the first king of the Fourth Dynasty—and was the oldest true pyramid of the group. It is also the first that meets the eye of the traveler as he comes down the Nile from Upper Egypt, upon the confines of which it stands, opposite to Atfih (Aphroditopolis). In its present condition it resembles a tower standing upon a platform. Hence, the Arabs call it El Haram el Kaddab, 'the false pyramid.' Against its eastern face was a courtyard and chambers, forming a small sepulchral temple, built of limestone. Here stood an altar, between two tall stelæ, rounded at the top, like those of the First Dynasty, but uninscribed. The walls were perfectly plain. They were built in the rough, but were trimmed afterwards. A peribolos wall enclosed both the temple and the pyramid. It was reached by a causeway, walled on either side, leading up from the plain.[1] From a neighboring tomb came the fine statues of Ra-nefer and Nefert. In that of Nefer-mat, an officer of Snefru, we are introduced to a new style of decoration—square depressions filled with colored paste—which produce the effect of mosaic and prepare us for the 'cloisonné' technique of the Twelth Dynasty jewels. It is worthy of notice that, under the Sixth Dynasty, at Abydos, the true arch appears in a tomb discovered by Mariette. The arch is unfinished. It rests upon two limestone slabs, closed by a wedge-shape stone. Bricks of ordinary form are used, between which stones are forced.[2] At one time the Etruscans were regarded as inventors of the keystone. Subsequently, however, older Grecian arches were found; and others still more ancient

[1] See Flinders-Petrie 'Medum.' 1890; also 'History of Egypt, vol. i (1899), Scribner.

[2] See Perrot and Chipiez, 'Histoire de l'Art,' 4, vol. i.

were brought to light by the excavations at Nineveh, where was discovered at the city gate of Khorsabad an arch with a span fourteen to fifteen feet in width. None of the early Babylonian arches are keystone arches, and nowhere are the bricks fashioned so as to fit in the radial scheme of the arch (voussoirs). A fine arch of elliptical form has been found at Telloh, near the palace of Ur-Nina (B.C. 4000). It is regular, and is composed throughout of the plano-convex bricks typical of the pre-Sargonic period, the date of which is still a subject of controversy. It cannot well be later than B.C. 3000, however, and may be much earlier. It is not a keystone arch. Its top is formed of broken bricks filled into the space between the last two bricks. According to Mr. Clarence Fisher, the architect of the expedition sent by the University of Pennsylvania to conduct excavations at Nippur—the site of ancient Calneh—the arch discovered in that locality is of about the same size as the Telloh specimen—viz. : 30 inches high by 20 inches wide —inside measurement—and is finished in the same manner. It is rougher, and of inferior construction, and extends about three feet, connecting with a finely built water conduit. A small section of a four-inch pipe was found inserted. A smaller arch also occurs at Fara. All were outlets for drains.

The examination of the buildings, monuments, and other works of the early empire forces upon us the conclusion that the Egyptians of the First Dynasty had already attained a degree of culture very many centuries removed from the beginnings of civilization. Indeed, earliest Egypt marks the close of a long epoch in the history of the human race, the best legacy of which is the ancient Egyptian monuments. The peculiar nature of the soil demanded a vast amount of labor in order to render possible the existence and the subsistence of so numerous a population, and effected here a more rapid advancement than elsewhere. Still Egyptian civilization, even at its dawn, had so far advanced beyond that which would have sufficed for the mere protection of existence, that between such an epoch and the beginning of the dynasties a considerable space of time must have elapsed. This we can perhaps estimate by reflecting how long a period man requires in order to go forward from building a clay hut to the erection of an edifice of granite. The existence of a system of writing even in the most ancient time so perfected that, apart from such improvements as will arise in every human invention, it remained the same through millenniums, and showed itself adapted to the preservation of a rich literature, leads us to conjecture that its origin long preceded Mena, and must be sought for during the proto-historic period. The graphic system of the Egyptians passed very anciently beyond its primitive stages. Its relation to other systems of writing, and especially to the Phoenician alphabet, once gave rise to much learned discussion. The additional material furnished by the discovery of a written script used in very early times throughout the Mediterranean area has complicated, rather than cleared, the problem which remains unsolved. Without entering upon these difficult inquiries, a brief sketch of the Egyptian system may properly be introduced at this place.

In the last year of the eighteenth century a French engineer, in erecting a redoubt at Rosetta, found an inscribed black stone, known as "the Rosetta Stone" (PLATE VIII.). It was to be taken to Paris; but after the victory of the English under Nelson it fell into their hands, and is now in the British Museum. The stone consists of three divisions: in the uppermost, which is more damaged than the others, are the hieroglyphics; then follows the demotic part, which is best preserved, and below this the Greek text. This invaluable tablet contains a decree of the priests' college at Memphis of March 27, 195 B.C., in honor of King Ptolemy V., Epiphanes, on account of his merits respecting the prosperity and protection of the country, ordering that a statue, a shrine of gold, and an image of the king, be erected in every temple, and on feast-days be adorned and venerated; that this decree should be set up in every temple of the first and second class, engraved upon a tablet in hieroglyphic, demotic, and Greek characters. As it was already known from the study of the obelisks at Rome that the specific signs of the kings' names appear enclosed in a kind of ellipse or cartouche, comparison was made of the names of the kings occurring in the Greek text with the cartouches (royal shields) of the hieroglyphic text, and thus it was possible to determine a series of signs. Thus was the key furnished for deciphering; but to ascertain the meaning of many hundred hieroglyphic signs, and to connect the known with the unknown, was still a difficult task, demanding genius and patience. The Egyptian language survived even into the first Christian century, and was then

PLATE VIII

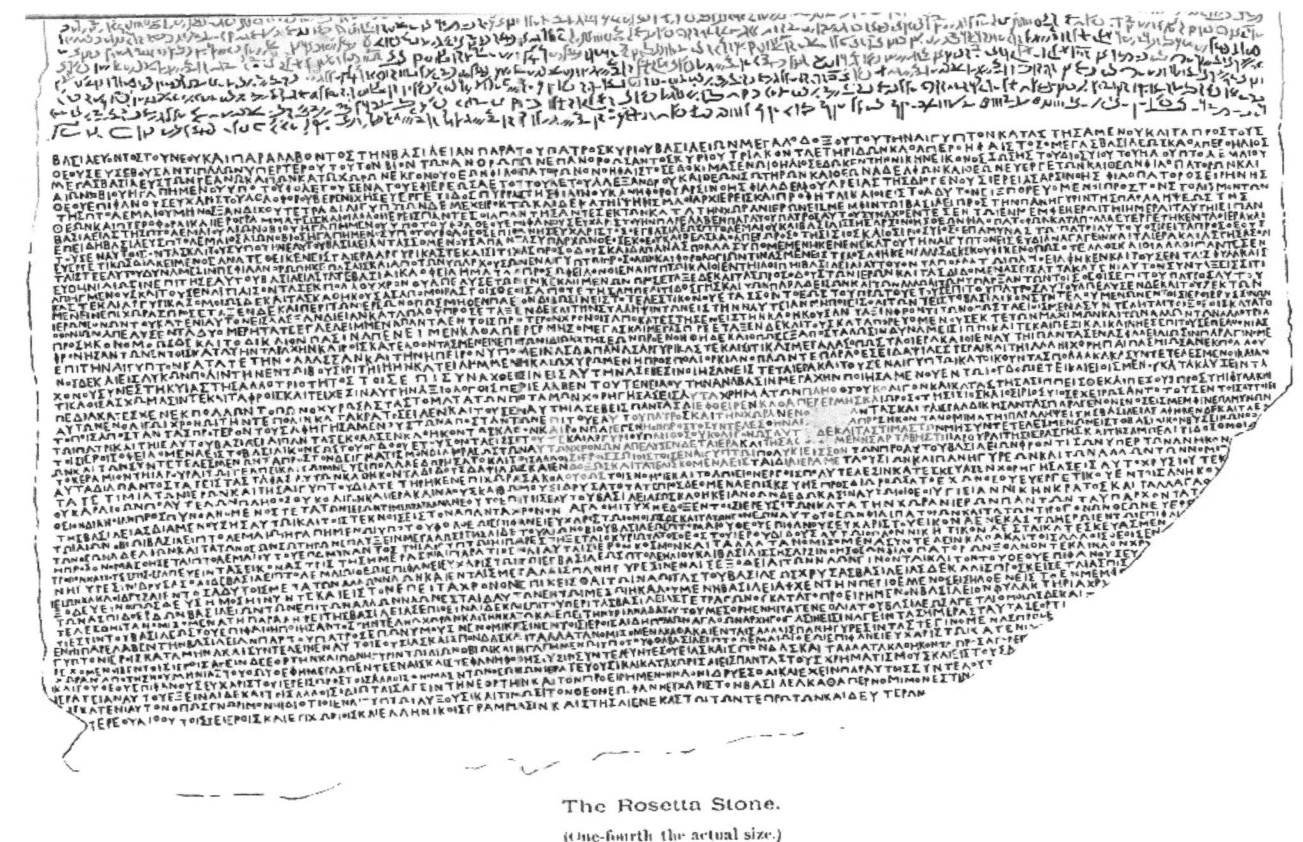

The Rosetta Stone.
(One-fourth the actual size.)

perpetuated in the Coptic, in which the translation of the Bible and a Christian literature have come down to us. The daughter tongue thus afforded valuable aid in the translation of the ancient texts. The merit of bringing the hieroglyphical system to the knowledge of the modern inquirer, and thus acquiring again the art, unknown since the death of the last priest of the religion of ancient Egypt, of writing and reading hieroglyphics, belongs to the younger Champollion (1790–1832).

The foundation of the Egyptian system of writing, as also of the Chinese, of the cuneiform, of the Hittite, and of all others, is picture-writing. The Chinese and the cuneiform lost their distinctness, and became conventionalized by abbreviation. It is characteristic of Egyptian conservatism, however, that although, from early time, the signs were cursively rendered for current use, it preserved to the end picture-writing, so that the writer had to be at the same time an artist. The manner in which abstract conceptions are rendered is remarkable: 'seeing' is naturally represented by two eyes or pupils,  ; 'fighting' by two arms, one of which is equipped with a shield, and the other with a battle-axe,  ; 'king' by a bee, , since it lives in a monarchical state. Some signs are compound; for example, 'silver' is represented by a crucible, which is the symbol of gold, combined with the sign of a white onion  , so that the united sign suggests the conception, 'white gold.' It is common to hear 'hieratic' writing spoken of as distinct from hieroglyphic writing; but the two are as identical as are our own written and printed characters. One was the cursive form of the other. Two styles of 'hieratic' writing, however, may be noted. One, formal, like our engrossing; the other a rapid cursive in which all the letters of a word are linked together. It was from the latter that the Demotic of later times was evolved. The entire list of some two thousand hieroglyphs, of which about five hundred were in common use, may be divided into three classes: First, phonetic signs which, whether alphabetic or syllabic, represent sounds. Second, ideograms, which represent certain words or ideas, and which often serve to represent homonyms. Third, determinatives—that is, signs placed after the word to indicate its meaning.

To the Egyptians writing was of divine origin. The god Thoth had taught it to the men of the Nile Valley. There is reason to believe that in prehistoric times it passed through an earlier stage when it was purely phonetic. At least, according to Erman—the highest authority on Egyptian philology—only the consonants of the words were written, as is the case in Semitic languages, where the vowels are added as a rule to indicate the grammatical forms. To use Erman's own illustration: in the Arabic word 'qatala,' he killed, the meaning of 'killing' rests on the three consonants q t l. The vowels representing only the active tense. The passive form is 'qutila'; the imperfect is 'qutl'; the imperative 'qtul'; the participle 'qâtil.' Only the consonants are invariable, and they alone are written. According to this system, the original Egyptian alphabet consisted of twenty-one consonants.

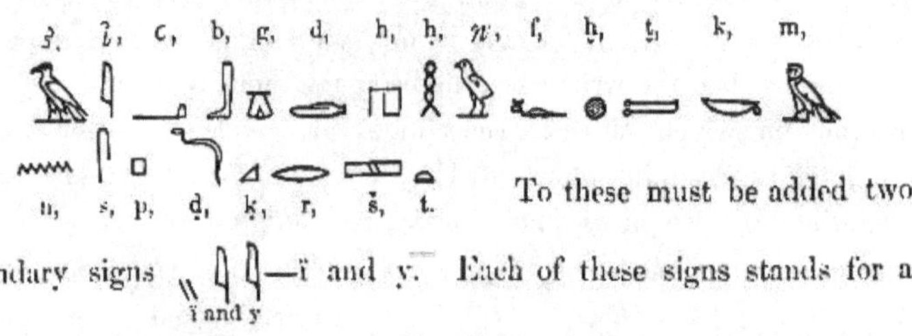

To these must be added two secondary signs —ï and y. Each of these signs stands for a short word with similar sound, from which it derives its phonetic value. Thus = t is probably 'ta,' a loaf; , d, a hand, 'dot'; , n = water, 'nu'; , r, the mouth, 'ro,' and so on. Only in cases when the vowel was important to the correct reading of the word did the Egyptians try to indicate the same in their writing. For this purpose they used three consonants, , ꜣ, i, and w. Not satisfied with this simple system, the Egyptians, even in prehistoric times, began to develop it by the use of ideograms, in order to add to the clearness and brevity of the writing. These, in time, often superseded the purely phonetic form of the word. For instance, , pr, the house, came to be written , the house itself. Many abstract words could not be drawn—i.e., 'good,' 'son,' etc. They therefore used for the purpose homonyms. To write 'nefer' = good, they used 'nefer,' a lute; and for 'sa,' a son, they used sa , a goose. These, and such adapted signs practically lost their original concrete values, and became mere conventional syllabics—purely suggestive of sound. As an illustration: The picture of a checker-board with the figures 𓏠 is called *men;* but it expresses also the syllable *men* in the name of the god Amen, 𓇋𓏠𓈖; here the original object was lost sight of and 'men' came to represent mainly the syllable. A word can be written in several different ways; for example, the word *ā n k h* ('life') can be expressed by the hieroglyphic mark, a cross with a ring 𓋹, symbolizing life; or this mark can be applied acrologically—that is, one may designate therewith only the letter *ā,* and must then add *n* and *kh* 𓋹𓈖𓐍; moreover, the alphabetical sign *ā* might be placed before *nkh* 𓂝𓈖𓐍. Again, the form of writing, *ā, ānkh, kh* also is used. 𓂝𓋹𓐍 in which the middle sign stands for the *n;* or finally, *ā, n, ānkh* 𓂝𓈖𓋹, where the ideogram stands for *kh,* and by itself represents the sound *ānkh.* Sometimes the first sound is doubled, that is to say, the hieroglyphic is first given as a figure, and then again the sound with which it commences; for example, the conception "god" is rendered by the figure of an axe 𓊹, and pronounced *neter;* again, one may write axe, *t, r,* 𓊹𓏏𓂋, where in like manner the axe represents only the sound *n;* or axe, *n, t, r,* as if *n* (*eter*) *n t r* 𓊹𓈖𓏏𓂋. This diversity in the manner of notation would be misleading were it not limited by usage which forbids many combinations.

With regard to the syllabic signs that have been mentioned there is an additional difficulty to be considered, in the fact that the greater part of them are polyphonous, that is, they may have various sound values. Thus, for instance, the circle with a point ☉ has the sound of *ra* ('sun'); but it may also, as a sign used by metonomy, be read *hru* ('day'). Although in many cases the connection of the sentence leaves no doubt with regard to the choice between such different sounds, yet for greater clearness the so-called phonetic-complements, or supplements by means of sounds added, were invented. Thus there is a hieroglyphic which originally represented a metallic bracelet in spiral form 𓎛: it has the meanings 'to encompass; a fold or curve; a pound' (for in place of the coined money of to-day, rings and other metallic pieces, which were originally weighed, were used), and may be pronounced in three ways: *rĕr, kĕb, tĕn.* If after the hieroglyphic the letter *r* is written, the combination can be read only *rĕr* (not *kĕb* or *tĕn*). But when *b* or *n* is written after it, it can be read only *kĕb* , or *tĕn* . Since *rĕr* is a verb, one finds besides the hieroglyphic formed of two striding legs, which indicates the category of the verb. If the word "pound" is meant, a square ('weight') is subjoined as an explanatory figure. Hence the syllabic signs can be used singly, or connected with one or more alphabetic signs; and indeed in the latter case they may be put before, after, and between the alphabetical signs.

Very frequently the hieroglyphic figures appear only as determinatives; that is, a word is given phonetically, and for greater clearness to the eye a picture is also added; for example, 'diseased' is *mĕn-t; men,* the syllabic sign, is written; *n,* the phonetic-complement, *t,* the article, and then the picture of the determinative of evil: . Again, 'bread' is *āq;* this is written with a swan, the syllabic sign *āq,* to which is added the alphabetical sign *q,* in order to secure the proper pronunciation; the word is then further determined by the figure of a long loaf, so that no doubt can exist either as to sound or as to meaning, . This picture of bread is a special determinative. In addition to these there are general determinatives, or such as designate entire categories of words; for instance, all conceptions that in any way stand connected with the mouth, to which belong not only eating and drinking, but also numerous other conceptions, including such as suggest a motion of it, as to speak, to know, to judge, etc.; this determinative is represented by a man sitting, who lays his hand on his mouth ; for example, *swrī,* 'to drink,' is written , *s, w, r, ī,* determinative. Similarly, the active voice of the verb receives as determinative an arm with a club, which is also the determinative for 'strength' . Likewise a bark upon the water is employed as determinative of 'ship,' 'navigation,' and 'voyage'; the sail determines the words for 'wind,' 'coolness.' A roll of papyrus tied together is the determinative for expressions referring to writing, books, painting, and for all abstract conceptions. The Egyptian language itself, such as we know it, is related to the

Semitic languages (Hebrew, Arabic, Aramaic) to the East African languages (Bishari, Galla, Somali, etc.) and to the Berber languages of North Africa. But its affinities with other tongues, whatever they may be, are sufficiently distant and rudimentary to warrant the belief that Egyptian belongs to a philological understratum, and became separated from other linguistic groups at a period so remote that it acquired its own individuality, and early became crystallized, while the others pursued their evolution. However this may be, the old Egyptian of early days continued as the literary language of Egypt well into the Roman period. Its most archaic forms may best be studied in the pyramid texts—sepulchral inscriptions, prior to that epoch, being short statements or brief invocations. The so-called 'Middle Egyptian' is the popular language of the Twelfth or Thirteenth Dynasties; and the 'late Egyptian' is the popular language of the New Empire. Demotic is the language of the Graeco-Roman epoch. To these linguistic forms, long dead as spoken languages, the key is furnished by the Coptic—the language of Christian Egypt—written in Greek characters. It only died out three hundred years ago, and furnishes the only attainable information with regard to the structure and vocalization of the mother tongue. Authorities are divided as to the transliteration of Egyptian. The French school still adheres to its own system, while the German school is generally followed by English and American scholars.

Most of the literature preserved is written in the hieratic script. Such is the Prisse papyrus, which dates of the Twelfth Dynasty (B.C. 2500), although the maxims which it contains were written in the Fifth Dynasty. Many papyrus manuscripts exist containing prose and poetical literature. We have elegies of the Nineteenth Dynasty; hymns to the gods, as that to the Nile, composed by Enna in the time of Merenptah, some passages from which were quoted above; and to the Pharaoh, wherein it is said: "Let well-being, life and strength be the king's! This call comes to the ears of the king, to the royal hall of the friend of truth, to the great heavens in which he is the sun. Hear me, thou sun, who liftest up thyself; enlighten the earth with goodness, thou sun-disk of men, who dost fright away the darkness from Egypt; thou art as the image of thy father, the sun-god, who exalteth himself in the heavens. Thy rays reach down to hell. No place is without thy goodness. Thy speech is law for every land. When thou art at rest in thy palace thou hearest the speech of all lands. Thou hast millions of ears. Shining is thine eye above the stars of heaven, able to look into the sun-disk. When something is spoken with the mouth even in Hades, it comes into thine ears. That which also is done in secret, thine eye seeth it. O Ba-en-ra Meri-Amen ('soul of Ra, friend of Amen, Merenptah,') gracious Lord, creator of life." Further, we have the lament of Isis and Nephthys over the dead Osiris (in the time of the Ptolemies). A "Praise of Wisdom" describes the different occupations and their several drawbacks, in order to place the vocation of the scribe, that is, of the learned, above all others (composed during the Sixth Dynasty). Also we have narratives, preserved in a late form in the demotic writing of the first century before Christ, from the hand of Setnau, wherein appear the dead, who are called back into life by means of a book kept in seven coffers at Coptos, and guarded by serpents; the description of a journey into Syria; the voyage to the land of frankincense and to the isles of the blessed. In the 'History of the Two Brothers,' likewise composed by Enna, and belonging to the library of Seti II., the wife of the elder brother calumniates the younger brother in the same manner as the wife of Potiphar did Joseph; and the innocent man is obliged to flee before the dagger of the deceived husband. We commonly associate the Egyptians with religious fervor and with the grave; but besides hymns and epitaphs there also exist medical and magical treatises, maxims, fairy tales, official and personal correspondence, reports and accounts, school texts, epics, popular songs, etc. The following is from a collection of love songs (Harris 500):

"The voice of the dove speaks, she says:
'The world is light, observe it.' Thou, thou bird dost entice me.
Then I find my brother in his room, and my heart is joyful . . .
I will not turn from thee, my hand remains in thy hand,
When I go out with thee in beautiful places."—

And again:

. . . "All the birds of Arabia flutter over Egypt, anointed with myrrh:
The one that comes first seizes my worm. He brings fragrance from Arabia.
His claws are full of incense. My heart longs for thee,
That we may open the snare together, I with thee alone.
How beautiful is he who comes in the field because one loves him."

Among the sciences fostered by the Egyptians, their astronomy has at all times awakened admiration. Though the famous Zodiac, constructed at the temple at Denderah under the Romans (in Paris since the year 1822), is not so ancient as it was first supposed to be, the achievements of the Egyptians even in very early times are highly memorable. The calendar which we use, "the most famous relic of ancient times that has exerted influence in the world," was brought from Egypt by Julius Caesar, and by him introduced into the Roman Empire. While other nations connected childish notions with the stars, the Egyptians even at the beginning recognized the distinction between the planets and the fixed stars, and assigned to the former the names of the gods, as we are still doing. It appears also that they observed the retrograde motion of Mars, which lasts some seventy days, and even the movement of the earth, that is, its character as a planet. They observed the rising and setting of the stars for many centuries continuously; and if one possessed no further proof with regard to the extent of their astronomical knowledge, the numberless dates in their writings show what importance was attributed to the careful reckoning of time. The astronomy of the Greeks had its development at Alexandria, where doubtless Egyptian tables supplied the basis for all computations. Among the fixed stars, in the foremost rank stand the 36 or 37 stars of the Equator, which correspond to the 36 decades of the year; every second year has 37, on account of the twice five intercalary days. We possess catalogues of stars in which are found among others Sopd (Sothis, Sirius, or Dog-star); Sah (Osiris, Orion); Art (the Hyades); Khau (the Pleiades). The solar year contains 365 days; but the Egyptians perceived that its proper astronomical length was 365¼ days. At the theoretical commencement of the year, Sirius should rise at the same time as the sun (heliacally), and indicate the beginning of the inundation. In the progress of time the diff'rence would be constantly increasing between the astronomical year, that is, between two heliacal risings of the star Sirius and the civil year. In forty years it would amount to ten days, until at the end of the 1460th astronomical year it would include the civil year 1461. As now the commencement of the civil year again coincided with that of the astronomical year, the civil year began once more on the first day of the first month (Thoth), at the moment of the heliacal rising of Sirius. Accordingly the period of 1460 astronomical or 1461 civil years forms the Sirius (Sothis) or Dog-star period. Such a period ended or began on July 20, 1322 B.C., and the next on July 20, 139 A.D. In a tomb at Beni-Hassan (Twelfth Dynasty) mention is made of the celebration of a festival commemorating the rising of Sothis. Since it was only in the two or three centuries before or after the year 3285 that the heliacal rising of Sirius coincided so exactly with the summer solstice that this concurrence could be observed, it is evident that this determination of the beginning of the year must have existed as early as the fourth millennium B.C. At the present time, however, the rising of Sirius, on account of the further recession of the equinoxes (precession) takes place two and a half months later than it did 5000 years ago. With regard to the reform of the calendar under Ptolemy III., Euergetes I. (238 B.C.), the so-called decree of Canopus (found at Tanis) gives information. It sought to remove the inconvenience occasioned by the fact that on account of the difference between the astronomical and the civil year, the religious festivals lost in the latter constantly about one day in every four years, and by degrees lost the entire year.

Scribe of Gizeh. (After Maspero.)

CHAPTER III.

THE MIDDLE EMPIRE.

DURING the last period of the Ancient Empire[1] the centre of government had been already transferred to Thebes in Upper Egypt. From this point the Pharaohs of the Twelfth Dynasty guided with a powerful hand the destinies of the nation. By the successful repulse of Libyan and Asiatic foes, and of those also who menaced them on the south, by means of long-continued commercial relations with Arabia, by the abundant revenue resulting from the richness of the soil of Egypt, — to which must be added the products of the mines in the Sinaitic peninsula, — and by gorgeous structures which they had reared, they had led the country onward to enjoy an increased prosperity. At Korosko, about midway between the first and second cataracts, an inscription of Amenemhat I. has been found, which announces the conquest of the Nubian Wawa, in the vicinity of Assuan. Here the power of Egypt extended far toward the South. We learn by inscriptions at Beni-Hassan, on the tomb of a local governor, that Usertesen III. pushed the frontier forward as far as Semneh in the land of Heh, beyond the second cataract, and there built fortresses on both steep rocky banks of the river. These fortresses are built of square brick tiles with beams of wood embedded; they are high, the walls on the ground are thirty to thirty-three feet thick, and have towers, moats, and glacis. Near the stream stands the west fortress immediately over the precipitous rocky shore, while the east fortress, also near the river, has a glacis at the side. The latter

[1] The reader is reminded that the Ancient Empire closed with the kings of the Eleventh Dynasty, the history of Dynasties VI.-XI. being somewhat obscure. The Middle Empire comprised the reigns of the kings of the famous Twelfth (beginning with Amenemhat I.) and of the Thirteenth-Fourteenth Dynasties; then followed a second period of obscurity, within which fell the dominion of the Hyksos, or Shepherd Kings, which continued over five hundred years. The New Empire begins with the Eighteenth Dynasty and extends through the Twentieth.—ED.

has a square form with buttresses; the ground plan of the other is shaped like an *L* with the lowest line near the river. In the work of Perrot and Chipiez a view in perspective of the latter fort is given, drawn according to the measurements of Lepsius and de Sauley. Usertesen III. also set up a pillar to designate the boundary, with an inscription in which that country is called Aken. Brugsch recognized in this name the Acina mentioned by Pliny, in the time of Nero, as lying south of Primi (Kasr-Ibrim, west of Korosko). Nevertheless, Usertesen III. was obliged at different times subsequently to contend with the negroes. His successes as conqueror secured his elevation later to a local divinity, and Thothmes III. (Eighteenth Dynasty) erected for him, as such, a temple at Semneh. Amenemhat III. likewise established a fortress opposite Pselcis; there are found at Semneh numerous records of his time with regard to the height of the Nile on the rocks at that point, from which the state of the river in Egypt proper could be estimated. This Pharaoh gave special attention to the regulation of the canal works, and generally of the waters of the Nile. The accounts given respecting the height of the Nile are therefore of interest, since they show that the Nile rose over twenty-seven feet higher at that time than it does to-day, for then it had not broken through the rocky barrier at Selseleh and lowered its level. There is also a series of small monuments bearing the name of Amenemhat I., in the northern parts of the kingdom; and on the spot where at a later day the great temple of Karnak (Thebes) was reared a group of statues and an altar inscribed in his name have been discovered. Several papyri belonging to the later period of this king's reign, when he had established Usertesen I. as co-regent, are preserved. One of these contains the instructions of the king himself to his son. Others relate the interesting experiences of a shipwrecked sailor on a fabulous island; and those of Sa-nehat, an Egyptian nobleman who, probably for political reasons, fled to the land of Edom. Another tells the history of a peasant who was robbed of his ass by a tyrannical officer, and who brought his complaint before King Nebkara (the last king of the Third Dynasty).

The chronological sequence of this Dynasty is satisfactorily established. But its date is difficult to determine. Recently Dr Borchardt, basing his calculation upon an astronomical date found in a papyrus from Kahun, obtained the date B.C. 1876, for the seventh year of Usertesen III. But much difference of opinion still exists with regard to the matter. Approximately we may place the beginning of the Twelfth Dynasty, with the powerful administration of Amenemhat I., between B.C. 2500 and 2000. The successor of Usertesen I., Amenemhat II., was for two years co-regent; and three years before he was murdered by eunuchs he appointed his son Usertesen III. to be his own co-regent, of whom the Louvre possesses a statue of carnelian. He has often shared with Rameses II. the honor of being identified with the Sesostris of Manetho, of Herodotus, and of other classics. Tacitus reports that under Sesostris a Phoenix-period closed. But he means by this a Sirius-period; since from his statement that the Phoenix-period according to some lasts 500 years, and according to others 1461 years, it follows that one of these epochs occurred in the reign of Sesostris, and the other in that of Amasis (572 B.C.); yet these two rulers do not lie 500 years apart, but even still farther than a Sirius-period,—a proof of the slight dependence that can be placed on chronological reckonings of this description. Under Usertesen III., whose statue is in the Berlin Museum, the building of the Labyrinth was begun; it was completed under his successors. His son, Amenemhat IV., married his own sister Sebek-neferu (Scemiophris). The Labyrinth and Lake Moeris were the chief monuments of the Twelfth Dynasty; and these works have been fully described by admiring Greek and Roman writers. Both are situated at the entrance of the 'lake land,' or Fayum, an oasis in the Libyan desert, separated from the valley of the Nile only by rising grounds of moderate elevation. 'Joseph's canal' (in Arabic, Bahr-Yûsuf) leaves the Nile at Siût (Lycopolis), and goes northward, piercing the hills at its entrance into the Fayum, and by numerous ramifications watering a region renowned to-day and in ancient times for its climate and the abundance of its splendid fruit-trees, cereals, and rose gardens. In the deepest part of this depression lies a great lake, the Birket-el-Kurun, at whose southern extremity stands a temple (in Arabic, Kasr-Karûn) of the Roman period; behind it rise the mountains of the Sahara. The present chief town of the Fayum, Medinet-el-Fayum, lies a little south of the ancient city of Pa-sebek, or Crocodilopolis (from the worship of the crocodile, and of Sebek, the crocodile-headed god of the inundation); and a mosque of the modern chief town, with many Corinthian pillars of marble, was built out of material of the age of the Ptolemies, when the city was called Arsinoë. Farther north lie the ruins of Biahmu (Fig. 40), in which search has been made for the pyramids of which Herodotus speaks as standing in the middle of Lake Moeris, i. e., two platforms of stone surmounted by seated colossi of Amenemhat III., monoliths of quartzite, thirty-nine feet in height, some fragments of which are now in the Ashmolean Museum at Oxford. On the margin of the Fayum, north of the mouth of the Bahr-Yūsuf, lies the brick pyramid of Hawāra. It was the tomb of King Amenemhat III. Adjoining it are the ruins of the

Fig. 39. -- Tanis Sphinx. (After Maspero.)

Labyrinth, an immense building 1000 by 800 feet, built by Amenemhat and his daughter and successor, Sebekneferu. Its axis extends directly from north to south. On the south side of the pyramid there is a court, formerly covered, as is probable, with colonnades, nearly sixty acres in extent; and on three sides this is encompassed by a bewildering mass of brick walls. At the present time a canal runs through the ruins. Herodotus says that the Labyrinth was vast beyond all description; that what the Greeks had brought to pass in the erection of walls and of various buildings would not equal, if taken together, the Labyrinth in cost and labor; the temples of Ephesus and Samos were worthy to be mentioned, but the pyramids surpass all description; and

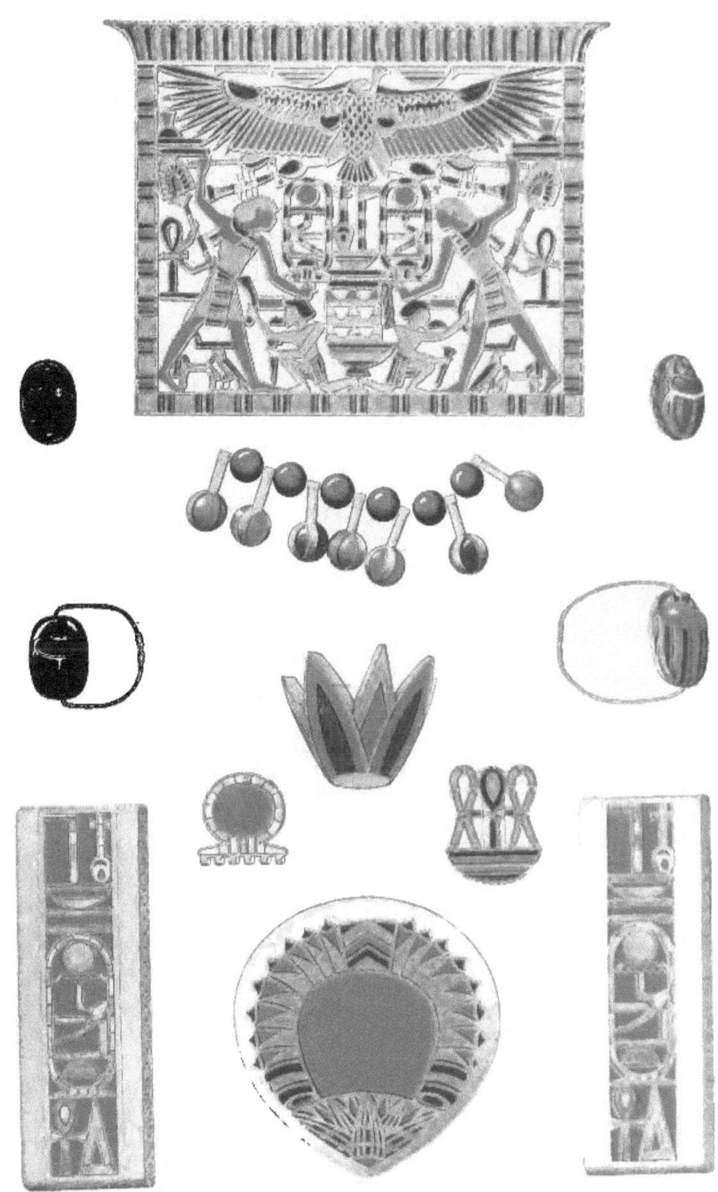

JEWELRY FROM DASHUR. XII. DYNASTY. GIZEH MUSEUM
AFTER DE MORGAN.

History of All Nations, Vol. I., page 120.

any one of them outweighs a multitude of the best Grecian works, while the Labyrinth still excels the pyramids. His description seems less credible than that of Strabo, who represents the Labyrinth as a royal palace, in which the governors of the Egyptian provinces assembled, to each of whom belonged a special court-room and chamber; all the courts were encircled by colonnades, and the corridors were so numerous and complicated that a stranger could not go in or out without a guide. The pyramid, examined by Mr. Petrie, is peculiar: The passages to the central chamber are elaborately complex, and provided with gigantic trap-doors in the roof, leading to other passages and to dumb chambers. The only access to the sepulchral chamber was obtained through its roof. This was formed by three immense

Fig. 40. — The Ruins at Illahun.

blocks, one of which, weighing forty-five tons, was dropped into place on closing the pyramid. The chamber itself is a marvel. It is hollowed of one block "of glass-hard yellow quartzite cut and polished with exquisite truth." It is 22 by 8 feet inside and is over two feet thick, weighing 210 tons. A trace of these building activities occurs at Hamamat, in an inscription of the ninth year of Amenemhat II., recording that, under the supervision of the head architect Usertesen, stones were brought thence for the building in the Fayum, and a sitting statue of the king, five cubits high, was carried thence for the temple of Sebek. The Moeris (in Egyptian *meri*, 'a lake'; or *hunt*, 'the water that flows off') covered the western part of the Fayum; it began at the Labyrinth, and extended to the vicinity of Medinet, while it spread far to the north and south. The aim which Amenemhat sought and attained by diking Lake Moeris was to secure an outflow of the water into this reservoir when the inundation was high, and, on the other hand, when the inundation was scanty, to draw off the gathered water from the lake to the land that was not overflowed; moreover some twenty thousand acres of fertile land were thus rescued from the lake. The sluices necessary for regulating this were placed at Illahun (in Egyptian, *la-hunt*, 'the mouth' of the Moeris) in the neighborhood of the city of Pa-ra-sekhem-khafer (the city of Osorkon I.), by the Greeks called Ptolemaïs. These sluices were arranged to prevent the further outflow of the waters from the Bahr-Yûsuf into Lake Moeris,

Fig. 41. — The Pyramid of Illahun.

and to cause them to run off into the extension of this canal in the region of Memphis. At Illahun is situated the pyramid (Fig. 41) of Usertesen II., excavated by Mr. Petrie in 1889–1890. The lower part of the pyramid is of unmoved rock, isolated by a deep cutting. On it arise walls of large blocks between which is filled in a brick pyramid. This consists of a framework of brick walls carefully constructed, which from each of the four sides run inwardly, and are connected within with two diagonal walls which cross each other. The whole was then filled up with stones, and cased with great slabs.

Even at this day the circuit of the former lake-basin can be accurately determined by depressions in the soil and the remains of ancient dykes at different places. The western shore reaches from Crocodilopolis to the modern Tulūn; and the northwest margin forms with it an obtuse angle, and extends to the vicinity of Sele. In Gizeh there is a papyrus containing a plan of Lake Moeris, together with the towns and temples on its shores; in the plan of the Labyrinth it confirms Strabo's statement by specifying with regard to each room for what province of Lower or Upper Egypt it was set apart. The same manuscript confirms what was long ago conjectured respecting the relation of the myth of Osiris and Set to the blessing-bearing floods of the Nile and to the desert; since it designates several places where the canal was led through portions of the desert as scenes of conflict between Horus and Set, in which the good god by a victory preserved the benefits conferred by his father Osiris. At the present time the water-works at Lake Moeris are no longer in existence; but engineering works of great magnitude are being carried on with a similar purpose by the British at Assuan and at Siût.

At Abydos, Mariette found, in great numbers, private tombs belonging to the period of the Twelfth and Thirteenth Dynasties. They are very much injured, yet their type can be completely established. They consist of a square substructure, containing a vault for the mummy. Upon this foundation rises a pyramid which has a hollow space within; this runs up to a hollow, pointed cupola, which is formed by every row of bricks projecting over that immediately below; hence the vertical section exhibits a pointed arch. Before the entrance is a small hall used as a tomb-chapel; this is often wanting, and in this case a table is constructed for the worship of the dead in the wall of the building, such as we have already seen in the mastabas at Memphis. Before this table the prescribed ceremonies were performed under the open sky. Evidently the outer surfaces of the building, which commonly is but sixteen to twenty feet high, were covered with stucco and painted white. Sometimes the tomb-chamber is sunk into the soil. This kind of tomb, with the chamber for the mummy and the chapel, either in front of the same or built upon it in the shape of a shrine with ascending walls and surmounted by a pyramidal top, is found also in the time of the New Empire and very generally at Thebes. In some Apis tombs of the Eighteenth Dynasty, the corners are adorned with columns; and they remind us of the Lykian type of sepulchre, to be described hereafter. The sarcophagi retain the usual shape of a chest, which is still treated as a house; and often its evolution from wooden architecture is indicated by painted depressions in the stone. There are also sarcophagi in which the stone carving exhibits the deceased partly as he was in life, with rich clothing, and partly as a mummy, i. e., the body swathed in mummy wrappings up to the head, and the extremities not visible. Far more interesting are the tombs originating in the time of the Twelfth Dynasty, which were excavated in great numbers from the rocks above Beni-Hassan (in Egyptian, Panubt; in Greek, Speos

FIG. 42. — Rock-tombs of Beni-Hassan.

Artemidos). The richer of these grottos consist of a vestibule in the rock, which has two pillars and a substitute for the architrave and cornice, that is seemingly supported by a row of columns; it opens outwardly, and in the middle at the rear is shown the entrance to a larger hall for the worship of the dead. The ceiling of this hall is supported by scattered columns, and, like that of the vestibule, is often carved into the form of a flattened arch. In the rear of the hall, which receives light only through the door, there opens commonly a niche or chamber in which is placed the statue of the dead. In one part of the hall the pit descends into the sepulchre. Some porticos of these rock grottos, at a distance, forcibly remind the spectator of Doric columns; near at hand, this resemblance is much lessened, for the columns at Beni-Hassan stand on a low, round socket, and have neither echinus nor, strictly speaking, abacus. Therefore, they have been called Proto-Doric. Here again we meet with a survival in stone of the wooden architecture of primitive days. The pillar was the wooden prop that supported the roof. Where it rested on the ground clay was heaped to give it solidity, and where the roof-beam rested on it a board was added to divide the weight. Both features were retained in the Egyptian column; they constituted the round base and the square abacus. The Egyptian column originated from a square pillar; and this, diminishing in diameter but a very little from bottom to top, is cut obliquely at the four corners, so that an octagonal body results. The corners cut in this manner lessen the mass of the pillar, and hence give freer admission to the light. The original form of the pillar is still indicated by a low quadrangular intermediate piece between the column and the architrave, which is of the same diameter as the column at its base, yet does not project, like the Greek abacus, but lies in the same plane as the architrave. The latter is smooth, without the distinction of parts which characterizes the Doric entablature, and it passes into a moulding which we may regard as a cornice. In the inner hall of a sepulchre the octagonal column is once more cut obliquely, so that it has sixteen angles, and besides, in order to render the play of light and shade more effectual, the flat spaces between the angles being somewhat deepened and rounded, were fluted. Two or four of these fluted interspaces were then brought together to form a broad, smooth surface, in order that hieroglyphics might be engraved upon it in a vertical direction; here the effort to make architecture everywhere subservient to figures and writing destroyed the aesthetic effect of the columns. In the time of the Eighteenth Dynasty this pillar appears, with its sixteen faces, in the western portico of the temple at Semneh, as also elsewhere. Here a polygonal pillar is used, the anterior part of which is entirely employed as a surface for inscriptions. Above it is displayed a mask of Hathor, that is, the head of a woman, with cow's horns, broad tresses of hair, and a diminutive temple on her head, in such a manner that at a distance it gives the impression of a mummy standing erect or that of the

Caryatides, that is, of human bodies bearing up the architrave.[1] While the original pillar, as it appears in the Temple of the Sphinx, and also in a tomb at Sakkara, where, however, a low socle is placed beneath to prevent the sinking of the pillar, is transformed into the column, on the other hand, the pillar retains its primitive character, and is covered with sculptures. Besides the square socle a square capital is added (Karnak). The façade is then adorned with these columns, the fronts of which are wrought into colossal figures, representing the royal founder as Osiris (Abu-Simbel). These figures, however, do not architecturally support the architrave, as do the Grecian Atlantes and the Caryatides of the Erechtheum. With these changes in the pillar there was developed a column which in the time of the Eighteenth Dynasty appears standing isolated, perhaps as the support of a movable piece of decoration; its capital has the form of a bell, but it represents in stone an elegant metallic rod, the head of which passes through a ring. More richly developed are the columns which grew immediately from the architecture in wood. In very ancient paintings appear representations of canopies of wood supported by wooden posts. These last are surrounded by canes and papyrus stems, which are fastened together with ribbons, and adorned with wreaths, a *motif* that is shown also in the mastabas, as before mentioned, while here between the rods of the lath decoration, the fasciated lotus-stems with their overhanging coronals of flowers serve as ornaments to the niches and the stone sarcophagi. Sometimes in such pictures there are also separate flowers tied together by ribbons under the masses of buds pendent from these reeds, and their stems are inserted in the spaces between the several rods, and their flowers are blended with the calyx of the capital. As simple decoration of one face of these columns this massing of lotus flowers appears in the tomb at Zawijet-el-Meitin (Sixth Dynasty). The imitation of the flowers with the ends of their leaves turned inwards presents a conventional design, which, according to some authorities, suggested the Ionian volute. As Egyptian art did not adopt this motive in stone, the volute remained in use simply as a decoration on a flat surface; it is thus often seen on the handles of mirrors and on many metallic implements.

[1] As to the antiquity of the Hathor head, see Introduction, page 9.

This covering of the supporting wooden post was copied in stone, and it formed the lotus column with the capital buds which occurs in a tomb at Beni-Hassan. Instead of buds, the unfolded blossoms can now come forth as the coronal of the reeds which are bound together, and then are transformed into the so-called calyx capital, which takes the form of a decided and beautiful curve; but it departs from the original conception in so far that the stems, which are bound together, have each not one but many buds at the top, as at Philae and Esneh, where the capital is entirely composed of a great profusion of flowers. Over this capital the early inner wooden post of the prototype is still visible as an impost of stone. The effect is confusing. The posts, which formed the shaft of the column, bound together beneath the capital, are now encompassed with a cylindrical covering, so that the section of the shaft forms a circular line. Above the socle, where the column shows a considerable enlargement (entasis), we see indications of the derivation of the column from reed stems in the painted bulrush leaves used as a decoration. It has been pointed out, and too much stress cannot be laid upon it, that the forms and details of Egyptian architecture, as we know them, were rarely originally intended for the use made of them. These delicate stems, buds, and flowers could never have been meant to be executed in stone with a diameter of twelve feet and a height of sixty feet. The entire scheme of Egyptian architectural decoration betrays its development from wood and brick material.

The first tomb of Beni-Hassan concealed the mummy of the nomarch Khnum-hotep. The inscriptions here relate numerous experiences in the life of the deceased, and are of great importance for the history of the Twelfth Dynasty. The princes of the provinces, the Egyptian feudal nobility, had endeavored to extend their authority, after the passing away of the most ancient and powerful royal houses and during the decline of the central government in the time of the Seventh and subsequent Dynasties. The royal power was, however, again strengthened; and they were thereby confined to the circuit of their several nomes, and were obliged to content themselves with filling the highest position next to the Pharaoh. We learn from the inscriptions that Khnum-hotep was appointed (confirmed) by Amenemhat I. as nomarch and hereditary prince of the sixteenth nome. This principality had, however, come to his father, Nehera, son of Sebek-ankh, as the dowry of Beket, his wife, who after the death, without children, of her brother Nakht, was the bearer of the dignity of hereditary ruler. The father of Beket had been called by Amenemhat I. to the nomarchy of the province of Mah (Sah); and under Usertesen I. his brother had become governor of Mena-t-khufu (the modern Minieh), a dignity which belonged to the oldest princes of the house, before they succeeded their fathers as nomarchs. Khnum-hotep died in the eighteenth year of Usertesen I., after holding the office for twenty years. He had married Kheti, an heiress, who brought him as her dowry the seventeenth nome (Cynopolites). His son, the offspring of this marriage, who was named Nakht, was confirmed by Usertesen II. in the nomarchy of the seventeenth province, his mother's heritage; and he obtained the dignity of governor of all the provinces lying between Thebes and Aphroditopolis. Ameni, another son, inherited the Nome of the Gazelle. A full record of his life appears in his tomb at Beni-Hassan in an inscription dated the forty-third year of the king. He enumerates the warlike services which he had rendered to his king, whom he followed in his raids in Nubia, returning laden with gold, and extols the excellence of his administration, telling how he had cared for the entire nome, and had held all the inhabitants to labor, so that no one could be found who suffered from hunger; how he had sought to be friendly to every one, had brought sorrow to no child, had oppressed no widow. Making all due allowance for the egotism of these statements, as well as for their grandiloquence, their substantial truth is corroborated by the activity and industry manifested by all classes of society in their occupations, as is clearly and abundantly shown by the figured descriptions in the sepulchre at Beni-Hassan. Such a development is possible only in a flourishing country, and with a population at once energetic and skilful, and living under a peaceful rule. Our conception of the high degree to which the moral feelings and humanity of the Egyptians were cultivated is enhanced when we compare inscriptions of this kind with those by leaders or kings of other nations, who with rude complacency portray the horrors of the wars waged by them, and yet for this count upon the approval of heaven. The painted reliefs in the tomb of Khnum-

Figs. 43, 44. Paintings on the Wall of a Tomb at Beni-Hassan. Semitic family asking admission into Egypt.

hotep show the farmer with his cattle in various kinds of labor, the gardener engaged in setting out his shrubs and other plants, the vine-dressers, the hand-craftsmen, the joiners, the currier, the saddler (with the semi-circular knife for cutting pieces of leather), shoemakers, potters, glass-makers, and women employed in weaving and cooking. The remarkable representation—now unfortunately much defaced—of the arrival of a Semitic family (Amu), who having left their home, ask to be received by the nomarch (Figs. 43, 44), although it has frequently been published and commented upon, cannot be overlooked when dealing with this tomb. The company is introduced by the scribe Nefer-hotep, who delivers to the nomarch a tablet with the following inscription: "In the sixth year of king Ra-kha-kheper (Usertesen II.) is the account rendered concerning the Amu who bring to the princely son Khnum-hotep the *mesd'emt*, a green paint for the eyes. Their number amounts to thirty-seven." The third figure in the painting is, according to the inscription, the prince (Heq Setu) Absha. The second is Khiti, an officer who is conducting them before the nomarch, who awaits them with dignity, accompanied by his son and three dogs. The chief delivers to the nomarch a wild goat from Sinai. The representation is important in the history of art; since it is the most ancient picture of the Semites, and shows their costume in its peculiar colors,—blue, white, and red. The chief and a number of the men, as well as all the women, wear the sleeveless tunic, which extends over the left shoulder, and leaves the right arm bare. A number of the men wear merely a fringed gown reaching from the hips to the knees; the chief also has fringe on his dress; the white woollen stuff of his coat is ornamented with stripes running vertically, between whose waving lines run lines shaped like bars and scales separated by dots; the white dress of a woman shows also green waving stripes (meander pattern). Their weapons are spears, bows, and a kind of club or boomerang. The chief is barefooted, as also the women; but the latter have rings on their ankles. A man is playing on a harp or cithern with a plectron in the right hand, and with the fingers of the left hand. The asses led along with them carry, among other things, peculiar vessels, with feet, double mouths, and horizontal handles; these contained the *mesd'emt*. We saw that the most ancient tomb-statues have a green streak under the eyes; this ungnent has been found used as early as the prehistoric period; and the Semites beyond the isthmus prepared it at this time. In the same tomb appear also swarthy men with red hair, carrying lances and boomerangs; they are performing mock combats; one of these men is also figured in the tomb of Seti I. (Nineteenth Dynasty). According to Newberry, who last studied Beni-Hassan (1890), these men are Libyans.

Among the many representations of Egyptian life, there is found in the tomb of the nomarch Thoth-hotep, — the son of Kai and grandson of Nehera, that is, the nephew of Khnum-hotep at Bersheh (Antinoë, in the nome of Hermopolites) the picture of the transportation of a granite statue of a king, in a sitting posture; it belongs to the time of Amenemhat II. This statue is placed on a sort of sledge, and is made fast by means of a great metallic ring and ropes that are drawn in different directions around the colossus; mats are carefully arranged beneath, in order to protect the polished surface of the granite from being rubbed by the cords. By means of four ropes made fast to a ring the sledge is drawn by four rows of men, consisting of twenty-one (three times seven) pairs, and one special pair in advance of them all, thus in all 172 men. The commander of the men who are at the ropes stands upon a knee of the colossus; the cords and the planks over which the sledge is moved, are wetted to prevent their igniting. Seven rows of eleven men each may be seen bearing palm-branches in their hands, thus giving a festal character to the procession. This recalls a similar scene depicted on a bas-relief at Kuyunjik (Nineveh). Indeed, Layard reports that he employed this same method of transportation in removing an Assyrian colossus.

To the time of the Twelfth Dynasty belongs the oldest extant monument of Heliopolis, the city of Ra. The scanty remains of An (the 'On' of the Bible) lie at the village of Matarieh, northeast of Cairo. Here in early times was the centre of the worship of the Sun. Tum, the evening sun; Ra, the hawk-headed sun-god in the fulness of its power; Ra-Harmachis ('the rising sun'): Shu, and Tefnut were the principal gods. The sacred bull of Ra, Mnevis, with his black cows; lions also, beasts with shining skin, and symbols of the greatest strength of the sun's heat; and finally the bird Bennu (the phoenix) formed the zoölogical pantheon of this city of the Sun. The numerous company of priests connected with the sanctuary, on whom, as sons of Ra, gifts were lavished by the Pharaohs, maintained also a school of a high order, which enjoyed a great renown in ancient times, and was resorted to by many Greeks. Here Plato, Eudoxus, Thales, Archimedes, Pythagoras, Anaxagoras, and Chrysippus, as the Greeks themselves have testified, derived much of their wisdom. Amenemhat I. restored the temple of Tum, and founded the temple of the Sun. The site of the latter is at this day indicated only by the most ancient of the great existing obelisks (sixty-eight feet high) which was erected in front of the temple by Usertesen

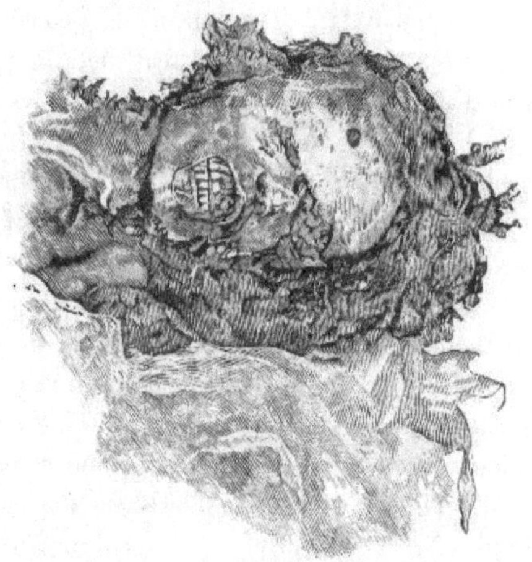

FIG. 45. — Head of Seqenen-Ra Ta-a-qen (Seventeenth Dynasty).

I. From the position of the obelisk the conclusion may be drawn that it occupied the space before the pylon or gateway of the temple, as later in the New Empire, and that the arrangement of the great temple in the Ancient Empire was the same as at a later period. This is also confirmed by many building-plans that have been preserved, in conformity to which edifices were erected in subsequent times. The Arabs tell also of numerous other colossal statues, the products of marvellous labor. The polished obelisks (in Egyptian *tehen*, later *men*, 'standing erect') were dedicated to the sun; upon them, as on shining pillars, the vault of heaven seems to rest. They are at the same time symbols of the generative power of the Sun-god, Amen in Thebes, Ra in Heliopolis. Apparently the obelisks, the tips of which were touched with gold, were regarded furthermore as lightning conductors: "they break the storms of heaven" (inscription in the temple of Edfu); and something similar is reported of the masts with their pendent streamers upon the pylons. We have seen that there was one type of monument consisting of a substructure, and a short obelisk standing upon it. Several of the obelisks which have been transported from Egypt had their origin at Heliopolis (Egyptian On), around which centred Sun-worship. It was called 'the house of Ra,' Per-Ra, and also the 'house of obelisks,' 'Hat-Benben.' In texts of the Old Empire, Heliopolis is rarely mentioned. Yet the great temple of Ra, which dates of the Twelfth Dynasty—if we believe a leathern manuscript at Berlin—was not the first sanctuary there erected, and a temple of Tum was enlarged at the same time. Under Rameses III. the temple of Ra was at the height of its renown, 12,963 persons were attached to its service. And Herodotos and Strabo praise the learning of its priests even in their day. The obelisk of Usertesen stood until the thirteenth century. The same Pharaoh erected the obelisk of Ebgig (Fayum), which has two narrow sides and two that are wider; the last are arched in the shape of a roof whose gable ends are formed from the tops of the narrow sides rounded off. The broad sides do not present the usual columns of hieroglyphics, but five rows of figures; a notch at the summit serves to fasten a metallic top-piece. In the time of the Eighteenth and Nineteenth Dynasties, nearly all the Pharaohs set up obelisks, especially at Thebes and Tanis. At Karnak there is a pair of obelisks erected by Thothmes I., between the sanctuary and the great pillared hall; the one now overthrown was still standing in the middle of the last century. A second pair of similar monoliths was erected by his daughter, Hatshepsut Makara; but of these also only one is now standing. It is the highest (109 feet), although one is mentioned which is said to have measured 200 feet (120 cubits); according to the inscription on the socle seven months were expended upon Hatshepsut's obelisk, and it came from the quarries at Syene. The tops were overlaid with the metal *asem* (electrum—gold mixed with silver—but in this case probably a sort of brass). Thothmes III. caused many obelisks to be erected at Heliopolis, especially the two brought to Alexandria at a later day, which became famous under the name of Cleopatra's Needles. One of these was conveyed some years since to London, the other was brought to New York. The central column of inscriptions shows the name of Thothmes III.; on two sides Rameses II. also has engraved columns of writing. On the top is represented the god Tum, to whom Thothmes III., in the form of a sphinx, is presenting a drink-offering, with the words: "The gift of fresh water of the good god, the lord of the two lands, Ra-men-kheper" ('giver of eternal life,' that is, Thothmes III.). Beneath the sphinx stands "the mighty bull, crowned in Uas (western Thebes), son of the sun, Thothmes." On another side of the obelisk is placed the wine-offering. On the third side, not Tum, but Ra-Harmachis, is depicted: and the offering consists of frankincense. The fourth side of the obelisk represents Thothmes as a sphinx on the pylon, making two offerings of incense. In 1877 it was discovered that the obelisk now in New York was placed upon four bronze crabs, only one of which remained, the others being replaced by stone. This crab has a Greek and Roman inscription, according to which the obelisk was erected in the year 13–12 B.C., in front of the Caesareum, or Sebasteum at Alexandria. The middle column runs as follows: "The royal Horus, wearer of the crown, king of Upper and Lower Egypt, the golden hawk, who smote the kings of all lands that approached him, according to the command of Ra. Victory over the whole world, and strength of the sword are there when he openeth his hand for the extension of the bounds of Egypt; son of the sun, Thothmes the life-bestower." "The royal Horus, the mighty bull, crowned in Thebes, lord of the diadem, whose kingdom is far extended as that of the sun. Beloved of Tum, the Lord of Heliopolis, son of his loins; Thoth created him, Thothmes. In the perfection of their members they created him, in the great dwelling-place, so that he has established an extended dominion for hundreds of years. The king of Upper and Lower Egypt, Ra-men-kheper, beloved of Tum, of the great god, and of the gods of his circle, bestowing all life, joyfulness, felicity, immortal as is the sun." From Thothmes III. came also the obelisk which was set up, in the year 1588, before the Lateran in

Rome; it was brought by Constantine to Alexandria, and by Constantius to Rome, where it served in the *spina* of the Circus Maximus. The second obelisk belonging to him was brought by Theodosius to Constantinople, and placed in the Hippodrome. An obelisk of Amenhotep II. is to be found at Sion House, the country seat of the Duke of Northumberland at Brentford. From Seti I. came the obelisk on the Piazza del Popolo at Rome, originally set up by Augustus on the *spina* of the Circus Maximus. From Rameses II. are derived the two obelisks of Luxor (Thebes), one of which, separated from its companion, has stood in the Place de la Concorde in Paris since 1833. This splendid square, on account of its great size, seriously lessens the effect naturally produced by the height of this granite needle, which was brought from Egypt and erected here at a cost of three million francs. In Tanis eleven obelisks of the time of Rameses II. are lying in ruins on the ground. From this Pharaoh came also the obelisk in the Boboli Gardens, behind the Pitti Palace in Florence. The obelisk in front of St. Peter's in Rome originated with Merenptah, the son of Rameses II. Caligula caused it to be carried from Heliopolis, and set up in the court of the Vatican. The obelisk in the Piazza della Minerva, which Bernini, in 1667, placed on the back of an elephant, was made under Hophra (Twenty-sixth Dynasty). Augustus ordered a similar one, of Psammetichus II., to be removed; it now stands in the Piazza di Monte Citorio. In the Piazza Navona is the so-called Pamfili obelisk, and an obelisk of Nectanebo I. is in the British Museum. The obelisk of latest date is the Barberini obelisk, on the Pincian Hill, on which occur the names of Hadrian, of the Empress Sabina, and of Antinoüs. The obelisks, as is known, are polished granite monoliths, which were worked out in the quarry, then separated from the rock, and transported on a ship to their position. The difficulty of setting up such a stone may be perceived from the fact that modern engineers have been obliged to avail themselves of all the resources of their art in order to remove and re-erect the obelisks.

The dwellings of the priests that encircle the inner sanctuary at Karnak were due to Usertesen I. They were restored at a later day. To the same ruler are traced also the fragments of columns which are identical with those at Beni-Hassan, having sixteen faces; a granite statue also from the same site is now at Luxor. The Middle Empire was an era of great literary activity. The first attempt at alliteration and at tales of adventure appear. Art also received a strong impulse, as well as architecture and engineering. The colossal granite statues, no less than minor works, are highly finished. In 1894, M. de Morgan attacked the north brick Pyramid of Dashur, which proved to be the tomb of Usertesen III. At the corners of its peribolos walls were wells connected by passages and burial chambers of royal personages: Henut-taui, a 'royal wife'—probably of Usertesen III.—and two 'king's daughters,' Sent-s-Seneb and Sat-Hathor, whose splendid jewels enclosed in a casket had been overlooked by former grave robbers. In similar connection with the south brick Pyramid of Dashur was found the burial place of a king, Hor-aua-ab-Ra, who has no place in the official lists of this dynasty. A box of his sepulchral deposits, however, sealed with the undisturbed stamp of Amenemhat III., was found. Near-by was buried a princess of King Amenemhat's family, wearing the asp and vulture of queens; and with her another set of wonderful jewels was found. Pectorals, inlaid with precious stones and colored paste, pendants, two beautiful crowns of the most delicate and elaborate workmanship, gold, amethyst, emerald beads attest the splendor as well as the artistic goldsmithery of the period. (PLATE IX.) Two large galleys, some thirty feet long, were also found. They were richly painted and well preserved. They, no doubt, are specimens of the funeral barges, often portrayed on the walls of the Egyptian tombs, in which the defunct was conveyed from the eastern to the western side of the Nile on the first part of his journey to 'Amenti.'

After the Twelfth Dynasty there follows an obscure period, which continued until the accession of the Eighteenth Dynasty. Manetho assigns to the Thirteenth Dynasty (at Thebes) and the Fourteenth (at Xois), together, 136 kings; the Turin papyrus has 130–159 names of sovereigns, unfortunately for the most part illegible, and, so far as the numbers are preserved, giving brief reigns. In the Thirteenth Dynasty the name of Sebek-hotep occurs about ten times. The duration of 500 years, which was formerly accepted, is so short for the period indicated that, if it comprehends only the Thirteenth and Fourteenth Dynasties, every ruler would have reigned a little less than three years. The monuments of several of the reigns are spread over all Egypt.

Furthermore, some kings of the Shepherd Dynasties (Hyksos) that followed also left monuments in all Egypt; they therefore could not have reigned contemporaneously with the former.

The Fifteenth and Sixteenth Dynasties are those of the Hyksos, or Shepherd Kings. Manetho alone gives an account of their first appearance and of their rule; but the fragments of his writings bearing on this subject were so worked over by Josephus (who has preserved them for us), through his desire to enhance the high antiquity and nobility of the Jewish nation, that for a long time they misled the judgment of scholars, and confirmed the opinion that the Hyksos, who are named Aatu in the Sallier papyrus, where their final expulsion is alluded to, must have been of Semitic stock, a sort of Bedawin Arabs. It has been suggested that the Hyksos invasion was the indirect result of the Elamite and Chaldean military movements of the late third millennium B.C. But who they were, whence they came, is still doubtful, although no historical problem ever aroused more interest among scholars. They have in turn been identified with Semites, Cushites, Mongols, Hittites, and others. To the Egyptians themselves they were 'Shasu'—pillagers—a word applied by them to the Bedawin; or 'Sheman'—strangers (under Queen Hatshepsut), or 'Aatu'—scourges. They were nomadic tribes which were attracted to Egypt by its fertility and wealth, and in whose wake it is probable that many different Asiatic tribes followed. Among them, perhaps, the Beni-Israel. Be that as it may, they swept over the Isthmus, established their stronghold at Hat' nar (Avaris) in the eastern extremity of the Delta, and thence conquered, or dictated terms to the entire country. That this had become possible, although only after stubborn conflicts in which the strangers showed all their barbarous cruelty, confirms the supposition that the Dynasty of Xois, weakened perhaps by internal dissensions, and contests of the feudal nobility with the crown, were easily thrust from the throne. According to the narrative of Manetho, it was at the time when Timaeus (Timios) was reigning, that God, for unknown causes, was unfavorably disposed toward the Egyptians. Suddenly a people of inglorious origin seized the land, and conquered it with little difficulty, without determined opposition. The rulers were taken captive, cities were burnt, and the sanctuaries of the gods laid waste; of the male population a portion were slain, the wives and children of another part were dragged into slavery. The king of these foreigners was named Salatis. He chose Memphis for his capital, and occupied the towns with large garrisons; in Avaris (Pelusium), west of the Bubastic-Pelusian mouth of the Nile, he established a great encampment, and there kept his troops in training. His five successors, Bnon, Apachnan, Aphobis, Annas, and Asseth, reigned for a long time; in fact, the sway of these six Hyksos kings lasted 260 years. During this long period the Hyksos gradually yielded to the influences of Egyptian culture. They became Egyptianized. They adopted the protocols of the Pharaohs; and, notwithstanding the supremacy of their god Sutekh, these 'princes of the desert' (Heq Setu) became known as 'sons of Ra' and 'divine Horuses.' A mathematical papyrus is dated the twenty-third year of Apepi II., who also bestowed a scribe's palette (Berlin Museum) upon one Atu. Traces of Khian occur from Gebelen to the Delta and even in Crete. A granite socle in the Louvre bears thirty-six names of conquered Nubian provinces, and inscriptions attest their control of the Assuan quarries. They, therefore, ruled over all Egypt and held the Theban princes in subjection. The Sallier papyrus No. 1, however, shows us the latter ready to shake off the yoke. A command, the sense of which is obscure, issued by Apepi II. to the 'prince of the south,' Seqenen-Ra, with regard to a certain canal; and in which the worship of the god Sutekh is mixed up, seems to have precipitated the crisis. The war of independence followed; and we know that King Seqenen-Ra Ta-a-qen was probably killed on the battle-field. To this, his hastily mummified body, found in 1881, bears eloquent testimony. (See Fig. 45.) A battle-axe had opened his left cheek exposing his teeth and breaking the jaw. A second blow had fractured his skull. A spear had pierced his forehead above the right eye, which is covered with brain matter that oozed from the wound. How long he remained on the field uncared for no one can tell; but when embalmed his features were set. They still express the rage that filled his soul. The brow is contracted below his thick matted hair; the lips are drawn over the gums; and the tongue is caught between the teeth. He must have been forty years old when he died. Tall, vigorous, he resembles the Berber type. The fact that his body was preserved seems to imply victory for the Egyptians—which

Aāhmes I., his successor, brilliantly followed up. A long and grievous war followed, which finally ended with the deliverance of Egypt. Of the kings constituting the Seventeenth Dynasty, the names of eleven are known; several names are supplied from a very peculiar source, the Abbott papyrus in the British Museum. This contains the record of a suit at law against tomb-robbers in the time of the Twentieth Dynasty (Rameses IX.). After investigations made by engineers, record is made of the tombs at Thebes—which the culprits had robbed, and which they had spared. Four tombs of the Eleventh Dynasty, those of Antef-āa, of An-antef, of An-aā, and of Neb-Kher-Ra Mentu-hotep, were not robbed at that time. On the other hand, the tomb of Sebek-em-saf (Thirteenth Dynasty) and that of Seqenen-Ra I. (Seventeenth Dynasty) were robbed. Again, there were found to be unopened the sepulchres of Seqenen-Ra II., of Kames, of Aāhmes-sa-pa-ar, and of Amenhotep I., who was buried by the side of the Pharaohs of the Seventeenth Dynasty. The gilded sarcophagus of the third sovereign of the Seventeenth Dynasty, Seqenen Ra Ta-aa III., together with the mummy, was found in the year 1881, at Dēr-el-Bahri, when the pit that was completely filled up with a collection of royal bodies was laid open, as already mentioned. A costly sarcophagus of Aāh-hotep, the consort of the fourth Pharaoh, and mother of Aāhmes, the founder of the Eighteenth Dynasty, was disinterred by Mariette at Thebes, and is now in the Gizeh Museum. The whole sarcophagus, having the shape of a mummy with face and wide, opened eyes, is gilded; the margins of the eyes are encircled with gold; the white of the eyes consists of quartz, the pupil is of black enamel. Beneath the painted jewelry around the neck were found a serpent and a vulture, the insignia of sovereignty over Upper and Lower Egypt; the hieroglyphics give the name of the queen. The body was not enveloped with bandages, but only lightly wrapped in pieces of cloth. Upon it were found two hundred and thirteen ornaments, the head being adorned with a rich diadem, consisting of two golden sphinxes that guarded the cartouche of Aāhmes (her son, who had provided for her burial). There were jewels on the upper part of the arm, bracelets of gold with the name of Aāhmes wrought into the gold with pearls, lapis lazuli, carnelian, and enamel; a necklace, and a representation of Amen and Ra, who are sprinkling Aāhmes with living water as he is standing in a sanctuary upon a bark, and adorned with golden bees. A gold chain of nearly a meter in length, with heads of geese at both ends, on which the names of Aāhmes is legible, bears a splendid scarabaeus, whose breast and wings are woven of gold threads and blue enamel. Numerous objects are between the linen cloths and on the floor of the sarcophagus: a golden poniard; a hatchet with a gilded cedar handle, the edge of bronze inlaid with gold and otherwise decorated; a lion's head of gilded bronze; nine silver and gold *neter* with the name of Kames (the father of Aāhmes), symbols of nine principal gods; a black rod covered with gold plate; an ebony fan of similar workmanship; and finally, besides many other jewels, a golden bark with the cartouche of Kames, having twelve silver marines, and a steersman, the ship's captain, and a third figure in gold.

Aāhmes I., the founder of the Eighteenth Dynasty, reaped the benefit of the efforts of his predecessor. His part in the liberation of Egypt seems to have been finally to drive the oppressor from the Delta. Captain Aāhmes, to whose inscription at El Kab we are indebted for full information with regard to this stage of the struggle, fought in the war and commanded the Nile flotilla. His father, Abana, before him, had served under Seqenen-Ra. On the walls of Aāhmes' tomb is given an account of the taking of Hat'uar—the last Hyksos stronghold. He also claims to have served in the southern campaigns undertaken by Amenhotep I. and Thothmes I., and in the Syrian war of the latter's reign.

Monuments attributed to the Hyksos have been found in great numbers at Tanis by Mariette, and more recently by Petrie. Naville also discovered works attributable to the same school of art at Bubastis. Tanis (the biblical Zoan, Arabic San), on the Tanitic branch of the Nile, through which, according to myth, the body of Osiris was carried into the sea, had among its inhabitants in a remote antiquity Semites (Amu), who in that place worshipped their gods. In the book of Numbers (xiii. 22) it is said that Hebron was built seven years before Zoan, an enigmatical declaration which may, perhaps, be interpreted to mean that the Hyksos, seven years before their irruption into Egypt, where they made Tanis their special residence, had founded that city in Palestine. Wiedemann supposes here a connection with the 'era of Tanis, which dates from Nubti, the third king of the Second Hyksos Dynasty, as we learn from a monument of Rameses II. at Tanis, which speaks of the 400th year of the Nubti Dynasty. This would give, as a date for Nubti, about the eighteenth century B.C. Colossal statues of the Middle Empire attest its importance at that time. After the expulsion of the Hyksos, Tanis was neglected for a long time, but was again favored by the Nineteenth Dynasty. It appears in the writings of Isaiah and Ezekiel as an important place. It was conquered by the Assyrians, and in later times declined because other cities in the Delta became flourishing. A hieratic papyrus describes it as a splendid city, filled with all the delights of life. The great temple rose upon a beautiful terrace; its site is indicated by the broken shafts of granite columns, more than ten obelisks, sphinxes, colossi, and among them one of granite with remains of polychromy. The greater part of these belong to the age of Rameses II. Here were found in 1884 the remains of a figure in red granite of this Pharaoh — once erect — supposed to be ninety-eight feet in height, and thus higher by far than any other existing statues. Tanis is made interesting to us, not only by these ruins, but also by the decree of Canopus in the time of Ptolemy Euergetes, brought to light by Lepsius, executed in three languages, and of importance for deciphering hieroglyphics, being the duplicate of the copy in the Louvre. Among the remarkable monuments which have been attributed to the Hyksos is a huge sphinx of black marble, inscribed in the name of the Hyksos king, Apepi II. The face is very different from the Egyptian; the eyes are small with strongly marked under-lids, the nose is very large and flat, cheek-bones and chin projecting, but especially noticeable are heavy whiskers framing in the face. Maspero, however, thinks that he has found under the cartouche on the breast of the sphinx a more ancient figure chiselled out, which renders it doubtful whether the work should not be assigned to an earlier date. Three other sphinxes, preserved in a fragmentary shape, show the same type of countenance. A very remarkable work represents Nile gods before a high, narrow structure, like a double altar, on which fish are lying, and from which fish, waterfowl, and lotus stalks are hanging. The lower parts of the arms of the men lie on the sides of the altar, and are adorned at the wrist with long pendants; especially striking are the heavy beards on cheek and chin, while the mustache is wanting as on the sphinxes, and the flowing hair is parted like a long periwig over the shoulders, and falls down to the breast and behind to the shoulder-blades. The work was long attributed to the Hyksos; and it was thought that Psusennes (second king of the Twenty-first Dynasty) had caused his name to be engraved on the statue. But M. Maspero now regards it as belonging to the Twenty-first Dynasty. Another piece of sculpture belonging to the Hyksos has been found in the capital of the Fayum, a statue of gray granite, with the same type of face as the statue at Tanis; over the shoulder hangs a panther's skin. There is also a head in the Ludovisi Villa in Rome, which is considered to be the head of a Hyksos king. And the colossal heads found at Bubastis are striking examples of the type which has been attributed to that period. Lately, however, much doubt has been cast upon the origin of the entire series. Mr. Golenischeff sees in them works of the Twelfth Dynasty, while Ed. Meyer regards them as belonging to invaders of Egypt in the obscure period between the Seventh and Tenth Dynasties, and as having been appropriated by the Hyksos kings. The fact remains, however, that the type which they represent differs from any of those with which Egyptian art has familiarized us. A type which, it is said, still may be detected among the modern inhabitants of the lake region in the Delta.

Hyksos head and woman of the Delta. (After Maspero.)

BOOK II.

ASIA.

ASIA.

THE BEGINNINGS OF HISTORY IN WESTERN ASIA (BABYLONIA, SYRIA, AND ASIA MINOR).

CHAPTER IV.

BABYLONIA.

THERE is every reason to believe that as early at least as 4000 B.C. civilization had developed to a high degree in the southern part of the region embraced by the Euphrates and Tigris, and which may conveniently be termed the Euphrates Valley. The chronology, however, beyond 2500 B.C. is still so uncertain that when we reach the period of 3000 B.C. we can deal in very general statements only. If reliance could be placed upon a date which the last king of Babylonia, Nabonidus (555–539 B.C.), has preserved for us in one of his inscriptions where he speaks of having found the foundation stone of the temple to the sun-god Samas at Sippar that revealed the name of Naram-Sin (the son of Sargon), who reigned, as he states, 3200 years ago, we would have a most important guide for the early chronology, but apart from the suspicion, naturally aroused by the round figure, there are serious difficulties in the way of accepting so high a date as 3750 B.C. for Naram-Sin. Up to the present, at all events, there are not enough rulers known to warrant us in going further back than some centuries beyond 3000 B.C. for the oldest of those whose names have been read on the monuments (and there are some older than Naram-Sin), so that the figures furnished to Nabonidus by his scribes may be some 600 or even 800 years out of the way. At the same time, in view of the fact that the oldest Babylonian inscriptions reveal a developed form of writing, a fully organized form of government, an elaborate cult, a flourishing condition of commercial activity, it is quite safe to fix the beginnings of the culture in the Euphrates Valley at a period earlier than 4000 B.C. The political picture unfolded by the inscriptions that belong to the oldest period is that of a series of states in the Euphrates Valley, each with its own centre, with now the one, now the other exercising a larger or smaller measure of control over the others. In a general way, it may be said that the course of political supremacy, like the course of culture, is from south to north, so that centres like Uruk, Ur, Isin, Lagash (or Shirpurla), Larsa, and Nippur represent the older centres of importance as against Sippur, Agade, and Babylon, which belong to a later period or which come to the front at a later time, though it must be borne in mind that this principle has only a general application and must not be too rigidly pressed.

The origin of the Euphratean culture is even obscurer than its early history. So much, however, may be stated definitely that the Euphrates Valley appears to have been at all times a natural meeting place for two distinct waves of migrations of peoples, the one entering the valley from the east and northeast, the other coming from the south and southwest. The peoples represented by these two waves belong to different subdivisions of mankind, and adopting the common though unsatisfactory nomenclature, the former represent the Turanian type, while those issuing from Arabia are Semites. The Euphratean culture in the oldest form known to us bears distinct evidence of being a mixture of non-Semitic with Semitic elements, with such a preponderance of the latter already at the period when historical certainty begins that if, as seems likely, the non-Semitic element represents the older stratum to which the beginnings of culture were due, its significance during the entire historical period known to us is largely theoretical and limited to the traces that remained of it in the script, in the language, in the cult, and in the forms of political and social life. At the same time, these traces are not of such a character or sufficiently pronounced to warrant any attempt at separating the Euphratean or Babylonian culture into Semitic and non-Semitic components. Granting the non-Semitic origin of the culture in the Euphrates Valley, the Semitic conquerors so thoroughly adopted the earlier culture—including the script—to their peculiar method of thought and expression and imparted to it such a distinctively Semitic character that, as intimated, the non-Semitic traces represent a *quantité negligeable* in any general view of the civilization with which we have to deal.

It must not be supposed, however, that all the Semites came to the Euphrates Valley at one time. Indeed, we may distinguish several distinct waves of migrations from Arabia, each one of which was fraught with political consequences of a more or less violent character, and which contributed certain elements further modifying the aspects of the Euphratean civilization. The oldest of these waves known to us belongs to the period before 3000 B.C., and evidence of its strength is to be seen in the establishment of a north-Babylonian state with Agade as its centre, followed about 2700 B.C. by the supremacy of Ur, whose rulers indicate by the title king of Sumer and Akkad their jurisdiction over northern and southern Babylonia. This supremacy lasted till c. 2400 B.C. By this time the first migratory wave had spent its force, and there becomes manifest a disposition of a return toward the earlier condition of independent states. The old centres like Lagash, Isin, Nippur regain their independence until a new unifying force appears, brought about by a fresh wave of Semitic migration. As a designation for this second wave the name "Canaanitic" has been suggested because the special type of Semitism represented by it bears a close resemblance to that which we afterward find in Phoenicia and in the interior of Palestine. The political centre shifts first from Ur to Sippar, where until the days of Hammurabi (c. 2250 B.C.) the members of the "Canaanitish" dynasty appear to have established themselves, and then during the reign of Hammurabi definitely to the city of Babylon, which with some interruptions retains its supremacy as the chief political centre in the Euphrates Valley, while its religious predominance outlasts the political career of the newly formed Babylonian power.

While thus establishing a state larger in extent and more definite in control than the older kingdom of Ur, the "Canaanitish" wave likewise spent its force, and the first dynasty of Babylon (as it is called) after furnishing eleven kings who ruled about 300 years is succeeded by one that appears to have come from the extreme south, known as the "sea land," and whose eleven kings maintained themselves for a period of more than 350 years. About 1750 B.C. Babylonia is conquered by a people coming from the east and north-east known as the

Cassites. For 576 years these Cassites ruled Babylonia, absorbing the old culture and retaining, after some vacillation, the city of Babylon as their political and religious centre. During the period of their supremacy a third distinct wave of Semitic migration enters Babylonia, and for which Winckler has suggested the name "Aramaean." Its most striking result is the formation of a new political centre much farther north, leading to the establishment of the Assyrian kingdom which was destined to become the arbiter of Babylonia's fate. Assyria, a far greater military state than any established in Babylonia, paid the penalty of her greater activity by exhausting her vitality before her southern rival, although at various periods Babylonian rulers had to submit to the humiliation of acknowledging their dependence upon Assyrian rulers. In 606 B.C. Assyria fell by a combination of her enemies in the south and east, Babylonia and Elam, aided by the advance of hordes from the north known rather indefinitely as Cimmerians ("Scythians"), while a new Babylonian empire is established by the "Chaldaean" Nebopolassar in 625 B.C. This empire, due to the advance of the district in southern Babylonia known as "Chaldaea" and which for some centuries had given Babylonian rulers considerable trouble, revives though only for a short period the glories of the last, and under Nebuchadnezzar II. (604–561 B.C.) the past is even eclipsed to such an extent that the term "Chaldaea" symbolizes for western peoples the sum and substance of the entire Mesopotamian culture and history. Nebopolassar, though largely occupied with making his rule secure, found time to embellish his capitol, Babylon, and to undertake the rebuilding of temples in Sippara and elsewhere. It was left, however, to his son Nebuchadnezzar II. to make the city of Babylon, by its palaces, its temples, its gates, its gardens, and canals, one of the marvels of antiquity. The political strength of the new empire was, however, soon exhausted, and in 539 B.C. Cyrus entered Babylon, and with scarcely a struggle the city yielded to the conqueror, whose coming meant also the triumph of Elam over her old rival Babylonia.

In so far as climatic phenomena help to explain the origin of culture and the course taken by it, it is of importance to note that the scene in which this history of almost 3000 years is enacted lies in a district along both sides and between the two rivers Euphrates and Tigris, in which we encounter natural conditions similar to those in Egypt. Here, too, the people were obliged to contend with the mighty waters with which the streams, when swollen by the snow melting in the highlands, destroyed the works of their hands. The waters of the floods, which begin in April and subside in June, must be conducted in canals, the swamps must be drained, and the towns protected by terraces. This was especially necessary in the southern portions of the country. In the northern portions numerous streams, belonging to the system of the Chaboras, water the intermediate country; but in the south the lands between the streams must be irrigated, mostly by artificial means. From this region, formed by alluvial deposits, arose the oldest Semitic civilization; although for centuries it had been exposed to the elements, and had been occupied by nomadic tribes opposed to culture. When the tribes, however, made for themselves a fixed abode, a desire for extensive buildings was awakened; but these had to be built of dried or burnt clay from the plain on account of the entire absence of stone. These vast walls of dried brick were protected by a covering of stucco. This in turn stimulated an artistic activity, just as the knowledge of surveying and levelling had occasioned the division of the year and the observation of the heavenly bodies, naturally connected with it. The necessity of recording the measurement and division of the fields led to the invention of a writing, which at first consisted of pictures, but which was at last developed into syllabic script. As the early records, which were made upon the bricks or clay tablets while they were still moist, were scratched with wood or metal, the original pictures lost somewhat of their distinctness. This caused the characters to become angular and to have straight lines; and since the sharp instrument was applied with great force the nail-shaped impressions of the cuneiform writing met with in Babylonia and Assyria resulted (Fig. 46). The Persian writing, which was engraved upon stone, has, however, characters that are longer and slenderer, of a wedge-shape, on account of the use of the chisel.

In the case of the cuneiform writing of Babylonia and Assyria it must be remembered that, like the Egyptian, it was originally pictorial in character, and on some of the oldest inscriptions this pictorial form is well preserved, though not in the case of all the signs. So it is easy to see that the sign for house, which finally becomes merely a

A

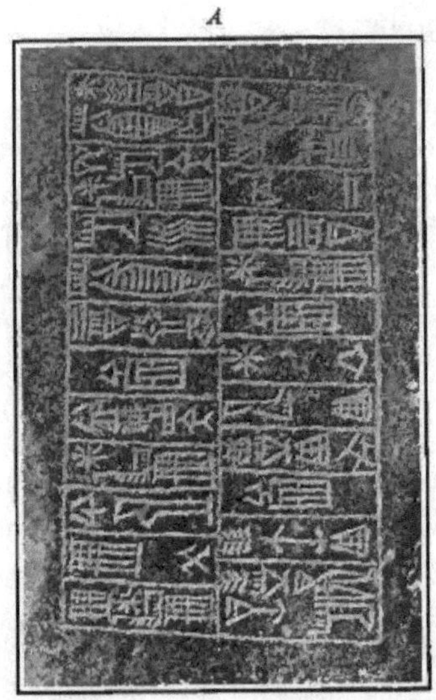

B

Fig. 46.—A, Inscription of Sargon I., king of Agade (old Babylonian characters). B, Business document dated in the 5th year of Darius (420 B.C.) (neo-Babylonian characters). [Reproduced by permission from Clay—Business Documents of Murashû Sons (Philadelphia, 1904).]

series of four perpendicular strokes preceded by two short horizontal ones, was originally the picture of a hut made of reeds placed horizontally and perpendicularly. Various complicating factors appeared in the course of development from a pictorial method of writing to a genuine script, only some of which can be described here. The Babylonian scribes, like the Egyptians, used compound groups also; for example, the ideograph for vault of heaven arose from the groups for star and vault, both of which hieroglyphics mean 'night' in Egypt. From the groups for light and gold arose the combined group for 'silver.' Since every writing with pictures was spoken by the reader, every picture gradually awakened the idea of a definite sound, or group of sounds, and every figurative or symbolic sign, which had heretofore been only an ideograph, received a fixed pronunciation; thus the sound alone began to be represented. The first step from the writing of ideas to that of sounds was made in this way: the sound which a definite ideograph had was expressed in similarly sounding words or syllables by one and the same ideograph, although the meanings might be different; just as if one should use the same picture for 'veil' and 'vale.' A dissyllabic word was also reproduced by two ideographs, one of which generally sounded like the first and the other like the second syllable, as one would express 'manhood' in a rebus by a 'man' and a 'hood.' The cuneiform writing of the Babylonians and Assyrians is syllabic, but it has preserved many ideographs from an earlier stage of development. If by means of italics we should distinguish the ideographs from the words written with syllabic characters, an inscription of Sargon would read as follows: 'Palace of Sargon, *great king*, mighty *king*, *king* of the universe, *king of the land of Ashur* (*land*).' Only the name Sargon (*Sharrukinu*), the expressions 'palace' (*ekallu*), 'mighty' (*dannu*), and 'universe' (*kishshati*) are represented by phonetic symbols. The endings expressing variation in declension are represented by phonetic symbols attached to the ideographs. The ideograph for 'land,' which occurs after Ashur as well as before it, is not to be pronounced, and only indicates that the name of a land precedes. The sign ⋰, which stands before Ashur, with the meaning 'land,' is the ideograph for 'land,' 'go,' and 'take.' It also, however, stands for the word *shadû*, 'mountain,' and judging from its form it has undergone but slight changes in the course of the millenniums covered by the cuneiform script; it still suggests a series of mountain peaks, so that the meaning 'mountain' is apparently older than that of 'land.'

Such a circumstance might be regarded as an indication that the inventors of the Babylonian writing came from some mountainous district. Various devices were introduced to avoid the ambiguity resulting from the use of the same sign for 'land' and 'mountain,' but despite this, in many cases, especially in names of temples, where the sign in question—to be pronounced *kur*—frequently enters, a doubt remains as to the interpretation to be preferred.

The name of the city Babylon was written upon the bricks of Nebuchadnezzar in ideographs, . These, which were originally pictures, are signs of 'Gate of (the) god of (the) region'; this group of pictures, according to their phonetic value in Sumerian, should be pronounced *kā-an-(ra)-ki*. The Assyrians, however, said *bâb-ilu* ('gate of El'), and wrote in phonetic symbols, , *ba-bi-lu-(ki)*. They allowed the last sign to remain, but did not pronounce it, since it only shows that the name of a district precedes. In the writing of polysyllabic words, a principle similar to that in the Egyptian prevailed. The sign that indicated 'shine' was pronounced *ur* in the non-Semitic (Sumerian) language; but the same sign was used in the name Artaxerxes, although the first syllable of this had nothing to do with 'shine.' The second ideograph in the name of Babylon means 'heaven,' or 'god' (*dingir, an*); but in the name of the land Mitanni (*mi-i-it-ta-an-ni*) it represents only the sound *an*. In this syllabic writing there is the disadvantage that frequently the signs were very different for the different forms of one and the same word; for example, in Assyrian 'mistress' is *be-lit*, written (*be-lit*), but the plural, *be-li-e-ti*, is written ; so that only the first sign remains the same. 'I place' is *ashkun* (*ash-ku-un*); but 'we place' is *nish-kun* (*ni-ish-kun*), so that the singular and the plural of the same stem, *shakânu*, consist of very different signs. If we compare with this state of things the Hebrew or Arabic, in which only the consonants of the root are brought before the eye, and there remain unchanged in all the inflections, while the vowels are not indicated at all or only by small points placed over or under the consonants, we recognize that the writing of the Hebrews and Arabians was adapted to the genius of their language. The Babylonians certainly did not invent their own writing, but must have derived it from a people who formed their language very differently, and for whom the difficulties mentioned did not exist, inasmuch as they appear to have expressed the varying shades of thought by prefixes and suffixes, without any internal change of the word. The Babylonians, however, continued to employ this complicated writing as a hieratic one; and not till later times did they begin to use to a limited extent as endorsements upon legal records or upon objects in common use, like weights, the Phoenician writing, which had begun to spread about 800 B.C.

Another element—the use of phonetic complements—ought to be mentioned, since it favors the idea that the cuneiform writing was adopted by the Semitic settlers, and was not an original invention on their part. Since it was possible to pronounce one and the same ideograph in different ways, there could always be a doubt which pronunciation was intended by the writer. The picture of the round disk of the sun, which was represented in the older form of the characters by a parallelogram because made by a stylus in the clay, or in the abridged form , could have different pronunciations according to its ideographic meaning; for example, *sham-shi*, 'sun,' and *ûmu*, 'day.' These two words could be more exactly expressed by placing after the first word the syllable *shi*, and after the second *um*: thus , *sham-shi*, , *ûm-um*. It does not follow from this that has the phonetic value *sham*, or *û*, for in these cases it has no phonetic value, but rather represents a meaning. On the other hand, sometimes it is used not to represent the meanings 'sun,' or 'day,' etc., but as the phonetic symbol of a large number of syllables other than those mentioned, such as *ut*, *tam*, *par*, *bir*, *khish*, *lakh*, *zal*. However, such a polyphonous character has only one phonetic value, if it is used as a simple syllable, that is, consists of a vowel and consonant, or a consonant and vowel; if the character mentioned forms with the character *mu* the syllable *mut* (*mu-ut*), it must be pronounced *ut*, not also *tam*, *par*, etc.

A complete discussion of the cuneiform writing cannot be given here; but one other peculiarity should be mentioned, which occurs also in the old Armenian, Pehlevi, or Parthian-Sassanian, Japanese, and other languages: this is the occurrence of one sound-value for another. The Assyrian language has foreign words derived from the old Sumerian, or Akkadian. The Assyrians retained the foreign character, but substituted an Assyrian word. It is just as if we should read 'in an instant' when 'in a moment' is written, or as the English write *d*, which was originally the sign for denarius, but read 'penny.' Thus the word for 'overflow,' 'blessing,' is written by means of two signs with the phonetic values *khe-nun*, but which are to be read in Assyrian as *nukhshu*.

The Babylonians and Assyrians themselves felt the difficulty and frequent ambiguity of this system of writing. They therefore prepared syllabaries, which fortunately have been discovered in Nineveh in the library of clay tablets of king Asurbanipal, and are now in the British Museum. Many of these have been published in two series of cuneiform texts issued by the British Museum, and by means of these syllabaries the phonetic values and meanings of almost all the signs used in the text have been determined or confirmed. These syllabaries, prepared by Babylonian and Assyrian scribes thousands of years ago as a practical means of teaching the language and the script to the students of those days, still serve their purpose to-day, and have been invaluable in unlocking the secrets of Babylonian lexicography, besides proving of great help in the decipherment of the texts. Various kinds, consisting of two, three, and four columns, are to be distinguished. In some, the syllabic values and what appears to be the names by which the series are known are furnished, the sign itself being placed in the second column with the syllabic values in the first and the name in the third column. Others furnish the syllabic values and the word or words for which the sign stands, while another class is formed by a combination of syllabic and ideographic values together with the name. In a general way, we may safely assert that the phonetic value of the ideograph must represent the word which the inventors of the writing used for it in their speech. If the character *d* means 'penny,' but is an abbreviation for *denarius*, a people which used denarius in their language must have introduced *d*. So the phonetic values of the Assyrian ideographs must belong to a language in which the sound of the ideograph corresponded with the meaning. Of this view, which required the presence in Babylonia of a people not related to the Babylonians or Semites in language, acute and learned critics have arisen, who regard the non-Semitic or Sumerian elements of the cuneiform writing as simply an hieratic or cryptic form of the Assyrian. A long controversy has been waged among Assyriologists in connection with this question, which involves, not only the origin of the cuneiform writing, but also the origin of the culture that arose in the Euphrates Valley. The leader of the anti-Sumerian party, which contends for the Semitic origin of the script, is Prof. Joseph Halèvy of Paris, who has defended his views with profound learning and great acuteness of reasoning. He has gained from time to time adherents, but the great majority of scholars have persistently clung to the view that we must perforce assume the existence of a non-Semitic language at the bottom of the phonetic values attached to the cuneiform characters, and this supposition carries with it the conclusion that the inventors of the cuneiform writing were not Semites. On the other hand, thanks to Halèvy and his followers, a reaction has been brought about against the extreme views formerly held by the adherents of the Sumerian theory, who claimed that the entire syllabary was non-Semitic. There can be no doubt, indeed, that many of the phonetic values of the signs represent truncated Semitic words. Thus, if the sign which is read *rabû*, 'great,' has the value *gal*, it is impossible to disconnect this from a Semitic stem *djalla*, which occurs in Arabic in the sense of 'great,' and in the same way there are at least one hundred syllabic values that represent parts of genuine Semitic words or stems. It follows, therefore, that if the Semites adopted the cuneiform writing from a non-Semitic people, they also adapted the system so thoroughly to their purposes as to give the syllabary to a large extent a Semitic character; and it must also be admitted that many of the texts which appear to be 'Sumerian' in form represent translations or rather transliterations of Semitic texts into the older 'ideographic' method of composition. Such factors complicate the problems connected with the study of the origin and development of this curious system, and it is not possible, on account of our lack of knowledge, to solve them all; and it will perhaps never be possible to separate the non-

Semitic from the Semitic elements in the culture that developed in the Euphrates valley, but the existence of Sumerian cannot be doubted in view of the hundreds of genuine bilingual inscriptions that have been found, in which the syntactical constructions in the one text differ *in toto* from those which characterize a Semitic language. It is claimed by many scholars that dialectic differences have been discovered within Sumerian itself. The two chief dialects recognized derive their names Sumerian and Akkadian from the country Sumer, or Southern Babylonia, and Akkad, or Northern Babylonia. The older Sumerian dialect is spoken of in the texts as the 'women's language.' The term has not yet been satisfactorily explained, but meanwhile it is interesting to note that 'women's languages' are found elsewhere. Thus the women's language in the South American and Polynesian languages is caused by taboo, which prescribes that certain words are to be changed, or omitted altogether; thus the women among the Chiquitos are allowed to use only the feminine forms of the pronouns, while the men use both the masculine and the feminine. A special study of these dialects was made by Prof. Haupt, who has shown that the Sumerian often has *m* where the Akkadian has *g*; thus *mal* and *gal* ('to be'), or *mêr* and *gêr*, 'foot'; *ng* and *mm* are also interchangeable, as in *dingir* and *dimmir* ('god'). This appears to show that the name Sumer, which may have been Sungir in the older dialect, is the same as the Shinar of the Bible, the region in which Babel, Erech, Calneh, and Accad were situated.

Between the mountains and the northern portion of the Persian Gulf there is an extended plain, which was in part covered by the sea even within historic times. Formerly, the Euphrates and Tigris, as well as the rivers of Susiana, emptied their waters into the gulf by separate mouths, without uniting with one another. The country along the coasts of Khuzistan and on the Shatt-el-Arab was called Gambul in the Assyrian inscriptions, and the principal city Sapi-Bel, while the region in which Susa was situated, toward the mountains, was called Cissia. Toward the north and east were the Luristan Mountains, among which Cassites dwelt, who bore the same name as the mountains, and of whose language some traces have been preserved; still farther north the Guti lived. Antigonus, in late antiquity, on his way from Eulaeus, near Susa, to Ecbatana, was obliged to go through Cassite territory. These people once had a town on the site of the present Mal Amir, which was called Idhaj in the Middle Ages. There are several mounds of ruins at this point of the plain, one of which is as high as that at Susa, and dates from the old Persian period. In the surrounding rocks there are caves, one of which contains two colossal figures cut in the rock, as well as a cuneiform inscription of thirty-three lines in the language spoken in this district, and to which the name Elamitic or old-Elamitic is now generally given. Inscriptions are also found in the valleys and ravines through which the main road from Susiana leads southward. The Atabegi road, a very ancient one paved with large stones, ascends from the plain into the mountains; at Telāt the road divides, and one may branch off for Ispahan and Persepolis. This road was restored in the Middle Ages, as its name shows. As early as the so-called Diadochi there was a paved road in the Klimax Megalē ('great stairway') leading from Susa to Persis; hence it cannot have been built later than the time of the Achaemenides. Numerous ruins in the neighborhood of Mal Amir have been described by de Bode, but most of them date from the time of the Sassanids.

Supplementing the inscriptions of Mal-Amir, but belonging to a considerably older period, are numerous bricks and tablets found of recent years at Susa,[1] which, containing dedicatory inscriptions of Elamitic rulers, chiefly of the twelfth and thirteenth centuries, and records of commercial transactions, have made it possible to distinguish various periods in the development of the language spoken in Elam and surrounding district. The first attempts at a decipherment of the texts of Mal-Amir were made by Sayce and Guyard, but their results have been considerably modified by the researches of Hüsing, who, following in the footsteps of Heinrich Winkler, is inclined to place the old-Elamitic language in the Caucasian group, and also maintains that there is a relationship between Elamitic and the language spoken by the Cassites. The later form of the Elamitic is represented in the monuments of the Achaemenides, who accompanied their Persian inscriptions with a Babylonian and what we may call a Susianian or neo-Elamitic translation, and which has been deciphered through the labors chiefly of Norris, Oppert, and Weissbach. The kings mentioned in them belong to both

[1] See next page.

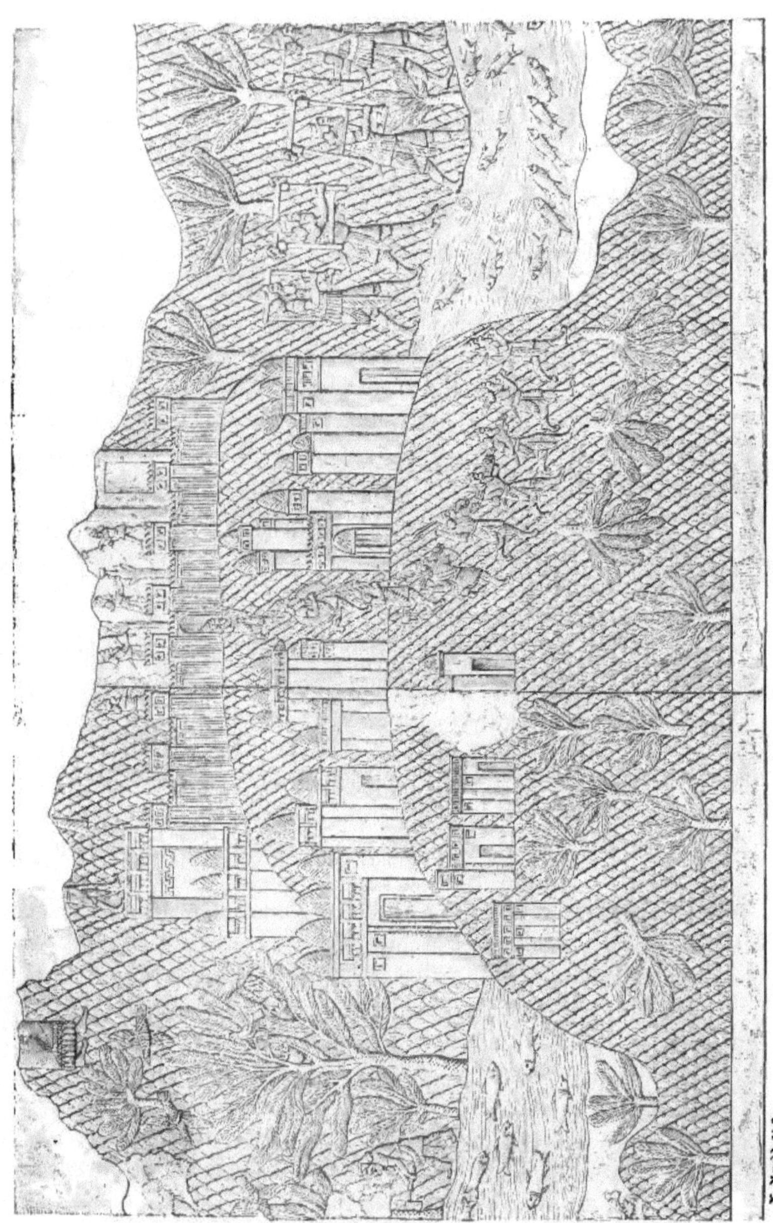

FIG. 47. — An Armenian Town Plundered. (Relief from Koyunjik.)

PLATE IX.—A.

Monument of Naram-Sin, King of Agade, with Superimposed Inscription of Sutruk-Nakhunte, King of Elam.

History of All Nations, Vol I., page 159.

very early and late periods. Thus Sargon II. (721–705 B.C.) speaks of one of them, Sutruk-Nakhunte, and of him (c. 1100 B.C.) many monuments have been found at Susa. He calls himself the son of Khallutush and the favorite of the chief god of Susa, known as Shushinak. It was this ruler, it appears, who brought the remarkable series of inscriptions found on monuments, as well as the code of Hammurabi from Babylonia as trophies to his capital at Susa, where they were found by the French Expedition in 1897–1902; on one of these monuments, a handsome stele of Naram-Sin (before 3000 B.C.), this same Sutruk-Nakhunte has added an inscription stating that he brought this monument which originally recorded Naram-Sin's victories from Sippar. (PLATE IX. A.)

As a result of these excavations, supplementing those conducted by Dieulafoy in another part of the city of Susa which contained the palaces and remains of the Persian or Achaemenidian period, we now know that a close contact existed from the earliest days between Elam and Babylonia, and we can follow the history of Elam in a general way from before 3000 B.C. The old king of Agade, Naram-Sin, and various rulers of the Ur dynasty, devoted themselves to the embellishment of the temples to the gods in Susa. Babylonian deities are met with here by the side of Elamitic gods and goddesses. The Elamitic rulers of this early period are not called kings on their inscriptions, but *patesis*, a title which indicates a dependency upon Babylonia. About 2300 B.C., however, the Elamites made themselves free, and from this time on their rulers, setting up their inscriptions in their own language, claim to be kings. The time came, though not for almost a millennium, when the Elamites in turn overran Babylonia and carried away some of her splendid monuments, including, besides those already referred to, a statue of the goddess Nanâ, which the Assyrian king Asurbanipal boasts of having recaptured 1635 years later. But though after 2300 Elam did not have anything to fear from the Babylonians, a formidable foe arose in the Cassites, who, coming from a district to the east and northeast of Elam proper, brought Elam as well as Babylonia under their subjection. In Babylonia the Cassite rule lasted for 576 years (c. 1780–1200 B.C.), and Elam likewise does not appear to have had any independent rulers till the close of this period. When, however, her independence was regained she rapidly rose in power and succeeded in maintaining herself for five centuries even against the onslaughts of the mighty Assyrian empire; even Sennacherib, although he was victorious, did not conquer the country. The conquest was not accomplished till the time of Asurbanipal, who was almost the last Assyrian king. Esarhaddon, the son of Sennacherib, conquered the Dakkuri, a Chaldaean people who dwelt upon the borders of the desert of Babylon and made incursions into the Babylonian territory, captured their leader, and burned him alive; he subjugated also Bel-ikisha of Gambul, which was, as has been mentioned, the part of Elam in the lowlands, and fortifying his principal city, made it a bulwark against Susiana. Nevertheless, this same prince, in the year 650 B.C., was an ally of Urtaki of Elam against Babylon. When Asurbanipal came to the throne, in 668, Elam was afflicted with a famine, and Elamites fled to Assyria. Although the Assyrians received them, and gave them protection till the return of rain, Urtaki began hostilities against them upon the advice of his general Marduk-shum-ibni; he secured the aid of the prince of Gambul and an Assyrian governor in Chaldaea. Asurbanipal approached, and the allies took to flight. In the following year Urtaki took his own life; and Bel-ikisha, from his concealment in the marshes, engaged in plundering Elam, which had become Assyrian. Later he was taken prisoner, and put to death. Asurbanipal made a second expedition, and chastised Gambul, destroying its chief city.

Susa, the ancient royal residence, was also the real capital of the empire in the time of Persian sovereignty, and did not decline until the neighboring cities, Gondi-Shahpur, Shuster (Sosirate), and also Ctesiphon had become powerful; coins are still extant which were struck in Susa in 709. The ruins of the city form a mound, largely composed of bricks, which is three miles and a half in circumference; and it is within this area that the successful excavations of the Frenchmen Dieulafoy and de Morgan have been conducted. Reserving an account of the former's work until we reach the Persian empire, upon which it exclusively bears, let us come to Babylonia and Chaldaea proper, where the first ancient site to be thoroughly explored was, Telloh, situated on a branch of Shatt-el-Hai, not far from Zerghul. With rare devotion the French consul at Basra, M. Ernest de Sarzec, spent no less than twenty years (1877–1900) at these mounds, and to him we owe our first definite knowledge of the construction of an ancient Babylonian city. Telloh represents Shirpurla or Lagash, the importance of which at one time may be gleaned from the existence of several distinct quarters, each with its own special patron deity. Beneath the remains of a palace of Seleucidian days, de Sarzec came across a series of nine magnificent statues of diorite covered with inscriptions in the old Babylonian style of cuneiform writing. These statues represented a famous ruler of Shirpurla, whose name was Gudea (c. 2800 B.C.), who, however, no longer occupies an entirely independent position, but owes allegiance to the Ur dynasty. The chief sanctuary at Shirpurla was known as E-ninnu, 'House of Fifty,' and was sacred to Nin-girsu, who is identical with the god generally known as Ninib. Two large cylinders of Gudea containing accounts of his deeds, are of inestimable value in the reconstruction of the history of this early period, while the discovery of an exceedingly extensive business archive, containing upwards of 30,000 tablets recording temple and private business transactions from a period that may be roughly defined as c. 3000 to 2300 B.C., illustrates the commercial activity of those days. A feature of the temple area was a stage-tower of seven stories, known as E-pa, 'the summit house.' A large number of clay cones and statuettes with entire inscriptions were found, and among these objects a tablet representing Ur-Ninâ, a ruler older than Gudea, aiding in the construction of a sacred edifice, and accompanied by his eight children and chief officers, is noteworthy (PLATE XVI.); and still more remarkable is a monument, unfortunately only partially preserved, furnishing a pictorial illustration of the campaign of E-annatum against the Gishbanites, his victory over his enemies, and the burial of his own warriors who fell in battle. Accompanying the monument is an inscription setting forth the details of the campaign. (PLATE XIII.) The excavations at Telloh are now being continued by M. Cros.

At some distance south of the Euphrates is the ruin Mugheir, the ancient Ur, which in high water forms an island (Fig. 18). The ruin is about half a mile in diameter, and consists of a collection of hillocks composed of rubbish. These are surrounded by numerous graves, which form an oval around them. Mugheir, which means 'covered with bitumen,' is made of bricks united with bitumen. It is the largest northern ruin, on a hill about seventy feet high. Like most

Babylonian structures, it is placed with the angles toward the four cardinal points. Rarely is a building placed with the sides toward these points. Therefore it was not customary to remove the corner-stone; and later kings, when they restored a building, gave the assurance in inscriptions that it had not been disturbed. These records in regard to the building were inscribed upon ellipsoidal bricks, which were built into the corner of the temple. The long side, toward the southwest, is 198 feet long, and has nine pilasters, while the short side, toward the northwest, has only six; the other sides are as yet

FIG. 48. — Ruins of the Temple of Mugheir (Ur).

uncovered. The lower story is twenty-seven feet high; and its top is reached by a stairway eight feet wide, which ascends within. The second terrace is 16 feet high, 119 feet long, and 75 feet broad. This is not placed centrally upon the lower terrace, since it is much nearer the northwest side than the southeast; it contains a vaulted passage-way, and is covered on top with the *débris* of bricks, vessels, and lamps. A second stairway with balustrades, leading from the lower terrace to the top of the second, occupied the whole of the southeast side. Here we have a typical example of a temple in stages (*ziggurat*); the first staircase was within, in order that the line of the wall might not be broken; the second and third story were reached by a stairway which was without upon the terrace. Upon the highest story the little shrine was situated, not in the middle of the rectangular space, but nearer the northern end, for the stairway required more room at the southern end. The brick coating of this temple of the moon, called E-gish-shirgal in the inscriptions of Nabonidus, is ten feet thick; the massive interior consists of burnt and dried bricks. Taylor found an inscription at the south corner and duplicates of it at the other corners. The Arabians assert that half a century ago a chamber still existed on the top of the second story; and this is also indicated by the enamelled bricks which formerly adorned the interior of it, and which lie scattered about. Upon the bricks, imbedded in the bitumen, is stamped the inscription: 'Ur-gur, king of Ur, builder of the temple of Sin (the moon).' This king, as well as others of the Ur dynasty, is well known to us from inscriptions found at Nippur, over which these rulers once claimed control and where they were actively engaged in rebuilding and enlarging the ziggurat or stage-tower in honor of Bel. The bricks of the upper story of the ziggurat at Ur, which were laid in a cement composed of lime and ashes, bear the inscription: 'Dungi, the mighty hero king of Ur, king of Sumer and Akkad.' The sanctity of this ziggurat is illustrated by the anxiety of the last king of Babylonia, Nabonidus (555–539 B.C.), to restore it. The reign of Ur-gur is probably to be assigned to about 2700 B.C. Bricks found in Warka, Senkereh, and Zerghul also bear his name as well as that of other members of this dynasty, which is noteworthy as representing the oldest attempt in the Euphrates Valley, so far as known to us, of the establishment of a kingdom uniting all of north and south Babylonia under one rule. For several centuries this empire maintained itself, though it would appear that the rulers during this time represented several dynasties. Hammurabi's policy of uniting north and south Babylonia was in a measure a continuation of that pursued by the kings of Ur. Opposite the southeast end of the temple of Ur was a second building with projecting wings, adorned without with perpendicular recesses. The bricks have the name of Ishme-Dagan, meaning 'Dagan has heard,' stamped upon them. Remains of beams of the roof, made of the palm-tree, still exist. Nearer the centre of the ruins is a large mound with graves, provided with a system of drainage. The graves of different families are separated from one another by long strips of masonry. The dead bodies lie upon a pavement eight feet below the surface, and have over them a cover of clay shaped like a dome, or oval like a boat. The body always rests upon one side, with the fingers of the right hand reaching into a copper vessel, which contains the food for the dead, and is supported by the left hand. Usually an inscribed cylinder rested upon the arm. In the graves of the women ornaments of gold and copper were found, agates, rings for the ears and toes, bracelets and shells. The successive layers of brick project, and approaching each other at the top form the vault, while the ends are closed by a wall. The whole ruin was a great city of the dead, for there are no traces of dwellings. There is also an inscription of King Gungunu, son of Isme-Dagan. The latter is also the name of one of the oldest rulers of the city of Ashur (c. 1850 B.C.), a fact of importance for the extent at one time of the cult of Dagan. The date of the Assyrian Isme-Dagan can be fixed by a statement in an inscription of Tiglath-Pileser I., living in the twelfth century B.C., that he restored a temple which was built 641 years before by Samsi-Adad, a governor of this city, and a son of Isme-Dagan. In the southeastern portion of Ur, Bur-Sin seems to have erected buildings; and he is also mentioned in connection with Nippur and Abu-Shahrein. In this last place, covering the site of the ancient city of Eridu, two stages of a temple of Ea are exposed to view; and on the southeast side is a marble stairway. There is evidence that a shrine existed upon the second terrace; for various ornaments have been discovered, such as agates, alabaster, marble, small gold plates, and copper nails with gold heads for fastening the gold plates to the shrine. At the foot of the staircase stand two columns composed of alternate layers of sandstone, obtained from the neighboring hills, and marble slabs. The columns thus formed are incrusted with several layers of clay. Among the ancient relics are numerous longish clay cones, whose bases are enamelled with different colors. They were embedded in the cement of the wall with the bases exposed, so that they furnished an ornamentation of various colors; besides, there are knives made of flint for cutting inscriptions, chisels of stone with straight edges, and of clay with semi-circular edges, stone rivets, also flat, pear-shaped punches made sharp at the edge by means of flint and bent adzes of burnt clay. The use of sandstone and granite in the construction of ziggurat of Eridu is quite exceptional in the buildings of ancient Babylonia. In Tel-el-Lahm, which is three hours south of Suq-esh-shujueh, clay coffins were found, consisting of two jars fastened together with bitumen. The mound Zerghul, situated near Nasshajet on the left bank of the Shatt-el-Hai, and the mound El-Hibba six miles distant, are noticeable chiefly as forming an ancient necropolis, the exploration of which in 1887 by two German scholars has thrown much light upon the Babylonian methods of burial. About twenty miles further south upon the Euphrates stands Senkereh, the site of the ancient city of Larsa, and one of the chief centres of sun-worship in Babylonia. The temple at this place, dedicated to the worship of Samas, and known, like that at Sippar (see page 170), as E-barra, 'the brilliant house,' dates back to the old kingdom of Ur, and while Larsa played an important political part for a limited period only, it was one of the last places to succumb to Hammurabi in his attempt to unite the old states of northern and southern Babylonia under one rule. Nebuchadnezzar II. built the surrounding wall and the upper portion of the temple, and from the inscriptions of Nabonidus, the last king of Babylonia who, in his devotion to the temples in the old religious centres of the country, also restored the sacred edifice at Larsa, we learn that Hammurabi (c. 2250 B.C.) and the Cassite ruler Burnaburiash (c. 1450 B.C.) were among those who devoted themselves in earlier days to the enlargement of the same temple and tower. Numerous clay tablets that turned out to be business contracts were found in portions of the mound where the dead were buried, from which it would appear that after a certain period, when the city had perhaps been abandoned, the site was used as a necropolis.

Farther up the Euphrates, upon the left bank, is an elevation about six miles in circumference, which is surrounded by water during the larger part of the year. Upon this are the imposing ruins of Warka, or Uruk, called Erech in the Bible, and known to Greeks, who were acquainted with the astronomical school there, as Orchoë. Near the centre, is the chief ruin, Buwarijeh, 'reed-mat' so called, because reeds were there used for the protection of the bricks against the weather. The walls were strengthened, as in many Babylonian buildings, by pilasters cemented with bitumen.

Upon it is the stage-tower and temple of the goddess Nanâ. Several names are preserved in inscriptions: that of Ur-gur (2700 B.C.) of the Ur dynasty is found on bricks on the southeast side; that of Singashid, who ruled somewhat later, is inscribed on the foundation of the shrine. The second building, west of the first, is called Wuswas, said to have received its name from a negro, who searched for treasures here, and disappeared in a mysterious manner. It encloses a rectangle 650 feet long and 500 feet broad. In the eastern part of this is a court with two gateways, and to the north is also a smaller one. The southwestern portion of the building, which was perhaps built by Nebuchadnezzar, exhibits a very ancient style of panel ornamentation (Fig. 49); it is derived from the work of a joiner or carpenter, as seen upon doors, for example on a stone door at Sidon.

FIG. 49. — The Wuswas ruins (Warka).

The upper part of the façade has narrow but tall niches; many of these consist really of two or three niches, one within the other, decreasing in size as they recede from the surface. Under these are groups of seven vertical half cylinders in imitation of a block-house. In the somewhat broad spaces on either side of each group of niches and half cylinders are depressions extending to the top of the wall, and like the niches having two different depths. This façade, incrusted with stucco two inches thick, has been repeatedly copied from the original woodcut given by Loftus. The tower with stages, at Khorsabad, dating from the eighth century, is a good example of this style.

Reliefs in Nineveh, which represent houses and towers, repeatedly give this style of ornamentation. The Sassanian palace of Firuzabad in Persis has only single depressions in the face of the wall; on both sides of the pilasters, however, double ones, closed at the top by an arch. Tak-Kesra in Ctesiphon, dating from the sixth century after Christ, has something similar. In Asasif, near Thebes, is a long wall, enclosing graves belonging to the Twenty-sixth Dynasty; it presents an alternation of two vertical depressions and of two similar ones surrounded by a depression receding from the surface like a frame, in the same manner as the niches described previously. This style of decoration is, however, met with in the time of the pyramids in the façades of the mastabas. There is another building which is ornamented with the clay cones, which have red, white, and black bases, arranged in lozenges, zigzag, and in straight lines. Near Wuswas stands a kind of a tower, which is decorated differently; it has the appearance of wickerwork; between several layers of tiles are three rows of jars embedded in cement with their bases, which are pointed, in the wall and the openings outward.

Warka is the largest necropolis in Chaldaea: to it the dead bodies were brought for burial from all directions, even as late as the time of the Parthians. Several styles of coffins are here found: some like those in Mugheir, others consisting of two jars or urns with their mouths cemented together, and others still of a peculiar kind, made of clay and resembling a slipper, or more exactly the swaddling-clothes of a child. (Cf. PLATE XV., sarcophagi of this form, from Nippur). The glazing on the outside is green (oxide of copper) and on the inside blue. The threads are carefully imitated. That these graves belong to a late period is shown by the Parthian decoration on the surface of the garments, also by the Parthian coins found near the coffins, and by small figures, as for example of a reclining warrior, some of which have a Grecian character. The coffins are placed above one another in great numbers, being separated only by thin layers of sand. Loftus, who conducted excavations at Warka in 1854, also found some terra-cotta figurines, some inscribed clay cones, and to the east of Buwarijeh some forty contract tablets with the names of Nabopalassar, Nebuchadnezzar, Nabonidus, and Cambyses. He also found eight tablets containing many impressions of seals, representing very varied objects, and cuneiform writing, in which Greek names, like Seleucus and Antiochus, occur. At the same place was a vaulted tomb with an Himyaritic (South-Arabian) inscription.

To the northeast is Bismya, where Dr. Banks is conducting excavations for the University of Chicago, and which have already resulted in the excavation of an exceedingly ancient temple with a statue of a ruler who appears to belong to an earlier period than any as yet discovered. (PLATE IX.—*B.*) There are still other extensive ruins here, some of which have been hastily examined, and others only seen from a distance.

To the north is Nuffar, the Assyrian Nippur; it is situated at the point where the Shat-en-Nil is lost in the Affej marsh. The canal, which branches off from the Euphrates near Babylon, formerly ran beyond this marsh, and emptied into the Shat-el-Kahr. The most conspicuous feature of the imposing series of mounds at this place is a cone-shaped eminence rising to a height of about ninety-five feet, and called by the natives Bint-el-Amir ('Daughter of the Princess'). An examination of the ruins was made by Layard in 1851, but it was left for an American expedition to explore them thoroughly.

In 1888, Dr. J. P. Peters, at the time connected with the University of Pennsylvania, organized an expedition, and for two years directed excavations at Nippur. The funds for the expedition were provided by a number of public-spirited citizens of Philadelphia. Dr. Peters' work, especially during the second year, was eminently successful, and was continued by J. H. Haynes as director, to whose endurance we owe most of the discoveries, including that of the temple archive, made at Nippur. With an interval of only two years Haynes continued the excavations alone until 1900, in which year he was joined for a few months by Prof. H. V. Hilprecht, of the University of Pennsylvania. To this institution belongs the credit of having unearthed one of the oldest and largest temple-areas in ancient Babylonia, and the inscriptions and discoveries made in the mounds throw much light on the oldest period of Babylonian history.

The material results of these labors of Peters and Haynes at the mounds may be summed up as follows: Upward of 50,000 clay tablets of various sizes have been taken out of the ruins from that section of the temple area which harbored the archives, both the official business records of the temple organization, the judicial archives in which copies of contracts, commercial transactions, and judicial decisions were de-

Oldest Statue found in Babylonia. (University of Chicago Expedition at Bismya.)

History of All Nations, Vol. I, page 168.

PLATE X.

Arch of burnt Brick laid in clay mortar (Nippur).

[Reproduced by permission from Hilprecht, *Old Babylonian Inscriptions, chiefly from Nippur.*]

History of All Nations, Vol I., page 169.

PLATE XI.

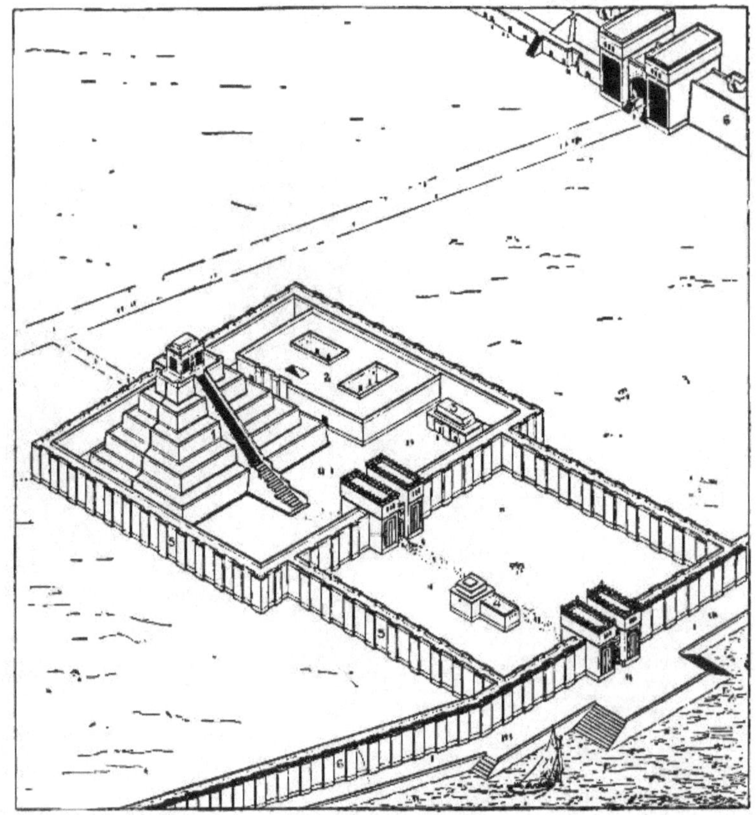

Ekur, the Temple of Bel at Nippur. (First attempt at a restoration by Hilprecht and Fisher.)

[Reproduced by permission from Hilprecht, *Explorations in Bible Lands*, Philadelphia, 1902.]

1. Stage-tower with shrine on the top. 2. The temple proper. 3. "House for honey, cream, and wine." 4. "Place of the delight of Bur-Sin." 5. Inner wall (Imgur-Marduk). 6. Outer wall (Nimit-Marduk).

History of All Nations, Vol. I., page 169

PLATE XII.

Inscribed Bas-relief of Naram-Sin.

History of All Nations, Vol. I, page 169.

PLATE XIII.

Eannatum's Campaign against the Gishbanites.

History of All Nations, Vol. I, page 161.

PLATE XIV.

Northwestern Facade of the first stage of Ur-Gur's Ziggurat (Nippur).

[Reproduced from Hilprecht, *Old Babylonian Inscriptions, chiefly from Nippur.*]

History of All Nations, Vol. I., page 16[illegible].

posited, and the literary collections—the incantation texts, hymns, ritualistic texts, and astronomical-astrological computations—which in the course of many centuries were gathered by the priests of Bel. In addition, about 20 so-called door-sockets with inscriptions of the Babylonian rulers extending from the earliest period well down into the rule of the Cassites in Babylonia. Sargon I. and his son Naram-Sin (see PLATE XII.) are represented by numerous bricks stamped with their names and titles, and particularly noteworthy is a long inscription of Lugalzaggisi, who belongs to a still earlier period than Sargon, and which has been skilfully pieced together by Prof. Hilprecht out of a large number of vase-fragments. Beneath the sanctuary remains of a remarkably constructed arched (PLATE X.) tunnel have been found which apparently served for purposes of drainage. The construction is interesting as the oldest specimen known of the true arch in architecture. Its date cannot be accurately fixed, but there is every reason to believe that it belongs to the period before Naram-Sin. Votive inscriptions to Bel, Belit, Ninib, Nusku, dating chiefly from the Cassite period (c. 1780–1200 B.C.), furnish the proof for the devotion to the cult of Nippur shown by these foreign rulers, and the University of Pennsylvania's Expedition has satisfactorily shown that the sanctity of Nippur was maintained up to the Assyrian period. Asurbanipal (668–626 B.C.) appears among the restorers of the ziggurat or stage-tower of Bel, and indeed after the conquest of the Euphrates Valley by the Greeks, Nippur continued to play a rôle, though the old temple of Bel and the stage-tower are converted into a Parthian citadel, and replaced by Parthian palaces. From what has been said it will have become clear that the chief work of the Nippur expedition has been confined to the temple area, and within this area to the stage-tower, which appears to date back to the days of Sargon. (PLATE XIV.) The accompanying plan of restoration, on the basis of the excavations at Nippur (PLATE XI.), will furnish a general idea of the temple area, known from the chief sanctuary as E-kur—*i.e.*, 'Mountain House.' Of the epigraphical material two volumes of historical and votive inscriptions have been published by Prof. Hilprecht, and two volumes of business documents of the Persian period (c. 500 to 200 B.C.) by Prof. A. T. Clay, of the University of Pennsylvania, forming part of a series issued by that institution.

Farther north, where the Tigris and Euphrates approach the nearest, are several large places in ruins. The most prominent of these is Babylon, which, although dating back beyond the days of Hammurabi (c. 2250 B.C.), and perhaps in existence already in the days of Sargon (c. 3000 B.C.), was so thoroughly rebuilt after its destruction by Sennacherib (689 B.C.) that an account of the ruins and excavations here may be postponed till we reach the neo-Babylonian empire (Vol. II., p. 128). The modern ruin, Tel-Ibrahim, is probably Cutha, which is often mentioned in connection with Babylon and Borsippa. It is situated northeast of Babylon, on the Habl-Ibrahim canal; this connects the canal El-Muth, which flows along the road from Bagdad to Babylon, with the Shatt-en-Nil. Shalmaneser, as the Bible relates (2 Kings xvii. 24, 30), carried from here to Samaria certain colonists who worshipped the god Nergal, a destructive war-god.

On the canal Habl-es-Sûq, or Nahr-Malka, which connects the Euphrates with the Tigris at Seleucia, is the ruin of the celebrated city Sippar, now called Abu-Habba. According to Berosus, the god Ea here announced to Xisuthrus (i.e. Khasisatra, 'the very wise one')[1] the approach of the Deluge, and commanded him to bury the tablets containing the divine law and the oldest memorials of men. The mounds here measure 1422 yards long by 875 yards wide, or about 250 acres, of which about 39½ acres are taken up by the temple area alone.

There was another city of the same name near by, and to distinguish between the two, the one was called Sippar-sha-Samas, 'Sippar of the Sun-god'; the other Sippar-sha-Anunit, or 'Sippar of the goddess Anunit.' The identification of the place was due to Hormuzd Rassam, who began excavations here in January, 1881, and soon came across inscriptions of Nabonidus, the last king of Babylonia, in which he tells us of his finding the foundation stone of the old temple E-barra or E-babbarra ('brilliant House') sacred to the Sun-god at Sippar, bearing the name Naram-Sin, and of his satisfaction in coming upon a foundation stone of the temple E-ul-mash, dedicated to Anunit,—a form of Ishtar,—with the name of the Cassite ruler Shagarakti-shuriash (c. 1300), though the latter could not have been the first builder of the

[1] One of the epithets of the hero of the Babylonian Flood, generally known as Utnapishtim (see p. 188).

PLATE XV.

Sarcophagi from Nippur.

[Reproduced from Hilprecht, *Old Babylonian Inscriptions, chiefly from Nippur.*]

sanctuary. In a hall containing a large altar he found under the floor an earthen chest. In the chest lay a tablet made by Nabupaliddin (c. 880–840 B. C.), a cuneiform inscription and a representation of the Sun-god, having a long beard and a high tiara, in a long garment with wavy folds, sitting upon a sort of stool (Fig. 50). He is under a *baldachino*, which rests upon wooden columns. Upon the side of the stool Gilgamesh, the hero of the great Babylonian epic, and his companion Eabani, are represented in relief; from the *baldachino*, which serves also for the sky, two gods are lowering the disk of the sun by cords upon an altar. The inscription over the image of Samas runs: 'Image of Shamash the great lord who dwells in E-barra at Sippar.' A worshipper—probably the king himself—is being led into the presence of the god by a priest, and behind the worshipper is a personage intended perhaps also to represent a priest. Before Shamash stands an altar on which the sun-disk rests, held by means of ropes by two attendants. The inscription itself, after recording the disappearance of the former image of the Sun-god from his temple during a period when nomadic tribes ravaged parts of Babylonia, commends Nabupaliddin for his efforts in having a new image made after ancient models that fortunately were found. The king also bestows rich offerings of food-stuffs and garments for the service of Samas and for the support of the priests in attendance at the temple of Sippar. Rassam was fortunate enough to find a part of the business archives of the temple with several thousand tablets containing records of commercial transactions. The work of Rassam was continued in 1894 in a measure by an eminent French scholar, Vincent Scheil, who concentrated his labors on the temple, and more particularly on that portion of it which contained the archives. A series of rooms, in which numerous syllabaries and other texts, clearly serving a purpose like modern text-books for teaching the cuneiform script and language.[1] Scheil concluded represented the ancient school of the temple. Tombs of various periods were also found in other portions of the mound, some in which the dead were placed in large jars, others containing coffins of slipper and bath-tub shape, similar to those found at Nippur (see PLATE XV.), while in some cases vaults were built to contain the human remains.

[1] See also page 154.

East of Bagdad is situated Tel-Mohammed, where Layard found Babylonian bronzes and utensils of clay. Hit (Is) on the Euphrates, celebrated for its bitumen, which was used as a cement in the buildings of Babylon, serves as a natural boundary between Chaldaea (Babylonia) and Assyria; north of a line running from this point to Samarra on the Tigris the country is slightly undulating, while south of it is a plain of alluvial formation, once the bed of the sea. In this plain are numerous mounds of ruins still unexplored, where

Fig. 50.—Adoration of Samas. Tablet from Sippara (after Perrot).

long ago there was a dense population and fruitful cornfields of great extent, and along the river fine groves of palms. To-day the date-palm extends no farther up the Euphrates than Anah; and the country, traversed by Arabian shepherds, has become a desolate tract through a lack of irrigation and by reason of robber hordes. Above the ruins rises in each case a tower-like temple, and we can picture to ourselves its former appearance by means of the remains still at hand and by the Assyrian reliefs. It is generally a shapeless mass; for the upper portions have fallen in, and destroyed its distinctive features, and the rains have also washed away much.

Although there were pipes and channels to carry off the water, yet, unless great care was exercised, the very severe thunder storms injured the outside covering, and then the moisture destroyed the inside, which was made of crude bricks. Diodorus, upon the authority of Ctesias, reports that the temple of Marduk in Babylon, which Nebuchadnezzar built, was ruined in this way even in the Persian period; and Strabo represents that it was completely destroyed in the time of Augustus.

The style of the buildings was determined largely by the character of the materials which were available. Since stone could be obtained only from a great distance, it was used only for ornamental work, such as statues, the facing of the walls and door-sockets. To strengthen the building, and to resist the lateral pressure, very strong brick walls were built with arches. The abundance of metals found in the mountain range on the other side of the Tigris, which was rich in silver, copper, iron, and lead, was the cause of a style appropriate to metal; not only the architectural portions of the interior of the palace, but even the furniture, was covered with a layer of metal. The furniture was made of wood, and then metal plates were fastened on; and this style of applied metal work continued to be dominant even after the practice of casting metals had come in vogue. Even the columns were designed more for furniture than for architectural purposes; for they did not serve as supports of architrave and roof, but as pillars of pavilions and holders of censers and garlands. Tables, chairs, *baldachins*, and chariots were similarly treated. It was very different in Egypt; for there the character of the wooden furniture was determined by the art of the cabinet-maker, whereas the articles in metal, as chariots, did not exhibit the influence of the old *repoussée* work, but had a style determined by the fact that the metals were cast.

The Babylonian temples proper, as well as the stage-towers, have massive terraces; and therefore in the case of the latter the staircases or inclined ways, which led to the upper shrine, were placed upon the outside. An altar stood at the foot of the tower, and on the highest story there was a small shrine. There was no uniformity in the number of the stages; sometimes there were three, corresponding to the three divisions of the universe, sometimes five, as in Calah, on account of the five planets; and sometimes seven, as in Borsippa, where the sun and moon were added to the preceding five. In the tower at Mugheir the ascent was made by staircases, in the tower at Khorsabad by a spiral inclined way. At present there remain at Khorsabad only four stories; but the panel and pilaster ornament is still preserved, also the balustrade of the inclined way and the coloring of the stories. V. Place represents the order of the colors, beginning at the bottom, to be white, gray (black), red, and blue.

The palaces in Chaldaea do not furnish us a clear idea of their appearance, since they are so much in ruins; but as Assyrian art is derived from Babylonian, we can think of the Babylonian princes as living in palaces similar to those of Assyria, although in Babylonia the stucco walls, with frescoes, took the places of the alabaster slabs which lined the walls in Nineveh. Perhaps the ruins of Arban on the Chaboras, which are older than those of Nimrud (ninth century), exhibit the transition. The portals on both sides of the palace are covered with stone tablets, on which winged bulls are chiselled in archaic style. The walls, which were built of dried bricks, are destroyed. A lion found in the centre of the mound resembles the Hittite lion at Ancyra, which will be spoken of later. Hittite art is a branch of the Old Babylonian, not of the Assyrian. The heads of the sphinxes have thick lips and broad noses; quartz and metal are inserted to represent the pupils of the eyes. The clay coffins found in Arban resemble the Babylonian, although the inscription on the winged bulls found there is written in neo-Assyrian characters. The Egyptian scarabaei of the Eighteenth Dynasty, which Layard here found, were secured in the expeditions of Thothmes and Amenophis, rather than later by exchange in trade. It was later than this that the region on the lower Chaboras, where Arban is, was conquered by the Assyrians, and apparently by governors partially independent.

FIG. 51.—Head of Gudea from a statue found at Telloh (Shirpurla).

PLATE XVI.

Ur-Nina and his Family.

History of All Nations, Vol I., page 175.

We obtain an excellent idea of the oldest sculpture from the objects found by de Sarzec in Tello: namely, the reliefs, and from the statues of king Gudea. (Compare PLATES XIII. and XVI., and Figs. 51, 52.) That they belong to the earliest times is shown by the very ancient cuneiform writing, arranged in vertical columns, as in Egypt, and by the names of the kings mentioned in it. The statues are made of the hardest diorite from the country Magan, which is to be sought, as Winckler has shown, in Arabia. Of the heads only two have been found, and on these unfortunately the nose is injured. The eye, as compared with the almond-shaped Assyrian, may be called round, while the brows are strongly arched. There is no beard; and the head is shaven, and covered with a close-fitting cap, which has a turban-like brim, and is shown to be a wig by its rows of round ringlets. The hands are longer than the Assyrian, and are made with great care. A long garment, reaching to the feet, leaves the right arm bare. Loftus found similar statues of black basalt at Hamman and the neighboring Jocha. With this statue of the older period may be compared the Assyrian art in the statue of the god Nebo, found in Nimrud (Fig. 53). The sitting statue of Gudea holds upon its lap a detailed architectural plan: beside the tablet a metal stylus is represented, such as was used for writing in clay, and on the front edge of the plan is a measuring-scale divided into sixty parts; this is of very great importance for metrology. The inscription, which is placed at the lower part, at the sides, and on the back of the statue, begins: 'In the temple of Ningirsu, his

FIG. 52. Statue of Gudea from Telloh (Shirpurla).

FIG. 53. — Statue of the god Nebo, found at Nimrud. Limestone. (British Museum.)

king, is erected the statue of Gudea, governor (*patesi*) of Shirpurla, who has built the temple of E-ninnu. 1 *ka* of drink, 1 *ka* of food, ½ *ka* of flour, ½ *ka* of crushed (?) barley shall constitute the fixed offerings.' These offerings were to be made to the statue of the ruler to whom in this way divine honors were accorded; and, indeed, we find in the days of the later rulers of Ur, Gudea designated as a god, just as the sign for god appears in an inscription of Sargon I. before the ruler's name, as well as before the names of quite a number of the members of the Ur dynasty. Upon the right bank of the Tigris, above its junction with the Little Zab, at Kalah Shergat (Assur), a sitting statue of Shalmaneser II. (859–825) was found, which is similar to these oldest Chaldaean statues. Still the Assyrians do not seem to have developed this type any further. These statues remind one of those of the Sacred Way of Branchidae, near Miletus, which date from about the year 536 B.C. The Egyptian statues of this kind are superior to the Chaldaean and Ionian; for the former represent the body naked, while the latter have a garment reaching to the feet, which is very stiff, and without folds. This same defect causes the numerous Babylonian clay figures to have a clumsy appearance, especially as the heads are too large. The back of these clay figures was flat, as they were made in a mould consisting of only one piece; while the Assyrian were formed in a double mould, or were modelled by hand. There are also Babylonian bronzes, of which a basket-bearer, found at Bagdad and now preserved in the Louvre, is especially interesting (Fig. 54). It holds the basket upon its head with both hands, only the lower portion of the figure is clothed with a kind of a case, which is ornamented not with designs, but an inscription of Kudurmabuk, an Elamite king of the sixteenth century, etc. De Sarzec found, in cubical sockets, and packed in sand, remarkable earthen rivets, with figures of the god Bel, of a basket-bearer, and of an ox. Articles of this sort were placed in the sand under the thresholds of houses, and on graves, in order to avert evil. Of later origin are the Babylonian clay statuettes of the mother goddess Ishtar, who is represented sometimes as placing the hands upon the breast, and sometimes as suckling a child. The statuettes of the goddess, with a tiara and a long fringed garment, are ruder and more infrequent. There is a Babylonian clay figure of this goddess-mother. The mother holds in her arms her child, which rests its little head upon her breast (Fig. 55). These figures, which are only four or five inches high, are especially associated with the dead, and are therefore frequently met with in Warka and other cemeteries. They gave rise to a widely extended species of works of art, which exhibited the same indecent characteristics as the rites of this goddess. Schliemann discovered in the second city at Hissarlik, a lead idol of the same goddess, which also bears the

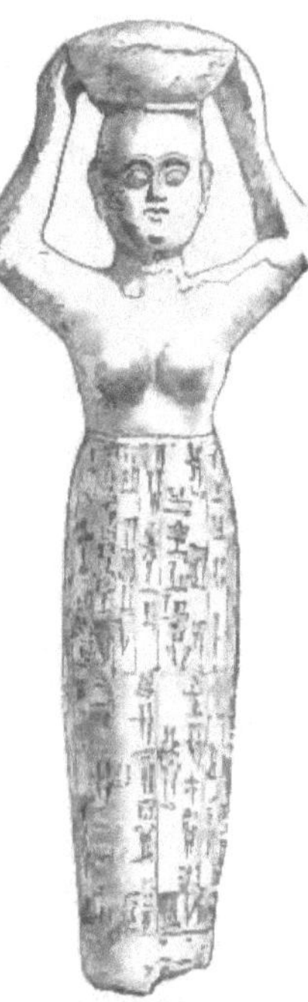

FIG. 54. — Bronze Canephorus, from Bagdad. (Paris, Louvre.)

Hittite mark of the *swastika* upon the private parts. Similar figures were found in Cyprus by Di Cesnola, and in graves in Attica and the Cyclades. The Greek sculptor was the first to transform the vulgar attitude of the Asiatic Venus into one of gracious modesty.

From the twelfth and later centuries we have a number of stone reliefs of Babylonian origin. Among these is a representation of Marduk-nadin-akhe, now in the British Museum (Fig. 56). This Babylonian ruler conquered Tiglath-Pileser in the year 1112 B.C., though subsequently he was obliged to succumb to the Assyrian king. He is crowned with a tiara, cylindrical in shape, upon which a tree pattern appears to be embroidered between two sphinxes; around the top runs a crown of feathers, and at the bottom a band with rosettes. The clothing consists of a double tunic, of which the under one has long, close-fitting sleeves, and reaches with its fringe down to the feet; the outer one is thrown over the shoulders like a mantle, and extends with its border of tassels nearly to the knee. Both garments are richly embroidered with rosettes, sacred trees, rows of half-circles, and a network of hexagonal form. The king has two daggers in his girdle, two long arrows in his right hand, and a bow in his left. The shoes, which envelop the feet and look like felt slippers, together with the garment, which resembles a sort of dressing-gown, prevent the figure from having a royal appearance.

FIG. 55.—Statuette of Ishtar and child.

As a specimen of the later glazed-tile work, the lion recently found in Babylon (PLATE XVII.) may serve as an example. It dates from the days of Nebuchadnezzar II. (604–562 B. C.).

Babylonia is highly important for the history of the art of engraving precious stones, since thousands of seals in hard half-precious stones were manufactured by Babylonian lapidaries. In the East it has never been customary to subscribe one's name, but to use a seal, formerly upon clay and wax, now also with ink. Some of these Babylonian seals are cylinders, which were rolled over the clay or wax by means of a copper axle, and others are stones set in rings. Great numbers of the seals themselves and the clay impressions have

PLATE XVII.

Lion of Babylon.—Forms the pattern of the decoration of the wall of the sacred procession street in the city of Babylon during the days of Nebuchadnezzar II.

been found; and on them we find the name of the owner and of his father, and often of the god honored by him. There is an impression in clay of a double seal which is highly interesting; one of these seals is Assyrian, and the other that of Pharaoh Sabaco (Fig. 57). These seals may have belonged to an agreement struck between Egypt and Assyria. In the seals the writing is reversed, and should be read in the impression or in a looking-glass; but there are talismans with direct writing. Among the Babylonians, as the priest-physician muttered sacred formulas to avert sickness, so certain stones were thought to have the virtue of warding off certain evils: hematite was a safeguard against hemorrhage; topaz against hemorrhoids; while the diamond prevented the execution of plans of murder, preserved the reason, and repelled wild animals; agate averted danger, and brought

Fig. 56. — Relief of Marduk-nadin-akhi (London, British Museum).

power and reputation; amethyst gave wisdom and prevented drunkenness. All the ancients believed that stones had a certain secret power, especially if mystic figures were also engraved upon them. In the Middle Ages there were books treating of stones, and this superstition is preserved even to recent times in medical books. These talismans were worn next the body as amulets, being suspended about the neck, just as is the custom to-day among the Arabs and in Southern Europe. The ancient Greeks received their cut stones from Egypt and Babylonia. The first attempts that the Greeks and Etruscans made to imitate Asiatic work were rude. Success crowned their efforts only a short time before Alexander. Except in the case of seals containing the names of rulers, it is impossible to determine exactly the age of the cylinders, since they are undated, though the general style and the character of the writing furnish a relative chronology. The oldest are made largely of black serpentine or of black and green jasper; also of hematite, which was a favorite in all periods, because it was so easily worked. They are easily recognized by means of the garments, which are wrapped spirally around the figures, as upon the cylinders of Ur-gur and Dungi, kings of the Ur dynasty, which are, however, preserved only in copies. The invention of the turning-wheel or lathe, furnished with a drill, divided the Assyrian work into two periods. In the first the hand-drill was used, which was turned by means of a handle, while the stone remained still. To make a straight line, holes were drilled at the ends, and a connecting line was drawn by means of a diamond point. After the introduction of the wheel, the precious stone, fastened in a wooden handle, was held by the left hand in contact with a small wheel, which was set in rapid motion by a large wheel moved by the foot. The tools for engraving were fastened to the little wheel; and the stone was cut more or less deeply, according as it was moved forth and back. The instruments used were a burin with round point, and saw, or

FIG. 57. — Seals of the Pharaoh Sabaco and the King of Assyria.

sort of file with a sharp point. By means of the right hand the tool was moistened from time to time with diamond dust mixed with olive-oil; formerly emery was used. It was impossible to make curved lines before the use of the wheel. The new Babylonian stones exhibit more life; a house or a tree indicates the background. The art of engraving stones reached its highest point in the Persian period. The red carnelian was now used for the first time, but the yellow not till later under the Sassanids. The Persian cuneiform writing upon them shows that the stones belong to this period, and other characteristics, such as the drapery, and the turban instead of

FIG. 58.—Cylinder of Mushezib-Ninib (London, British Museum).

the tiara, distinguish them from the Babylonian. The Babylonian work differs from the Assyrian in representing the forms as more slender, and in not betraying the life and movement so well. A sitting goddess, to whom another person is conducting a woman, is frequently seen on the Babylonian cylinders; the turbans often have two bent horns. The objects represented on the seals are very various. Gilgamesh, the Babylonian Hercules, is very common, strangling the lion, or as a winged genius grasping by the neck ostriches ('cruel birds of the wilderness,' Lamentations iv. 3); this is shown on the jasper of King Urzana of Muzazir, south of Van. The chief god of the later pantheon, Bel-Marduk, in contest with the dragon; Sin, the moon-god, riding upon a bull; Adad with the thunderbolt, Ishtar, and other deities; and offerings of animals are figured. The sacred tree is especially frequent, resembling at once the palm and a kind of pine. Associated with this are winged genii, or bulls, and worshipping kings, as is shown upon the cylinder of Mushezib-Ninib (Fig. 56), whose name is found in Arban; and surrounding these are winged horses, goats, and imaginary animals. This tree reappears as the Persea tree of the Egyptians, the *Hauma*, or paradise tree, of the Persians, which gives perpetual life, the Tūbā and Sidretel-muntahā of the Arabians, and was employed in all imaginable ways, upon furniture, dress, weapons, and religious reliefs. With endless variations, as a motive for decoration it extended over Asia, and by means of Arabian craftsmen was carried to Sicily and the rest of Europe. Even in antiquity it came through Hittite art to Greece, where it appeared first in the celebrated lions over the gateway of the citadel at Mycenae. Later, cones containing the seal in their bases took the place of the cylinders. Intaglios were used much more than cameos. There is a cameo of Sargon II. from Khorsabad, and in the Vaini Cabinet one of Nebuchadnezzar (Fig. 59); the head of the latter is given in profile, with a round, low-crested helmet. One is reminded somewhat of the helmet in the sculpture at Bayazid; the head also resembles that of Seleucus I., represented on his silver coins as Heracles. The technique strongly suggests Greek art. It cannot be regarded as a modern forgery, since it was discovered long before the cuneiform script was known to the modern world. It is barely possible, however, that it was made a short time after Alexander, when the cuneiform writing was still used.

FIG. 59.—Seal of Nebuchadnezzar.

The deities in whose honor the great *ziggurats* or stage-towers had been built were in part the same which the Semites worshipped in other lands; but there long persisted a primitive belief in many demons, coming from earlier times, which was being transformed into polytheism. The characteristics of this belief in spirits can be ascertained partly from the names of the higher beings, and from the use, in the ancient incantation rituals which we have in late Assyrian copies, and partly from the fact that those beings represent religious ideas different from those with which we are familiar in Semitic religions. The Semitic influence subsequently overpowers this foreign element, or assimilates it; for it is generally true that religions which fail to advance from a belief in spirits and spectres are overpowered by the more highly developed ones. This is illustrated in the case of the Kheta (Hittites), among whom only Syrian gods are mentioned. This non-Semitic people anciently had its own peculiar beliefs, which perhaps only had to do with spirits of the air and mountain goblins, beings similar to the Dactyli and Telchines of the Greeks, like those still found in Caucasian fairy tales. When they came into contact with the Syrians, and became acquainted with a religion which was more perfect and more imposing, their own superstition may have seemed so childish that they left it to the common people, while they adopted the foreign religion as the official one.

There are numberless evil spirits in the Babylonian-Assyrian religion, which, dwelling in the air, upon the earth, and under the earth, cause misfortune, bring on the pestilence (Ira), produce all manner of diseases, take up their abode in the possessed, and cause bad dreams. These numerous spirits could not be warded off except by mighty powers, whose friendly aid must be secured by worship. At the head of these stands a triad composed of Anu, god of the heavens; En-lil or Bel, god of the world inhabited by man; and Ea, god of the waters. These three gods, originally local deities whose worship was associated with certain centres, Anu with Uruk, Bel with Nippur, and Ea with Eridu, underwent a symbolizing process through the theologians of ancient Babylonia, who developed an elaborate cosmological-astrological system based on the general principle that the events on the earth are paralleled by occurrences in the heavens. A second triad was composed of Sin, the moon-god; Samas, the sun-god; Adad, the god of the thunder-storm; while at times Ishtar is associated with this triad and Nin-lil or Belit or Nin-khar-sag, the consort of En-lil, is added to the first triad. Of the other chief gods, Ninib represents the morning or spring-time sun and Nergal the noon-day and summer solstice sun. The latter is also chief of the world of the dead and the god of destruction and of war. In many of the incantation texts which were compiled into elaborate series, Marduk who, as the chief

Fig. 60.—Daemon, or Genius, with Eagle's Head. (London, British Museum.)

god of Babylon, becomes the head of the pantheon, is introduced as the mediator between man seeking relief from the evil spirits, and Ea who is viewed as the god of mankind *par excellence*. From Ea Marduk seeks advice when invoked by sufferers, and this advice, generally involving purification rites with various other ceremonies, is also bound up with the recital of certain magic formulas. In other rituals, the chief part is played by Girru, the god of fire, the guardian of the hearth and of the family, who is invoked as the one without whom no sacrifices to the gods can be brought, since fire consumes the sacrifice. In his name, therefore, magic rites and formulas are prescribed; for fire, both in nature and in the hands of man, is a most effective instrument. A religion can have no grand ceremonial which has not given definite forms to its gods; in that case the religious acts will consist mainly of incantations; representations of the demons are thrown into the fire, and at the same time wishes are expressed that the evil influence may be destroyed as the object was burned. Great numbers of such magical series and rituals have been found in Assurbanipal's library and published. At the entrances of cities and palaces it was customary to place winged bulls and lions with human heads,—representations of the most powerful daemons,—which should serve to prevent the other destructive spirits from entering, frightening them by their fearful appearance (Figs. 60, 61). As a specimen of one of these incantation formulas the following may suffice:

The *Utukku*[1] of the field, the *Utukku* of the mountain,
The *Utukku* of the sea, the *Utukku* that sits in graves,
The bad *Shedu*, the shining *Shedu*,
The evil wind that knows no fear,
The bad *Utukku*, which has torn the skin from a man,
By the spirits of heaven and earth be ye foresworn.
The *Utukku* that seizes hold of man,
The *Ekimmu*[2] that seizes hold of man,
The *Ekimmu* that creates evil,
The *Utukku* that creates evil.

Frequently attached to these formulas, however, are most impressive prayers to gods and goddesses which, full of lofty religious conceptions, illustrate the survival of primitive rites and beliefs long beyond the age which had outgrown them.

[1] Name of a class of daemons.
[2] Shade of the dead—conceived as a daemon or evil spirit.

The cosmological legends and the mythological traditions of the Babylonians are also preserved in Assyrian copies, which have been brought in thousands of fragments from the library in Nineveh, and deposited in the British Museum. It has been necessary to exercise great care in arranging and combining these, since they had fallen from an upper story in Nineveh, and had broken in pieces, and were in great confusion. There are several accounts of the Creation; and, besides many other legends, there is also an account of a destructive Flood, which appears to be older than the accounts of creation. The translations are in many points still uncertain. The story of the creation begins as follows: "When above heaven was not named, and below the earth had no name (the name is the sign of existence), there was Apsu ('the deep') the primaeval begetter, Mummu (the son of Apsu and of) Tiamat ('the waters' or 'seas') the mother that bore them all—their waters were united. No field was formed, no marsh was seen. When none of the gods were in existence, none bore a name and destinies were not determined; then the gods were created in the midst of heaven; Lakhmu and Lakhamu were called into being . . . ; The gods Anshar and Kishar were then created (according to Damascius, Assorus, and Kissare, 'the upper and lower space'); and long days afterward . . . the gods Anu, Bel, and Ea . . . (according to Damascius, Anos, Illinos, and Aos or Ao)." The story passes over into an account of two conflicts, one with Apsu and Mummu in which Ea is the hero, and a second and much more significant one in which Marduk overcomes the great monster Tiamat, the symbol of primaeval chaos, pictured at a time when the waters covered everything and were in unrestrained control. After the overthrow of Tiamat, order is established in the universe, the dry earth appears, vegetation ensues, and man is created. This creation myth, related in a series of seven tablets, and consisting of about 1000 lines, bears a sufficient resemblance to the Biblical story of creation to warrant us in tracing both to a common source. Even in the present entirely transformed form of the old tale as found in the first chapter of Genesis, there are certain features that point to Babylonia as the original scene of action, and the same applies to the Biblical story of the Flood, where the Babylonian system of metrology is the basis of the measures of Noah's ark. The Babylonian story of the Flood is introduced incidentally in connection with a great epic related on twelve tablets detailing the achievements of a semi-mythical hero Gilgamesh, who lives a life full of strange adventures, and to whom as a favorite

FIG. 61. — Winged Daemon in an Offering. Alabaster relief from Khorsabad. About 10 feet in height. (London, British Museum.)

personage, stories belonging to others (in some cases gods) are attached, and who is brought into connection with other myths that were current in Babylonia. He exercises a tyrannical rule in Uruk, but a rival Ea-bani, especially created by the goddess Aruru to curb

Gilgamesh's audacity and power, becomes his intimate friend. Together they proceed against Khumbaba, who is appointed as the watchman over a sacred cedar forest. Khumbaba is slain, and Gilgamesh's next adventure is with the goddess Ishtar who has fallen in love with him. The hero rejects Ishtar's suit, and in her rage she asks her father Anu, the god of heaven, to send a divine bull to kill Gilgamesh and his friend. Instead, however, the bull is killed. The pair return to Uruk and are received with demonstrations of joy as heroes. So far the six tablets of the epic. The second half of the epic is sad and sombre in character. Ea-bani is stricken with disease and dies. Gilgamesh bewails his friend, and begins a series of wanderings in which he encounters lions and scorpion-men, enters a wonderful park and reaches the sea. The goddess Siduri-Sabitu at first tries to hinder the approach of Gilgamesh, but yields to the hero's threats, and after a long dialogue between the two, in which Gilgamesh, fearing lest Ea-bani's fate may also be in store for him, asks how he may proceed to a certain Ut-napishtim, who alone of human beings has escaped death. The goddess tells him to reach his goal, which after much difficulty he attains. Face to face with Ut-napishtim, Gilgamesh inquires how he came to secure immortal life, and in reply Ut-napishtim tells the story of a great flood which the gods had brought on, and from which he and his wife were saved through the intervention of Ea. Ut-napishtim and his wife try by various magical manipulations to impart to Gilgamesh the power to resist death, and finally direct him to a plant "Restorer of the aged to youth," which grows at the bottom of the water. Gilgamesh secures the plant, but on his way to Uruk comes to a cistern, at which he halts to wash himself. A serpent comes and snatches the plant out of Gilgamesh's grasp. The hero's fate is thus sealed. He returns to Uruk and must look forward to death. In the last tablet of the epic we once more find Gilgamesh wandering, this time to find out what has become of his friend Ea-bani. The god Ea grants him a sight of Ea-bani's shade, and from the latter he learns of the sadness and gloom that prevail in the world of the dead. An honorable death and proper burial, however, secure for the dead at least rest and comfort, while he who is unburied and for whom no one provides endures hunger and discomfort. The same gloomy view of the life after death appears in the story of Ishtar's descent into the lower world, a nature myth based on the change of seasons. The goddess is represented as proceeding to the 'land whence there is no return';

> "To the house of darkness, the dwelling of Irkalla,
> To the house whence no one issues who has once entered it,
> To the road whence there is no return when once it has been trodden,
> To the house whose inhabitants are deprived of light,
> The place where dust is their nourishment, their food clay;
> They have no light, dwelling in darkness;
> They are clothed like birds in garments of feathers.
> Over gate and bolt dust is scattered."

Ishtar passes through seven gates, leaving some of her garments and ornaments at each until when she reaches the nether world she is entirely naked. This part of the story symbolizes decay of vegetation; while the second half, in which, after being sprinkled with the waters of life, she passes through the seven gates again, receiving at each the apparel and ornaments she had left there, and emerging in her full glory, marks the return of the spring and summer season. The religious literature of the Babylonians abounds in such stories, in which myths of a popular origin and other tales are taken up and made the medium for illustrating doctrines and views developed by the priests in the various religious centres of the Euphrates Valley.

Fig. 62. The god Ea (Oannes)

A Fish-god, who is represented on monuments, is none other than Ea, and he again is identical with Oannes, of whom Berosus relates a myth which makes Ea-Oannes the deity who instructed mankind in all the arts and gave them laws and laid the foundation of the Babylonian civilization (Fig. 61). The Babylonian gods were especially potent in opposing the hostile forces of nature, and were worshipped in order that their aid might be secured. The Assyrians, however, were warlike in their character, and were constantly busied with military preparations; and therefore most of their gods had a warlike stamp. The seven planets were the abode of the great gods: Mercury, of Nebo, the Babylonian Hermes; Venus, of Ishtar; Mars, of Nergal; Jupiter, of Marduk; Saturn, of Ninib; the moon, of Sin; and the sun, of Shamash. This belief, however, was not a popular superstition, but an integral part of an astronomical and astrological system devised by the priests, of which the outcome is to be seen in the extensive reports, records, and calculations of movements and phenomena of the heavenly bodies—the sun, moon, and stars—found in Asurbanipal's library at Nineveh. On the basis of this system an elaborate science of oracular lore and portents grew up. The fact that there were seven planets gave rise to the sacredness of the number seven, to the division of the week, which is a quarter of a month, into seven days, and to the seven chief demons. Every hour of the day has a planet as its tutelary god, as also every day has that planet that marked its opening hour. This is the origin of the names of the days of the week that are now used by us, the names being derived from the gods.

Numerous allusions in religious texts, of which some illustrations have above been given, reveal to us the views held by the Babylonians in regard to existence after death. They conceived of a shadowy existence in the next world, similar to that which other Semites held. Such beliefs, however, as we find alluded to in the story of Ishtar's journey to the better world, did not prevent the rise of a more earnest religious feeling and of true reverence for the gods, as is manifest in the numerous hymns which, though frequently forming part of incantation rituals, are not only couched in impressive and fervent diction, but also marked by elevated thought. The flower of the Babylonian-Assyrian religious literature appears in the so-called penitential psalms, some of which are worthy of a place by the side of Biblical religious poetry.

As far back as our history extends, the Semites dwelt near the Sumerians and Akkadians, and it must have been in an earlier period that these latter had exclusive possession of the land. It is generally supposed that the Semites originated in southern Arabia, and this view is now gaining the preference among scholars over the one which advocated Mesopotamia as the original abode.

Among the Semites we may distinguish two broad and general divisions,—the southern and the northern; to the former belong the Arabians, with numerous nations and races; and the latter consist of several groups, the Babylonians and Assyrians, the Aramaeans (who retained the name of Syrians), and the people of Canaan. The northern Semites were conquered, and carried away in such large numbers, at first by the Assyrians, that they lost their peculiarities of race; and through the conquest of Islam the territory of the Arabic language was extended over the north Semitic lands, so that only peoples here and there not subject to Mohammedanism, like the Nestorians and Mandaeans, preserved the Aramaic language. The Chaldaean population of Babylonia is the result of the union of the Semites with the oldest inhabitants of the land; and it would seem that the latter had the greater influence in the earlier periods, while in the later Babylonian empire Mesopotamia can be regarded as a Semitic land. Many names of the earliest rulers are Semitic, while others are Sumerian. The inscriptions furnish many names of kings, some of whom it is impossible to arrange chronologically with any exactness.

Berosus, a priest of Bel, who was born at Babylon about B.C. 330, and who in the time of Antiochus Soter (280–263) wrote apparently in Greek a work upon Babylonian history, is supposed to have made use of old records. Vitruvius, Seneca, and Pliny mention him only as an astronomer. Eusebius, whom we have already become acquainted with as the one who preserved the fragments of Manetho, quotes from the Babylonian history; he does not, however, know it in its original form, but only through an extract of Alexander Polyhistor, who lived in Rome in the time of Sulla. Since other ostensible quotations from Berosus are made only through this Alexander, the fragments in Eusebius and Josephus that treat of the creation and mythology are not a reliable source. The fragments of Berosus in Eusebius, however, contain, in addition, a list of Babylonian kings, likewise probably derived from Alexander Polyhistor. This list is cited in various works, and has given rise to ingenious combinations. It begins with the mythical kings, who were both before and after the flood, and whose reigns are arranged chronologically. The kings before the flood reigned 432,000 years, that is twelve times ten *sars*,—a *saru* being 3,600 years, or twelve solar cycles, or periods between two complete returns of the equinoxes. The others reigned 39,180 years, or twelve periods of 1805 years, or lunar periods of 22,325 synodical months (21,660 years or 361 *sosses*), together with twelve Sothis-periods of 1460 years (17,520 years or 292 *sosses*). The time from the flood to the birth of Abraham is 292 years (originally *sosses*), and there are 361 years from that time till the end of Genesis, making in all 653 years instead of *sosses*, which would make 39,180 years. Then follow the seven historical dynasties; but the chronology of these is not certain, since the duration of two is not given. The only two established dates are B.C. 747, marking the beginning of the Sixth Dynasty and also the era of Nabonassar, and 539, which marks the end of the Seventh Dynasty, coinciding with the capture of Babylon by Cyrus.

In the inscriptions chronological data are occasionally given, which assign some of the old rulers to a definite period, but complete reliance cannot be placed upon them. The Babylonians had a system of reckoning time, and had fixed the length of the year, but they had no long period like an era. They reckoned their years from the beginning of the reign of their kings or from some important event. On the other hand, we find for a considerable space of time perfectly reliable chronology indicated by the Assyrian *limmu*, or eponymous years. Every year received the name of a high officer, a city prefect, and one that of the king. In one place the list mentions the eclipse of the sun which occurred June 15, 763 B.C.; and by means of this date we can complete the series of years forwards and backwards, from 893 to 666. Moreover, the years from the 26th of February (1 Thoth), 747, the era of Nabonassar, to the time of the Ptolemies, are made entirely certain by the so-called Canon of Ptolemy (the geographer), who lived in the first half of the second century. This important record was derived from the tables which were added to the Almagest, an astronomical work, in order that the eclipses mentioned in it might be easily taken into account. From Nabonassar, who probably introduced the reckoning of time by solar years, the canon gives twenty Babylonian kings, ten Persian, thirteen Ptolemies, and the Roman emperors down to its own time, with the exact number of years of each reign.

Lists of the early Babylonian rulers, arranged according to the centres in which the rulers lived, will be found in the recent histories of Rogers and Radau, but in many respects these lists are still to be regarded as provisional, and will be modified and extended by further discoveries and researches. It is not worth the while to repeat these lists, though it may be of interest to supplement the general sketch of the earlier periods of Babylonian history at the beginning of this chapter by further data selected here and there from the historical records now at our disposal.

A Babylonian ruler of Elamitic origin is Kudurmabuk, son of Simtishilkhak; he calls himself king of Sumer and Akkad (south and north Babylonia), ruler of Martu or 'Westland' and of Emutbal, that is, Susiana. This would indicate that he extended his sway over Syria. He had a son Eriaku (or Rim-Sin), who succeeded to the empire of his father. With this should be connected the narrative preserved in Gen. xiv. 1–10, which is one of the later elements of the Pentateuch. The kings Amraphel of Shinar, Arioch (Eriaku) of Ellasar (Larsa), Chedorlaomer of Elam, and Tidal, king of the Goiim (who have been identified with the Guti, north of the Cossaeans), made war with the kings of Bera of Sodom (this name is still applied to the mountain Uzdum at the southwestern corner of the Dead Sea), Birsha of Gomorrah, Shinab of Admah, Shemeber of Zeboiim, and with the king of Bela, which is there called Zoar. They did this in order to bring them into subjection; for these had rebelled against Chedorlaomer, who had subdued them twelve years earlier. The Canaanitish kings were defeated in the vale of Siddim (which is probably the most southern portion of the Dead Sea, where there are marshy lowlands covered at times with water), and their cities were captured and plundered. Amraphel may be identical with the famous Hammurabi, though this is by no means certain. Chedorlaomer ('servant of the god Lagamar') was, perhaps, an ally of Kudur-mabuk; Lagamar was the name of a goddess, which Asurbanipal captured in Susa.

Of this important period in which Kudur-mabuk lived we now have considerable data through the historical and votive inscriptions of his contemporary Hammurabi (c. 2250 B.C.), through official letters of this same ruler and of other members of the dynasty to which he belonged, and through a most valuable chronicle which, so far as preserved, records many events in the reigns of the first ten members of this so-called first Babylonian dynasty. It was still customary in the days of this dynasty to use as a date some event in the reign of the king, and since this method is followed in the business documents of this period, of which now many hundreds are known, it is clear that the chronicle in question was drawn up to serve as a guide in determining the year to which a date in a business document refers. So, for example, it is from this chronicle as well as from the corresponding indications in no less than four contract tablets that we learn of the conquest of Emutbal, over which Kudurmabuk once claimed control in the thirty-first year of the reign of Hammurabi. As a specimen of such a method of dating, an example from one of the tablets in question may serve:

"The year of Hammurabi the King, in which with the help of Anu and Bel, he established his good fortune and his hand subdued the land of Emutbal and Rim-Sin (or Eri-aku the son of Kudurmabuk) the king."

Ordinarily, however, the dating formula is much briefer. Thus in a document of the reign of Sin-idinnam, the contracting parties swear by the name of the god of Ur and of the king Nur-Adad; and the date is expressed as follows: "Month Tebet (December), of the year in which he adorned with gold a high throne for the god Shamash." In the contract tablets dating from the time of Rim-Sin, who built a fortification around the city Larsa, together with a tower, and also constructed and restored several temple buildings, the capture of the city Apirak is mentioned; thus, "Month Tishri (September), thirtieth day, in the nineteenth year after Apirak had been captured by the ruler Rim-Sin, who is still alive." This event was of sufficient importance to mark the beginning of an era. The site of Apirak has not yet been determined; but it was apparently important that a dynasty should possess it, for it is announced that Naram-Sin, one of the oldest rulers, captured Apirak. The capture of cities like Kish and Dur-Ilu in Babylonia is used in the same way to indicate a date. Upon one tablet the year is mentioned in which the Tigris, the river of the gods, was connected with the sea; that is, a canal was constructed connecting it with the Persian Gulf. The building of temples was also used as a basis for dating, and thus by merely placing dates together we obtain considerable historical material for this early period.

It is not surprising that when we pass beyond the age of the first dynasty which ruled in the city of Babylon our knowledge should be less precise, for even to the Babylonians of later times this earlier period appeared in a half-legendary light. This may be concluded from the story about Sargon I. found on a tablet of Asurbanipal's library, in which we find the same *motif* as in the stories about Moses, Cyrus, and Romulus. The tablet so far as preserved reads:

"I am Sargon the mighty king, the king of Agani (Agade). My mother was of noble birth (?); my father was unknown.[1] My father's brother used to dwell in the highlands, and my native city was Azupiranu, which lies on the banks of the Euphrates. My mother, of noble birth (?), conceived me, and bore me in secret. She put me in a basket of *shur*, and closed up the opening with bitumen. She cast me into the river, which did not flow over me [?]. The river carried me along to Akki, the irrigator. Akki, the irrigator, took me up. Akki, the irrigator, reared me as his child. Akki, the irrigator, made me a gardener. While I acted as gardener, Ishtar showed me favor. Forty-five years (?) I ruled over the black haired race (i.e., the Babylonians): I . . . axes of bronze, . . . : [I ruled] the upper land, I governed [the kings] of the lower land. . . ." The remainder of the inscription is incomplete, and hardly intelligible: it seems to refer to the conquest of Dur-ilu on the borders of Elam, and of Dilmun, the island city in the Persian Gulf.

Again, events in Sargon's reign became for later times the basis for the interpretation of omens—an indication likewise of the "symbolical" aspect acquired by the remote age in which he was placed. This tablet that recounts the deeds of Sargon is divided into fourteen sections, each of which gives at the beginning the condition of the moon. From this we learn that Sargon made an expedition against Elam, and that in an expedition which lasted three years, he reached the shore of the Mediterranean Sea. He also repulsed an enemy who besieged him in Agade, and at last seized the kingdom of Subarti, from which he carried booty back to his capital. His son, Naram-Sin, is called "King of the four regions" upon an alabaster vase which was found in Babylon, and which is described as a piece of booty from Magan (Arabia).

[1] A phrase indicative of the non-royal birth of Sargon, whose father, as we now know from the inscriptions found at Nippur, was Itti-Bel.

Next to Sargon, the name that made the deepest impression upon the memories of the Babylonians was that of Hammurabi—the sixth member of the first dynasty of Babylon—who ruled for forty-two years (c. 2300–2250 B.C.). It was under Hammurabi, preëminent alike as a military leader and statesman, that Babylon, the origin of which may indeed go as far back as the days of Sargon, rose to political supremacy. From this time the title "king of Babylon" generally replaces the older one of "king of Sumer and Akkad"; and amid the frequently changing fortunes of the succeeding fifteen hundred years, the city of Babylon with only rare intervals and short interruptions maintained itself as the centre of the entire Euphrates Valley. The union of Euphratean states thus brought about by Hammurabi was of a more permanent character than the earlier one represented by the Ur dynasty, and even after it was dissolved through the rise of the independent state of Chaldaea in the extreme south, its effects were felt throughout the period of Babylonian history; and when, after the fall of Assyria, a Chaldaean dynasty succeeded in erecting the neo-Babylonian empire, not only was Babylon chosen as the political centre, but the example of Hammurabi evidently influenced the neo-Babylonian kings, notably Nebuchadnezzar II., who even imitated in his inscriptions the style of the cuneiform characters current in Hammurabi's days.

Besides a large number of tablets from Hammurabi to his officials and to contemporary chieftains, and of inscriptions which enable us to penetrate even into the details of occurrences during his long reign, in which he succeeded in making all of Babylon and Elam subject to him, we have records of his many undertakings, such as the cutting of canals for the internal improvement of the country, and of his activity in embellishing the temple of Marduk and of other gods worshipped in Babylon. Most precious of all, however, is a magnificent monument of diorite, over seven feet high, found in 1902 by the French expedition at Susa, and which proved to be an elaborate code of laws set up by Hammurabi for the government of his empire (Fig. 63). The monument stood originally in the temple to Shamash—the sun god—at Sippar, and was carried as a trophy to Elam probably by Sutruk-nakhunte, of whom we have spoken above (p. 159). The design at the top shows Hammurabi in an attitude of adoration before the sun god—who is the god of justice and right-

FIG. 63. — King Hammurabi of Babylon before the [illegible]
(Code of [illegible])

History of [illegible], Vol. I, page [illegible]

FIG. 64. — An Armenian town stormed; removal of prisoners. Marble relief (After Layard.)

cousness *par excellence*—and in accord with this sentiment Hammurabi in the body of the inscription calls himself king of righteousness, impelled by consideration for the welfare of his subjects to draw up laws that might ensure justice to all and to establish peace and security throughout the land. The laws themselves, consisting of about 300 paragraphs, represent a combination of customs derived from primitive days, with regulations that are the outcome of more advanced social conditions. While the punishments meted out for offenders—theft, fraud, assaults—are exceedingly severe, great precautions are taken against miscarriage of justice. Parental authority is recognized as paramount, but the son is protected against an unwarranted exercise of this authority, and similarly the wife is protected against neglect on the part of her husband. The *lex talionis* is in full force, but the era of "blood-avenge"—so characteristic of primitive Semitic society—is past.[1]

The exact relationship of this code of Hammurabi to the Pentateuchal codes has not been ascertained, but so much is clear that conditions prevailing in Babylonia as reflected in Hammurabi's code, as well as specific stipulations, exercised considerable influence on the Hebrews and on their leaders, to whom we owe the Hebrew codes embodied in the Pentateuch, and that date from various periods from the ninth to the fifth centuries.

The dynasty to which Hammurabi belonged was succeeded about c. 2150 B.C. by a series of eleven rulers who appear to have come from the extreme south of Babylonia, known as the "Sea land," and to have secured control of the city of Babylon. A more serious change is represented by the Cassite invasion of Babylonia, which took place about 1780. Of the 36 kings, extending over a period of 576 years —as a Babylonian chronicle informs us—only about a dozen are known to us through inscriptions—chiefly boundary stones and small votive tablets—but our knowledge of the period is somewhat enlarged by the records of rulers of Assyria, which during the reign of the Cassites forges to the front, while the archaeological interest of the last king of Babylonia, Nabonidus, prompts him to mention several of the

[1] For a full translation of the code, see Johns, "The Oldest Code of Laws in the World" (Edinburgh, 1902), also in the same author's "Babylonian and Assyrian Laws, Contracts, and Letters" (New York, 1904), and R. F. Harper, "The Code of Hammurabi" (Chicago, 1903).

Cassite rulers whose names he finds on records of the temples which he is engaged in enlarging and rebuilding.

At first the relations between the Cassites and Assyrians seem to have been friendly, though if, as has been supposed, the district of Khani whence Agumkakrime brings back the captured statue of Marduk and his consort Sarpanit, is a part of Assyria, it would seem that hostilities had broken out between the south and the north in the seventeenth century. Afterward, however, we hear of treaties and alliances between the Cassite and Assyrian rulers in the days of Kara-indash and Burnaburiash I., while a little later (c. 1500) a Cassite king, Kara-chardash, marries Muballit-sherua, the daughter of the Assyrian king Ashur-uballit. The alliance, however, was also fraught with danger, for when, after the murder of Kara-chardash, unsettled conditions prevailed in Babylonia, it was through Ashur-uballit's interference that (c. 1400 B.C.) his great-grandson, Kurigalzu II., was placed on the throne. Bel-nirari, the successor of Ashur-uballit, begins the hostile attitude toward the south which finally leads, under Tukulti-Ninib I. (c. 1300), in the practical subjection of Babylonia to Assyria. A revolt against Tukulti-Ninib in Assyria is followed by the temporary decline of the Assyrian power, but when a new period of strength and military glory sets in under Tiglathpileser I. (c. 1130), Babylonia too is involved, and soon thereafter the Cassite rule comes to end, and dynasties of various origin, though more or less under control of Assyria, followed, until in the eighth century the rulers of Babylonia became practically viceroys in the service of Assyrian kings.

CHAPTER V.

SYRIA AND ASIA MINOR.

BEFORE we begin to describe the struggles of the Egyptians with the various peoples of Syria, it will be well to speak of the geographical and ethnographical characteristics of the latter country, as well as to give some of the more salient points in its history. In order to present the subject connectedly, it will be necessary to touch upon many things which really occurred later than these struggles. It will also be necessary to discuss the oldest Assyrian history later, although it is connected with events touched upon at the close of the preceding chapter.

Syria is the country lying between the Mediterranean Sea, the Arabian Desert, and the Euphrates River. It is traversed by mountain ranges running north and south, which touch Mount Taurus in the north. The chief rivers of the country run in the valleys between these mountain ranges. As the land is the highest at the centre, some of them, as the Orontes, flow to the north, and some, as the Litany and Jordan, to the south: the Orontes flows through Coele-Syria, and after passing Antioch empties into the sea; the Litany, turning to the west, flowing through a valley, enters the sea north of Tyre. At the foot of Mount Hermon are three fountains, whose waters unite with smaller streams, and form the Lake Hûleh, from which the Jordan flows into the Lake of Gennesaret, or Sea of Tiberias (Fig. 65). The Jordan, soon after leaving this lake, enters a broad, barren valley, which has a tropical climate. At first it is a small volume of water: but its waters are soon increased by the Yarmuk, which comes from the region of Bozrah, and by the Jabbok, which flows through Gilead, rich in forest and grass. The waters of the Dead Sea, into which the Jordan empties, are increased by still other streams, as the Arnon in Moab (Fig. 66). East of the Jordan the land is well watered, but on the west it is to a large extent barren and unfruitful. The race of Lot, whom the genealogical history of the Bible represents as the nephew of Abraham, must be located in Moab. Lotan was a chieftain in the mountains of Edom (1 Chron. i. 38; Gen. xxxvi. 20). The well-known legend of the sensual conduct of Lot must have arisen out of hatred felt toward Moab, who was said to be a descendant of Lot; the pillar of salt into which his wife was transformed stands above the Dead Sea at its southwestern extremity, at Uzdum (Fig. 67). This lake is remarkable from the fact that its waters are strongly impreg-

FIG. 65. — Lake Tiberias, or Gennesaret.

nated with minerals; and on this account no fishes can live in it. It varies greatly in depth, being in its northern portion 1,082 feet deep, while in the southern portion it is less than 10 feet. Its surface is nearly 1,300 feet below the level of the Mediterranean.

The narrow strip of land lying along the shore of the Mediterranean, between it and the mountains, is very fertile, being visited by frequent rains. The Philistines occupied the southern portion, — a warlike people who emigrated from the island Caphthor, probably Cyprus, and lived in a confederacy of five cities under princes (Seranim). Three of these cities were on the coast. Gaza, with the temple of Zeus Marnas, that is, "our lord;" Ashdod, with a temple of Dagon; and Ascalon, with the temple of Derceto and her daughter Astarte. In the interior were Ekron, now called Akir, east of Jebna (Jabneel), and Gath, probably the modern Tel-es-Safie, situated between Beth Jibūn and Ekron.

Farther north along the coast dwelt the Phoenicians; they occupied the fruitful region, bordered by splendid forests and mountains abounding in metals, which extends from a point in the north opposite Cyprus to Carmel on the south: Carmel is the boundary of the plain of Jezreel, through which the river Kishon flows. The

FIG. 66. — Mouth of the river Arnon, or Mojib.

original home of the Phoenicians is still a matter of uncertainty. Herodotus preserves a tradition that they came from the Erythraean Sea (Persian Gulf). This is possible only on the supposition that centuries were occupied in the migration, and that it was aided by colonies established for purposes of trade. The Greek name

FIG. 67. The salt columns at Uzlum.

of the people (*Phoenices*) seems to have been derived from *phoinix*, the date palm. Their native name, Poeni, or Puni, was used by the Romans to designate the Phoenician Carthaginians. They must not be confounded with Punt named on Egyptian monuments, which designates the district along the southeastern coast of Arabia and the corresponding strip on the African coast whose inhabitants established a close intercourse between Africa and Arabia. The language of the Phoenicians became the prevailing speech of the country. It is identical with the Moabite, Hebrew, and other dialects of Palestine. The Phoenician religion is a type of the old Canaanitish nature worship, modified by Babylonian and Egyptian elements. The sun, moon, and planets were worshipped, being regarded as living, intelligent forces, having the power to influence the will and fate of men. The male creative power of the sun is personified by Baal, while Ashtoreth represents the productive power of the universe. The scorching heat of the sun is represented by Moloch, who is portrayed as a bull, or as a man with a bull's head. The wild boar, which is made furious by the summer's heat, is sacred to him; he is therefore only a form of Baal, and they sought to appease him by burning children alive. The Phoenicians had the idea that the angry god should receive the best of their possessions as a sacrifice; and this primitive rite prevailed among them, notwithstanding their high culture, even till a very late period, as, for example, in Carthage. Similar sacrifices were offered to Moloch by the Ammonites and Jews: Solomon built a shrine to Moloch upon the Mount of Olives (1 Kings xi. 7); Ahaz caused his son to be offered up (2 Kings xvi. 3); and it was not till the time of Josiah that the service of Moloch was abolished in the valley of Hinnom (2 Kings xxiii. 10; Jeremiah vii. 31, 32). Baal was worshipped under many forms, as Baal Shamim, or 'god of heaven'; Baal Hamon, or 'Sun-god'; Baal Berith, or 'god of the covenant' (at Shechem); also as Baal Gad, or 'god of good luck.' This god was worshipped at the foot of Hermon, and therefore was also called Baal Hermon. In Ekron of the Philistines he was called Baal Zebub, 'the god that wards off flies.' Other names were derived from the places where he was worshipped, as Baal Peor from Mt. Peor in the northern part of Moab; Baal Meon, from a place (likewise in Moab) now called Main, where stone altars are found. The name of the god appears in composition in many Jewish names, as Baal-iada, a son of David (1 Chron., xiv. 7), though in the parallel passage (2 Sam. v. 16) El-iada occurs, in which El is substituted for the objectionable Baal. It would appear, therefore, that at one time the Hebrew god Jahveh was also known as Baal.

Another deity was Astarte, the Hebrew Ashtoreth, honored by all the Syrian peoples as the productive power of nature, the Assyrian Ishtar, the Arabian Attar, who is represented also as a male, and is, therefore, androgynous, as the god is represented with the attributes of the goddess and the reverse, symbolized at the festivals by the exchange of garments (cf. Deut. xxii. 5). This goddess was called Dereeto by the Philistines, and was honored as Atargatis in the celebrated temple at Hierapolis (Membidj) near the Euphrates. The lion is sacred to her; and she is represented as standing upon one, or in the form in which she appears among the Greeks, as riding in a wagon drawn by a lion. Her worship was attended with licentiousness, and her women turned over their ill-gotten gains to the temple treasury. Such temple slaves are frequently mentioned in the Old Testament, and were distinguished by their peculiar attire. The Phoenician merchants and sailors had such women everywhere in their colonies. The symbol of Astarte (Ashtoreth) was the *asherah*, a trunk of a tree with a meaning similar to the 'idol' of 1 Kings xv. 13, a priapus, like the *emah* of the Babylonians (Jer. l. 38). The animals sacred to her are those distinguished for their generative power, — the ram, he-goat, doves, and fishes. In the temple of Aphrodite, at Paphos (Fig. 68), a cone-shaped stone stood between two pillars in a cella: before it there was a cage for doves, and a fish-pond in each of the two courts. Such a house for doves is still preserved in the temple of Gozzo, where there are several rows of rectangular holes, one above the other, for the doves: in front of it there was a bench or stone table on which the food was strewn. A coin of Antoninus Pius represents such a dove-house: the fish-pond is also often seen on coins of Cyprian cities. The festivals of Ashtoreth were accompanied by many strange rites which her devotees practised in an ecstatic state amid the din of drums, cymbals, and pipes. The goddess herself, according as the ecstasy or remorse that attends sensual excesses had sway, was viewed either as the voluptuous or as the chaste goddess, — Dido, or Elissa, in Carthage, the pure Artemis, goddess of the

Fig. 68. — Bronze coin of Paphos. Emperor Caracalla (211 217 A.D.).

chase, or the Magna Mater, at Ephesus. The Amazons, who were hostile to men, were her servants, and danced in arms at her festivals.

The Phoenicians had another god, Melkarth, or Baal, of Tyre, called also Cadmus, and by the Greeks identified with Hercules, a mediator between the world and the real Baal; mythically viewed as the champion of the god. Out of ruin he brings new life, destroys the injurious influences of the twelve signs of the zodiac (the Labors of Heracles), and tempers the winter's cold and the summer's heat (that is, kills the lion). During the winter he remains asleep, or is far away in Gades, near the Pillars of Hercules, where was his resting-place (1 Kings xviii. 27). He was a god who wandered over the earth, established Phoenician colonies, and delivered them from destructive forces. He was the first to wear the purple, and to direct the affairs of nations; he appeared as Minos in the Phoenician colonies. Herodotus saw a temple to him in Tyre, in which were two columns of gold and emerald (green glass); and in Gades there were two columns of bronze in his temple; the god himself had erected for his own honor pillars in the mountains of Calpe and Abyla, and the Phoenician workmen of Solomon placed the pillars of Jachin and Boaz before the temple.

Tammuz, who was called Zerach ('the appearing one') in northern Syria, was worshipped in Byblus. He is a god of spring, a beautiful youth, who is killed while in his prime by the boar of Ares, and is mourned by Baaltis (Baalat); he is also known as Adonis—a title which has the force of 'lord.' The Adonia were celebrated in the month which was named after him. The boar symbolizes the summer's heat and the rainy season, during which the sun is not seen. The river of Byblus, the Adonis (Nahr-Ibrahim), becomes swollen in the autumn; and its waters are colored by the red soil, which indicates Adonis's death in the mountains. The image of Adonis was carried about and bewailed by women with the lamentation *hoi adon we hoi hodoh*, 'Woe Adonis, woe his splendor.' They prepared the Adonis gardens, consisting of vessels filled with quickly fading flowers; but upon the approach of spring the resurrection of the god was celebrated with many excesses. In the plain of Jezreel, at Hadadrimmon, south of Megiddo, where a lamentation for Adonis likewise was made, this lamentation was transferred at a later time to King Josiah, who fell there in 608 B.C. (Zech. xii. 11; 2 Chron. xxxv. 25, cf. Ezek. viii. 14). A later version of the Osiris myth joined Adonis with Osiris, and represented the dead body of the latter as driven about in a chest, but at last found by Isis.

The different gods of the Phoenicians, as worshipped in their cities, are grouped together in the sacred number of seven, as Cabiri, ('the great'). They are called also Titans, or children of El, Benē Elohīm, represented as elementary or cosmogonic spirits in the form of children. Eshmun is added as an eighth; and all are called children of Siddik, 'the righteous,' that is, of Baal Shamim. The Greeks, who found their worship in Lemnos, Samothrace, and Rhodes, regarded them as children of the sun-god, or of the Egyptian Ptah-Hephaestus, and adopted into their own worship with the mysteries of the Cabiri, secret teachings in regard to the idea of life after death, which treat of the discovery of the wandering goddess of the moon Ashtoreth by Melkarth, and of the marriage of the two. The chief of the Cabiri was Chusor, the director of the world, the inventor of navigation and of the manufacture of iron. His image is represented upon the coins as Hephaestus, with hammer, tongs, and leathern apron. Chusartis, or Harmonia, the personified law or Thaurō (Hebrew Torah), is a female Cabira; she is alike moon-goddess, or Ashtoreth, and spouse of Melkarth, or Cadmus. Therefore this Cadmus was also reckoned among the Cabiri. He brought writing to the Greeks, taught them the science of mining, and established marriage after he had found Harmonia. The god Eshmun of Sidon unites in himself the qualities of the seven others. He is, in the myth, their chief, or Adon; in philosophic conception the order, the cosmos, of the others. Upon Phoenician coins eight rays encircle his head, and, like Aesculapius, he bears a snake, which on account of its annual change of skin is the symbol of recovery from disease.

Philo Byblius — who in the second century of the Christian era translated an historical work of Sanchuniathon, claimed to be Phoenician, fragments of which have been preserved by Eusebius — regarded Gebal, the Byblus of the Greeks, now called Jebel, as the oldest city of Phoenicia. Near the little city is a Phoenician burying-place. Near Kassuba, not far from the sea, Renan discovered the foundation of a great temple, probably that of Adonis, and besides, in different places in the vicinity, many gravestones with steplike ornaments, grottos containing beautiful stone sarcophagi, Egyptian antiquities, the winged disk of the sun formed in Phoenician style, and peculiar funnel-shaped wine-presses provided with stone covers. The temple of Baalat is represented upon a coin of Macrinus, 217–218 A.D.(Fig. 69). There is a court open to the sky, in which arises a pyramid or cone; also a porch containing an altar for offerings with its flame of fire. Upon a stele of King Jehumelek (first half of the fifth century) this brazen altar (*mizbach*) is mentioned, as well as the pyramid; the space where this was entered from the porch by a golden door (*patach*), with golden uraeus-serpents (*art*) on the sun-disk (*aten*) above the door. Unfortunately the goddess is represented here wholly as Egyptian, as Isis-Hathor, and not as Phoenician.

FIG. 69.—Bronze coin of the city Byblus. Emperor Macrinus (217, 218 A.D.).

Passing southward, before one reaches Beirut, he must cross the Nahr-el-Kelb ('dog's river') with its bridge. The paved way among the rocks above the sea was constructed during the latter part of the reign of the emperor Marcus Aurelius, who died 180 A.D. Still higher up is an older path, which is adorned with ancient sculptures, both Egyptian and Assyrian. The Egyptian tablets are all flat at the top, and the Assyrian rounded. The first tablet, as one comes from Beirut, was cut by Rameses II., who made short excursions into Syria in the second and fourth years of his reign, before the great war against the Hittites broke out. The second tablet is supposed to be that of Asur-rish-ishi; the third that of his son, Tiglath-Pileser I. (about 1130 B.C.). Higher up, where this older path enters the Roman road, is the fourth tablet, facing the northwest, of Asurnazirpal, the builder of the northwest palace at Nimrud, and as a companion to this is the tablet of Shalmaneser II., both of which date from the ninth century, B.C. The sixth and eighth tablets were the work of Rameses II., while the seventh was made by

Sennacherib. His son, Esarhaddon, caused the last to be cut in 670 B.C., after the conquest of King Tirharka of Egypt. The road ascended from the coast, passing over Lebanon to the south of the celebrated cedar groves in the vicinity of Bsherre (Fig. 70), and then continued northward in the valley of the Orontes. In the upper region of the Nahr-el-Kelb are the ruins Kalat-Fakra, two graves in the form of pyramids. One of these is now merely a heap of stones, but the other is preserved. The base of the pyramid has vertical faces; but above the structure is broken into steps, and ends at the

FIG. 70. — Cedars of Lebanon.

top with a platform twenty-five feet square, which is adorned with a moulding. The interior contains the grave and long galleries. There are pyramids similar to this in Greece, between Argos and Epidaurus, at Lessa west of the latter, at Cenchreae upon the Isthmus, and upon the Laconian coast opposite the island Elaphonesus.

The city of Beirut is situated upon a magnificent bay, with the snow-capped heights of Sannin rising behind it. It is mentioned along with Gebal (Gubla) in the Tel-el-Amarna Tablets (c. 1400 B.C.) and acquired prominence under Roman rule; to-day it is the busiest port of Syria. The only thing that recalls its antiquity is the foundation and fragments of the columns of a temple near the convent

(*Dêr*) El-Kaa in a southeasterly direction, situated above the Nahr-Beirut in a ravine; an inscription says that the temple was sacred to Baal Markod, the lord of the festival of dancing.

Sidon, now called Saida, was the chief of the Phoenician cities from the seventeenth to the twelfth century. It appears to be older than its rival Tyre, and it founded Aradus in the eighth century. The political and commercial importance of Sidon made the name at one time a designation for Phoenicia in general. The city had two harbors between the mainland and a rocky promontory and cliffs formerly built up with large blocks of stone. The southern one was the Egyptian; but to-day the Arabian boats use only the northern one, the entrance of which is guarded by a citadel belonging to the Middle Ages; this is upon a cliff, which is joined to the mainland by a bridge with nine pointed arches. The oldest sepulchres of the necropolis, situated southeast of the city, are entered by shafts ten or twelve feet long, in the walls of which holes are cut to aid in descending. Below are several chambers, but they are seldom connected. The arched grottos, entered by means of steps, and having rectangular cavities for the bodies, are of a later date. Besides the richly sculptured sarcophagi, they contain mummy-like chests made of stone, after Egyptian models. An example of this work, with an inscription, was found in 1855, and is now in the Louvre; it is the coffin of king Eshmunazar II. (Fig. 71), son of Tabnit and of Am-Astarte, daughter of Eshmunazar I. and priestess of Astarte. He died in 386 B.C., after a reign of fourteen years. In the inscription he says, among other things, that the lord of kings (i.e. Artaxerxes Mnemon) gave to him as a reward for his deeds Dôr (north of Caesarea), Joppa, and the land of Dagon in the plain of Sharon. Magnificent sarcophagi of the Greek period have also been found at Sidon. (PLATE XVII.—*A*.) Upon the sea-shore near where the dead are buried are mounds of muscle-shells, which accumulated from the manufacture of purple. One of these, nearly 400 feet long and 25 to 30 feet high, consists of the shells of the *murex trunculus*. These shell-fish were opened by a blow upon the side with an axe, treated with salt, and macerated. The coloring material consisted of azure cyanic acid and red purple oxide, yielding an amethyst purple. The wool was colored by being brought into contact with the color-glands in

PLATE XVII .1

Sarcophagus of the Greek Period found in Sidon.

History of All Nations, Vol. I., page 21[illegible].

the throat of the fish. Other mounds are formed of the shells of the *murex brandaris* and *purpura haemastoma*. The former were caught in the Adriatic Sea, and furnished the yellowish-red, or Tyrian purple; the latter, the so-called Gaetulian purple. The manufacture of Sidonian glass was carried on in Sarepta (Sarafend), south of Sidon. Nearer Sidon, in the mountains above the Nahr-Senik, a stairway 330 feet long, cut in the rock, leads to a castle of the Middle Ages, near which is a rocky grotto, formerly a temple of Ashtoreth, and now a chapel to the Virgin Mary.

FIG. 71. — The Sarcophagus of King Eshmunazar II. (Paris, Louvre.)

In the year B.C. 761 a portion of the inhabitants of Sidon, in consequence of party-strife, left the city, and established themselves at Arvad (Aradus), now called Ruâd, which controlled a considerable territory along the shore, and had great importance in the time of the Seleucids. Upon the hewen rocks along the shore are the remains of the Phoenician walls. Between the shore and the island there was a spring of fresh water, which was collected in a bell-like receiver and conducted above the surface of the sea by a copper pipe. Somewhat farther south along the shore is Marathus, now Amrīt, already in ruins in Strabo's time. Among the numerous Phoenician monuments, a temple (El-Maabed) is prominent, having the form of a cube, open in front, and covered with a large stone; it is in a court, which is enclosed upon three sides by rock, and

Fig. 72. — Sepulchral Monuments at Amrit.

which once formed in part a holy pond, with the ark, or *theba*, of the deity. The necropolis east of the temple contains a large number of graves, still in a good state of preservation, which have been sunk into the rock, and are generally surmounted by a large cippus, or monument (Fig. 72). By means of stairs or inclined passageways, one reaches a chamber, into which from the rear one or more somewhat long rooms open as receptacles for the dead. Sometimes the chamber is connected, by means of a shaft, with rooms still lower down. One of these monuments has a square base, on which rests a pedestal with so-called Roman contours; from this arises a cylindrical column about 31 feet high, which is rounded off at the top, and around which runs an Assyrian moulding resembling staircases. At each of the four corners of the pedestal, there stands forth the forward part of a lion, which is Grecian in style. The date of the monument cannot be determined, as there is no inscription. There is no doubt that the meaning of this column is the same as that of the phallus stones upon the Tantalis graves at Smyrna, and upon the mound of Alyattes at Sardis; it was to give expression to the thought that new life springs from the mould of the grave. Similar monuments are found in Etruria, as at Tarquinii, and upon the island Minorca (the Talayot); from the round towers arose the Roman tombs, such as that of Caecilia Metella and of the Tossia family (St. Helena) in Rome, and that of Theodoric in Ravenna; on the other hand, the tomb of Esther in Hamadan is similar to that of Amrit. Different styles are represented in other tombs: some have a square base, from which arises a cylindrical or a cubical pediment, both capped with a pyramid. (Fig. 73.) This is illustrated in the 'Tomb of Absalom,' at Jerusalem, which is adorned with Ionian columns, Dorian architraves, and Egyptian cornices. These architectural types often repeat themselves in distant lands and times. Another example is seen in the tomb of a sheikh in Ba-Azani, in Assyria. In this case, upon a large cubical stone, rests an octagonal one, from which rises a cylindrical surmounted by a fluted pyramid. In other cases the pyramid rests immediately upon a large cube, which contains an upper and a lower chamber with niches. This arrangement is the same as is seen on the pyre of the coins of Tarsus, on the 'Tomb of Zachariah,' at Jerusalem, and on the tomb of Mashaka, which is adorned with an encircling row of columns. This type can be traced back to Egyptian models, such as are preserved upon the heights west of Thebes. Still other tombs are square; and the space within, which is reached by deep openings on three sides, is contracted at the top into a flue, and is covered with a stone slab.

The city of Tyre arose later than Sidon. It was called in Hebrew, Tsōr; in Egyptian, Tar as early as an inscription of Thothmes

FIG. 73. — Tomb at Amrit.

III.; in Latin, Tyrus (from the Greek), and Sarra; and its present name is Çur. Since the name means 'rock,' the first settlement must have been upon the island, and not upon the mainland, which has been regarded as the site of the older town, but which is by no means rocky. Therefore the Papyrus Anastasi, from the time of

Rameses II., knows only of the island town. King Hiram, son of Abibaal, is said to have connected the double island with the mainland by a dyke and an aqueduct. The small outer island, upon which a temple stood, forms now the southwestern portion of the island town. Upon the large island was the royal citadel, the temples of Baal (Agenor), and of Ashtoreth, and the market-place. Upon the highest point stood the temple of Melkarth. The town was besieged at different times, once without success by Shalmaneser II.; but Nebuchadnezzar, after a thirteen years' siege, captured and destroyed it in 585 B.C. Alexander destroyed the town upon the mainland, using the ruins to construct a dyke about 200 feet wide, with which he approached the island-town and besieged it. This dyke was gradually increased by alluvial deposits, and the island became permanently united with the mainland. Antigonus also besieged it fifteen months. The harbor is the old Sidonian, or northern one; old remains of buildings with large blocks can still be seen. An ancient aqueduct, which furnished the city on the mainland with water, can be traced as far south as Ras-el-Ain, where there is a large reservoir. Beyond this aqueduct are mounds formed from the *débris* of an old suburb and the numerous ruins of a burying-place. On the road to the southeast, toward Cana, are many ancient remains; and at the distance of an hour and a quarter from Tyre is the 'Tomb of Hiram' (Kabr-Hiram, Fig. 74). This tomb is undoubtedly Phoenician: the base consists of large blocks about thirteen feet long, upon which rests an immense flat stone. Upon this rests the sarcophagus, which is closed by a large stone, making the whole about twenty feet high. In front of this, steps lead into a rectangular chamber in the rock, whose cross-section represents an irregular oval.

At quite a distance south of Tyre, the promontory Ras-en-Nakurah, 'the Staircase of the Tyrians,' extends out into the sea. Near this Renan found ruins of a citadel, which received the name Umm-el-Awāmid, 'Mother of the Columns,' on account of its Grecian columns. Some sphinxes were found here, and also stone coffins, one of which is rectangular and about six feet long; on the front side is a small altar, and the cover is shaped like a roof, with horns at the four corners. Other coffins have the form of mummies, being long stone receptacles, showing the outline of the head and shoulders;

these coffins resembling a human form are not older than the time of the Achaemenides and Macedonians. An inscription which has been much discussed states that Abd-elim, son of Matan, the son of Abd-elim, the son of Baal-Shomer, made a tomb-door in fulfilment of a vow to Baal-Shamim.

If one proceeds southward along the shore he comes to Ecdippa, a town mentioned in the Assyrian inscriptions, and then to Acca (Acre, or Ptolemais), at the northern end of the plain of Megiddo, which is bounded on the south by Carmel. Under the Persians and

FIG. 74.—'The Tomb of King Hiram' of Tyre.

the Diadochi the town flourished, but it did not attain its greatest prosperity till the time of the Crusades. Sailing around the promontory, one comes to Tantūra, the ancient Dōr, the last Phoenician town; its ruins, though of no great importance, extend quite a distance along the shore.

The Phoenicians, having even in early time directed their attention to navigation and trade, secured wealth and power. In the large cities kings ruled with the aid of counsellors selected from the oldest families, and of an influential order of priests. The cities became the centres of business in the trade carried on with the East, which introduced both Phoenician and imported goods and products into the interior of Asia. The Phoenicians were assured of the safe passage of the caravans by means of agreements with the rulers, and warehouses were established along the roads. The Phoenicians were aided in this by the fact that in many cases the roads passed through the territory of related peoples. They furnished purple woollen goods to the whole ancient world, and the manufacture of glass was so prominent among them that they are said to have invented it. In Egypt there are very ancient representations of glass-making (grotto of Beni-Hassan), and glass vessels have been found in graves dating even from the Fifth Dynasty. It is reasonable to suppose that a people like the Phoenicians, who were in the habit of seeing slag constantly in the preparation of ores, should even in very early times discover glazing for their pottery, and then should make glass itself. The Egyptians of the Eighteenth Dynasty mention among their booty Mesopotamian glassy flux, *kheshet*, or artificial lapis lazuli. Dr. Schliemann discovered in the second city of Hissarlik and in Mycenae glass balls and buttons of Phoenician and Egyptian manufacture; and Phoenician glass balls have been found even in the pile-houses of Switzerland and among the old Britons.

The shores of the Mediterranean, even as far west as the Straits of Gibraltar, were occupied by Phoenician colonies and trading-stations, which had the greatest influence upon the spread of the early Asiatic culture. The Phoenicians had warehouses in the Egyptian delta in Tanis, Mendes, Bubastis, Sais, and Memphis. Their first effort at colonization was in Cyprus, which was celebrated in all antiquity for its abundance of wood, metals (especially copper), fruit-trees, and vines; it was also very active in trade, and exported its carpets, clothing, leather-work, and ointments everywhere. Although the island was subsequently colonized by the Greeks, and experienced various vicissitudes, yet recently very many graves have been opened, which have revealed wonderful treasures of historical and artistic work. In very early times, Paphos was founded by citizens of Byblus; and Sidon and Tyre likewise sent out colonies. Larnaka stands upon the necropolis of Citium. In the Bible Cyprus is called Kittim; and there Di Cesnola found more than 2,000 graves, most of them belonging to the last four centuries before the Christian era, a Phoenician and a Greek temple; in the former were fragments of marble vessels and bowls with inscriptions of consecration to Melkarth and other gods: also a marble coffin with a head in high relief, Egyptian alabaster vases with Phoenician inscriptions. In Dali (Idalium), 15,000 graves were found, mostly Phoenician, with thousands of figures in terra-cotta, belonging to a very early period. In Golgi, also, there was a necropolis containing two ruined brick temples; in one of these were found about a thousand statues of Egyptian work and bas-reliefs of Assyrian. At Salamis no remains of antiquity were found; since its materials were used for the construction of Constantia and Famagusta, in the time of the Lusignans. In Curium, upon the southern coast of the island, Di Cesnola discovered a treasure-house with several underground chambers, from which he obtained an incredibly rich treasure, which had probably been secreted there in time of war; it is now deposited in the Metropolitan Museum at New York. It contains all kinds of valuable works made of silver, gold, bronze, precious stones, alabaster, and clay, which the Phoenicians manufactured in Egyptian and Assyrian style. This furnishes the richest information in regard to this transitional tendency in art.

Hittites, also, as well as Phoenicians, formed a portion of the population of Cyprus. This is embodied in the Greek tradition, which tells of the coming of Cinyras, son of Sandacus, from Cilicia. This Hittite population becomes of great importance in the history of the culture of the island; and it may be that they gave it a writing, which existed beside the Phoenician, and was employed by the Greeks, in Cyprus after the eighth century. In it the word *basileus* ('king') was not written with the eight letters forming the word, but with five syllabic signs, *ba-si-le-r(e)-s(e)*; in the genitive, *ba-si-le-ro-s(e)*. The Hittite monuments of the mainland have hieroglyphs, or picture-writing, which has not been deciphered. It is supposed, however, that the alphabet of the Cyprian Greek inscriptions may have been derived from those hieroglyphs. Fifty-five characters have some resemblance to them, though no conclusions can be drawn from this circumstance until the Hittite inscriptions shall have been satisfactorily deciphered.

After the occupation of Cyprus, the Phoenicians settled in the islands of the Aegean Sea and upon the coast of Asia Minor, where they exchanged their manufactures for slaves, skins, and wool, worked the mines, and collected the snails which furnished the purple. This intercourse was of incalculable importance to the Greeks, who at the beginning of the colonization, about the twelfth century B.C., were still in a primitive state, but who were also very quick to adopt new conditions. Thus both in the arts and in trade the Greeks became acquainted with the products of a culture centuries old, and copied them, and were enabled to interchange their thoughts by means of the Phoenician writing. The Phoenician mythology also played an important part in the religious belief of the Greeks; indeed, it can be shown that Phoenician sculpture on metal bowls was the occasion of the composition of mythological poems by the Greeks.

There were also Phoenician colonies in Crete, — at Itanos, Leben, and Araden. The coast of Sicily was dotted with their trading-stations, as Catana, Ortygia (Syracuse), Pachynus, Camarina, Megara or Rûs-Melkarth (Heraclea Minoa), Mazara, Motya, Eryx, Makhanath (Panormus, now Palermo). The Tyrian cities of the west coast as well as Selinus, Himera, and Agrigentum, were subject to Carthage (from c. 410). This circumstance brought on the Punic wars, in which two mighty powers, Carthage and Rome, contended with one another. The struggle was between the Semitic Orient, under the leadership of one of the greatest of soldiers, and the ancient Graeco-Roman civilization, whose overthrow would have caused incalculable consequences in the history of Europe.

The Phoenicians at a very early period occupied the islands Malta and Gozo, also Sardinia, which became partially subject to Carthage; they even went beyond Gibraltar, and founded Gades (Cadiz); and in company with the Iberian Turdetani and the Libyo-Phoenician agriculturists established a civilized empire in southern Spain, in the rich valley of the Baetis. This was seized by Carthage in the third century, and after long struggles yielded to Rome.

Sidon and Tyre established numerous colonies in Africa, — as Leptis, Hippo, Hadrumetum, Ruspina, Thapsus, Utica, and especially Carthage. These, in turn, extended their influence to coasts still more distant and into the interior of the land, establishing many towns, until Africa from Cyrene to the Atlantic Ocean became subject to them. They had commercial intercourse even with Cornwall in England, which furnished the countries bordering on the Mediterranean with tin, and amber was brought by them from the shores of the Baltic.

The influence of the Phoenician colonies was not limited to the extension of intellectual culture of various kinds. The Phoenicians brought with them from the Syrian coast to Europe plants designed for use and ornament. Victor Hehn has shown that the flora of the countries bordering on the Mediterranean, especially Italy, is totally different from that prevalent originally. This people succeeded in acclimatizing in more northern countries a great number of excellent fruit-trees and nut-bearing plants, which belonged to the sub-tropical region extending to the 34th degree of latitude. The cypress, introduced at an early period from eastern Iran into Babylonia and Canaan, the pomegranate, laurel, myrtle, olive-tree, fig, vine, — originally an Armenian plant, — cedar, quince, crocus, and numerous evergreen plants were carried beyond the Phoenician settlements to the west and north. These plants were connected in the mythology with the gods, who were likewise wholly or in part of Asiatic origin; and these wanderings of the plants, as well as the colonization, were treated mythologically, in that they were represented to have been effected by the sons of beneficent gods. Asiatic plants even from other portions of Asia continued to spread long after the Phoenicians gave place to the Greeks and Romans. Animals also accompanied their masters as they journeyed over the sea; only the donkey need be mentioned, which betrays its Phoenician origin in its name (*asinus*).

The tribes or clans who inhabited Palestine before the advent of the Israelites are enumerated many times in the Old Testament. The lists vary considerably, however, in the number of names included. That in Gen. xv. 18–21 contains ten, and even then omits one (that of the Hivites) found in nearly all the others. Several give only five or six. That which is perhaps the oldest of all names 'seven nations' — Canaanites, Hittites, Hivites, Perizzites, Girgashites, Amorites, and Jebusites (Josh. iii. 10; cf. Deut. vii. 1). Our knowledge concerning them is very scanty and fragmentary. The Jebusites were a small but energetic and warlike clan, who maintained their independence until the time of David. Their stronghold Jebus is repeatedly identified with Jerusalem (Jud. i. 21; xix. 10). Until recently Jebus was supposed to be the older name of Jerusalem; but the Tel-el-Amarna tablets, discovered in 1887, show that the latter name, in the form Urusalim, is the more ancient. When those tablets were written, about a century before the exodus, Palestine was subject to the king of Egypt, and ruled by satraps or viceroys of his appointment, who sometimes were the native princes. Such was evidently the governor of Urusalim, of whom a number of letters to the Egyptian sovereign are preserved in these tablets. There is no trace of Jebus or Jebusites in them; whence it follows that the Jebusite possession of Jerusalem was yet future. When and how it began, it is impossible to say; but it lasted several centuries. The Jebusites at last succumbed to David (2 Sam. v. 6 ff.), and seem to have become incorporated into Israel (Zech. ix. 7). Concerning the Girgashites, we only know that they dwelt west of the Jordan. They appear in only a few of the lists, and would seem to have been of small importance. The Hivites are met with in more places than one — at Shechem, Gibeon, and at the foot of Mount Hermon. If, as many think, their name originally signified 'dwellers in tent-towns,' it had certainly become inappropriate long before we meet with them. The Perizzites are the 'villagers,' peasants dwelling in unfortified places. The name would suggest a peaceable people, devoted to agriculture. The Hittites are named in all the lists, but are little heard of otherwise. One of David's 'mighty men,' who shamefully betrayed Uriah, whose wife became the mother of Judah's royal line, and Ahimelech, one of David's companions when hiding from Saul, are both styled Hittites. The narrative of the late, so-called priestly, writer (see p. 473) concerning the purchase of a sepulchre by Abraham, exhibits the Hittites, or 'Sons of Heth,' as settled inhabitants of a district near Hebron. Whether that was in part their location is a question of less interest than another which scholars find it difficult to answer satisfactorily. This concerns the relation of this Hittite tribe to the North Syrian peoples of somewhat advanced civilization, and bearing what appears to be the same name, known to us from Egyptian and Assyrian inscriptions, and through monuments of their own (cf. below, pp. 226 ff.). Were the Palestinian Hittites a division or offshoot of this great Syrian nation? That view is favored by passages of the Old Testament in which the name, without any closer definition, seems clearly to be applied to the larger, far more powerful group (1 Kings x. 29; 2 Kings vii. 6). But it is opposed by the fact that, so far as we know at present, the two peoples did not speak the same language. The Palestinian Hittites are classed by the table of nations in Genesis (x. 15–18) among the descendants of Canaan, Sidon being the elder brother of Heth. They must therefore have had the same general family marks, and have spoken the same language, as the Phoenicians, which we know was very nearly identical with Hebrew. The proper names of Hittites found in the Old Testament — Ephron, Zohar, Uriah, Ahimelech, Beeri, and Elon (the fathers of Judith and Basemath, wives of Esau) — agree with this, being all of decidedly Semitic, in fact Hebrew, type. On the other hand, althought it is impossible at present to determine the actual ethnic relations of the Syrian Hittites, it is tolerably clear that they were not Semites nor spoke a Semitic tongue. All things considered, the most plausible conjecture is, that the Palestinian Hittites, having long been separated from the main body, had become Semitized, or what is the same thing Canaanized, and yet, contrary to what usually happens in such cases, had retained their separate clan existence (like some remnants of Indian tribes in the eastern part of the United States), leading later times, oblivious of their true origin, to include them among the Canaanite tribes. The two remaining names of our list, Canaanites and Amorites, are both used as collectives, to denote the whole pre-Israelite population, — the former by one (J), the latter by two others (E and D) of the chief writers whose works form the basis of the first six books of the Old Testament, and by later writers after them. Primarily, however, both names must have denoted particular tribes. No writer would include either one or two names of the whole in an enumeration of the parts, unless they were also part-names. But the difficulty in many places of determining whether the names are intended to carry the larger or the more limited sense, makes it nearly impossible to gain any information concerning the particular tribes. Reasonings based on etymological interpretations are frequently precarious and misleading; and there is nothing to justify the view formerly held that Canaanite *meant* 'lowlander' and that Amorite signified 'mountaineer,' though such a distinction agrees with statements in the Old Testament. The Amorites are said to 'dwell in the mountains,' and the Canaanites 'by the sea and by the side of Jordan' (Num. xiii. 29). No doubt the two tribes illustrated the general rules of history: the lowlander, especially when seated by the sea, always surpasses the highlander in all the arts and pursuits of civilization.

Far more important than anything we can learn concerning the individual tribes, is the fact that they were all members of one approximately homogeneous group of nations, the same to which the Phoenicians and the Israelites themselves also belonged. According to the Genesis table of nations, Sidon (the representative of the Phoenicians) and the Hittites, the Jebusites, the Amorites, the Girgashites, the Hivites, and others who do not concern us here, were all descendants of Canaan, the son of Ham. This statement asserts what we may call the homogeneity, i.e., the essential likeness, notwithstanding all diversities, of the tribes specified. It seems, indeed, to go back of the fact, and to explain its existence upon the theory of physical descent and kinship; but that is mere form. At all events, the simple fact of homogeneity, however brought about, is all we here need; and as to that, all the evidence accessible at this late date is favorable to it. All these tribes spoke a common language. Their religion, notwithstanding marked differences, resulting from different degrees of culture and peculiar historical or local influences, was essentially the same. Their political constitutions and institutions had, in general, the same character. And all this applies to the Israelites also, except in so far as their religion was nearer the nomadic type. It is true, the table derives them, not from Canaan the son of Ham, but from Shem; but this unwarranted separation of the Hebrews from the Canaanitish groups is due to political history, which is illustrated in the curse pronounced upon 'Ham the father of Canaan' by Noah as related at the close of Chapter IX. of Genesis (vv. 25–28). The curse originally applied to Canaan, and when the term Ham came into use as a kind of ethnological purgatory, Canaan was made a 'son' of Ham. Incontestable facts warrant the inclusion of Phoenicians, Canaanites, Israelites, Aramaeans, Assyrians, Babylonians, and other less prominent peoples, into one great group of nations, distinguished from all others by many common features: and that, while it is convenient to call them Semites, it is not intended thereby to assert that all must have sprung from a common ancestry. It follows that the Israelites, when they entered their promised land as permanent settlers, did not, like the settlers of North America, come into contact with barbarous tribes of entirely alien speech and wholly strange institutions and manners. They encountered a civilization whose radical character was like their own, only in most respects much farther advanced. Their own religion was, indeed, greatly superior; but in its central features so recently received as to be scarcely more than put on, while that of the people of the land was akin to what had been, and so far as the mass of the people was concerned, practically still was their own. These are facts of great significance, and explain much in their subsequent history.

The Canaanites were not the aborigines of Palestine. They were preceded by a people of large stature and strength, who were known to the Israelites as Rephaim and Anakim. The list in Gen. xv. 19–21 names only the former, probably because it was a general term including the latter. The English version sometimes obliterates the name Rephaim by rendering it 'giants' (cf. Deut. ii. 11. iii. 11, 13). They appear to have been most numerous on the east of the Jordan, but were also found on the west side. The Emim, Zamzummim, Zuzim, were clans or local communities of them. Of their race relations nothing can be stated with certainty. The Israelites seem to have come into contact with mere remnants of them. The feelings of mystery and awe, and the legendary exaggerations that pervade Israelitish references to them, look more like the outcome of stories told about them by the Canaanites, than of Israel's own experiences transformed by tradition. These earlier populations may have been largely absorbed by the Canaanites, or they may have faded away before their superior civilization.

The list in Genesis speaks also of Kenites, Kenizzites, and Kadmonites. The last named are mentioned nowhere else, unless it be in Gen. xxv. 15 (Kedemah). Their name signifies 'Eastrons,' and may denote Ishmaelites (cf. Gen. xxv. 6). Two Ishmaelite tribes, Nebaioth and Kedar, were at home in northern Arabia. The Kenizzites were an Edomite tribe, a clan of which, represented by Caleb, the companion of Joshua (Num. xxxii. 12), and Othniel the deliverer of Israel from Mesopotamian oppression (Jud. iii. 9 f.), was incorporated into the tribe of Judah. The interesting Kenite clan also called Kain (Jud. iv. 11, R. V. margin), is by some Old Testament passages connected with the Midianites, an Arab tribe of considerable attainments in the arts of civilized life. Other notices (1 Sam. xv. 6; Num. xxiv. 21 f.) suggest relationship with the Amalekites, an old and prominent Bedouin tribe of the Sinaitic peninsula. Perhaps the greater weight of critical opinion favors the latter view; but a decision is difficult. The Kenites were nomads. According to Israelitish tradition, Moses married into the clan. A part of them cast in their fortunes with Israel, and entered Canaan with them. We meet them in the pasture lands of the south of Judah as late as the time of David. At an earlier day some of them are found far to the north, near Kadesh-Naphtali. They had adopted both Israel and the religion of Israel, and were passionately attached to one and the other. For one part of this statement, see Judges, ch. iv.; the other depends on the accuracy (which there is no sufficient reason to doubt) of 2 Chron. ii. 55, according to which the Rechabites of later days were Kenites (cf. 2 Kings x. 15 ff.). There is nothing to show that either of these three tribes or clans held lands in Canaan before the advent of the Israelites, as the Genesis list seems to imply. The list is of a comparatively late date.

The immediate, permanent neighbors of Israel, besides the Phoenicians and Philistines, already spoken of (pp. 201 ff.), were cognate nations, who were in possession of their respective territories long before Israel's settlement in Canaan. The Edomites occupied the mountainous region between the Dead Sea and the Gulf of Akabah. Their country, ill adapted for agriculture, made them a people of hunters, traders, and marauders, quite after the type of their reputed ancestor Esau. Of their religion nothing is known with certainty; yet there is some reason to believe that it resembled the religion of Israel (in its popular form) more nearly than any other. The Moabites, on the contrary, were devoted to the Canaanite or Phoenician religion, in its softer, sensual form, though not without occasional recourse to its severer features, as exhibited in human sacrifices (2 Kings iii. 27). Their land, the northern boundary of which varied at different times, lay along the eastern side of the Dead Sea. It was mountainous, suitable for pasture ground, yet also largely arable, fruitful, and fairly well watered. The Mesha stone with its inscription, belonging to the ninth century before Christ (discovered in 1868), evinces a good degree of literary culture among the Moabites of that early day. The Ammonites were near relations of the Moabites. Their territorial possessions are less certainly definable. They seem never to have touched the Jordan or the Dead Sea, but to have lain east and northeast of Moab. Rabbath-Ammon, the capital city, was situated near the southernmost sources of the Jabbok, in a district suitable for agriculture. The main body of the people were keepers of herds and flocks. They were less civilized than the Moabites, and in religion leaned more to the severer form. Their Baal was Milcom, or Moloch, the most terrible of all the Semitic gods, to whom human sacrifices, especially children, were offered.

Farther to the north and northeast we meet the Aramaean Semites, holding the broad plains that stretch from Mount Hermon and Iturea (Jetur and Geshur), by way of Damascus, to the Euphrates and beyond it into Mesopotamia, where a fusion took place with earlier inhabitants of the land between the two great rivers. Only in later days did the Aramaeans spread also into the Lebanon region and the Taurus lands, where formerly the Hittites and their allies bore sway.[1]

Concerning the Hittites, to whom we are thus led back, very many and reliable notices are contained in Egyptian and Assyrian inscriptions. The former name them Kheta, the latter Chatti. The conjecture that the inscriptions of Hamath on the Orontes were Hittite memorials has been confirmed by the fact that hieroglyphic writing similar to that in Hamath was found in excavations at Jerablus on the Euphrates, which Assyrian inscriptions declare to have been the site of Carchemish, the chief city of the Hittites. A similar style of writing, subsequently discovered upon monuments in

[1] The six paragraphs preceding (pp. 220-226), on the Palestinian tribes, are by Rev. Professor P. H. Steenstra, and replace material in the German original.

Syria and Asia Minor, has led to the inference that the term Hittites was employed to denote groups of peoples who spread over Syria and a great part of Asia Minor. The fact that the Assyrians did not succeed in getting lasting possession of the right bank of the Euphrates until after several centuries of conflict goes to prove the existence of a large Hittite kingdom. Egyptian monuments prove that the Pharaohs also regarded the conflict with the Kheta as a matter of grave importance, and the Tel-el-Amarna tablets dating from the fifteenth century show that at this time the Hittites already played a considerable role in Syria. Some of the Hittite monuments are accompanied by inscriptions, so that we have become acquainted with the characteristics of Hittite art, and are enabled to recognize it even when we come across monuments without inscriptions. A brief review of some of these antiquities will give the reader a clearer idea of the extent of the power of this group.

Hamath on the Orontes is the most southerly place where Hittite monuments have been found. This city was at the head of a small kingdom extending from the watershed between the Orontes and Leontes to Jisr-hadîd, where the Orontes turns westward. Burckhardt was the first to make known (in 1812) the five inscriptions imbedded in the wall of the bazaar. They are now in Constantinople, and casts were brought to England in 1863. Burton and Drake gave an incomplete copy of them. Wright and Ward were the first to call them Hittite.

At Aleppo a stone was found built into the mosque, upon which was a figure with a partially effaced Hittite inscription consisting of two lines. Carchemish, now called Jerablus, lat. 36° 50', formed with its walls the half of a circle, which was completed by the curved line of the Euphrates. The citadel is in the northern part, on an elevation. Fragments of Hittite sculpture were found here, a lion and human figures, among which was a very well preserved one of a king. His shoes are turned up in front, which is a marked characteristic of the Hittite attire, as well as of the Etrurian. The nine inscriptions from Carchemish, now in the British Museum, are still among the most important of the Hittite remains, though discoveries of inscriptions elsewhere have added material for the study of the Hittite language.

Birejik (Assyrian Tel-Barsip) is farther up the Euphrates than Carchemish, at an important crossing, where the road through Mesopotamia begins, used in the time of the Parthians as also to-day. The paved slope and artificial elevation of rock, upon which the citadel stands, are of Hittite origin. Within are arched passages; even in Pococke's time (1740) this was equipped with catapults and other Roman instruments of defence. There is a stone in the British Museum with the figure of a praying king, having the high Hittite tiara, from which a wig descends behind, and shoes with pointed toes; over the whole the winged disk of the sun.

Marmier found a relief in Rum-Kalah, a neighboring place. It represents a man with a long robe, tightly bound with a girdle, holding a kind of club in the right hand, while a cylindrical object (perhaps a wallet) is suspended from the arm; the left hand holds an object which has not yet been explained; perhaps a sort of shepherd's flute.

Still farther north is the territory of Kummukh (Commagene), the chief city of which in later times was Samosata. This city had control of a road which crossed the Euphrates at this point, on its way from southeastern Cappadocia to Edessa and Haran (Carrhae). In the southern portion of this kingdom, which was closely connected with that of the Hittites, was Doliche, now called Dulluk, north of Aintab. Gargar is an inaccessible cliff on the Euphrates, where the river breaks through a rocky gorge with great force. There is a footpath cut in the rock, and in a niche the relief of a king with an inscription. Farther in the mountains, on the Kiachta River, at Nemrud-Dagh, is a monument with a Greek inscription, erected by Antiochus of Commagene in honor of his ancestors and of certain gods, including the patron goddess of the district. Near by the Bolan-su is crossed by a Roman bridge, which has an inscription of Septimius Severus, in which the river is called Chabinas. In Marash, Puchstein found four reliefs and a lion, some of which had inscriptions; and farther south, in Saktshe-gözü, a lion-hunt upon three smoothed rocks. Inland from Alexandretta, which is on the bay of Issus, sculpture was found upon the rocks by an English officer. This region belonged to the Patinai, allies of the Hittites, as did also the region of Arpad, now called Tel-Erfad, north of Aleppo, where stones are met with having ornaments like those in Carchemish.

The largest monuments are in Cappadocia. Milid (Melitene) is the southeastern portion of this district, where the Tabal, or Tibareni, anciently lived. Here in a ravine of the upper Kamunas (Tochma-su), which flows into the Euphrates at Melite, is Gar-naka, now called Gurun, where there are two Hittite inscriptions. The Cappadocian sculptures have a somewhat different style from

FIG. 75. Sphinx of the Palace Entrance at Euyuk

those in Carchemish, in that the attire differs more from the Babylonian, and there is more movement. Between Amasia on the Iris, where there are ancient royal sepulchres in the steep mountain-side above the city, and Amisus on the coast, Ramsay found two stones with rude sculptures, representing a king with servants in Hittite dress, while prisoners in Phrygian dress are conducted before him. There is a cuneiform writing above the scene; the characters of the inscription upon a second stone are wholly unknown. Schrader has shown that the first representation is in imitation of a known relief in Kouyunjik (Nineveh), upon which Jewish prisoners from Lachish are being conducted before Sennacherib. Not far to the northeast of Alaja, where there is a Hittite tomb, is the village Euyuk. It has a gateway, with a wall fourteen feet long on each side. The doorposts (Fig. 75) are monoliths twelve feet high, representing sphinxes with wings, the claws of lions, and human heads, whose locks are arranged as in the Egyptian masks of Hathor. The reliefs cut upon the lowest course of the wall are a god, having an altar before him, and a priest bringing a goat, followed by three oxen; also a man with a stringed instrument, a snake-charmer, a flute-player, and two men with the plan of a palace. There is a remarkable double-headed eagle carved upon the inside of the eastern door-post (Fig. 76). It is the bird of the Thunderer, originally the winged lightning or thunderbolt, as wielded by the god Bel-Marduk, and as represented also upon the Greek coins of Elis and Sicily. The Seljuks, after their conquest of Cappadocia and Lycaonia, in 1217 A.D., adopted this ancient symbol, and stamped it upon their copper coins.

Boghaz-keui is situated upon the road from Adaja to Juzgat, southwest of Alada and north of Nefez-keui, which is thought to be the city Tavia. It is a village lying 3,150 feet above the sea, on the site of the ancient Pteria, which Croesus destroyed upon the approach of the Persians. The ravine, through which a stream flows that empties into the Halys, expands near this village into a plain. The mountains remain near the river on the right bank; but on the opposite side they recede toward the north in terraces, which were occupied by the ancient city. The walls are high upon the mountain, and have a circumference of from three to three and one-half miles. Near the little river the ground-plan of a building (palace) can still be recognized: it consists of a large hall about 89 feet long and 75 feet wide, in front of which is a double porch with three gateways. About thirty rooms can be distinguished. Upon the side away from the town, a broad stairway led to a platform 160 feet long. The stones of this structure are often sixteen to twenty feet long, and are dovetailed together like wood-work, instead of being placed side by side as in Persepolis. The stone is marble (limestone), but the porch is tra-

Fig. 76. — Double Eagle on the Door-posts of the Palace at Eyuk.

chyte or basalt. The upper portion of the walls, which consisted probably of sun-dried brick, were destroyed by Crœsus. A throne ornamented with lions was found upon the platform. An underground room extends from the brook toward the terrace. The rock to the west has been prepared for a walk; to the south a portion of the wall of rock has been cut at a slight inclination, smoothed and divided into sections by means of ten bands with hieroglyphics. Upon the side of the hill away from the brook are the remains of ancient fortifications; within and without the wall are several rocky

77.

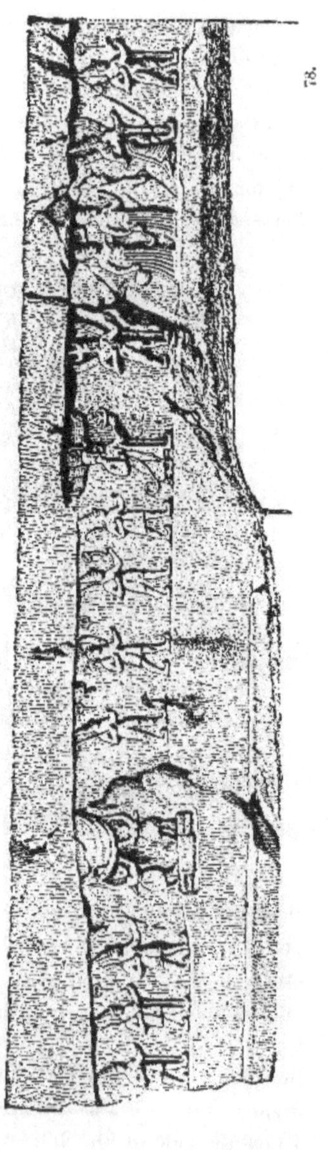

78.

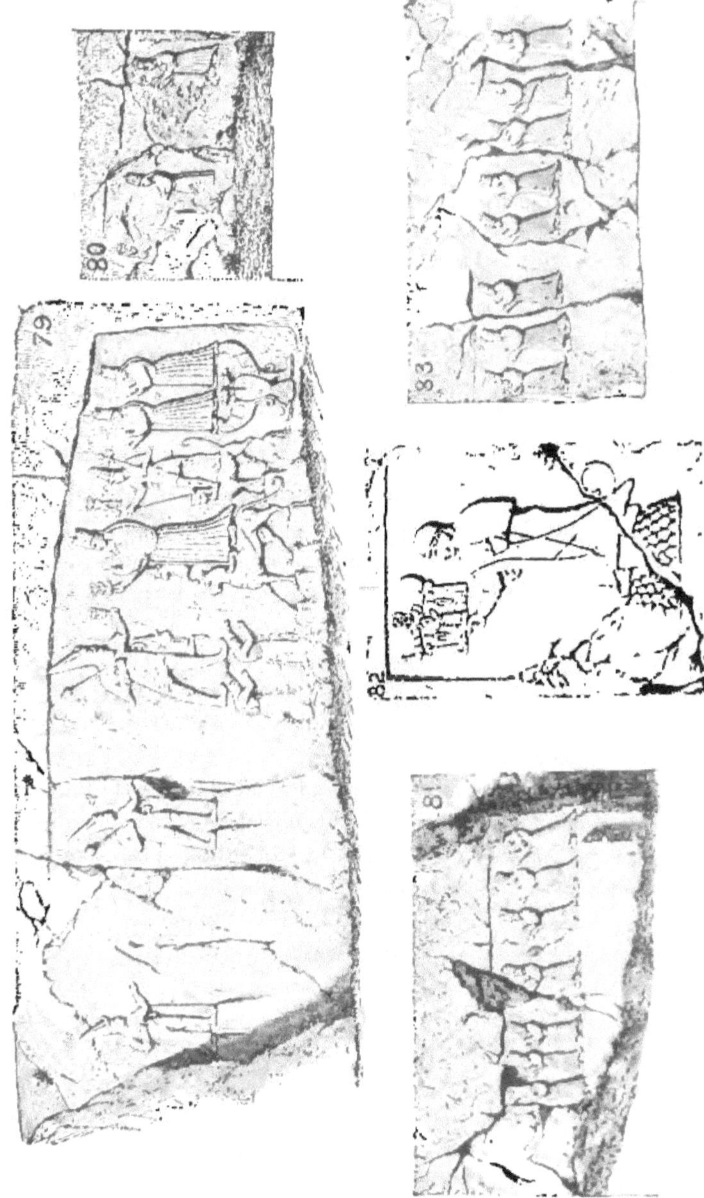

FIGS. 79-83.—A Hittite Religious Procession of Men and Women. Relief at Pteria, Boghaz Keui.

points occupied by walls, and the wall was also protected by a trench and a sloping glacis. Within are passages, which open into the trench. One of these, under the highest part of the enclosing wall, consists of five courses of rough stones. These project from both sides: and the space, which is closed at the top by inserted blocks, has the appearance of a vault having straight, instead of curved, sides. A very similar passageway is found in Tiryns; the Cyclopian walls, which are frequent in Asia Minor, Greece, and Etruria, and served for walls and substructions of long rows of buildings, were perhaps of Hittite origin. This Hittite citadel was destroyed more than 2400 years ago; but there are natural caves in the rocks, called Jazili-Kaja ('inscribed rock'), which are just as remarkable. They are about forty minutes distant from the citadel, and have their entrance upon that side. The rocks surrounding this space form a perpendicular wall 30–50 feet high. A rock projecting from the eastern wall marks the entrance. Immediately upon entering, one finds himself in the broadest part of the room. Near the ground a seat has been hewn out, which is still visible in some places. Upon a smoothed surface, some feet from the ground, are sixty-five figures in relief (Figs. 77–83); the largest, representing the chief persons, are five feet high, their attendants three and a half feet, and the rest only two and a half feet. The whole design, which is a very remarkable one, is covered with a yellowish stucco. There are two processions, which start at the entrance, and meet at the rear of the room, the one passing around to the right and the other to the left. The procession upon the right consists of women, all of whom wear long garments fastened about the waist with girdles, ear-rings, and high mural crowns, from which long hair falls down behind. There is only one male figure. The woman heading the procession, and at the rear of the hall, stands upon a lion, as do Ishtar and Atargatis; and by her side the forward part of a leaping gazelle or chamois is visible. Her left hand is extended, and contains an ornament resembling a plant. The Hittite inscriptions show that this is the ideograph or hieroglyph representing her name. She wears beak-shaped shoes, as Juno of Lanurium had *calceoli repandi.* Behind this goddess follows a god, who stands upon a leopard (?), just as the Cilician Sandon is represented upon the coins of Tarsus as standing upon a lion. The god, as well as almost all the human figures, wears a high, pointed, fluted tiara, which rises from a sort of a low helmet. This is also worn by later princes of Cappadocia and Commagene, such as Ariaramnes of Cappadocia, Mithradates of Commagene, and Sames of Samosata. His dress, as well as that of the remaining male figures, consists of a short robe (apron); in his left hand he holds a double axe with a cross at the end, and in his right a staff crooked at the end. The hilt of a Hittite sword is seen at his side. In front of him is the hieroglyph representing his name. Behind him are two women, under whom the eagle with two heads is poised. Some of the women that follow also carry in their hands characters representing their names, and the rest hold bent staves turned downward. In the corner next the entrance, that is, at the end of the procession of women, is a priest; one can determine this by means of the lituus which he holds in his left hand, pointed downwards. The occurrence of this in Asia Minor, in the neighborhood of Lydia, and among the Roman-Etrurian augurs, as well as much else, shows the connection of Asia Minor with Etruria. He wears a mantle over his under-garment, thrown back over his shoulder, and a tight-fitting cap, like that of the Kheta on the Egyptian sculptures. He stands upon a mountain, and holds in his right hand a peculiar symbol, which can scarcely be a hieroglyph indicating his rank or office. It consists of a somewhat reduced temple or shrine, with a winged disk of Hittite style for its covering; above which there is still another; and upon the sides are the supporting columns, with volutes clearly marked; within these end-columns are two high objects, which may be regarded as caryatides; and in the middle the representation of the goddess, with wings instead of arms, can be seen. This representation is repeated, but on a smaller scale. Turning now to the opposite side, to the procession of men, at the end we find a priest above whose head is the winged disk; in his right hand the lituus, and in his left the hieroglyph indicating deity. This procession is more varied than that of the women. The figures are in profile, except that we have a front view of the breast and shoulders, in order that there may be a freer movement of the arms. The figures of the women are entirely in profile, so that of the right arm only the hand is visible; and the left arm, which is raised, conceals the breast. The male figure at the head of the procession, who therefore meets the goddess in the rear of the hall, is standing with his feet upon two slaves. He has a beard, and carries a club in his right hand. He is shown to be a god by the hieroglyph held in his left hand. A horned animal is springing forth near him. Behind him are two figures standing upon a rock, which are also bearded, as well as the last one before the priest. This one has wings; and upon the upper part of the tiara, or of the high helmet, cone-shaped points like the *shairetana* of the Egyptian art. A group of thirteen running or dancing youths remind one strongly of the Egyptian groups which accompany the sitting colossal figures as they are transported. At quite a distance in front of the rocky hall, in a recess of the rock, are two human figures with the heads of a dog and a lion, and apparently with wings, perhaps to frighten demons away from the procession. Southeast of this, and adjoining it in a somewhat long rocky chamber, are twelve armed warriors cut in the rock, and opposite them a Mylitta, curiously carved; upon her head is a high tiara; her shoulders consist of lions' heads, her sides and belly are formed by two outstretched lions with head down; and the body terminates like a Greek Herma. In front is a god (Fig. 84), who holds in his extended right hand a hieroglyph, resembling a child with a large head, and whose left arm is thrown about the neck of a priest, who reaches up to his shoulder. He is conducting this priest into the presence of the goddess. Above the figures at the right is the winged disk. It is difficult to conjecture what gods are represented. The goddess related to Astarte may be Anat, the goddess of Kadesh; and the god Rezeph, or the Phoenician-Hittite war-god, who is called Baal-Sutekh in the treaty of peace between the Hittites and Egyptians, which is to be mentioned later.

Cappadocia was probably the place from which the Hittite power spread.[1] The country is called Khammanu in the Assyrian inscriptions: but in the northeastern section of it there lived the Kaskai, and in the direction toward Melitene, the Muskai. Later the Phrygian-Armenian races crowded in from the west, and drove back the

[1] Professor W. M. Ramsay maintains that the Hittites merely inherited, but did not originate, the art of Cappadocia, and that the ancient people of Cappadocia were accordingly of a very different stock. — ED.

Muskai, together with the Tabal in Milid, toward the northeast, where the ancient writers became acquainted with them as small mountain tribes under the name of Colchians, Moschi, and Tibareni. Other Hittite races dwelt farther south, as far as the Cilician coast; and even Cicero mentions a part of the Tabal, under the name Tibarani, in Pindenissus on Mt. Amanus, above the bay of Issus.

Fig. 84. — Relief from Boghaz-keui.

In Kaisariyeh (Mazaca), at the foot of Erjish-dagh (Argaeus) Ramsay found five clay tablets with Cappadocian cuneiform writing together with a scarabaeus and a terra-cotta whorl, similar to that represented in Schliemann's Ilios as No. 1490. In Galatia, Perrot and Guillaume found a lion built into the wall of a spring before the gates of Angora, which is like the one discovered by Layard in Arban. In Giaur-Kalesi, nine hours southwest of this place, upon the old road from Cappadocia to Pessinus and Sardis, there are Cyclopian walls made of polygonal stones, prepared upon the surface and at the joints; and upon the rocks below are two Hittite warriors (Fig. 85). These are on the very ancient military road leading to the western part of Asia Minor. A second road farther south ran westward from Cilicia, upon which also Hittite monuments are found. The so-called tomb of Sardanapalus, at Tarsus, is perhaps of Hittite

FIG. 85.—Cyclopean wall at Giaur-Kalesi, with two Hittite warriors in relief.

origin. Ancient Tyana, now Kiz-hissar, in Cataonia, whence the descent was made over the Cilician passes to Tarsus, was built, according to Strabo, upon a terrace, by Semiramis: and it was therefore in existence even in the Assyrian period. Ramsay discovered inscriptions which were not in raised relief like the rest, but sunken. Southwest of here, between Tshifteh-khan and the silver mines of Bulghar, is an inscription almost effaced by the weather; and near it, in relief, are a god and two small figures with an inscription. In Bulghar-Maden itself, Davis found some hieroglyphs. He also discovered the great relief in Ivris, three hours southeast of Cybistra, or Heracleia, on the borders of Lycaonia. The place lies under the chain of the Bulghar-dagh, in a ravine watered by a clear brook, and abounding in fine nut-trees. There is a bridge from Ivris over the stream; and a canal runs along at the foot of a rock, whose smoothed front bears the relief. About eight or nine feet from the water is a figure twenty feet tall (Fig. 86), the god of Cilicia. He has a beard upon his chin; and his head is covered with a pointed hat, around which twigs with projecting points are wound. His garment does

Fig. 86. — Relief from Ivris.

not reach the knees; the legs are very muscular, as in Assyrian figures; the shoes are high and pointed, like those now used by the natives. In his left hand, which is uplifted, the god holds tall stalks of wheat with bearded heads; in his right hand a vine with clusters of grapes; he is like Aptuchos, the Libyan god of fertility, upon a carnelian in the Demidoff collection, and Baal upon the Hellenized coins of Tarsus, with the legend Baal Tarz. Between the heads of grain and the face are hieroglyphics. The smaller figure before the god is a priest (?), who is holding his hand to his face as a mark of adoration. He has a beard, shoes with pointed tips, and a long garment girt at the waist, which has the Hittite pattern of squares with points in the centre. The mantle covers the left arm, and hangs down at the side; and on the edge of the skirt in front there is a tassel. Behind him are four lines of hieroglyphics. Lower down, just above the water, there is a third inscription. Not far from Ivris, in the neighborhood of Frahtin, other Hittite sculptures have been found.

In Iflatun-Bunnar, in Lycaonia, west of Iconium, near Lake Beishehr (Lake Carillis). there is, upon a building constructed with large blocks of stone, a group of ten figures; one of these is that of a god wearing a small hat, to the right of whom is a goddess, who has her hair dressed in a peculiar manner, like the sphinx of Euyuk. On the road from Chonos, south of the ancient Colossae, to Isbarta, north of Sagalassus, is Lake Jarishli. Upon this lake, on the site of ancient Lysinia, are sculptures, which are probably of Hittite origin. Only a short distance west of this, at Kara-atlu, are two weather-beaten figures. Hittite sculptures seem to have been found also northeast of Cibyra.

From Sardis, where the two great roads mentioned come together, only one continues to Smyrna. The influence of Hittite power and culture reached even this place; for here are the sculptures of the so-called Sesostris and Niobe (Cybele), which have been known since the earliest times. The figure of Sesostris has improperly received this name through the influence of Herodotus (ii. 106). Half an hour south of the road running from Smyrna to Sardis, and southeast of Nimfi (Nīf), in the Karabel ravine between Nīf-dagh (Olympus) and Mahmūd-dagh (Dracon), there is the figure of a Hittite prince in relief represented as walking in the direction of Ephesus. It is high up on the face of the rock. in a shallow niche, which becomes somewhat contracted at the top. Here we have the pointed tiara, the short robe, and the peaked shoes. The left hand is extended, and holds an upright spear; the right, a bow: and the hilt of a short sword is visible in front, in the girdle. There are hieroglyphics in front of the face, which Sayce has copied. Ten minutes distant, and just above the path, is a second figure, very much injured, upon a rock between the present road and the small river Karasu. It resembles the other, only there is less energy of movement; its face is turned toward Sardis. This figure appears to be the one described by Herodotus; but, as the present road runs behind the rock, Humann was the first to discover it in 1875. At Ali-agha, in the plain of the Hermus, southeast of the ancient Cyrene, is a pre-Hellenic fortification with Cyclopean walls: and near it is a relief similar to the one at Nimfi. Farther on are the mounds known as the Tombs of Tantalis; they are round, and are surmounted with pyramids. Texier describes one which was constructed in this way: walls radiate from the centre to the circular enclosing wall, and the intervening spaces are filled with refuse stones. The chamber is vaulted over with a pointed arch; but this is not constructed with keystones, but is hewn out of the rock. The stylobate of the tumulus, the chamber, in fact the whole character of the tomb, are the same which the cemeteries at Caere, or Tarquinii, in Italy, exhibit. Near Magnesia, on Mount Sipylus, is a figure of Cybele, which is probably the oldest work of art in Asia Minor; but it has been greatly injured by the weather, and its artistic qualities have been almost concealed by incrustation. It is more than twenty feet high, and is in a sitting posture, like the Athena in Troy (Iliad. vi. 297). The figure is not in relief, like those previously described, but half round. This peculiarity may indicate that here in a very ancient Lydian kingdom, from which the Greek tradition has preserved the names of Tantalus and Pelops, and which later developed into the kingdom of Sardis, we have forms of art differing somewhat from the Hittite. This city upon Mount Sipylus, in whose circuit these monuments are found, was visited, as Pausanias says, by a divine judgment, and swallowed up in the marshy lake of Saloe. This stagnant body of water is two hours distant from Magnesia, and the statue of Cybele is visible about a hundred feet above its surface. The throne of Pelops is said to stand above the statue: and Humann there found remains of the Tantalids, — rock houses, and cisterns shaped like bottles. The highest southern block of stone has been hewn out in the shape of a prism, large enough to form a seat for a man. It is claimed that the figure of the goddess Cybele still shows that it had a diadem around its head. Dennis discovered hieroglyphs on the northeast side, above the head. Gollob distinguished two other inscriptions under the Hittite one; namely, a cartouche of Rameses II., and a second Hittite inscription. The Egyptian characters are not made very correctly; but their existence here indicates that the coast of Asia Minor had begun to feel the Egyptian influence, and causes us to assign this work, with some probability, to the time of the Pharaoh mentioned; that is, to the fourteenth century B.C. About 1600 feet eastward is a vast fissure (Turkish, Jarikkaja, 'the rent rock'), more than three hundred feet wide in places, whose walls rise five hundred feet high. This is the Achelous of the Iliad (xxiv. 616), where Niobe mourned after being changed into a stone. It has been thought that the figures of Cybele and of Niobe were one and the same, but Pausanias speaks of two. One is that of Cybele, the Mother of the Gods, upon the rock of Coddinus, near Magnesia, which, according to Pausanias, is the oldest sculpture found on Grecian soil, and which Broteas, the son of Tantalus, made; the other is the figure of Niobe, which near by looks like a natural stone, but at a distance appears to be the bowed form of a woman weeping. Upon the northern slope of Sipylus, about ten minutes east of the figure of Cybele, is a cone-shaped stone (phallus) with a niche on both sides, which also belongs to the pre-Hellenic period. Of special interest are two Hittite inscriptions found in Babylon, an inscribed bowl, and a magnificent stele of diorite found by the German Expedition in August, 1899, with a picture of the Hittite storm god Teshup, together with an inscription of a little over six lines. The monument must have been carried to Babylon as a trophy from some Hittite centre. (PLATE XVII.—*B.*)

Besides the monuments which have been referred to, and which are still in position, and none of which are later than the eighth century, because the Hittite kingdom was at that time destroyed by the Assyrians, there are many smaller antiquities, more particularly seal cylinders. Especially worthy of mention is an embossed seal (Fig. 87), made from a thin plate of silver in the form of a segment of a sphere; it was attached to the hilt of a staff or dagger. This came to light in Smyrna, but disappeared again after an electrotype copy had been made for the British Museum. On each side of the figure of the Hittite prince are six hieroglyphs, corresponding to one an-

PLATE XVII. B

Hittite Monument found in Babylon

History of All Nations, Vol. I, p. 42

other and having the same meaning, which is evidently reproduced in the Assyrian cuneiform writing running around the edge. This begins opposite the left hand with the perpendicular wedge; this wedge indicates that a proper name follows; the three following wedges read *tar*, the next nine *qu*, then *dim* follows, expressed by five wedges, then *me* is expressed by a vertical wedge with a small one upon its side; the next six form the ideograph for 'king,' the next three with their points together mean 'land;' the next five read *er;* then the syllable *me* occurs again; and the last are *e*. The meaning of the whole is *Tarkudimme, king of (the) land Erme.* From this one would judge that the Hittite characters within the field should be interpreted as follows: the head of the animal represents *Tarku;* the figure under it *dimme;* the obelisk would indicate 'king'; the double mountain, 'land'; and the two remaining characters would be *er-me.* The first part of the name of the king appears to be that of a god, Tarku; and this occurs also in Tarkhulara, the name of a king of Gurgum, and in Tarkhunazi, that of the king of Meliddu. It is worthy of notice that this Hittite name appears several times, even in late antiquity; for example, in the time of Augustus there lived the princes Tarcondimotus and Tarcondarius. Plutarch mentions a Tarcondemus. A tribe in Mylasa in Caria was called Tarcondareis; and there was a Tarcodimatus, bishop of Aegae in Cilicia. The land Erme was perhaps that of the Arimi, whom Strabo locates in southern Cilicia, on the lower Calycadnus. While certain conclusions to be drawn from a study of this seal are of considerable importance, they do not suffice to solve the mystery of the Hittite script.

FIG. 87. Seal of Tarcondemus

Various works of a Hittite character have been found. In the brick library of Asurbanipal at Nineveh, eight clay impressions of Hittite seals were found, but four of them are identical. The presence of these in the Assyrian capital can be explained by the marriage of the Assyrian king with the daughter of Sandasharme of

Cilicia. Also eighteen clay impressions of seals, which Schlumberger secured in Constantinople, should be mentioned. Upon one of these there is a god upon a lion, having in his right hand a bow, as in the relief of Nimfi; there are also five stone seals in Berlin. A large number of hematite cylinders were found in Cappadocia, the Taurus, and Northern Syria, which have figures resembling those in Boghaz-keui. In Naples there is a gold seal-ring with the figure of a Hittite warrior raising up a hare. Di Cesnola found a seal in Cyprus, containing a figure resembling that of Nimfi, which represents a gazelle contending with a dog, and a hunter thrusting his spear into the neck of the gazelle; the inscription upon one side consists of two Hittite hieroglyphs, that upon the other of the two Cyprian syllabic signs *ja* and *po*. Various antiquities from Asia Minor have Cyprian characters, and these cannot therefore be regarded as Hittite memorials; still, they show that the Greeks as well as Lycians, Carians, and others before the adoption of the Phoenician alphabet made use of a script, — called by some 'Asian,' — which is derived from the Hittite hieroglyphs. This was employed a long time, especially in Cyprus. The letters which were lacking in the Phoenician alphabet were supplied in the writing of Asia Minor from the 'Asian;' the arrangement of the lines, running alternately from left to right, and right to left (*boustrophedon*) is Hittite, as the hieroglyphs upon the stones of Hamath clearly show. It also appears that a mystical sign, which was widely diffused, and which has been designated by a Sanskrit word *swastika*, is of Hittite origin. It consists of a cross, the four ends of which are bent toward the side. It is thought that it really represents the oldest means of striking fire; namely, two pieces of wood, which were rubbed at their intersection by a third, until the wood ignited. As in the mythological picture-language conceptions were frequently united, so the generation of fire is united with fertility, life, and good fortune. Countless examples of this sign are found upon vessels in Asia Minor and in the Greek islands, also upon objects from Schliemann's Troy. The *swastika* occurs much later in India; it passed thence, with Buddhism, to Tibet and Eastern Asia, even to Japan, where it forms the coat-of-arms of the Daimio family Hachisuka.

The eastern portion of Asia Minor was occupied by Hittites and cognate peoples, who in the earliest period ruled the whole peninsula. The Lydian dynasty of the Heraclidae seem to have been of Hittite origin. The western portion, however, gradually passed from under their influence, because independent kingdoms arose which became hostile to Asia, especially after the Hittite kingdom was destroyed by the Assyrians, and after the Median power spread beyond Armenia. The chief people of western Asia Minor were the Phrygians, who crossed over the Hellespont from Europe. The monuments found in Phrygia probably belong to the Hittite period, for Greek art had not yet made its influence felt so far inland; but they are later in time, for the inscriptions upon them are in a writing derived in the eighth century B.C. from the Ionian, and containing also some Phrygian characters. Here belong the monument called Deliktash ('the excavated stone'), at Harmanjik, upon the Rhyndacus; and the graves at Doganlu, south of Dorylaeum (Eski-Shehr), upon one of which (Fig. 88) is the name of Midas. At the latter place is an entire citadel, which, together with its approaches, is cut out of the solid rock. These monuments show a close connection with the Cappadocian. The outside of the tomb presents a large flat façade, above which runs a geometric embroidery pattern. The pediment is also flat, and ornamented with rows of squares, and is crowned at the top with spirals. These decorations were colored, as appears on the Deliktash. This latter is covered in many places with stucco, and shows still black, red, and white coloring. The cap-piece of the door was adorned with red rings, and its under side is decorated with beautiful foliage. The façade has the appearance of a wall hung with Phrygian carpets. There appears to be a door at the bottom near the ground; but it is not a real one, for the entrance is from the top. But the opening of the shaft is concealed by the growth of plants, so that it has been found only in the case of a single grave.

The ancients affirm that the Mysians, who were a warlike race in the north of Lydia, spoke a language between the Phrygian and Lydian. Although the statements of the Greeks upon linguistic matters cannot be relied upon, since they did not treat of the relationship of languages upon scientific principles, yet this view can perhaps be regarded as correct, as it is favored by the geographical position of the people. The Carian language is also believed to be related to the Lydian, although the Carians in many respects occupied a peculiar position. Cognate with the Lydians and Carians were the Leleges, to whom many Cyclopian walls and pre-Hellenic

FIG. 88.—The Tomb of Midas.

fortifications are ascribed. Adjoining the Lydians are the inhabitants of the Troad; adjoining the Phrygians are the Bithynians, the Mariandyni and Paphlagonians, who, like them, came from Thrace. The Thracians built the lowest city of Hissarlik, the pottery and stone remains of which are the same as those discovered in the so-called Hill of Protesilaus on the European shore of the

Hellespont, which belong to the stone age of the Aryan race. The Phrygian is an Aryan language, which is connected on the one hand with the Thracian and Lithuanian, and upon the other with the Armenian. It is probable that the Cappadocians, whose name does not appear till the inscriptions of the Achaemenides, is that portion of the Aryans which conquered the old Hittite Khammanu. It can be assumed that many Indo-European peoples entered into Asia Minor even in very ancient time, just as the Cimmerians did later, mingled with the earlier inhabitants, and adopted the culture of Asia Minor. The origin of the Lycians, whose native name was Termil, is wholly uncertain. Greek tradition says that they are related to the Rhodians and Cretans. Their numerous inscriptians, many of which have a Greek translation, show that the language was not Indo-European. Their civilization became later wholly Hellenized; and only their language, and the rock architecture of the graves, which will be treated of later, are pure Lycian.

Asia Minor lay at the centre of the ancient world, and was adapted to commerce because it is washed on three sides by the sea; its rich soil and fine climate fitted it to be the home of an early civilization. The lack of a great river, or of a large plain, such as Mesopotamia and Egypt possessed, prevented the formation of a central power, to unite the different nations and the countries, which are to some extent separated by mountains difficult to cross.

The chief significance of Asia Minor in the history of the human race lies in the fact that it was the transmitter of the civilization and culture of Asia to Greece and thus to Europe.

Until, however, the Hittite inscriptions, of which we now have some thirty of a substantial character, besides single Hittite signs on many seal cylinders or clay impressions of seals, shall have been satisfactorily deciphered, many of the problems presented by the history of Asia Minor, and more particularly the relationship of the various groups in this district to one another, cannot be solved. Despite some progress made in the determination of some signs and in the general pictorial interpretation, chiefly by Sayce, Jensen, and Messerschmidt, the key to the language has not yet been found. A solution proposed by Jensen in 1894 has not been accepted by scholars, and one proposed by Sayce in 1903 still remains to be tested.

BOOK III.

EGYPT AND WESTERN ASIA.

THE NEW EMPIRE IN EGYPT AND THE RISE OF ASSYRIA.

EGYPT AND WESTERN ASIA.

THE NEW EMPIRE IN EGYPT AND THE RISE OF ASSYRIA.

CHAPTER VI.

THE RELATIONS OF THE NEW EMPIRE TO SYRIA.

THE Egyptians in earlier times had business relations with foreign peoples, and were also often obliged to engage in war with Libyans and roving Asiatic races. These wars, however, had for their main object the defence of Lower Egypt. Only toward the south was the kingdom extended by conquest. With the Eighteenth Dynasty there set in weightier campaigns against the greater powers in Asia to vindicate Egypt's greatness, and to enrich the land by spoils, as well as to gain workmen for the great architectural works from the captives taken in war. Aāhmes (Amasis I.), the first king of the Eighteenth Dynasty (seventeenth to fifteenth century B.C.), had, with the aid of the Ethiopians, driven forth the Hyksos. The inscription on the grave, already referred to (p. 140), of the king's namesake, Captain Aahmes, found at El-Kab, gives full details of the siege of Avaris, the Hyksos' fortress. We learn from it that the attack was made both by land and water. "We besieged Avaris, and I had to fight on foot before His Holiness (the Pharaoh). I was conveyed on board the ship Khasen Mennefer ('Rising in Memphis'); we fought on the canal Pazet-ku of Avaris. Here won I a prize. I carried off a hand, which was communicated to the chronicler of the king. For my valor the golden chain was given me. . . . A fight took place at Takem, south of Avaris, where I captured a man alive. I went into the water, leading him with me. To avoid the streets of the city I went with him through water. . . . We took Avaris. I took thence, as captives, one man and three women, which I presented to His Holiness as slaves. We besieged the city of Sharuhen in the sixth year of his reign, and His Holiness captured it. I took with me two women as captives, and carried off a hand. . . ." Sharuhen (Joshua xix. 6) lay on the road to Gaza. We know from the inscription of another officer—Aāhmes-pur-Nekhbet—that Aāhmes I. pursued the Hyksos to Phoenicia. After capturing Avaris, the king, hurried against the mountaineer of Khent-nefer in Nubia, and scarcely were these subdued, when a still mightier southern foe appeared. This also was conquered. The general, Aāhmes, captured the ship of the commander, and was rewarded by large possessions. After bringing his wars and two rebellions to a successful issue, the king devoted himself to the enlargement and decoration of temples. Prisoners from the northeast frontier — among them the Fenkhu, a foreign coast-people in the eastern Delta — were employed in the quarries of Turra. From this time forward, Thebes came more to the foreground than under the Seventeenth Dynasty, and saw a series of great structures arise. Memphis, in virtue of its commerce and its being the seat of government for the Delta, remained a city of high importance; but the days of its glory were departed. During the last dynasties, however, the seat of empire was again transferred to Lower Egypt.

The portrait of Aāhmes is preserved on a stele in Turin. His well-preserved mummy shows him to have been about fifty when he died. The head is small, the hair is thick and wavy. Erman has pointed out that the entire organization of the country changed as the result of the war of independence. The invasion had weakened the old feudal houses. The territory recovered fell into the hands of the crown. Egypt had become a military power. Army chiefs stepped into ancient civil offices, replacing the feudal aristocracy. The crown, the priesthood, and the army divided the wealth of the land. Aāhmes married his sister, Aāhmes-Nefertari, through whom descended the rights of the pure solar line. For centuries she was worshipped on a par with the great Theban gods as the 'great ancestress.' In her coffin—over ten feet high—the mummy of Rameses III. had been secreted along with her own. The Mahdi war that followed upon the find of royal bodies caused these to remain neglected until 1886. It then was found

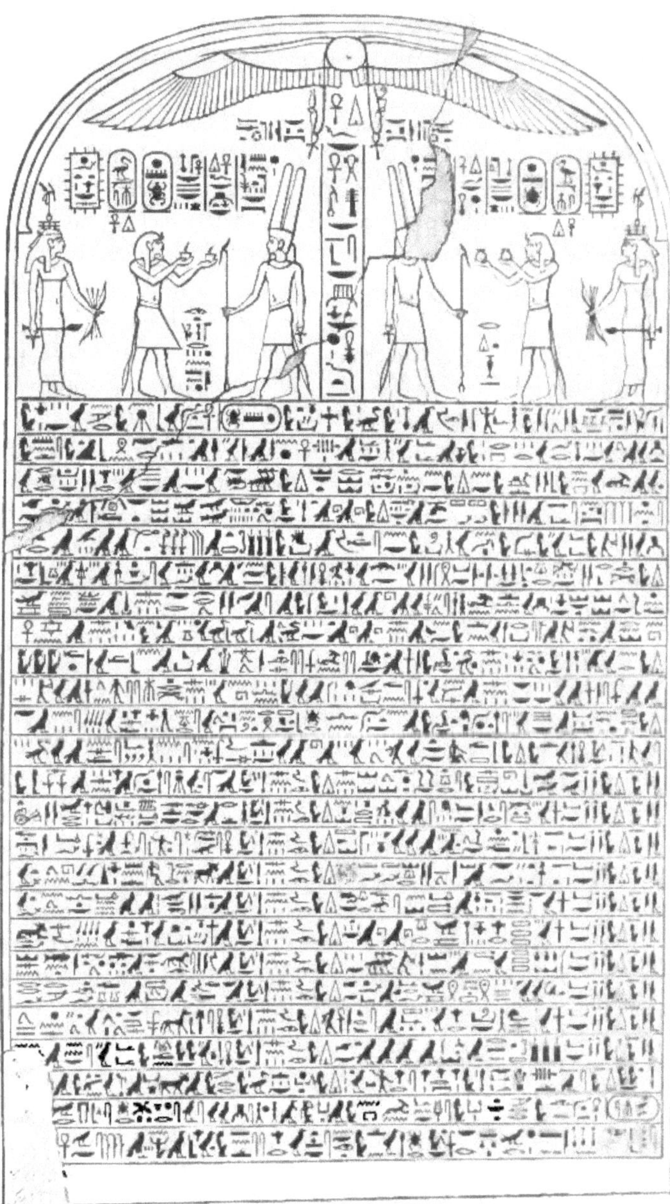

FIG. 89. — Tablet of Thothmes I.

that the mummy of Nefertari—after having survived 3500 years—was decomposing, and, in Mr. Maspero's absence, she was hastily buried anew.

Amenhotep I., son of Aāhmes, reigned at first jointly with his mother. He fought in Nubia and in Asia.[1] The dominions which he left to his son extended from Nubia to the Euphrates. Thothmes I. (Fig. 92) vanquished the Nubians of Khent-nefer, and set up a monument at Kerman, opposite the island of Tombos (Fig. 89). He then entered Asia, marched through the land of the Rutennu into northern Palestine and Syria, and erected memorial-stones at Niy on the Euphrates. The hoary hero, Aahmes, the king's lieutenant, appeared for the last time here in the field, and captured a battle-chariot. The victories in Asia did not secure for Egypt any real sovereignty in these parts. Tribute only was required, without any change in the political relations. On the other hand, the conquered Nubian possessions were practically incorporated into the kingdom by the establishment of strong places, the introduction of Egyptian culture, and the appointment of the Prince of Cush as governor, an office often filled by the crown-prince. Thothmes II. married his sister, Queen Ma-ka-Ra Khnumt-Amen Hatshepsut (Fig. 90), whom Erman and Edward Meyer suspect of doing away with him. The feebleness of his frame, however, and the ravages of the disease, still visible on his skin, sufficiently explain his early demise. The relationship of the Thothmeses is still a matter for discussion. But whether Thothmes III. was a brother or nephew of Hatshepsut, as is generally believed, or, as recently suggested, was an usurper and her consort, Hatshepsut's right to the throne is unquestioned. She organized a great commercial maritime expedition to the land of Punt whose details are represented in a series of very beautiful reliefs, with descriptive inscriptions, in the temple at Der-el-Bahri, in Thebes. (PLATE XVIII.) Parihu, the Prince of Punt, appears as an old man of dark-brown skin; his wife and daughter, portrayed with realistic humor, are anything but slender beauties. The freighting of homeward-bound vessels, on some of which men are already giving the

[1] In the reign of this king the horse first appears on Egyptian monuments. —ED.

[2] The coffin and the mummy of Thothmes I. were found at Der-el-Bahri. The head bears a strong likeness to that of Thothmes II.—ED.

PLATI

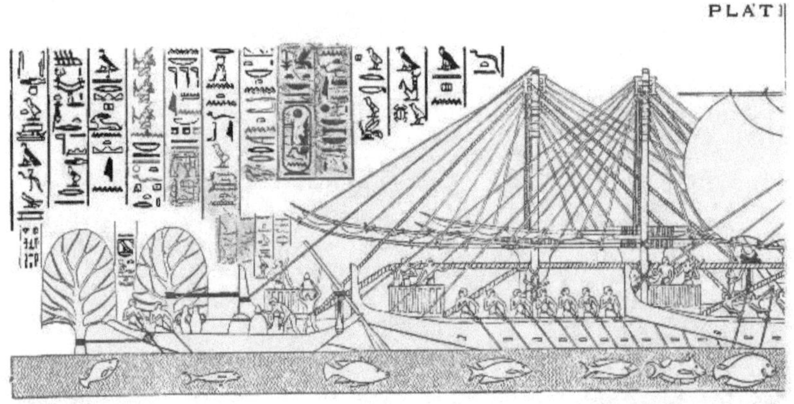

1. Arrival of the Fle

(One-sixteen

2. The Freigl

(One-ninth t

Bas-relief on a wall in the temple at Der-el-Bahri, repro

ıg of a Ship.

ctual size.)

ing a fleet sent by Queen Hatasu to the land of Punt.

sails to the wind and moving the rudder, is represented on the lower part of our plate. The fish in the water are depicted so truly that it is possible to determine their species. The wares are enumerated in the inscriptions. Among them we find frankincense plants, ivory, etc.; also apes (*kafu*, Hindostanee *kapi*), peacocks (*aanau*), and other foreign animals, as well as thirty-two fragrant shrubs, which were acclimated in Thebes. The reader can recognize many of the names in the subjoined determinatives, or elucidatory picture-signs, on the plate. In Thebes their arrival was celebrated by a festival, and the cargoes were consecrated and entered in the temple-books. The god Thoth, and Safekh, the goddess of libraries, record the weight, and number the articles. In the one scale of a balance held by Hor are thirty-one metal rings (coins); in the other, the 'tens' or pound-weights in the form of ox-heads or gazelles (rock-goats). The queen reigned twenty years. Her empty coffin has recently been found.

FIG. 90. Queen Hatshepsut.

With Hatshepsut the legitimate line seems to have come to an end; for Thothmes III. nowhere mentions his mother, Hest, her name appearing only on the mummy-bands of his corpse. Scarcely was the queen Ma-ka-Ra, descended from the queen of Aāhmes, dead, when he avenged the indignities he had to endure from her, and his banishment to Buto in the Delta at her dictation, by causing her name to be chiselled out from all the monuments and replaced by his own.[1] The reign of Thothmes III., covering nearly fifty-three years, is glorious, both by reason of his success in arms and the

[1] We are told that during her lifetime Hatshepsut wore male attire, and put on the robes and ornaments that belong to kings. She honored the memory of her father, Thothmes I., by erecting to him two magnificent granite obelisks at Karnak. — ED.

noble works of art raised by him. But his name has been probably kept more vividly before posterity than that of any other of the Pharaohs, from the fact that he himself had his annals first inscribed on a leathern roll, preserved in the archives of the temple of Thebes, and, from that, engraved on the stone walls of the great hall that encloses the sanctuary. Here they have suffered by restorations; yet, in connection with the splendid pictorial illustrations, they furnish priceless information touching the deeds of this Pharaoh, and the degree of civilization then attained by the countries of Asia. On a stele of black granite, now at the Gizeh Museum, the victories won by Thothmes are celebrated in lofty diction, and the subdued nations enumerated. Another original source of information for this reign is the inscription on the grave of the commander Amen-em-heb, discovered by Ebers in Gurnah. The sculptures are remarkable for their life; in the battle pictures one looks down, as from a bird's-eye point of view, on the whole action, the combatants being arranged in rows one over the other. Some passages of the text consist only of names of the conquered peoples and cities; these names appearing on shields or cartouches, over which are seen the half-length figures of the inhabitants with their arms bound behind them. These shields, arranged in rows one over the other, are fastened on cords, and are being presented by the Pharaoh to Amen and the other gods.

As under Thothmes I., so in this reign, the Rutennu appear as the dominant people of Syria. Immediately after the victory over this people, there came from Asia to Egypt numerous works of highly developed art-industry, which exercised a very distinct influence on Egyptian art. These exhibit a style of ornamentation mainly motived by the metal (bronze) in which they are worked, whereas, before this time, Egyptian decorations were based on textiles and on work in wood, as well as on the imitation of natural objects.

The annals of Thothmes III. report that, in the twenty-second year of his reign, when he appears as sole ruler, he marched by way of Gaza to the fortress Yehem, where tidings were secretly brought him that the hostile prince of Kadesh (northwest of Merom, or Bahr-Huleh) had garrisoned Megiddo, rightly conceiving it to be the key to northern

Syria. This city occupied the site of the modern Khan-Legum (from the Latin *Legion*), near which Tel-Mutesellim indicates the old fort. Thothmes approached Megiddo through the Wadi-Kanah, on which he rested his right wing, while the left extended itself northwest of the town. The enemy was defeated and the fort stormed, which later, under the supervision of Egyptian architects, was made a point of support for future campaigns. The booty captured in Megiddo, and that taken from the petty kings who made their submission, is detailed in the inscription: living prisoners, 340; hands (cut from the fallen), 83; horses, 2,041; fillies, 191; bulls, 6; a war-chariot inlaid with gold; a gilded chest; a royal gilded chariot; 892 other war-chariots; a bronze suit of armor; the armor of the king of Megiddo; 200 suits of bronze armor; 502 bows; 7 silver-plated tent-poles; innumerable cattle, goats, etc. The Pharaoh captured and razed the fortress of Kadesh on the Orontes, where Amenemheb broke through a newly erected wall and performed other feats, and then entered the land of the Rutennu, where he strengthened three captured fortresses, — Anaugasa, Herenkal, Inenaa. The Egyptian arms were carried still farther, to Naharena (Mesopotamia): and mention is made of a land, Afrit, lying behind Niy, where Thothmes erected boundary pillars. On one inscription, mention is made of the tribute (homage-gift) of the king of the Kheta (Hittites), consisting of 96 pounds and 2 ounces of gold (the pound, or 'ten,' is 10 ounces: the ounce, 140 grains apothecary weight), 8 negro slaves, 13 boys as servants, oxen. In continuation, there are cited as booty from Syria, Remenen, and Naharena: silver and gold; vessels of Phoenician (Zahi) work: silver rings (used as money or for ornament), 8 of which weighed 301 Egyptian pounds; gold rings (the weight only, not the number, told): green stones (malachite); lapis lazuli: turquoises (real, and artificial of blue glass from Babylon); bronzes; iron articles; lead; emery: bitumen; silver goblets; white vases mounted in gold; 'Adonis-gardens' (vessels with flowers); wine amphoræ; vases of felspar: chariots, some inlaid with silver and gold, and plated and painted; armor of leather and bronze; battle-axes with stone heads; of living beings, male and female — slaves, horses, asses, bulls, oxen, goats, foreign birds, geese, — nay, in one representation the Rutennu bring not only a bear, but an elephant, probably from the plain of the Euphrates; of natural products and articles of food—bread and cakes, corn, barley, meal, grape- and date-wine, honey, figs, balsam, teak (for chariots), fauteuils of cedar or acacia (*ses*) and other fine woods, tent-poles beset with bronze and precious stones, colors, and the like.

The campaigns were soon renewed. In the twenty-ninth year of his (Thothmes III.) reign the fortress of Tunep was taken. It was afterward destroyed. From this point Amenemheb, the Pharaoh's general, made a sally against Carchemish, on the Euphrates—the capital of the Hittite kingdom—and then followed his lord toward Aradus, on the Mediterranean, overtaking him at Tyre. There seemed to be no limit to the conqueror's activity. The annals of his reign are very full, and show him extending Egypt's power from the banks of the Tigris to the mountains of Armenia and those of Abyssinia. There are records of his wars from his twenty-second to his fifty-fourth year. Almost each year marks a new warlike enterprise. After placing under tribute the nations of Phoenicia, Northern Syria, Mesopotamia, Cyprus, Punt, and Ethiopia, in his forty-second year, he dedicated the long inscription at Karnak, commemorative of his exploits. His fiftieth year saw him in Ethiopia. At this time he cleared the canal of the cataract. He was a great builder. He must have been over sixty when he died. His mummy and coffin have survived. He was short, robust, and his features recall those of Thothmes I. and of Thothmes II. (p. 287). The forehead is low, the eye deep-set, the jaw heavy, the lips thick, with high cheek bones. His type is that of the fellah—"coarse of fibre and expression, but vigorous." The long list of conquered peoples and places has been studied by various scholars from Mariette and Brugsch to W. M. Müller and Breasted, and furnish valuable clues to the ancient world, about B.C. 1500. Never was respect for Egypt so widespread over distant regions as under Thothmes III. Yet the constant repetition of the campaigns proves that the vanquished provinces were unsubdued.

Amenhotep II., son of Thothmes, was obliged to march to Mesopotamia to enforce payment of the overdue tribute. His mummy was found in 1898 by Loret (Fig. 91). His tomb had served as hiding-place for other royal mummies—among others for that of King Merenptah.

Thothmes IV.,[1] immediate successor of Amenhotep II., also maintained the boundaries established by his ancestors. Amenhotep III. (Fig. 92), the Memnon of the Greeks, was a worthy successor of the great Thothmes. He conducted expeditions in Asia which seem more like triumphal progresses than like wars. And he maintained Egypt's supremacy over Tunep, Kadesh, Carchemish, and Northern Mesopotamia. He made raids in the south till all the land to Ethiopia was subject to him. His edifices reach even to the city of

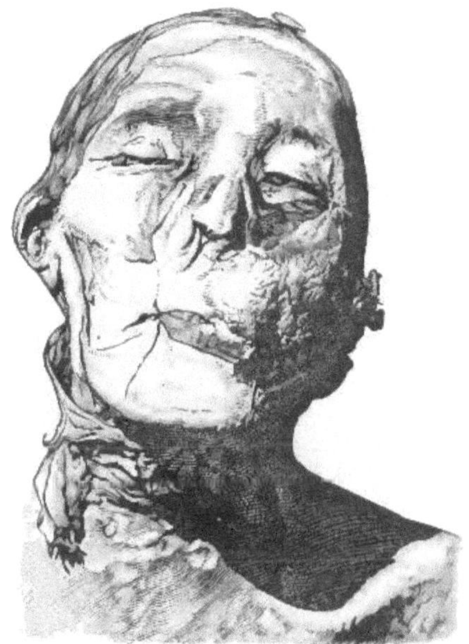

Fig. 91. — Mummy of Amenhotep II. (From Annales du Service des Antiquites, iii. 2e fasc.)

Napata, on the mountain Barkal, above the great southern bend of the Nile. In the history of art he is famed through his erection of the magnificent south-temple of Thebes, where Luxor (i. e., the 'palaces') now stands, and of another on the western bank, of which nothing now

[1] He is interesting to us as repairer of the Sphinx at Gizeh. A tablet set up by him between the paws of the Sphinx relates that in an afterdinner sleep Harmachis appeared to him promising the crown of Egypt if he should clear his image—i.e., the Sphinx—from the sand. This he did in the first year of his reign.—Ed.

remains but the Memnon colossi. The latter are blocks of stone nearly seventy feet high, in the form of gigantic sitting figures, portraits of the king as the representative of the god. The features are dilapidated; but one can reproduce them from several still existing likenesses, as, e. g., that in his tomb.

Four important events in the life and reign of this king are recorded on some large steatite scarabs. One celebrates his lion-hunts, where he is said to have slain 102 lions with his own hands—perhaps in Armenia; another records the coming to Egypt of Kilgipa, the

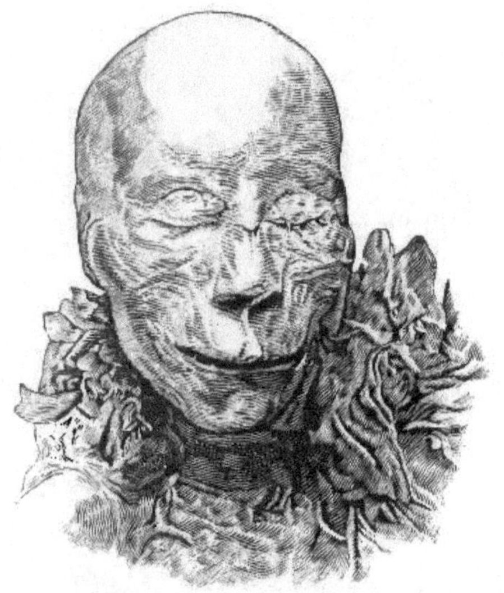

Fig. 92. — Head of Thothmes I.

daughter of an Asiatic father, Sutarna, son of Artatama, king of Mitani, with 317 of her women; another, his marriage with Tyi; and the last, the building for his queen of a large lake near the town Tarukha. The Tel-el-Amarna tablets prove that Amenhotep had as his wife not only Queen Tyi, but also a sister and a daughter of Kallima-sin, king of Babylon, as well as Gilukhîpa and Satumkhîpa, princesses of Mitani (Armenia), and the sister and daughter of Dushratta, king of Mitani, while the son of the Egyptian king—i. e., Khu-en-Aten—married Tadukhipa, Dushratta's daughter, whom Petrie identifies with Nefertiti.

Under Amenhotep IV. a religious schism took place. The learned priesthood had reached an intellectual plane from which the multiplicity of Egyptian gods seemed but the manifold manifestations of the divine essence. In different localities various names might be given to the Supreme Power. But by the process known as henotheism, each deity was endowed with the attributes of all. Of this amalgamation of divine types, the sun-god was the central point. If they did not reach monotheism, it was because in this, as in all other branches of their civilization, the Egyptians progressed without abandoning the ancient teaching, upon which they engrafted the new. Amen, the 'hidden' one—originally a harvest-god, the local god of Thebes during the Eighteenth and Nineteenth Dynasties—had reached supremacy in the pantheon. His priesthood had become all-powerful. Amen became the invisible god who manifests himself in the sun—i. e., Amen-Ra. But around him—albeit often identified with him—were still grouped the entire plurality of the gods. Amenhotep III. had ruled in the old faith, although, in the light of subsequent events, it is significant that the bark in which he sailed on the artificial lake which he constructed at Zaru for his bride, Queen Tyi, was named Nefer-Aten—'the beauties of the disk.' This betrays in his mind the leaning toward Aten, which his son, later, developed. At his death, Amenhotep IV. began his reign in the old faith. While he announced his intention to erect at Thebes, in honor of Ra-Harmakhis-Aten, a Hat-Benben or 'house of obelisks' like the temple of Heliopolis, a tomb was begun at Thebes in which he appears in the conventional way. But during the process of construction things reached a crisis: at least, in part of the mausoleum he assumes the name of Khu-en-Aten—'splendor of the disk.' The fact that it remained unfinished attests the political as well as the religious revolution that took place. The local cultus was too deeply rooted into the very life of the people of each locality to be changed. It might readily be added to, but it never could be supplanted. Breaking with the Theban priesthood, Khu-en-Aten left Thebes. He established his court in Middle Egypt, at Tel-el-Amarna, where he erected a new capital—Pa-Aten. The god is here represented as a disk, shedding upon the world its beneficent rays, each of which terminates with a hand, often holding the sign of life (Fig. 93). If this form was original, however, the Aten itself was no new or foreign god. His worship had long existed at Heliopolis. What was new to Egypt was the intolerance which its worshippers evinced toward other gods. 'The doctrine,' as it was called, taught adoration of "the living sun-disk, beside whom there is no other"; and its converts erased the names of other gods, directing their special fury against Amen. Only Maāt, the goddess of truth, found favor in their eyes, while Aten

Fig. 93.—Amenhotep IV. and his family, sacrificing to the Sun. Relief in a tomb at Tel-el-Amarna.

alone was worshipped. The remains of the palace, the temple, and other structures of Khu-en-Aten have been found (Petrie, 1891). The temple was called Hat-Benben. In the refuse heap of the palace much Aegaean pottery and glass was obtained; and amid the rubbish in the palace, probably left by those who carved his statues, the death-mask of the king—now in the Gizeh Museum—and an unfinished relief-portrait were found. The latter, now in the Museum of the University of Pennsylvania, still retains after 3400 years the ink-tracings of the artist where the stone is uncut. A block found at Gurob, also in the last-mentioned museum, represents the disk in the Assyrian style, as a rosette from which depend short, straight, arrow-like rays. The conventional art of this interesting period represents the king as quite altered from his former self. Indeed, every man and woman is portrayed in the same unattractive as well as unegyptian form, which, as Wiedemann has wisely suggested, belongs to the peculiar school of art of the time. The early likenesses of the king show him with a normal body and the features of his race. A great hymn to Aten has been

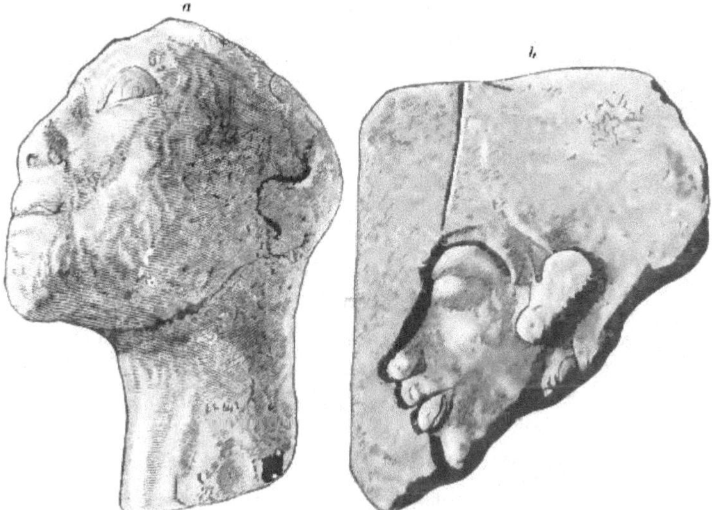

FIG. 94.—*a*, Mask of Khu-en-Aten (Gizeh Museum). *b*, Relief portrait of Khu-en-Aten (Museum of the University of Pennsylvania).

preserved. It has been published by Bouriant and also by Breasted. It is worthy of remark that in this invocation to the sun-god all trace of the old Heliopolitan anthropomorphism, as well as of polytheism, has disappeared: . . . "Thou createst the earth according to thy will, when thou wast alone. Men, herds, flocks, all that is upon earth and goeth upon feet, all that is on high and flieth with wings. The lands of Syria, of Kush, of Egypt; thou settest each in its place: thou providest each with that which pertaineth to it. . . . Their forms are according to the color of their skins. . . . Thou makest the Nile, . . . that it may give life to men whom thou hast made for thyself. Lord of all. . . . Thou art the Only One, when thou risest in thy form, as the living Aten, splendid, radiant, fair shining. Thou createst the forms of the beings who are in thee. Thou art the Only One. . . . All behold thee in their midst, for thou art the Aten of day, above the earth. . . ." Most of the inscriptions of Khu-en-Aten breathe the same religious fervor. In some of them, however, he lays aside conventionality and appears as a loving husband and father. His tomb was unfinished, his sarcophagus destroyed, and only fragments of mummy wrappings exist of this strange monarch.

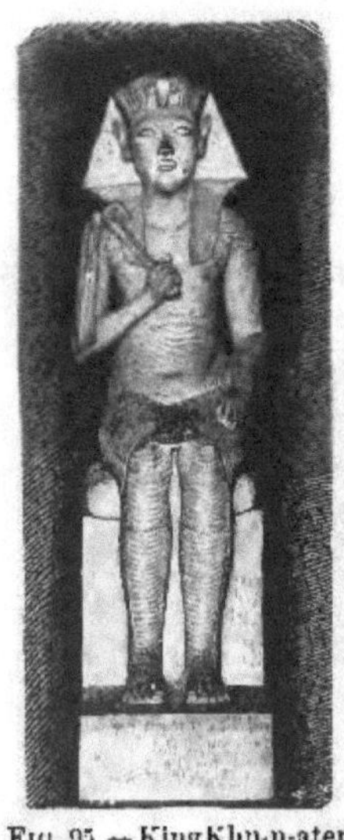

Fig. 95. — King Khu-n-aten (Amenhotep IV.).

The close relations with Asia resulting from the treaties and marriages that followed upon the great wars of the preceding reigns, had led Asiatics to flock to the Egyptian court. At the new capital there were scribes in charge of the correspondence conducted in cuneiform script with the tributary or allied Asiatic princes, as well as with Egypt's lieutenants in Syria. In 1887, at Tel-el-Amarna, some three hundred and twenty cuneiform tablets forming a portion of these archives were found in the loose sand at the foot of the hills back of the village by a peasant woman in search of antiquities. The Semitic dialect used is Assyrian, and—in some important details—is related to the Hebrew of the Old Testament. The tablets are of the clay peculiar to the various localities represented. They were written from about B.C. 1500 to 1450. They are inscribed on both sides, and are annotated in red ink and in hieratic by the Egyptian scribe. They vary in length from two to twelve inches. At present, they are distributed between the British Museum (82), the Berlin Museum (160), and the Gizeh Museum. The tablets are, for the most part, letters written to Amenhotep III. and Amenhotep IV. by their subject princes or deputies in Syria and Palestine, and by the friendly rulers of Babylon, and are either diplomatic messages, friendly communications, or official reports. The correspondence with Babylon consists of eleven letters, the principal subjects of which are matrimonial alliances; three from Kallima-sin, king of Karaduriyash (Northern Babylonia, nearest to Assyria), to Amenhotep III.; one, perhaps a first draft, from the latter to the former; and seven from Burraburiyash of Babylon to Amenhotep IV. As a specimen of this correspondence, we quote a part of the letter from Amenhotep III. Kallima-sin had been asked to send Sukharti, his daughter, to the harem of the Pharaoh, and had replied that since the marriage of his own sister to the king of Egypt, she had never been seen, and that it was not known whether she was alive. To these and other objections Amenhotep III. replies: "To Kallima-sin, king of Karaduriyash, my brother, thus saith Amenhotep, the great king, the king of Egypt thy brother: 'I am well, may it be well with thee, with thy government, with thy wives, with thy children, with thy nobles, with thy horses, and with thy chariots; and may there be great peace in thy land,'" etc. The king then states that he has understood the message concerning Sukharti. He replies that none of the members of the embassy sent by Kallima-sin for news of his sister were acquainted with her: "Since thou sayest 'my messengers cannot identify her,' I answer: Who can? And I ask further, Why dost thou not send a wise man who might give thee a trustworthy account of thy sister here? . . . and see for himself the honor in which she is held by the king." He calls upon the great gods to witness that "the kings of the land of Egypt" are not wont to act deceitfully. Kallima-sin had stated that it was his custom to give his daughters to the "kings of Karaduriyash," who treated their escorts with generous hospitality and sent back handsome gifts. Amenhotep answers that he possesses and will give more than they.[1] Another letter (Berlin No. 3) shows Kallima-sin complaining that when he asked for the hand of an Egyptian princess the king had answered that "the daughters of the king of the land of Egypt have never been given to a nobody." He asks: "Why not? Thou art king, and if thou givest who shall say a word?" The matter must have been adjusted finally to their mutual satisfaction, for another letter (Gizeh No. 1) shows Kallima-sin writing to Amenhotep: "With reference to thy request that my daughter Sukharti be given thee to wife, she has now reached

[1] See Bezold-Budge, 'The Tel-el-Amarna Tablets in the British Museum'; Winckler-Abel, 'Der Thontafelfund von El-Amarna'; Delattre, 'Lettres de Tel-el-Amarna,' in Proc. Soc. Bib. Arch., 1890-91, vols. xiii., xv., 1892-93. Sayce and others have also contributed to the elucidation of the subject.

the proper age. If thou wilt write unto me, she shall be brought unto thee." None of these Asiatic princesses, however, was acknowledged queen of Egypt. Tyi alone was described as "royal daughter, royal mother, royal wife, great lady, mistress of the North and South." Her portrait shows her fair with blue eyes. Her father was Yuaa, and her mother, Thuaa—and she was the mother of Khu-en-Aten, the 'Napkhuriya' of the El-Amarna tablets—a transliteration of his throne name, Nefer-Kheperu-Ra.[1] According to a tablet (No. 3, British Museum), the latter's daughter married a son of Burraburiyash. It has been suggested that this was Karakhardash, who succeeded his father on the throne of Karaduriyash in the time of Ashur-uballit, king of Assyria. An interesting tablet gives the terms of a commercial treaty between Kallima-sin and Amenhotep III., according to which any Mesopotamian travelling in Egypt with merchandize shall pay certain duties to the king of Egypt. Should the traveller refuse, the duty may be forcibly exacted. Among dutiable articles are mentioned gold, silver, oil, clothing, and other commodities. So far, this is the oldest commercial treaty of which the terms are officially recorded. Burraburiyash in a letter (No. 2, British Museum) alludes to a treaty of offensive and defensive alliance made between his father, Kurrigalzu, and the king of Egypt. In all these transactions astonishing stress is laid upon the respective value of the presents exchanged, and in return for Asiatic bronze, rock-crystal, lapis-lazuli, and chariots, gold, oxen, oils, furniture, or men are expected. The longest letter—of 518 lines—in the whole collection is from Dushratta, king of Mitani (Armenia), and relates to the marriage of his daughter (Sadukhipa) to Amenhotep IV. (Khu-en-Aten). We have already seen that the sister, and another daughter of Dushratta, had married Amenhotep III., whose throne name, Neb-Maat-Ra, is translated 'Nimmuriya.'[2]

Besides the letters from Babylonia, Assyria, and Armenia, already referred to, there are others from remote regions; several from a prince of Alashia (Cyprus and perhaps the adjacent coast), and one from

[1] Several scholars have identified Queen Tyi with one of these Asiatic princesses. Wiedemann, 'Aegypten Geschichte,' p. 393, and Ed. Meyer, 'Geschichte des alten Aegyptens,' p. 260, however, look upon her as a Libyan. Maspero sees in her an Egyptian.

[2] On the subject of the Asiatic marriages, see Erman, Winckler, and others in the Zeitschrift für Aegyptologie, xxviii., etc.

Tarkhundara, lord of Arzapi (Rezeph), a region held by the Hittites to the north of Palmyra.

A second group of letters, in some respects the most interesting, as they are the most numerous, there being over two hundred of them, consists of letters to their Egyptian suzerain, Amenhotep IV., from his viceroys and captains in Syria and Palestine, covering a period of only five or six years. In the reign of this Pharaoh the hold of Egypt upon Asia had been very much relaxed. By reason of his fanatical devotion to religious reform, the 'heretic' king has made a political failure at home, and suffered loss and humiliation abroad. These letters from Syria and Palestine reveal a painful condition of demoralization and disintegration, destined to be arrested only at a much later time by the conquests of Seti I., and his great son Rameses II. Garrisons and outposts are neglected; allied princes, in the court of each one of whom was the Egyptian *paka*, or resident, fail to receive needed succor from Egypt. Yet it was important to Egypt to maintain her sovereignty in southern Syria and Palestine, not as an end in itself, since these states were not at this time especially wealthy or powerful, but rather because through these regions passed the great trade-routes from Egypt to the north and to the powerful empire of Babylonia in the east; and it is noteworthy that the chief struggles are at points on or near the line of these trade routes, and not in the remoter inland regions. The main route led along the Mediterranean shore from Zoan (Tanis) to Gaza; thence to Ascalon (Ashkelon), Joppa, Accho, Tyre, Sidon, Beirut, and Gebal (Byblus). It continued to the cities of Arka and Simyra, or each side of the river Eleutherus. North of Simyra the shore route becomes difficult, and the road turns inland, passing through the plains of Emesa and Kadesh on the Orontes. The valley of the Orontes was held by the chariots of Egypt; and the main highway was continued as far to the north, under Egyptian protection, as Tunep (now Tenneb), an important station, and Doliche (now Aintab), which was a great city of the Hittites. Here the route turned eastward, descending a river valley to Zeugma on the Euphrates. A more direct route to the eastern country struck out from Tunep to Carchemish, the capital of the Hittite kingdom, farther south on the Euphrates. Here the Egyptians intersected the great trade highways, branching off northeast or east, to Edessa, Armenia, Nineveh, and Babylon. This royal road, on which embassies passed two and fro, was, from Zoan to the Euphrates, about six hundred English miles long. There were side routes to Damascus, which, with the parts adjacent to the Sea of Galilee (Gennesaret), appears to have been held in the interest of Egypt. The Amarna tablets contain official letters from many of these important posts and from places near,—Ascalon, Lachish, Gezer, Joppa, Jerusalem, Accho, Hazor, Tyre, Sidon, Beirut, Gebel, Tunep, while other familiar names are referred to in the text. From this correspondence, which is largely made up of anxious pleas for aid from the representatives of Egyptian power, it is possible to reconstruct with much detail the main features of a great war of rebellion.

The war began with a league between the Hittites, Cassites, and other tribes with whom some of the governors of the Syrian tributary provinces like Zimridi,[1] governor of Sidon and Lachisch appear to have joined. It is obvious throughout the correspondence that the attack was seriously complicated by the rivalries and jealousies of the local governors. Among the earliest operations was an assault on Damascus by Aidugama, the Hittite king of Kadesh, on the Orontes ; the whole country of Damascus was ravaged. Simultaneously with these operations, as we gather from the letters of Rib-Adda of Gebel and other loyal provincial governors, the Amorites descended upon the rich Phoenician cities on the shore road. Simyra was first taken ; then in quick succession Arka and Tripoli. Gebel, however, held out for five years, and fell only after a protracted siege. The war was also carried on at sea. The fleets of Arvad aided the Amorites, while the ships of Sidon and Beirut succored Gebel. During the blockade of Gebel the Amorites moved southward, and joining forces with the Hittites, who moved west, took Sidon by treachery, and beleaguered Tyre, cutting off its water-supply. As a result of this great war, the Egyptians, owing to a feeble foreign administration, must have lost some of their hold on Palestine and Syria ; though friendly relations were maintained with the Mitani and with the Babylonians. Abd-Ashirti—the rival of Rib-Adda, who describes him as the arch-rebel—while protesting his loyalty to the king, adds that in the days of old the Hittites were

[1] On the site of Lachisch (Tel-el-Hesy) Dr. Bliss found a cuneiform tablet written to Zimridi.

vassals of Egypt, but now they destroyed its cities, seized its gods, and made its liegemen prisoners (No. 36, British Museum). The independence of the Hittites, before their final conquest by Rameses II., seems to be implied in the language of the treaty of Rameses with Kheta-Sar, king of Kadesh.

Amenhotep IV. left no male heirs; but in conformity with the law of succession in the female line, in the absence of male heirs, he was succeeded by several of his sons-in-law. Of Saa-ka-Ra, husband of Mert-Amen, little is known. Of Tut-ankh-amen, husband of Ankh-sen-pa-Aten, there remain monumental traces. In the grave of Hui (Ai), prince of Cush, at Thebes, besides the seated king stand Hui and Amen-hetep, governors of Ethiopia. A brown princess, whose hair is interwoven with golden threads, rides on a chariot drawn by oxen, and surrounded by negro and Abyssinian servants, who bring gifts to the Pharaoh. Among these are thick gold rings (serving as coin), gold-dust in bags, leopard skins, cattle, fans, elephants' tusks, a gold pyramid standing on a gold enamelled pedestal, also a great cabinet on a table hung with skins and carpets, and resting on a golden column enamelled in the Egyptian style. Two golden pyramids stand on the table, one on either side, also a giraffe under a palm-tree, attended by three negroes, all of gold. Some of the men are ruddy brown, others white, with black beards and hair. They appear in a parti-colored woollen dress wound spirally round the body. Their white-skinned, black-eyed slaves, wearing only an apron, bring white horses, magnificent vessels, and lapis lazuli. As shown by his name, Tut-ankh-amen returned to Amen-worship. Even the queen's name becomes Ankh-sen-Amen. His successor, Ay, married Tyi, who is styled the great heiress. After building two tombs at El-Amarna, on returning to Thebes, he built another, in which he reverts to the 'Ka' formula—which under Khu-en-Aten had been abandoned. With Horemheb (Armais) we reach firmer ground. His wife, Nezem-Mut, was an 'heiress,' and his splendid tomb at Sakkara shows him to have been general and nomarch of Ha-Suten (Alabastron) before King Ay selected him for his successor. He zealously destroyed all vestiges of the Aten heresy, restored order, waged war in Ethiopia and Asia, and concluded a treaty with the Hittite king, Sapalulu, which, however, did not last longer than his life. Horemheb erected numerous structures, particularly at the temple of Karnak. A tablet speaks of the twenty-first year of his reign. With him the dynasty expired; although his successor, Rameses I., the founder of the Nineteenth Dynasty, appears to have been related to him; but his claim to the succession is unknown.

Rameses I. ruled but a short time. At his death, Southern Syria was in open rebellion. Among the records of Seti I. we learn of an advance of the Shasu upon the fortress Zal, which Aāhmes had erected for defence against Asia, after the destruction of the Hyksos city, Avaris. Egypt's internal difficulties under the last kings of the Eighteenth Dynasty had emboldened its neighbors. Along with the Rutennu, the Kheta (Hittites) now appear as a leading power. At the time when Horemheb made a treaty with their king, Sapalulu, they already occupied the region between the Mediterranean, the Lebanon, and the Euphrates. Their king in Seti's time was Mutnara, who fought against Rameses II. in the fifth year of the latter's reign. Later his brother Kheta-Sar appears. The father of both was named Mar-Sar, son of Sapalulu. The fortress Kadesh was again captured; and the march was continued through Lebanon back along the coast to Egypt. Seti is figured presenting the captives in triumph to Amen. Among them are the Kheta, the people of Naharena (Mesopotamians), the Upper Rutennu from the hill-land of Syria, the Lower Rutennu who inhabited the land between that and the Euphrates, the Senzar (i.e., 'Double Tyre,' from the second or insular Tyre), and many other Syrian and Canaanitish nations. A treaty was concluded with the Hittites, each country retaining its possessions. More decisive was Seti's victory over the Libyans, against whom he afterward turned his arms, and of whom henceforth nothing was heard for many years. The south also felt the edge of the Egyptian sword; and the king is named, in an inscription of the temple of Redesieh, 'conqueror of four negro peoples.' Four tablets on the hill Sese (near lat. 20°) show the limit of Seti's power. After these exploits, Seti became "the jackal that lurks about the land to guard it," rather than "the fascinating lion marauding along the hidden roads of four countries," i. e., he peacefully devoted himself to the administration of the empire and to the erection of superb edifices at Abydos, Luxor, Gurnah, etc. His highest claim to fame is the erection at Karnak of the marvellous Hypostyle Hall—his father's grandiose dream—executed by him. His tomb, discovered by Belzoni (1818), is a palace cut in the living rock and covered with elaborate paintings. The calm dignity of his face (see Frontispiece) shows him to have been "every inch a king."

Fig. 96. — Rameses II. as crown-prince. Relief in the temple at Abydos.

While yet alive, Seti associated his son, Rameses II. (Fig. 96), to the throne. From the accumulation of the heroic deeds of many Pharaohs laid by the Greeks on his person, a whole cycle of legends has clustered around him, which ascribe to him as Sesostris mythical campaigns, reaching to the ends of the world. His sixty-seventh year is on record. His likeness is known to us from many statues; and his admirably preserved mummy is at Gizeh. Rameses was in Ethiopia when his father's death left him sole ruler. He promptly returned, and after the prescribed ceremonies, turned his attention to the most pressing needs of the Empire. The growing importance of Syrian affairs since the increase of the Hittite monarchy, and the aggressive movements of the Mediterranean and Libyan peoples, drew his attention to the Delta. Thebes was too remote from the centre of these political activities. A new royal residence was erected as an advance-post near the isthmus, and called 'Rameses.' Passing over the usual raids into the south, as well as an inroad of the Libyans with their allies, the Shardana and Tulsha, we notice as the principal event in his reign the war in Syria. As early as the second and fourth years of his rule, small expeditions had been made to the Syrian coast, which are recorded on the before-mentioned rock-tablets at Nahr-el-Kelb, near Beirut. In the fifth year of his reign, the Hittite king Mutnara, the son of Marsar and the grandson of Sapalulu, warned of the approaching storm by the young Pharaoh's preliminary campaigns, made on a formidable scale his preparations to meet the threatening danger. Calling his allies to his aid, he summoned his forces from Babylonia to Lykia, from the Mediterranean to Cilicia. Rameses, warned in time, marched out to meet him. The armies came together on the Orontes south of Kadesh, where was fought a great battle. A minute account of it is given in an epic preserved in the Sallier Papyrus No. III. in the British Museum, transcribed by the scribe Pentaur, and in one of the Raifet papyri in the Louvre. The text was engraved on the walls of Karnak, Luxor, Abydos—and another account of the war appears at Abu-Simbel, where the scene of the battle is given, as it is also on the walls of the Ramesseum (Thebes). Kadesh occupied the site of the present mound Tel-Nebi-Mend. The old name is still attached to the lake. Jakut, the learned traveller and geographer (died A.D. 1179), names it Buhairat Kadasa. The relief shows us the camp of the Egyptians, surrounded by the shields of the warriors, as well as all the soldiers, Egyptians and Shardana, the camp-followers and animals, the tent of the Pharaoh whence he issued his orders, the troops on the march, — a truly impressive scene. In the fight the Hittites appear on horseback, or in threes in chariots, the warrior being attended by a driver and shield-bearer. Their garments are long, their beards shaven, and their skins of a clear red hue, by which they are distinguished from the yellow, black-bearded Semites, as also from the Assyrians. The Hittites had dominion over diverse lands in Asia, while others followed their lead. In the catalogue of their allies, we therefore have bands of Lykians (Leka), Maeonians (Manna), Mysians (Masu), people from Pedasa in Karia, or from Pedasos in the Troad (Patasu), who had joined the army of the Kheta. The names Kirkamash (Carchemish), Khirbu (Aleppo), Artu (Aradus), Naharena (the plain of the Euphrates), are also familiar; other identifications are less certain.

The Egyptian army was divided into four columns, named after the gods, Amen, Ra, Ptah, and Sutekh, a fact observed by Diodorus in his description of the Ramesseum. The division Amen was under the leadership of the Pharaoh, who approached the city of Kadesh, while Kheta-Sar lay in ambush to the northwest. On a sudden the latter dashed forth in an attack, which was foiled by the personal valor of Rameses, although only the van of the Egyptians was engaged. This moment is depicted in the official poem in the most extravagant style. Rameses, in his extremity, prays to Amen; for he stands alone, opposed to 2500 chariots. "He reaches his hand to me, . . . he calls from behind me: 'Thou art not alone, I am with thee—I, thy father Ra—my hand is with thee. I am worth more to thee than hundreds of thousands together. I am the Lord of Victory.' I take heart. . . . I am as Monthu—I shoot right and left. I am like Ba'al, as a plague among them." Accompanied by his lion, Smam-Kheftu-f ('Render of his enemies'), he bursts through his deadly foe in his chariot drawn by the two steeds, 'Victory in Thebes' and 'Valor is satisfied.' After he effected a junction with his main force, the attack on the Kheta was renewed, and they were cut to pieces: "Behold none of them are able to fight before me, their hearts melt in their bodies. . . . I make them rush into the river even as crocodiles rush into water. They fall over each other, and I slay them according to my will. Not one of them turns around. He who falls riseth not again." The garrison of the city made a sally, and brought the fugitives within their walls. Next day Mutnara sued for peace. On the west side of the pylon of the Ramesseum, in Thebes, the battle is depicted in a very animated manner—half as a battle-plan, half as a picture, executed as a flat decoration, in low relief. Originally it had been overlaid with stucco, and painted; but all this has disappeared. The Kheta, with horses and chariots, are driven into the Orontes. Across the river lies the city with its defenders. Instructed by the descriptive catalogue, we recognize, in the turmoil of the chariot-fight, Kemayis, prince of the Hittite phalanx, slain, probably by the Pharaoh, who storms forward over his body, darting his arrows as swiftly as a god. Farther off we see Khirep-Sar, the king's annalist; Targatas, captain of the archers; Grabatus, master-of-horse for the Kheta. On the other bank the king of Khilpu (Aleppo) is being dragged out of the water, and placed on his head, so as to discharge the water he has swallowed. Still farther off the king of the Kheta is seen, standing in his chariot, and surrounded by his guards, praying for mercy. The northern half of the west side shows the pursuit into the river. Here the lists name Tetar, chief of domestics, brother of the king Masrima; Rebasununa, prince of the people of Anunas; and Suaas, prefect of Tanis, who is being drawn from the water. On the water-girt fortress are inscribed the words "the Fortress Kadesh." Eventually, Mutnara, by a truly Oriental euphemism, 'succumbed to his destiny'—i.e., was probably murdered by his brother Kheta-Sar, who succeeded him.

In the eighth year of Rameses II. Galilee revolted, and the following year the rebellion spread to Sephelah. A relief in the columned hall of the Ramesseum represents the capture of the fortress Dapur (PLATE XIX.). This stood on Mount Tabor (Fig. 97), in Galilee, at the foot of which lies Daburiyeh. Down to the time of Antiochus the Great (218 B.C.) a city stood on the summit of the mount; and even in A.D. 67 Vespasian caused it to be besieged by Placidius, when it was surrendered, owing to want of water. On our relief the fort of the Kheta is besieged; and the Egyptians, recognizable by their red skins, storm it. Among them the reader discerns the six sons of Rameses, distinguished by the princely lock of hair. According to the accompanying hieroglyphic explanation, the princes are Kha-em-uas, Ment (-her-khepsh-ef), Men-amen, Amen-em-ua, Seti, Sotep-en-ra. The first of these, nearest the Pharaoh, was born of the queen Hes-t-

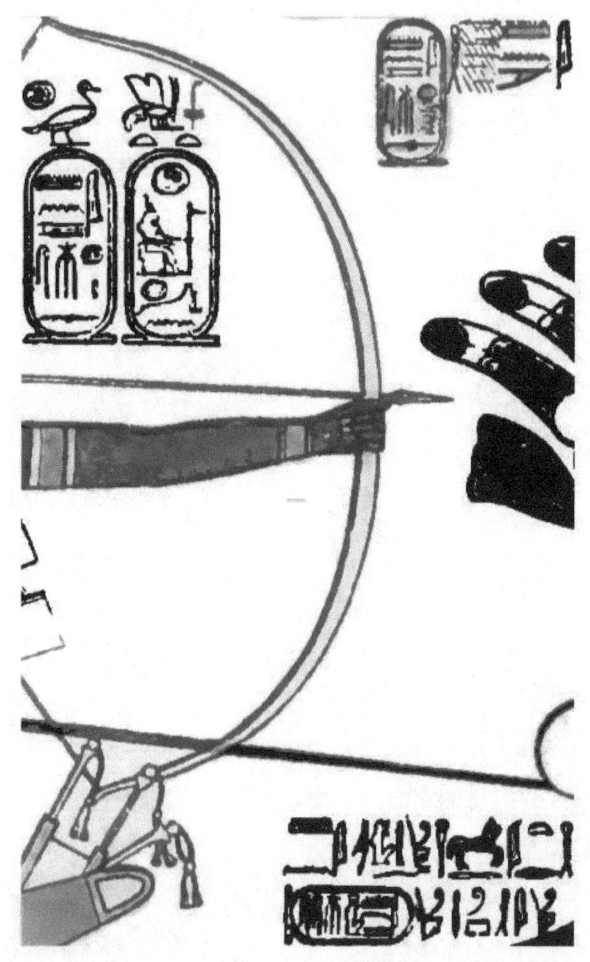

nefer, who was also mother of the future Pharaoh, whose twelve elder brothers died before their father. (Rameses had 111 sons and 51 daughters, of whom a list is in existence. Another list gives 60 sons and 59 daughters.) Kha-em-uas, besides being priest of Ptah in Memphis, was a priest of the royal house, and, in place of the monarch, presided over the celebration of the great solemnities.

Rameses's victories, however brilliant, were evidently not decisive; for fifteen campaigns took place, after the battle of Kadesh was fought in his fifth year, before the final treaty of peace was concluded in the twenty-first year of his reign. Its terms are an alliance offensive and defensive, based upon a perfect equality and reciprocity. Kheta-Sar is

Fig. 97.—Mount Tabor.

first named, and Rameses after him. Kheta-Sar is spoken of in the first person, Rameses in the third; it is therefore obvious the peace was not dictated by the latter. The treaty was engraved, in Egyptian and Hittite, on a silver plate, designed to be attached to a temple-wall. The Egyptian rendering alone is preserved. According to the words of this treaty—the oldest of which the text has been handed down by history—Rameses, when it was concluded, was in the city Rameses-meri-amen in the Delta. Two heralds—Tarti-bu and Rames—conveyed the silver tablet, which was set up under the protection of the thousand divinities, male (warlike) and female, of the lands of Kheta and Egypt, — Sutekh of Tunep, of Kheta, and of Arnema; Zaaranta, Pilka, Khisasap, Sarfu, Khilpu, Sarpaina: also of Astarte of Kheta, of the god of Zayatkherri, of the gods of the land, hills, and rivers of Kheta, of the gods of the land of Kazauatana; on the other hand, of the Egyptian gods Amun, Ra, Sutekh, of the male and female gods of Egypt, of the earth, sea, winds, and storms — all of whom were invoked to protect the observers, and punish the infringers, of the treaty. It established a league between both great powers forever, as well as an agreement for the extradition of runaway laborers and criminals.

The god Sutekh, who appears in this remarkable document as Hittite, is the same whom the Hyksos king, Apepi, made the one supreme divinity, and to whom Rameses's son Mereuptah founded at Avaris a cult, as god of strangers. He is represented with the high Hittite tiara, and the band hanging down behind, as one can see on the pedestal of the statue of Usertesen I. in the Berlin Museum, where a royal prince prays to him. Through the identification of this form of the Baal Zephōn with the Egyptian Set-Sutekh, this divinity acquired the character of the Egyptian evil genius Typhon. Astarte (Ashtoreth), whom, like Sutekh, the Hittites had borrowed from the Phoenician pantheon, was also worshipped in the Delta, where from an early period Canaanitish people were settled. She was represented as a lion-headed female warrior, guiding her chariot. On a stele in the British Museum, she is shown brandishing a battle-axe, and holding a shield and lance, like the war-god Rezeph (by the Greeks named Antaeus, also Apollo).

The treaty of peace was yet further confirmed by the marriage of Rameses with the daughter of Kheta-Sar. A relief in the temple of Abu-Simbel, dating from the thirty-fourth year of this king, depicts the Hittite king wearing the high tiara, and accompanied by the Prince of Keti (perhaps Cataonia), leading his child, in the attire of an Egyptian princess, to the Pharaoh. The daughter of Rameses appears to have married a Syrian prince; for on the granite statue which her father erected as a pendent to his own before the second pylon of the temple of Luxor, she is distinguished by a Syrian name,

Bant-Anat ('daughter of the goddess Anat'). Similarly the Hittite wife of Rameses received the Egyptian name, Ra-mãa-ar-nefru. A tablet between two pillars of the first hall of the temple of Abu-Simbel bears a eulogium of Rameses, in the form of an address of the god Ptah-Totunen. It was also engraved on the pylon of the temple of Rameses III. at Medinet-Abu. Among other things it says: — "King Rameses, I have exalted thee through so wonderful gifts, that heaven and earth leap for joy, and those who are therein extol thy being. Mountains, waters, and the stone walls of the earth quake at thy name; for they have seen what I have accomplished for thee, namely, that the land of Kheta is subjugated to thy house. I have seen into the hearts of its inhabitants, that they come before thee with obedience in the bringing of their gifts. Their princes are captives; all their possessions are the tribute of their dependence on the living king. The royal daughter comes at their head to soften the heart of Rameses. Her charms are wonderful, but she knows not yet the goodness of thy heart. Thy name is blessed forever. The successful issue of thy victories is a wonder, which men hope for, but such as from the time of the gods was never seen, a hidden remembrance in the house of the books from the time of Ra till the reign of life, health, and strength (i.e. of your Majesty). It was unheard of that Kheta-land should be at accord with Egypt:

FIG. 98. — Rameses II.

FIG. 99.—Sandstone statue of Seti II. (a ram on his knees). From Thebes. London, British Museum.

and lo! I have struck it down under thy feet, in order that thy name may live forever, King Rameses."

Rameses continued Seti's works at Karnak and elsewhere, and erected many monuments. In his thirtieth year he chose as co-regent and heir Kha-em-nas, his son by his sister Isis-Nefert. Kha-em-nas won fame as priest and magician, and built the Serapeum of Memphis. He died before his father, who then selected as heir Merenptah II., his thirteenth son. He was over sixty, when, after having been for twelve years co-regent, he succeeded his father. Merenptah's relations with his Syrian provinces remained peaceful. But in his fifth year the powerful king of the Libyans, Marayu, son of Titi, swept into the western Delta, and threatened Heliopolis. Merenptah caused Memphis, Heliopolis, and other cities to be fortified forthwith; for this was no ordinary raid. The Libyans had effected a great confederation of 'the peoples of the Sea.' These were the Libyan Mashuasha (the Matshiya of the Persians or Maxyans of Herodotus), the Tamehu and Kehak; besides the Shardana, Shakarusha, Akaiusha (Akauasha), Leku, and Tulsha (Tursha), piratical Mediterranean coast peoples, "who marched fighting to daily fill their mouths."

The Lebu, who, along with the Tamehu and Mashuasha, went under the common name of Tehennu (the western neighbors of the Egyptians up to the Abyssinian frontier), were tall and fair, with crisp, light, curly hair, ornamented by two feathers; and a side-lock hanging down to the shoulder. Like the Tuaregs or the Kabyles, they were tattooed. Some of them practised circumcision. Their arms were similar to those of the Egyptians. The Pharaoh's army completely overthrew the allies at Per-er-shepes (Prosopis). Great was the rejoicing. The paean of victory that sounded throughout Egypt was carved in stone and set in the temples. The great black stela found by Petrie (1896) at the Ramesseum is especially interesting, as it mentions Israel among the Syrian peoples in whom the victory struck terror: "No one raises his head among the foreigners. Tehennu is destroyed; Kheta is quiet; Kanaan is rid of all evil; Ascalon is sacked; Gezer is captive; Janoam is crushed; Israel is laid waste and seedless; Kharu is as a widow to the land of Egypt. The entire earth is quiet."

Merenptah has been regarded as the Pharaoh of the Exodus. But scholars differ on the subject; and the above-quoted passage—by showing Israel, in his reign, already established in Syria—has further complicated the problem. On the other hand, excavations in the Eastern Delta have proved that the construction of 'Rameses' and of Pi-tum dates from the Ramessids. This tends to confirm the view which sees in Rameses II. the Pharaoh "who knew not Joseph." However this may be, Seti II. (Figs. 99 and 100) did not come peacefully into his own; and although he left monumental traces, his tomb remained unfinished. A high priest of Ptah usurped the royal titles. A Semite, Ersu or Arizu, ruled "in the years of famine." . . . For a period "Egypt was governed by princes who killed each other in pride and arrogance, and did after their own pleasure, for they had no chief." The Harris papyrus (133 feet long) gives much information on this period. Ameumeses followed; then Si-ptah Mereuptah, who "ascended the throne of his father," thanks to his marriage with the heiress Ta-usert. His sixth year has been found; and he seems to have held the country and maintained its foreign relations. At last Set-nekht established order and ushered in the Twentieth Dynasty. Under Rameses III. (Rhampsinitus) Egypt once more enjoyed thirty-three years of glorious prosperity. He won over the priesthood by gifts and edifices—"he restored truth, destroyed untruth"; reorganized mining interests and commercial intercourse with Punt. Asia recognized his authority.[1] The Libyans alone were inimical. Again, with the 'peoples of the Sea' (the Akayasha, the Bikaua, the Kehaka, the Sabati) they had invaded the Delta to the canopic mouth of the Nile. Set-nekht dared not oppose them. Rameses, before doing so, reorganized his army, improved its equipment and discipline, and enlisted mercenaries. In his fifth year the crisis came.

FIG. 100. — Seti II.

[1] W. M. Müller, 'Asien und Europa,' p. 276.

The struggle was terrific; 12,525 dead were recorded by the conqueror, who scattered the vanquished in military colonies along the Nile valley. These formed a military cast called Mashuasha (the name of the dominant Libyan nation). The Delta to the Natron Lakes was recovered; but Libya remained powerful,[1] for Rameses had to face a more serious danger.

Migratory European hordes had been pouring into Asia Minor. They had overrun Northern Syria. The immigrants came in ox-carts or in ships with their families. The names of many had already

FIG. 101. — The captive Pulasati in the triumphal procession of Rameses III.

appeared in the Egyptian annals. But the Takekar, the Daen-euna, the Uashash, the Pulasati (Philistines) are now named for the first time. The latter represent the group of people whom the classics vaguely describe as Karians, whose ships scoured the Mediterranean. The Pulasati wore a feathered head-gear, sandals, the long copper sword of the north, strapped on the left side. They carried two daggers, two javelins, and, like the Hittites, used war-chariots. The Turu-ba (Tyrseni) came next in numbers, then came the Zakkala (Sikels[2]); the

[1] In the eleventh year of Rameses III. they again had to be repelled.

[2] W. M. Müller, loc. cit., pp. 362–386, regards them as a Lykian tribe.

Shakarusha, who wore the woollen cap still used by the sailors of the archipelago, the Shardanes, the Daen-euna, the Leku, the Uashasha, were nations of Asia Minor. Their ships resembled those of Egypt, but had no spur. "The islands had shuddered and thrown up their nations in one single effort." Khati, Godi, Karkhemish, Aradu, Alashiya, had been swept down. The empire of Kheta-Sar had crumbled before them. In the land of the Amurru they entrenched a camp, in which they established their families. Then they attacked the Egyptian provinces. Rameses arrived at Zar in his eighth year, and defeated them near Sephelah. They fled to the coast, and joining his fleet near Jaffa, Rameses again defeated them at sea. He then established the Pulasati at Sephelah, the Zakkala between Carmel and Dor, and erected migdols (watch-towers) to control and protect them, thus creating a bulwark between the Delta and Asia. These triumphs are immortalized on the walls of Medinet-Abu. After this, he devoted himself to the erection of superb edifices, and a 'renaissance' followed. But, if Egypt prospered, Rameses had troubles of his own. Pentaurt, his son by a secondary wife, plotted to secure the succession to the exclusion of his sons by Queen Tyi. The 'Great Judiciary Turin Papyrus' gives the proceedings of the trial. A certain Pa-hi-ben had made waxen images, some intended to excite hatred of the king, others to cause him to waste away. Denounced, the conspirators—six women and forty men—were executed. The extreme penalty was given to the leaders and Pentaurt: "They died themselves"; and Maspero believes this to mean that they were mummified alive, and that Pentaurt may be the "Anonymous Prince" found among the royal mummies of Der-el-Bahri. His viscera were not removed, but he was outwardly thickly coated with natron. The bands are tightly drawn. The limbs are stretched and the hands and feet are twisted as if in unspeakable agony, while the horrible expression of the face, as well as the contortion of the entire body, reveal atrocious suffering. Nameless, he was also doomed to annihilation. Rameses III. was followed by one of his eighteen sons, Rameses IV. His reign and those of the eight Rameses who composed the Twentieth Dynasty were of little importance. The influence of the priesthood had grown so powerful as to overshadow the throne. At length the high-priest of Amen, Herhor, seized the crown and established the Twenty-first Dynasty. The Abbott, Salt, Amherst, Mayor, and Liverpool papyri contain reports of commissioners appointed to examine the royal tombs, and to secure the royal mummies against grave-robbers. Herhor and his grandson Pinozem, unable to secure their safety, had them removed, until they were finally concealed in a pit southwest of Der-el-Bahri. Here they were discovered by Arabs, who exploited the rich mine and sold royal objects to tourists—until, in 1881, they quarrelled and one turned evidence. Emil Brugsch Bey was the first to enter the pit. It is impossible to do justice to his description of his feelings when—after crawling down a shaft about 39 feet and through a gallery 243 feet long—he entered a chamber 23 × 12 feet, and found himself in the presence of the august dead. Here lay pêle-mêle the coffins of some thirty royal personages of historic fame. It seemed like a fantastic dream. Wherever he turned to apply his light, he read names that had filled the ancient world with wonder: Seqenen-Ra, Aãhmes, Seti, Rameses, Thothmes III. (p. 287)—there were their very bodies. The garlands on that of Amenhotep I. were in such a state of preservation that they are exhibited as an herbarium at the Gizeh Museum. Along with the flowers was found a wasp that, allured by the odor,

FIG. 102. The Mummy of Rameses II., Gizeh Museum, Cairo.

had become shut in when the king's mummy was placed in its wrappings, and now came once more to light a mummy 3000 years old. The enamelled and gilded coffin of Thothmes I. was also found, but in it was the mummy of Pinozem II. That of Thothmes II., containing its proper mummy, and that of Thothmes III., with a body only five feet one inch long, had been broken and plundered. On the bands appear passages from the "Book of the Dead" and litanies to the Sun. Of Queen Maka-Ra, there was found only her liver embalmed in a casket. The name of Rameses I. was inscribed on a woman's coffin, probably because the robber had shattered the proper one. The mummy of Rameses I. was not found at first, but was identified later. Further, there were found the coffin of Seti I. (the stone sarcophagus remained in the original grave at Biban-el-Moluk); those of Rameses II. (Figs. 102, 103), III., and XII., of Pinozem I. and II., and of Masaherta. In addition to these remains of royal personages, there were found coffins and mummies of Ansara; of Aahmes-nefertari,[1] spouse of the liberator of Egypt (beside whom were found four vases of the dead); of Aah-hotep, sister and spouse of Amenhotep I. (not the ancestress of the Eighteenth Dynasty); of Queen Hent-meh, spouse of Aahmes, and of Mes-hent-meh, probably their daughter, whose mummy had been apparently replaced, after an earlier robbery, by a block enveloped by bands; of the young princess Sat-amen and the prince Sa-amen, infant children of Aahmes; the coffin of the priest Sonu, chamberlain of the queen, but with the mummy of the princess Merit-amen, sister of Amenhotep I.; coffins and mummies of Queen Notemit, spouse of Herhor; of Queen Hen-ta-ui, spouse of Pinozem; of Queen Hest-em-sekhet, spouse of her uncle, Ra-men-kheper, and daughter of Masaherta. By the side of the mummy of this princess, in her threefold coffin, lay a wooden image of Osiris, with a copy of the "Book of the Dead," bronze and clay articles, but especially a leather *baldachino* after the Assyrian pattern, decorated with Asiatic painted ornaments, and inscribed with religious texts. Yet further were found the mummy of the princess Nesi-khuns; the coffin containing the Queen Maka-Ra, spouse of Pinozem, and Mut-em-hat,

[1] This mummy, inscribed with the name of Nefertari, when unwrapped in 1886 proved to be that of Rameses III., and was in an excellent state of preservation.—ED.

their daughter; likewise the coffins of some private persons connected with the royal family. In all, this heterogeneous resting-place of princely bodies yielded a treasure of 6000 separate objects,

FIG. 103. — Head of Rameses II.

which were conveyed in solemn procession, under charge of the natives, across the plain, laden on a Nile steamer, and brought to Bulak, whence they were transferred to the Museum at Gizeh. The Mahdi war, which broke out soon after this remarkable discovery, for a time engrossed official attention, and it was only on June 3, 1886, that the unwrapping of the bodies of Rameses II. and Rameses III. took place with great ceremony before the Khedive, who enjoyed the unique privilege of gazing upon the face of his illustrious and legendary predecessor across a chasm of more than three millenniums.[1] History with all her tragedies can furnish none more impressive than the spectacle of the mightiest monarch of the ancient world—whose devotion to the gods, attested by countless magnificent monuments, was to secure to him a happy eternity—set up on exhibition as an archaeological curiosity, No. 5253, in the very heart of his ancestral empire.

Some years after this, another sepulchral hiding-place yielded eighty mummies of the high priests of Thebes. Since then other similar, though partial, 'finds' have been made. One of the most important of these was made by Loret, who, in 1898, discovered the tomb of Amenhotep II., where, in addition to that monarch's body, other royal mummies were found, notably that of King Merenptah.

Herhor's successor was his grandson Pinozem, son of the high-priest Piankhi. His name is not given as a royal cartouche, as are those of his wife and their little daughter Mut-em-hat, who died shortly after being born. The king nominally married this child in

[1] The following extract is from Maspero's report:

"The mummy (No. 5.233), first taken out from its glass case, is that of Rameses II., Sesostris, as testified by the official entries bearing date the sixth and sixteenth years of the reign of the High Priest Her-hor-se-amen, and the High Priest Pinozem I., written in black ink upon the lid of the wooden mummy-case, and the further entry of the sixteenth year of the High Priest Pinozem I., written upon the outer winding-sheet of the mummy over the region of the breast. The presence of this last inscription having been verified by His Highness the Khedive, and by the illustrious personages there assembled, the first wrapping was removed, and there were successively discovered a band of stuff [*sic*] 20 centimeters in width rolled round the body; then a second winding-sheet sewn up, and kept in place by narrow bands placed at some distance apart; then two thicknesses of small bandages; and then a piece of fine linen reaching from the head to the feet. A figure representing the goddess Nut, one meter in length, is drawn upon this piece of linen, in red and white, as prescribed by the ritual. The profile of the goddess is unmistakably designed after the pure and delicate profile of Seti I., as he is known to us in the bas-relief sculptures of Thebes and Abydos. Under this amulet, there was found another bandage; then a layer of pieces of linen folded in squares, and spotted with the bituminous matter used by the embalmers. This last covering removed, Rameses II. appeared. . . . The jawbone is massive and strong; the chin very prominent; the mouth small, but thick-lipped, and full of some kind of black paste. This paste being partly cut away with the scissors, disclosed some much-worn and very brittle teeth, which, however, are white and well preserved. . . . The hairs are white, like those of the head and eyebrows, but are harsh and bristly, and from two to three millimetres in length. . . . The expression is unintellectual, perhaps slightly animal; but even under the somewhat grotesque disguise of mummification, there is plainly to be seen an air of sovereign majesty, of resolve, and of pride. The rest of the body is as well preserved as the head. . . . The corpse is that of an old man, but of a vigorous and robust old man. We know, indeed, that Rameses II. reigned for sixty-seven years, and that he must have been nearly 100 years old when he died."

order to secure his title, thus avoiding possible future political complications. Pinozem's successor was Pa-seb-kha-nen. A second Pa-seb-kha-nen had two daughters, one of whom married Osorkon (Twenty-second Dynasty), conveying to him thereby the right to the throne. Rameses III.'s policy of establishing military colonies of mercenaries had resulted in the development of a military aristocracy, Shardana or Mashuasha, which grew in power until, under King Sheshonk, even high priests of Thebes and of Memphis were Libyans.

From the Twenty-first Dynasty Egypt had indeed become 'two lands': Theban Egypt, ruled by a theocracy—retiring more and more from cosmopolitan influence and the new civilization of the Mediterranean—and Northern Egypt, which had never lost touch with Europe and Asia. A struggle was shortly to begin between the two, in the course of which Ethiopia conquered Egypt, and in turn succumbed to its northern neighbor. Soon Ethiopia was to struggle with Assyria for the possession of Libyanized Egypt, and Persian, Greek, and Roman conquerors were to follow.

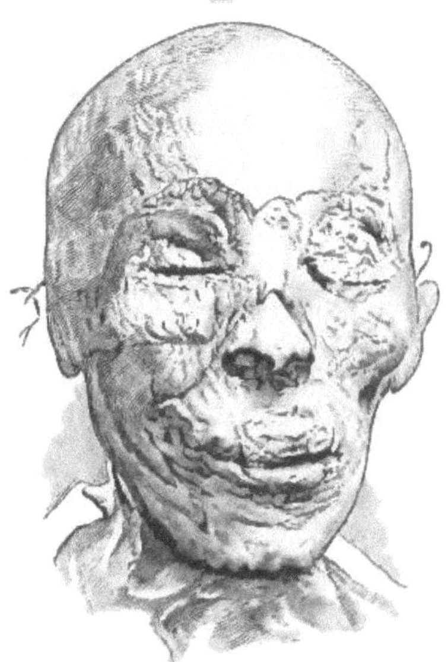

Head of Thothmes III. (After Maspero.)

CHAPTER VII.

ART UNDER THE NEW EMPIRE.

THE art of the New Empire has longer been known than that of the Ancient Empire. It is only since the time of the modern excavations in the necropolis of Memphis that we have been enabled to study the latter satisfactorily, while the gigantic remains of the temples of the New Empire, with their obelisks and granite figures, have, from very early times, attracted the admiration of mankind. The more ancient art is unquestionably closer to nature than the later. It did not show such technical dexterity in the handling and working great masses of the hardest stones, nor in overlaying its productions with durable stucco painted in colors; but it was guided by a truer and better instinct. Yet art reached a high degree of perfection, especially under the Eighteenth Dynasty. There are single pieces of sculpture of that period which are equal, if not superior, to anything in Egypt. The so-called head of Taïa (see p. 324) and that of Khuns (PLATE XXVI.)—the first for grace of expression, the second for depth of meaning—will bear comparison with any work of man. Nothing could be more realistic than the female acrobat of the Turin Museum. Her supple activity is such that—as Maspero has remarked—"one almost expects her to turn over and finish her caper." If we lose sight of such excellence, it is perhaps owing to the artistic exuberance of the period, and to the abundance of the more ordinary material preserved, in the mass of which such masterpieces are lost. The colossal statues grew out of the necessity to keep pace with the enormous proportions of the buildings. But these architectural colossi of sixteen and twenty metres, carved of the hardest substance, were as carefully proportioned as though they had been of natural size. Egyptian sculpture always retained certain archaisms. A statue, unless of wood, was never free. The back always rested on a pillar and the legs were not separated, and were badly modelled; the hands also were crude.

One must be accustomed to Egyptian art to fairly judge of its merits. Certain peculiarities of dress, symbolism, and traditional rule often interfere with our correct appreciation of the work. But the masterful way in which the Egyptian artist managed his material must be plain to all.

The statements of the inscriptions lead to the inference that, in the New Empire, the ground-plans of the older temples were utilized for the later. In order to realize the full effect of these edifices, it is best that we should set out from a consideration of their elements in detail.

FIG. 104. Quarries at Turra.

The walls of the temples are chiefly built of sandstone and limestone, seldom of granite. Brick we find only in the subsidiary buildings and in the outer wall enclosing the whole sacred precinct. Even the operation of quarrying the stones is regarded as worthy of perpetuation: and the officials tell us, in the inscriptions on their graves, with how much care they had watched over the transportation of great blocks. The quarries were worked in shafts, the hill being bored till the proper stone was reached; and we still see at Turra (Fig. 104), near Cairo, the oblong quadrangular cavities in the rocks due to the excavation of the immense square blocks for the pyramids. The opening of a new shaft was solemnly recorded in a writing meant for posterity.

The pillars and columns are the most important elements of the temple. Some remarks on their history will be found on p. 125. The so-named proto-Doric columns occur but seldom in the New Empire. We see them of an octagonal form in Medinet-Abu, with sixteen sides in Karnak, Der-el-Bahri, and Temneh; with twenty-four in Kalabshe (Talmis, in Nubia), where, however, four were left smooth for inscriptions. The calyx columns consist in Luxor of eight stalks clustered together, bound round three times by a quintuple band. The under part of the capital is enveloped; and immediately over the neck the bud is bent strongly outwards, and tapers in straight lines to a point at the abacus, which is not broader than the upper circumference of the bud. The shaft is usually sunk into the socle, so that the reed-leaf ornamentation gives it a bellied appearance. This column is either fluted, so that its original form is still plain, or it is covered with a round coating, enriched with ornaments or painted. The column with opened calyx is distinguished from the other only by its capital. On both sides royal cartouches run round the body like a garland. The open calyxes are only painted with reed leaves, from which stalks with crowns of blossoms arise. In Karnak we see, in the portions originating from Thothmes III., columns with inverted bell-shaped capitals (PLATE XX.); but this unlovely motive has found no imitators. The open-calyx capital shows, later, plastic elements. In Soleb, in the time of Amenhotep III., it is modelled into eight palm-branches with painted leaves. Papyrus-blossoms also serve as motives, and suggest the Greek acanthus leaves. A striking feature is the disregard of proportion between the inter-columnar distances and the height and thickness of the pillars, a matter which in Greek art was governed by strictest rule. Thus in the same temple pillars of the same diameter and entirely similar character are found of different heights. Similarly we find columns of different character, some with the bud, others with the calyx capital, in close juxtaposition; and although they are of the

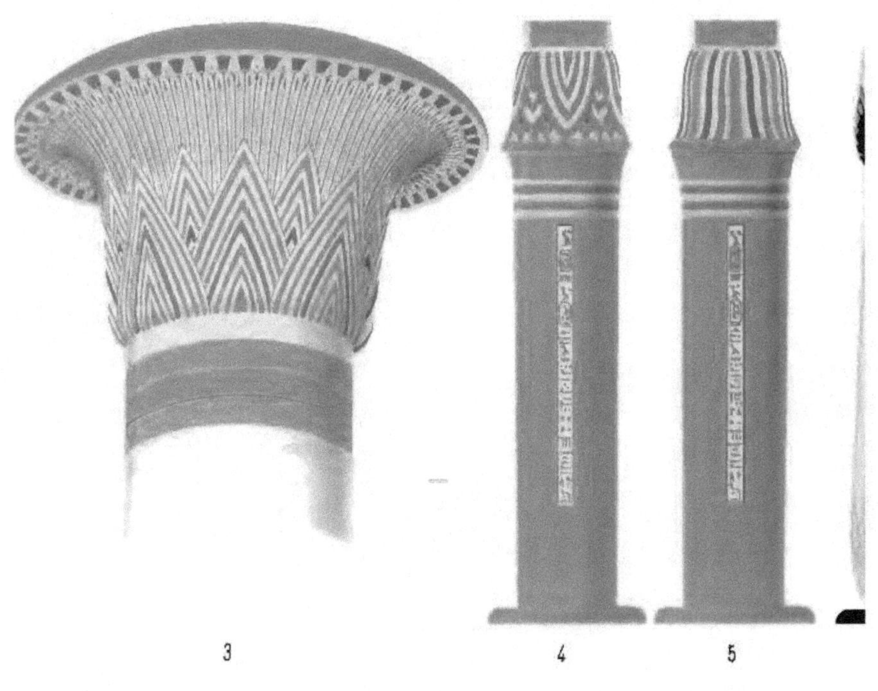

COLUMNS FROM THE GR

I and 3, Columus of the middle rows of the Great Halls of Seti and Rameses.
of the outer Hall of Thothmes III.

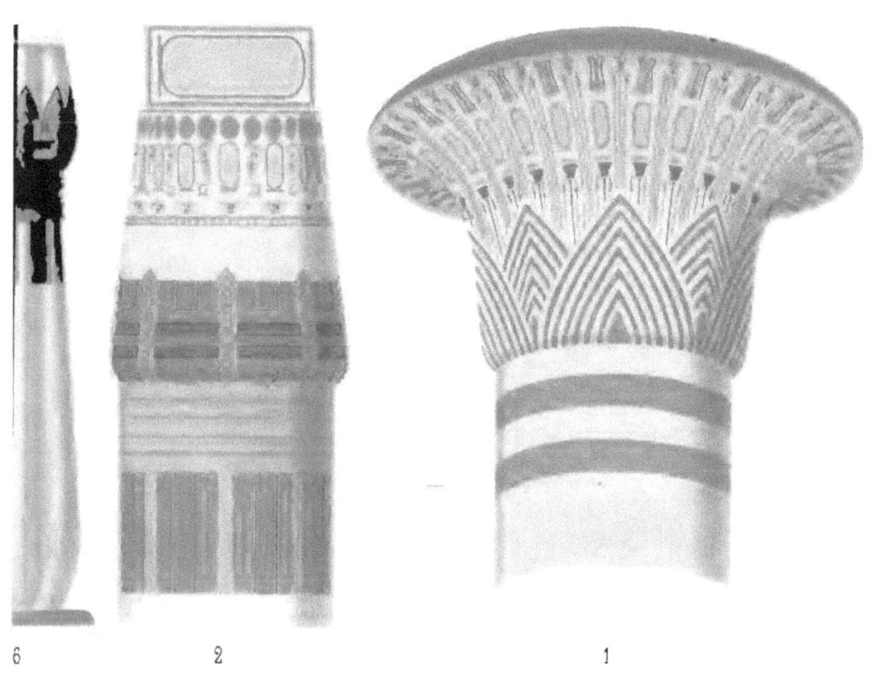

T TEMPLE AT KARNAK

One of the 122 remaining Columns of the anterior Hall. 4 and 5, Columns
Column from an adjoining Room.

(See page [illegible].)

same diameter, sometimes the one sort, sometimes the other, is the higher. On the other hand, again, there are columns of different character in the same edifice, of similar height and thickness. Finally, columns entirely alike are found with different inter-columnar spaces; so that the bearing-beam, or architrave, which is more prolonged over the wider spaces, is higher in one place than another, a circumstance to be frequently observed in the middle rows of columns of the hypostyle, which stand farther apart than the others. The entablature consists of the architrave, which is smooth, and affords a surface for sculptures, and the trochilus, with leaf ornaments. These are divided by the astragal, which, as we saw in the mastabas, has its motive from the embroidery-frames on which the decorations of carpets were covered. The cornice rises above the end, and thus constitutes a sort of breastwork. The gateways of the outer enclosing-wall are very high and deep, so that they jut out over the wall, both outside and in. On their far-projecting entablatures and cornices, as well as on all the doors, is seen the winged solar disk, the symbol of Horus of Edfu, Hor-Behûdti (see p. 46). It was formerly overlaid with metal. The enclosing-wall is built of Nile bricks, and has, therefore, merlons in place of a cornice. The passage hence to the temple-buildings proper was bordered by avenues of sphinxes. Before the temple-gate were erected colossi of the builder in a sitting posture, also two obelisks (Fig. 105). The temple-gate was flanked by pylons, that is, by quadrangular tower-like structures with plane surfaces inclined inwards, whose longer sides constitute the façades. An astragal covers the corners of the pylons, and runs under the base of the entablature. Stone rings project from its surfaces, to hold masts on which pennants were displayed. Passing through the gate we enter the fore-court, which on both sides, as well as on the third, is surrounded by colonnades. The spaces between the pairs of middle columns of the third side are very wide, so as not to contract the entrance to the first hall, or *usekhet* ('the breadth'), which lies some steps higher, and is supported by pillars. The hypostyle, or vestibule, is followed by the sanctuary, where in a separate shrine, often worked out of a single granite block, the statue of the god stands, or the animal sacred to him is kept. The sanctuary could be entered only by the Pharaoh and the higher priests, and the tabernacle could be opened only by him and the high priest. The lower classes awaited in the vestibule the appearance of the god. The latter was carried around the temple-bounds in a procession formed in the hypostyle, either in a consecrated vessel, — the bark that sails the heavenly ocean — or in a shrine borne on the shoulders of priests. Round the sanctuary lay various chambers, mainly dark, designed for religious purposes and for keeping the temple-treasures;

FIG. 105. – The Obelisk of Heliopolis.

also chapels and the lodgings of the priests. Farthest back of all was often an opisthodomus, or hall of columns, which, but for little openings in the ceiling, would have been quite dark. Candelabra were used to light dark rooms, one of which is represented at Tel-el-Amarna. The outside walls of all these apartments constitute one unbroken surface, only that, beside the pylons, admission is given to the fore-court by little side-doors, in the thickness of whose wall lies the entrance to the small passage, in the interior of the pylons, that leads to the roofs. This uniform wall-surface, that gives to the temple the appearance of a colossal chest, is everywhere cov-

Fig. 105. The Vestibule, with the First Pylons, of the Great Temple at Karnak.

ered by sculptures. The horizontal is here the dominant line, as it is in Egyptian landscape. The edifice is shut off entirely from the outside, and allows no glance into its interior, in conformity with the character of the land, in which man flees from the glare of the sun, as well as with the genius of the Egyptian religion, that enveloped itself, for the initiated, in the gloom of mystery. The temples in Nubia were hewn out of the living rock, partly because the Nile valley is occasionally too narrow to afford room for great structures, partly because, owing to the distance from Egypt, it was desirable to complete them very expeditiously: and a rock temple required neither foundations nor the tedious operations of quarrying and preparing great blocks of stone. In several instances the pylon and fore-court are built, and only the pillared hall and the sanctuary worked out of the rock. At the great temple of Abu-Simbel, the pylon and the sitting forms of the colossi before it constitute one immense rock sculpture.

The temples of Egypt are, as a rule, constructed on one uniform plan, which is most completely exhibited in the great national temple of Karnak in eastern Thebes (see Plan, PLATE XXI., with the following description). This great Temple of Amen (PLATE XXII.) stretches to the length of 1180 feet, and is at once the most magnificent structure in the valley of the Nile, and the greatest religious edifice the world has seen. It was begun in the period of the first Theban dynasty, and completed in the age of the Ptolemies. Some 450 androsphinxes (Fig. 107), symbols of Harmakhis, and of royal power, or rams lying prone (animals sacred to the fertilizing sun-god, and emblems of generation), border the various sacred avenues; while in the southwest a long street of sphinxes is added, leading to the temple of Luxor. On this passage, 6500 feet long, must have stood nearly 1000 sphinxes; for those still extant stand thirteen feet apart. When we approach the temple from the bank of the Nile, in the direction of its axis,—namely, from north-

FIG. 107.—Thothmes III., as Androsphinx.

PLATE XXI.

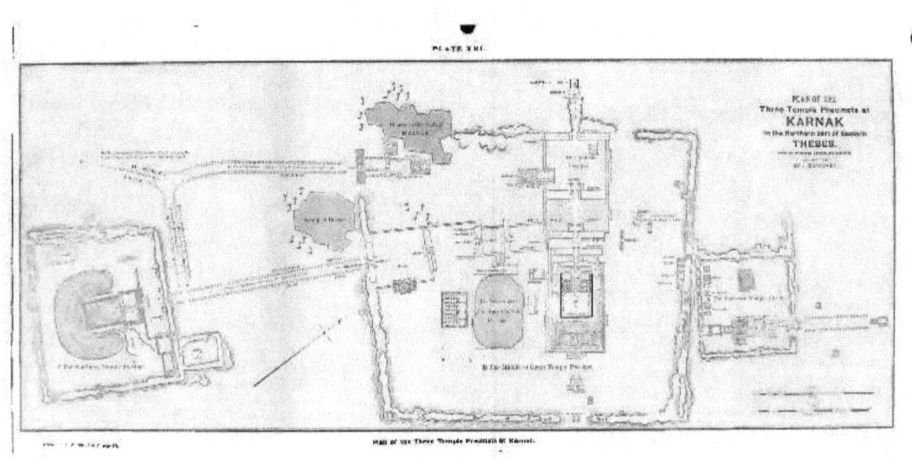

Plan of the Three Temple Precincts at Karnak.

PLATE XXII.

General view of the great Temple of Amun in the Middle Temple precinct of Karnak (from the south).

west to southeast,—we pass through a little gateway of Seti II., where formerly two obelisks stood, into an avenue of rams, laid out by Rameses II., and leading to well-preserved pylons of the time of the Ptolemies, 360 feet broad and 145 feet high. These lie in the range of the enclosing-wall of the *temenos*, or temple-area. The wall itself, 7500 to 8000 feet in circumference, and built of Nile bricks, is destroyed, and can be traced only by the mounds of fragments. Passing through the portal between the pylons, we enter an open court. Before this was laid out, a pair of pylons of the time of Rameses I., now constituting its back wall but overthrown, were the façade of the temple. Before these pylons there stood, on either side of the entrance, statues of Rameses II. in the act of walking. Over against these, there arose under Seti II., outside the buildings then existing but now enclosed within the fore-court, a sanctuary, consisting of three halls, of which little more than the foundation walls are preserved. Still closer to the façade, but with its axis at right-angles to that of the great temple, stood a temple founded by Rameses II., with pylons, fore-court, hypostyle, and sanctuary, as well as representations of the heroic deeds of this king. When, afterwards, the present great fore-court was formed, it enclosed the sanctuary of Seti II., above mentioned, and so impinged on the temple of Rameses III. that the pylon of the latter intruded on the court. The court-wall bears no inscription: only between the temple and the pylon of the next hypostyle are statues and inscriptions of Shishak I., relating to his campaigns in Syria. In the middle of the court was an avenue of five or six columns, 70 feet high, laid out under Taharka and Psammetichus II., in the beginning of the sixth century B.C. Only one of the columns is now erect. This avenue served for laying poles across during the processions, on which great carpets and baldachins were fixed to shade those taking part in them in their passage through the court. One of our illustrations (Fig. 106) affords a view of the back of the Ptolemaic pylon, to which the colonnade of the fore-court is joined. Farther to the left appear the pylons of the temple of Rameses III. and the two columns (of one of which only the half is standing) belonging to the middle avenue. In the background to the right we catch a glimpse of the Temple of Khuns (to be later noticed), and, on the left, of the pylons of Thothmes. These last, as we shall see, bound the great temple-court, whose axis is nearly

FIG. 108. — Relief at Karnak. Nekhebt, the Goddess of the South, conducting King Seti I. to the Throne of Amen. (Fourteenth century B.C.)

at right-angles to that of the chief temple. The extent of this fore-court — 295 feet broad and 330 feet long, and large enough to be

PLATE XXIII

The Obelisk of Thothmes in the Great Temple at Karnak.

History of All Nations, Vol. I., page 297.

Columns in the Great Temple at Karnak.

History of All Nations, Vol. I., page 207.

the site of a respectable cathedral—prepares us for the impression made by the hypostyle. No words have ever been found to adequately describe this impression. It can only be computed in figures. This hall, though over thirty centuries old, has a roof supported by 134 columns, whose gigantic proportions leave far behind all that even Egypt has elsewhere produced of a similar kind. An avenue formed by six pairs of columns with unfolded calyx capitals passes through the centre of the hall. On both sides of this are seven rows of nine columns with bud capitals. The columns of the middle avenue are 67 feet high, 11¾ feet in diameter, and 33 feet in circumference. The remaining 122 columns are only 26 feet lower. The hall, therefore, has a lofty central nave, as the middle passage carries a stone roof which is 26 feet higher than the roofs of the aisles on either side, and which rests upon a wall 26 feet high, borne up by the two adjoining rows of lower pillars. In this wall are windows in the form of small stone crosses. This arrangement is to be seen in the two accompanying illustrations, of which the one (PLATE XXIII.) gives a view of the part next in succession, where the obelisk of Thothmes stands; while in the other (PLATE XXIV.) we look towards the transverse axis of the temple, so that the gateway in the next-following portion is visible on the right. In several temples a similar mode of lighting by upper side-lights is observed. On the flat roof, immediately over the inner pillars, there rises a sort of *attica*, or clerestory, through openings in the walls of which light falls into the interior. Konrad Lange has shown that this arrangement of the hall of Karnak — a high middle nave with windows and two side-naves or aisles — is the prototype of the Greek *megaron*, and of the Greek, Roman, and also of the Western, basilica. Since the middle columns of the hall stand thirty-three feet apart, the stone beams of the roof are necessarily of the same length, while the others are somewhat over sixteen feet long. How the Egyptians elevated these stone beams, and the great flags lying on them (whose weight has been estimated to be about ninety tons) is unknown. All the walls, architraves, and ceilings are covered with colored pictorial representations, the walls chiselled in flat relief. Dreamed of by Rameses I., the hall was executed by Seti I., and its western half was erected under

Rameses II., who also completed the sculptural ornamentation. On October 3, 1899, eleven columns crashed down and several more were damaged. Some 1700 tons of stone had to be removed by Mr. Legrain before anything could be done toward repairing the damage. The catastrophe which inflicted so serious a loss upon the civilized world is attributed to the action of infiltrations of water saturated with saltpetre. While clearing and strengthening the temple of Khuns, which also seemed threatened, Mr. Legrain found among other valuable monuments the superb gray granite statue of the god Khuns—unquestionably the finest piece of sculpture of the New Empire. (PLATE XXVI.) In its execution it recalls the chisel which carved the beautiful head of 'Taïa'—now regarded as the portrait of the queen of Horemheb (see p. 324). Both evidently belong to the Eighteenth Dynasty, and Maspero suggests that the statue of the god was a portrait of the king, while the queen was represented as the goddess Mut. However this may be, the school of art which produced those masterpieces represents the highest plane to which Egyptian taste ever rose. The Khuns is not merely a clever piece of modelling—it embodies an ideal. The back wall of the hypostyle adjoins the pylon of Amenhotep III., which is followed by that of Thothmes I. Between them stand the obelisks of Thothmes I. and III., the former overthrown. Behind it is a headless statue of Queen Aāhmes-Nefertari. On the left this space is open; for here, on the outside, lie some lesser erections of the Twenty-sixth Dynasty, and farther off, near the opposite door of the outer wall of the temple area, a small Ptah-temple of Thothmes III., in front of which Sabaco and the Ptolemies placed porticoes. The right side is, on the contrary, shut in by a wall whose gate gives entrance to the system of courts of the time of Thothmes, already referred to. On the inner wall of the pylon of Thothmes III., a series of statues represents the king as Osiris; and on it, also, the elevation of Maka-Ra to be co-regent with her father is delineated. Behind this pylon lies a columned hall, in which the highest obelisk (seen to the right in PLATE XXII.) rises. This was erected by Queen Maka-Ra-Hatshepsut; its counterpart is overthrown. The inscription tells that the upper part of the obelisk was incrusted with *asem* (either electrum, or a sort of bronze), and that it was prepared in seven months. Obelisks were worked in the quarry, and then sawn out. Behind a second pylon of Thothmes I.,

FIG. 109. King Horus approaching Amen. Bas-relief on the Pylon of Horus south of the Great Temple at Karnak.

comes, in a sadly ruinous condition, a mass of halls, apartments, and corridors, in the midst of which a great quadrangular structure (colored black in PLATE XXI.) of the time of the Ancient Empire is recognizable, its ruins comprising a number of priests' chambers. We find here the cartouches of Antef, Amenemhat, Usertesen, and Sebek-hotep. The old sanctuary (restored by Thothmes III.) no longer exists, but is replaced by a new one constructed entirely of mighty squares of granite, of the time of Philip Arrhidaeus, who was raised to the monarchy after Alexander's death, B.C. 323, but was murdered B.C. 317. Two isolated pilasters of red granite, with lotus capitals, of the time of Thothmes III., still stand before the sanctuary (PLATE XX.). The most of these ruins, among them those of a hall surrounded by thirty-two pillars, and having its roof borne on fifty-two piers, are of the time of Thothmes III. Some, however, were begun by Amenhotep I., and completed by Thothmes. Among the latter were found a pair of granite sphinxes, now in Cairo, and an interesting inscription consisting of a sort of building-contract. According to the inscriptions on the wall south of the sanctuary, there were, among these portions owing their origin to Thothmes III., halls decorated with silver and bronze. They contained statues of this monarch and older kings, sacrificial tables, a harp incrusted with silver and precious stones, a chapel hewn out of one block of stone, cedar doors inlaid with gold and other metals, three large gates decorated with silver, and a great granite shrine whose interior was plated with gold. The inscription makes mention also of temple-servants, among them children of the Rutennu and Khent-nefer in Nubia. This whole portion of the temple was surrounded by a wall by Rameses II., and, through additions, extended by him to the outer enclosing-wall, in which, at this point, Nectanebo II., the last Pharaoh, inserted a gate.

Between the pylons of Amenhotep II. and Thothmes I. lies a free space, which divides the whole temple into two parts, and at the same time points to a complex of courts whose axes were at right angles to that of the main temple. A first court was cut off by pylons of Thothmes III.; a second, with two colossi of this monarch at its entrance, has in its fore part pylons of Thothmes I., before whose exterior sides stand two colossi of Thothmes II., and one each of Thothmes III. and IV. A gate in the east wall of this second court gives entrance to a little temple of alabaster. At some distance follows a third court, with two gates flanked by pylons of Horus, the one restored by Rameses II., the other erected by Amenhotep II. In the eastern enclosing wall of this court lies a temple of Thothmes III., consisting of a portico in front of the façade, and a hall with twenty columns and side chambers. An avenue of sphinxes' heads leads from the outer gate of this court to the southern temple bounds. Between the principal temple and

FIG. 110. — The Holy Lake in the Middle Temple at Karnak.

the courts of Thothmes lies the sacred lake (Fig. 110) Usher-ha, where the bark of Amen floated on festival days. Its embankments date from the reign of Thothmes III. A temple of considerable size on its southern side has disappeared, except the foundation-stone. On the other side of the court of Thothmes lies, among the houses of Karnak, a great temple of the oracle-god Khuns (Fig. 111), with its pylons facing the southwest, so that their backs are towards the great temple. The gate of Ptolemy Energetes, one of the most beautiful memorials of his time, is all that is left of the pylon structure, and lies in the outmost wall of the middle enclosure. An avenue of Rameses III., bordered by sphinxes, leads to the temple proper, which, again, opens through pylons on a court whose three colonnades are borne on twenty-eight columns in double rows. To the eight-columned hypostyle, lying a few steps higher, succeeds the Sanctuary of Khuns. The Pharaoh worships him here under the two forms of Khuns-neb-zam (Khuns of the Thebaid), and of Khuns-nefer-hotep, or the moon-god. The temple was erected by Rameses III., and, in its good state of preservation, is an instructive example of a temple of

FIG. 111. — The Temple of Khuns (southwest of the Great Temple at Karnak).

simple, uniform design. Beside it stands a square temple, of the time of the Ptolemies, sacred to Apet, the goddess of birth, who appears in the form of a pregnant hippopotamus. In the illustration (Fig. 111), the pylon of the Temple of Khuns is seen in the foreground, and farther back the Temple of Apet; while the houses of Karnak stand in the background under palms. In the other illustration (Fig. 110), we have a view of the Temple of Khuns in the background, on the farther side of the sacred lake; while to the right and left, in the middle distance, the ruined pylons of Thothmes and Horus (Horemheb) show themselves. At a considerable distance northward of the chief temple lies the northern temple with its surroundings, founded by Amenhotep III., with restorations of the time of the Ptolemies, and decorated with colossi by Rameses II. The outmost pylon, and a side-temple on the west, date from the time of the Greek monarchs. Besides the above, other Pharaohs endeavored to perpetuate their names by lesser contributions, which have, however, all fallen into ruin. To the south, on the other side, lies a greater congeries of temples, dedicated to Mut, likewise due to Amenhotep III., but now, with its later additions, entirely destroyed. In the fore-court, on both sides of an avenue of ten columns, stood a great many statues of the lion-headed goddess, part of which have found their way to European collections. Westward, and close to the boundary-wall of the grounds, lies a little temple of Rameses III. A semicircular sacred lake runs round the back of the temple.

This temple-city, constructed by the sacred art of Egypt in the course of two thousand years, constitutes only a part, though the most impressive one, of the capital of Upper Egypt. A glance at a general map of Thebes shows that the Nile Valley, especially westward towards the mountains, is covered with its ruins. A second temple, — 'the temple of Amen, in southern Apet,' — formerly separated from that we have been describing by the main mass of dwellings, including those of the kings and priests, lies on a terrace overlooking the Nile, and near the village of Luxor. The façade faces Karnak, whereas all the other temples look towards the Nile. In front of the pylon sit four statues of Rameses II. and his daughter, forty feet high, but deeply sunk in the sand (Fig. 112). Before these stood two obelisks, one of which is now in Paris (see p. 135). The pylons are decorated with representations of the Hittite War. The present Thebans, with their huts, nestle in the interior and on the roof of the temple. The relatively unimportant city that Thebes was, at the opening of the Eighteenth Dynasty, had spread into an immense town of splendid monuments and sumptuous edifices. It had absorbed most of the neighboring villages. Suburbs stretched within the walls of enclosures; and avenues of sphinxes connected the principal quarters composing the capital. Everywhere were the monotonous clusters of gray huts and muddy pools, where animals drank and the people obtained water. Markets and bazars, dwellings of the well-to-do enclosed in blank walls and reserving what comfort and charm they might possess for their occupants—such was the Thebes of the people. The population might reach one hundred thousand souls. Many were foreigners—Syrians, Libyans, Negroes, Mesopotamians. The nobles lived outside the town, each residence forming a small settlement. The conquests of the New Empire had brought streams of gold into Egypt. Although barter remained the fundamental principle of trade, a change took place: rings and plates of

FIG. 112. Obelisk, seated statues of Rameses II., and Pylons of the Temple at Luxor.

gold, silver, and copper of standard weight (Tabenu) were used in exchange for goods, stimulating commerce.

The buildings on the opposite shore, in Western Thebes, faced the Nile and the eastern city. Here lay 'the West-land of the buried.' Here, too, was practised the ancestor-cult of the kings, in great temples, which served the same purpose as the temples before the pyramids and as the chambers of the mastabas.

In the extreme southwest lies Medinet-Abu, and near it the imposing temple of Rameses III., in a tolerably good condition (Figs.

113, 114). We reach first a propylaeum structure of the time of Antoninus Pius. It gives entrance to a very graceful temple of Thothmes III., on whose pylon the Pharaoh Taharka had his victory over the Jews engraved. Beside this temple, and approached through a free-standing gate, erected at its side by the architect Petamenap, stands a tower-like structure of Rhampsinitus, a building quite peculiar of its kind. On coming up from the plain, one finds before him two small pylons of a parterre and two stories, crowned with curved merlons. Their walls are a little higher than the inner court wall, while this latter contracts towards the back on both sides; so that we have a wider fore-court and a somewhat narrower second court. The buildings surrounding the court open upon the great temple. Where the

Fig. 113. View of the plain of Thebes, with the two Colossi of Memnon in the distance. From the Temple of Medinet Abu.

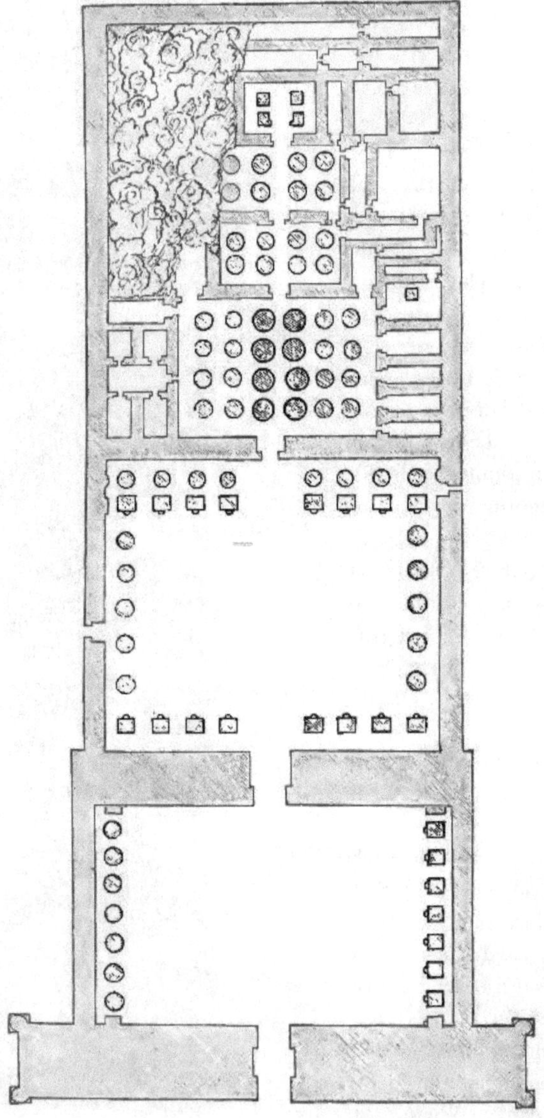

FIG. 111. Ground-plan of Memnonium of Rameses III., at Medinet-Abu.

court narrows, lie the stairs to the first and second stories. These were formerly divided by a wooden ceiling, while the top story is covered by a stone ceiling with beautiful lozenge-shaped ornaments. A broad frieze runs between this and the upper cornice of the windows, on which we see lotus-flowers, vases, pomegranates. Under this is a band covered with hieroglyphics, and, lowest of all, a series of uraeus-serpents, symbols of the kingly dignity. Among the sculptures we see some that represent the king amusing himself with his wives and at chess. From two places in the southern wall, there project the breasts, propped-up arms, and heads of four prone male figures, on which rests the bedding-slab of a horizontal stone tablet let into the wall. This 'pavilion' may probably be regarded as a triumphal gateway, in which, at the same time, chambers were contained for the king and part of his court, to be used by him in preparing for the festival pageants, while it might also serve as a sort of tribune for the spectator at the temple processions. The great temple consists of two fore-courts each behind pylons. In Fig. 115 the latter are seen towering in the background. The colonnade on the north side of the first court was borne on seven Osiris pillars; that of the south side on eight columns. The second court has eight Osiris pillars on its east side, arranged along the pylon, and an equal number stand opposite them. Behind the latter, eight columns arise, whose socles stand on a dais. The other sides have each five columns. This fine hypaethral hall is decorated with sculptures, painted in lively colors, and representing a great coronation procession, as well as the victories over the Phoenicians and Libyans, carefully indicating the great booty captured. The Coptic community has restored this hall as a church, and set in it five fine Corinthian columns. They had, at the same time, coated the wall with plaster, on which are depicted figures of Christian saints: whereby the old sculptures are maintained in excellent preservation. The view of the interior (Fig. 115) shows the hypostyle in the foreground, also a large second chamber, and on the left the adjoining chambers. On the south side lie the treasure chambers of the temple, whose vanished contents are commemorated by pictures on the walls. The gifts dedicated to Amen consist of gold in grains and dust, silver bars, perfect mountains of precious stones and metals, frankincense, statues, ornaments, spoils captured in the campaigns against the Syrians and negroes — all accompanied by devout dedicatory inscriptions.

Northeast of Medinet-Abu stood once a great temple of Amenhotep III., probably the Memnonium of Strabo, of which only the foundation walls remain, covered by the soil which now lies several

FIG. 115. — Vestibule of the Temple at Medinet-Abu.

meters deep over the temple site. As in Luxor, four colossi were reared in front of the vanished pylons, of which only two now stand upright, — the world-renowned vocal statues of Memnon. These own their origin to Amenhotep III. A large portion of the third colossus lies at a distance of 115 paces. The figures are of coarse, hard grit stone, mixed with chalcedonies, difficult to work. That on the north was broken by an earthquake, and its upper half re-erected by Alexander Severus. During the process of its decay, musical notes were elicited from it by the drops of early dew falling into the holes in the stone, which the ancients fancied to be the morning greeting of the Sun to his divine mother, Eos. Seventy-two inscrip-

Fig. 116. The Colossi of Memnon.

tions appear on the leg of the Memnon, engraved between the times of Nero and Septimius Severus, by strangers who had heard its tones. One of these is by the Emperor Hadrian and his wife

Sabina. The statues consist of two pieces, of which one forms the socle, the other the figure, which must have been lifted on to its pedestal. What this means will be understood when it is considered that the shoulders are nearly twenty feet broad, the middle finger four and one-half feet long, the tibia eighteen feet, and the foot (now lost) ten feet. The whole mass, pedestal and statue, according to the calculation of French engineers, must weigh nearly 2400 tons. The architect who erected the temple, and superintended the setting up the statues, bore the same name as his king, Amenhotep, and was the son of Hapi. Behind the ruined temple lies a second, in a similar condition, and also by Amenhotep. Near it are traces of erections of Thothmes IV. Deeper amongst the rocks are the graves of Gurnet-Murai, and, in a ravine behind these, a Ptolemaic temple

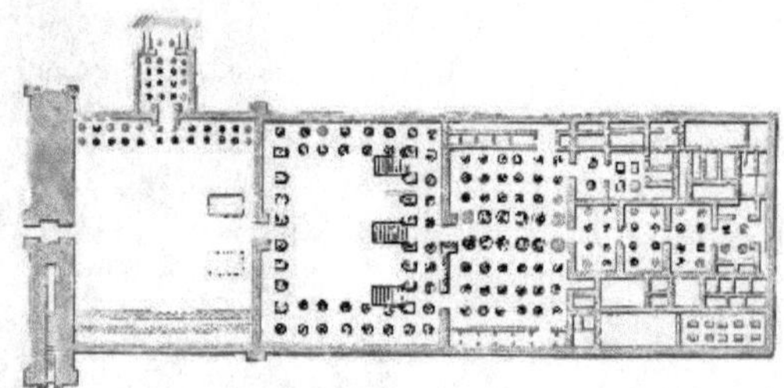

FIG. 117. – Ground plan of the Memnonium of King Rameses II.

of Hathor (Hekate) — Der-el-Medinet — in full preservation. Farther in the hills lies the so-called Tombs of the Queens. The nearest large, and partially preserved, temple is the famed Ramesseum or Memnonium (Figs. 117, 118), designed by Rameses II. for his cult when dead, and by the Greeks termed the grave of Osymandyas (i.e., User-ma-ra, the prenomen of Rameses). The first court had colonnades on both sides, each of eleven Osiris-pillars, with columns standing behind, the most of which are destroyed. It is strewn with blocks of stone, among them parts of a sitting colossus of the builder, and the sepulchral statue, which in old times was concealed in the *serdab*. The pedestal stands on the back wall, near the entrance to the second court. The figure was 56 feet high, and, like the Colossi of Memnon, worked out of a single block of syenite, and towered over the court. Head, breast, and arms lie now in one solid fragment on the ground.[1] It is much the largest statue in Egypt, and when perfect must have weighed over 1000 tons. Undoubtedly gunpowder was the agent employed by the wretch who shattered this work of art. On the other side of the portal stands a second, and smaller, pedestal for the statue of the queen. Although Diodorus, following the statement of Hecataeus, speaks of the statue, it is doubtful whether it was ever set up. Certainly no *débris* in-

Fig. 118. The Memnonium of King Rameses II.

dicating its presence is to be found. On the north face and propylaea of the second court is represented the war with the Kheta (Hittites), and the storming of their stronghold, Kadesh. In the

[1] I met a traveller from an antique land
Who said: Two vast and trunkless legs of stone
Stand in the desert. Near them on the sand
Half sunk, a shatter'd visage lies, whose frown
And wrinkled lip and sneer of cold command
Tell that its sculptor well those passions read
Which yet survive, stamp'd on these lifeless things,
The hand that mock'd them and the heart that fed;
And on the pedestal these words appear:
"My name is Ozymandias, king of kings.
Look on my works, ye Mighty, and despair!"
Nothing beside remains. Round the decay
Of that colossal wreck, boundless and bare,
The lone and level sands stretch far away.

SHELLEY.

second court (the Osiris-pillars of which with high columns are visible in the background of Fig. 118) stand two pedestals for statues nearly twenty feet in height, now lying in fragments. All of the hypostyle is destroyed save the four middle columns. Like the hall of Karnak, it consisted of a high nave with lower aisles. The columns are regarded as the most beautiful of any of the New Empire. The rear portion of the temple is covered with *débris*. The reliefs on the base of one of the doors show Thoth as 'Lord in the hall of books,' and behind him, the eye as God. Opposite is Safekh, as 'Mistress in the hall of books,' and behind her the ear as divinity. Conformable with this is Diodorus's statement that the library, as 'hospital of the soul,' was situated here. Alongside of and behind the temple lie numerous vaulted brick buildings, the bricks bearing the impress of the name of Rameses, a practice exceedingly ancient, and customary also in Babylon. Next follow the ruins of a temple of Thothmes III. and Rameses III.; and behind, in the hills, numerous rock sepulchres near Sheikh Abd-el-Gurnah, and in the north and south Asasif, where are graves of the Twenty-sixth Dynasty.

A vast and peculiar congeries of structures presents itself on the angle of the range of rocks near Der-el-Bahri (Plate XXV.), and at the foot of a steep declivity over which a path leads to the Tombs of the Kings. In conformity with the contour of the ground, the temple of Der-el-Bahri, lately excavated by Naville, stands on four terraces, some 300 feet broad, rising one above another, and each constituting a court. Traces of some 200 sphinxes, belonging to the avenue of sphinxes, were still visible in the end of the last century. Of the pylons we find only scanty remains. A street, in continuation of the avenue of sphinxes, intersects the whole place. Coming from the direction of the Nile, it here forms a junction with an avenue of sphinxes from Karnak, and ascends from one terrace to another by means of staircases. In the background of the second terrace the remains of a colonnade were discovered: on the third, close to the cliff, is a hall of columns, through which there is access to a niche in the rocks. The back part of this terrace shows double rows of pillars. On the fourth platform stands a mighty gateway of granite; and last of all follows the sanctuary, lying among the rocks, and dedicated by Thothmes to his wife Aahmes, to which the whole

PLATE XXV.

The Terrace-Temple of Der-el-Bahri (from the south).

(Prior to the excavations of Naville.)

History of All Nations, Vol. I., page 312.

of this most peculiar temple-system constitutes, as it were, only so many fore-courts. On both sides of the third terrace, also, lay rock-temples. The illustration shows, in the middle distance, in the shade, the long hall of the southern hall of columns, which terminates the third terrace. Before the wall lie the fragments of the double row of pillars. Quite behind are still seen the broad roof-flags. The strongly lighted wall in the foreground, with a pillar before it, separates the hall of columns from the southern side-temple, which opens by a gate on its portions lying in the rock. Under the high brick tower, belonging to the Coptic convent Der-el-Bahri ('the north convent'), is seen the wall of the fourth platform, and on the right, close to it, the granite portal, on the farther side of which rubbish covers the northern half of the grounds.

FIG. 119. — Seti's Temple of the Dead at Gurnah.

The most northern ruin of Thebes is Seti's Temple of the Dead at Gurnah, dedicated by this king to his father Rameses I., and the gods Osiris, Hathor, and the Theban triad, but not completed till the time of Rameses II. (Fig. 119). Of the sphinx avenues and the propylaea, only the pylons remain. The temple itself has a portico of ten columns with bud capitals, standing between antae. The middle and two outmost pairs of columns stand wider apart than the others; for behind these lie the three entrances into the hypostyle and two adjoining apartments, which, with their numerous chambers, each decorated with sculptures, are grouped in quite unique fashion.

The temple at Abydos, also begun by Seti and completed by his son, is peculiarly arranged (Fig. 120). Passing between two pylons

Fig. 120. — Columns of Rameses II. before the Hypostyle of the Temple of Seti at Abydos.

erected by the latter, we reach a row of twelve vast pillars decorated with religious scenes, standing before the hypostyle. Behind them lie seven entrances, of which, however, five are built up owing to their not harmonizing with the twelve pillars: so that only the middle entrance and the most westerly remain open. The base of several of the walls of the hypostyle consists of a socle-frieze, on which are depicted the symbolical figures of the Egyptian nomes, with their colors and escutcheons above their heads. This hall is borne up by a double row of twelve columns; and on its back wall there are seven entrances into a second hypostyle, in which are three rows of twelve columns, the third row somewhat higher than the other two. Here, again, we have seven openings in the back wall, which give admission into seven longish sanctuaries dedicated to Horus, Isis, Osiris, Amen, Harmachis, Ptah, and King Seti. These apartments have vaulted roofs, without, however, any keystone, but formed by layers of stone reaching inwards from both sides, and finished with roof-plates rounded out on the inner side by hewing (Fig. 121). As in the mastabas, the back walls are treated as screens. Only in the sanctuary of Osiris is there a door leading into the opisthodomus. On the south side an out-building of the same period joins on to the temple, which for this reason shows peculiar arrangement, as this necessitated a lateral entrance from the chief temple. One of the two doors of the second hypostyle gives access into a small passage, in which Dümichen, in 1864, found the great list of the kings, already given on p. 59. The relief shows Seti and his son adoring the cartouches of seventy-five kings. Another list of thirteen names, now in the Louvre, had already been discovered in 1818. A second temple in Abydos, built by Rameses II., is hopelessly destroyed. The *débris* of granite and alabaster gives evidence of surpassing magnificence. Here was found a geographical list enumerating the Egyptian cities. It has been interpreted by Brugsch.

The beautiful edifice of Amenhotep III., at Elephantine, gives an example of the arrangement of the smaller temples, or chapels. This was demolished, in 1822, by the Turkish governor of Assuan; but, fortunately, it is minutely described in the 'Description de l'Égypte.' It consisted only of a long cella in honor of Khnum, with a colonnade running round it, and a so-called peripteros, or exterior colonnade, such as we see in the little temple of Thothmes III. in Medinet-Abu. Along the longer sides stood seven pillars without pedestal or capital; the transverse sides had two columns with bud capitals between their corner pillars. The pillars and interior were sculptured. The whole stood upon a substructure of stylobate, with cornice: and, on the front, steps led upwards be-

FIG. 121. The arched hallways of Seti's temple at Abydos.

tween balustrades. This little temple reminds us forcibly of Greek architecture.

The numerous grottoes, or rock-temples, took their origin from the rulers of the Eighteenth and Nineteenth Dynasties. Of later date we have only the temple in Mount Barkal, erected by Taharka; and even it is only a copy of the older. The most northern is probably that near Beni-Hassan, dedicated to Sekhet (Artemis). Others lie in Upper Egypt, e.g., the grotto of Selseleh, founded by Horemheb; the most are in Nubia. The largest, that of Ipsambul, com-

PLATE XXVI.

Statue of the God Khuns, found at Karnak by Mr. Legrain, 1900.

History of All Nations, Vol. I., page 317

The Rock Temple of Abu-Simbel (Ipsambul).

History of All Nations, Vol. I., page 317.

monly known as Abu-Simbel (PLATE XXVII.) may be described as a specimen. The place where this astonishing work lies was called Pimas, or Pimsa, of which the Greeks made Psam-polis; the Arabs, Ipsambul. The pylons are here hewn out of the face of the cliff; and the colossi, which the founders were wont to set up before these members, are themselves part of the living rock, either of one piece with the pylons, or in close contact with them. The breadth of the façade at the base is 120 feet; its height, 93 feet. It is crowned by a concave moulding, bearing the cartouches of the kings, each surrounded by the uraeus-serpent. Above sits a row of twenty-two dog-headed apes, sacred to Thoth, each nearly eight feet high; and under the astragal of the entablature runs a band of votive inscriptions. Close up to this band, their kingly crowns towering aloft, their hands resting on their knees, and their eyes directed towards the far distance, sit four kings on thrones, whose arms are borne up by female figures. The last of the statues is half buried in the sand. Over the gates, which, with their cornices, reach to the elbows of the statues, stands, in a niche, the statue of Ra-Harmachis, with the solar disk over his hawk's head, with the royal builder in the act of adoration on both sides. A deep gateway gives entrance to the first hall, whose roof is borne up by two rows of four pillars. Before these stand statues of the king, thirty-three feet high, painted red, and wearing the white and red double crown. In his crossed arms is borne the crook of the shepherd of his people, and the scourge, the symbol of supreme power. His garment is a plaited yellow loin-cloth, or kilt, striped with red and blue. Several side-chambers issuing from this hall penetrate into the rock. A second hall is supported by four pillars, and to this, behind a broad passage, follows a third of the same breadth, but of very limited depth. Finally comes the sanctuary, in whose extreme niche, 180 feet from the portal, sit the four statues of Amen, Ptah, Harmachis, and Rameses II. All the walls and pillars are decorated with scenes from the wars in Nubia, Lybia, and Syria.

A second and lesser temple lies in the immediate neighborhood. Its façade has, in the centre, a broad pilaster, whose upper half shows the two cartouches of Rameses, while the lower is perforated by the door. To right and left, on each side, stand three colossal figures, thirty-three feet high, in high relief, and separated by narrow pilasters. The middle ones represent Nefertari, spouse of Rameses: the four others Rameses himself. The portal gives entrance into a great hall, with six pillars, showing, in the upper part of their front sides, huge heads of Hathor, under which three vertical fillets with inscriptions run down the pillar. In a niche in a second hall is the image of the cow of Hathor. Other temples of Nubia are only half grottoes; thus in the temple of Gerf-Hussein (or Girsheh, on the east bank), not only the fore-halls, but the hypostyle, are built outside the rock, only the sanctuary lying in the hill.

A characteristic feature of the New Empire are the hypogaea, or cavities penetrating far into the rock, consisting of several halls or chambers, to which long galleries give admission. A noteworthy work was discovered by Maspero in 1883, near Der-el-Bahri, on the hill-path leading to the Tombs of the Kings. This had belonged to a man named Hor-hotep, of the time of the Eleventh Dynasty. As the rock is brittle, the architect had lined the grave with limestone slabs, which he painted. The pictures exhibit the whole arrangements of the household of the deceased. The coffin is not, as usual, monolithic, but constructed of blocks cemented together. The grave had been plundered: still, there were found an excellent arm of a wooden statue and a portion of a wooden bark. In respect of decoration, both chambers and the coffin bore the greatest similarity to those of the Sixth Dynasty graves near Memphis; so this grave forms a connecting link between the ancient mastaba and the rock-vault of the Nineteenth Dynasty. The Pharaohs have rock-tombs at various points in Western Thebes, the most renowned being the twenty-five tombs of the Eighteenth (Amenhotep III. and Ai, successors of Tut-ankh-amen, and Rameses I.), the Nineteenth, and Twentieth Dynasties, in Biban-el-Moluk ('Gates of the Kings'). This is a gorge to which entrance is gained through a narrow pass or rock-gate, partially widened by art, and so entirely shut in by naked walls that it is never swept by the wind nor filled with the mid-day heat. Each of the graves opening into the ravine on either side has a great vault, called, after the yellow ground on which the pictures are arranged, the 'Golden Hall,' and lying in a range of corridors, niches, and chambers extending to the length of over 100 yards. The granite sarcophagi are mostly decorated with figures outside and in. The most elaborate tomb is that of Seti I., known as 'Belzoni's Tomb,' after the name of its discoverer. Its entrance, as that of all others, was blocked up after the sepulture of the king, and covered with sand. Over it is seen the yellow disk in which sits the ram-headed god, — the setting sun adored by the king: to the right is Nephthys: to the left Isis, representing the terminal point of the sun's course in the upper hemisphere. Beside the sun sits the beetle, the symbol of the second birth. Like the sun, the king descends in the west into the under-world, to reappear again in the east, and after his wanderings through Hades to arrive at the bosom of the divinity. In the corridor nearest the entrance is engraven the litany to the god Ra, which is noteworthy on account of its esoteric character. It constitutes an introduction to the numerous representations on the walls of the tomb typical of the course of the sun during the hours of darkness. A part of this litany is preserved in the Book of the Dead. Ra is here the greatest power in the universe; all gods are assimilated to him; and through him, whose various forms of manifestation they represent, they exist. "Adoration to thee, supreme power: exalted mighty one, that compasses the place of light: whose form is that of the spirit who comprehends the all; who conceals his form in himself: who lives in his eye (the solar-disk) and illumines the coffin: the invisible engenderer, who makes the spheres and creates bodies: from whose person, emanating from himself, those have come forth that are and are not, the dead, the gods, the souls: the mysterious hidden one, whom the spirits follow as he leads them: the eternal element permeating the heavens, in whose presence in Amenti (Hades) the spirits rejoice in the heaven of light: the prince of the powers in the sacred spheres: the bark of heaven: the gate of the spheres of light; the wanderer, the revolving illuminator, who causes darkness to follow his light: the lord of souls, who sits on his obelisk." Following an oblique downward-sloping passage, which at one point — obviously with the view of precipitating grave-robbers to destruction — sinks suddenly and unsuspectedly into a deep pit, leaving only bare room for walking close to the wall, one reaches, at a distance of 143 feet from the entrance, a great hall with four rock pillars, lying fifty-six feet under the level of the threshold. In this hall Horus is figured as leading the natives of Egypt and of foreign countries in four groups, of three representatives each. The Egyptians (Romêt, i. e., 'men') are depicted with skins of red hue and wearing white loin-cloths: the yellow Aamu, or Semites, with black beards, and loin-cloths striped blue, white, and red; the black Nehesu, or negroes, with white apron, over which falls a robe of diaphanous material, kept in place by a red embroidered girdle and shoulder-band; finally the Temehu, or Libyans, of white, partially tattooed, skins. This hall joins on to another: but the way to the tomb leads, not through this last, but down a steep stair, and through three other apartments. The golden hall consists of a vestibule with pillars and various side-chambers (in one of which is a noteworthy representation, with descriptive text, of the destruction of mankind by Ra and the gods), then of the main apartment, lying somewhat deeper, but with a flattish vaulting rising higher into the rock. On the left a door gives admission into a terminal hall with a row of four pillars. The sarcophagus is formed of a block of translucent aragonite, over nine feet long and three broad, and is now in the Soane Museum, London. The figures and hieroglyphics, filled in with blue, describe the voyage of the bark of the sun through the underworld, through twelve gates (the hours of night). Near it, on the left, but lower, are seen the damned: on the right, the blessed. On the inside of the cover are inscribed passages from the Book of the Dead. Behind the side of the coffin, there opens a slanting shaft, which has been followed for over 300 feet, without reaching the end. Here we are 180 feet under the level of the entrance, and 470 feet distant from it. In the course of excavating this and all other hypogaea, the rubbish must have been carried forth, along narrow, suffocating, ascending passages, whose heat was tempered by no breath of air. The whole surface is covered with fine, highly colored sculptures, all executed by torch-light, and under the conviction that they would be seen only by the dead, who, in virtue of the transformation of the images into actual existences effected by the prayers of those left behind, would revive and enjoy them. From the living they were believed to be hidden in everlasting night.

High officials also had elaborate rock-tombs. The tomb of

the priest Pet-amen in El-Wut-el-Khorkah, eastward of Sheikh Abd-el-Gurnah, scarcely yields in number of apartments to the graves of kings; many royal sepulchres are indeed much simpler. The sepulchral statues of the Ancient Empire occur also in the Theban tombs; but under the influence of religious ideas such images came to be, more and more, mere miniature imitations of the mummies in enamelled clay, and, as such, lost all value as works of art.

A peculiar variety of sepulchral architecture is constituted by the graves of the sacred bull Apis. The Apis became, after its decease, an Osiris, whence came its name of Asar-hapi, Greek Serapis, and that of its shrine, Serapeum. From the time of Amenhotep III., these animals were interred in separate tombs, consisting of chambers worked out of the rock, to which access was given by an enclosed path. Immediately over the tomb was an under-ground substructure, on which was placed a dado with columns at its angles, and over all was a pyramidal roofing. The son of Rameses II., Kha-em-nas, a learned high priest of Ptah (see p. 275) who resided in Memphis, and died before his father, laid out the renowned Apis graves. The exterior temple of the dead above ground has disappeared; but Mariette found the Greek Serapeum, which lay to the east of the Egyptian one, and was connected with it by an avenue of sphinxes. Here, in the necropolis of Sakkara, lived enthusiast devotees, who, in the service of Serapis, shut themselves out from the world, and in gloomy cells, into which food could be introduced only through air-holes, gave up their lives to the practices and visions of asceticism. To these recluses we have to look for the origin of Egypto-Greek and Christian monachism.

The subterranean Serapeum (or Apis-mausoleum), consists of a gallery 650 feet in length, tunnelled into the rock, on each side of which were spacious and lofty wainscoted chambers. After the dead Apis had been deposited in one of these, enclosed in an enormous coffin of granite or limestone, it was walled up. Under Psammetichus I., some of the vaultings of the older Apis-graves sunk in, and this new gallery was begun, whose 64 vaults are now visited by tourists. These contain 24 sarcophagi, of an average length of 13 feet, breadth of 7 feet 6 inches, and height of 11 feet. On the discovery of the coffins, only two were found unplundered. The most important objects contained in these catacombs of the sacred bulls are the numerous stelae, or tablets, which it was permissible to set up in the chamber, or before it, a certain number of years after the Apis had been laid to rest. These are now mostly in the Louvre, and contain dates of the highest value in determining the length of the reigns of the Pharaohs from the time of Psammetichus. On each of three coffins is an inscription of the times of Amasis II., Cambyses, and Khabash, respectively. The first is short, and says simply that the King Amasis had 'caused this mighty stone chest to be made out of red granite for the living Apis,' the word 'living' having reference to the life beyond the grave. A stela belonging to the coffin tells that this Apis was born and died in the reign of Amasis. He was born in the fifth year of his reign (B.C. 567), on the seventh day of the month Thoth (June–July); installed in Memphis, eighteenth Payni (March-April) the same — Egyptian — year; died sixth Phamenoth (December-January) of his 23d year (549); was deposited in his tomb on the fifteenth Pathon (February-March) of the same year. This Apis lived, therefore, 18 years 6 months, an age exceeded by other Apides. The sarcophagus dedicated under Khabash, owing to unforeseen circumstances occurring during his interregnum (between Darius and Xerxes) of only two years, was never set up, and stands to this day in a corridor, while its cover lies on the ground in the main gallery.

The dwellings of the Egyptians were constructed of brick and wood, and have entirely perished. Yet one gains a tolerably clear conception of them from the architecture of the tombs, which was borrowed from that of the dwelling-house, from little models that have come down to us, as well as from drawings and plans, both on papyrus and on the walls. One such plan found in Tel-el-Amarna, Chipiez has made the basis of a perspective bird's-eye view. This wooden house consisted of vertical and horizontal (never diagonal) beams, mortised, with the intermediate spaces panelled. Pavilions were wont to be erected on the flat roofs, under whose covering of carpets or matting the night was passed in the hottest season. The cleaving and twisting of the wood-work was remedied by lattice-work of small rods, from which originated handsome geometric designs, as is the case in all warm countries. Concerning the furniture also of the private houses, the monuments afford the fullest information. Couches, chairs, stools—massive yet elegant, with carved animal's feet and other ornamentation—were used. The walls were hung with variegated carpets or variously patterned straw plaiting. We can trace the dress of the Egyptians in all its forms, from the primitive loin-cloth up to the diaphanous robe of byssus. This loin-cloth, or kilt, is the dress not only of the peasants and workmen, but it is also the sacred vestment in which the king is shown in reliefs and statues. People pride themselves in having it richly finished; they starched and plaited it, and, bringing it up in front, folded it back on itself, so that its ends, decorated with colored stripes and ornaments, fell down over the girdle. In the case of women it was lengthened both upward and downward into a petticoat, which was held up by shoulder-straps; but these were sometimes replaced by a scarf or sash, which was tied in a large knot before the breast, under which the corners of the garment were tucked. Such a robe is worn by the goddess Isis; and even the noble granite statue of Rameses II., in Turin, is thus attired. Over this kilt a shirt-like garment of linen was worn, under which the under dress and the body appeared. Above all was occasionally thrown a sort of wrap, or calasiris. Generally people went barefoot, the rich only wearing sandals. The head was shorn, and protected from the heat by a sort of cap of cloth. It would lead us too far were we to detail all the articles of the toilet, especially those of the female sex.

On an earlier page, in the account of the famous discoveries of royal mummies at Der-el-Bahri, mention was made of the fact that the enamelled and gilt coffin of Thothmes I. was found, but that in it was the mummy of Pinozem. In 1899 Loret discovered the actual tomb of Thothmes, from which the coffin had been stolen. It is in the Valley of the Kings at Thebes. This chapter on the art and manners and customs of the New Empire may well conclude with a detailed description[1] of this tomb, the original burial-place of one of the greatest monarchs of the Eighteenth Dynasty. "This Pharaoh appears to have been the first to make his tomb in the rock of the valley instead of building it in the plain. The tomb is a small one and contains but

[1] *American Journal of Archaeology*, 1900, pp. 243, 244.

two chambers. In the tomb were a papyrus containing texts from the 'Book of the Dead' with colored pictures finely executed, a draught-board with a full set of draughtmen, some garlands, thirteen large earthen beer jars, and a large number of other vessels, weapons, two beautiful arm-chairs, and remains of food. The most remarkable piece of all is a large and beautifully preserved couch, consisting of a quadrangular wooden frame overspread with a thick rush mat, over which were stretched three layers of linen, with a life-size figure of the god of death, Osiris, drawn upon the outer layer. The figure itself was smeared with some material intended to make the under layer water-proof. Over this, mingled with some adhesive substance, soil had been spread in which barley was planted. The grains had sprouted and had grown to the height of from two and one-half to three inches. The whole therefore represented the couch whereon the dead Osiris lay, figured in greensward."

Taia, probably the Queen of Horemheb (Eighteenth Dynasty).

Plate XXVIII.

HEAD OF WINGED FIGURE FROM NINEVEH.

As type of the Assyrian Race and Proof of Painting on the Rock-sculptures.

(After Layard.)

CHAPTER VIII.

THE EARLIEST ASSYRIAN KINGS.

DURING the most flourishing period of the New Empire in Egypt, there was maturing in the Upper Mesopotamian valley a powerful nation which ultimately became dominant in Western Asia and gave decisive direction to the subsequent development of civilization,—the kingdom of Assyria.

Assyria was the region watered by the Greater and Lesser Zab,—streams that empty into the Tigris, about two hundred and three hundred and fifty miles northward from Babylon. Its kings gradually extended their sway—on the south towards the Adhem and Diyala; on the west, over the plains watered by the Chaboras and its tributaries; on the north, to the upper courses of the Euphrates. Thus they came into collision with the Babylonian empire, with the Aramaeans, and with the Hittites and their allies. The conflicts with their various neighbors continued down to the last days of the Assyrian people, so that their history is little more than a record of wars. The earliest seat of the Assyrian kings was Assur, the ruins of which now bear the name of Kalah Shergat. On the right bank of the Tigris, somewhat above the mouth of the Lower Zab, an immense terrace rears itself, with the ruins of a temple in platforms or stages, now covered by drifted sand. An excavation of these ruins is now being made by a German expedition which has already made notable discoveries. In the district of Assyria, on the left bank of the Tigris, and above the mouth of the Zab, lie numerous ruin-mounds of ancient cities, in particular of Nineveh, over against Mosul. Here are two rubbish-mounds, of which the southern, Nebi Yunus, is occupied by buildings; but, as the prophet Jonah is said to be here buried, excavations cannot be made. Certain trials with the spade, at the angle of the mound, revealed that an Assyrian palace lay here interred; and fragments of the annals of

Sennacherib, and bricks of the times of Adad-nirari III.[1] (811–783) and Esarhaddon, were picked up. The northern mound, Konyunjik (Turkish, 'the lambkin'), has been thoroughly ransacked, and found to be the ruins of a palace of Sennacherib and Asurbanipal, in the condition it was left by the Medes, who demolished it over twenty-five centuries ago. Nineveh is a very ancient city, but it does not appear as the capital till the later times of Assyrian history. Here stood a temple of Ishtar, which, as early as the nineteenth century B.C., was restored by Samsi-Adad, and, 400 years later, again by Ashur-uballit. A head of Ishtar, with a broad diadem around the curled hair, was found by George Smith. Shalmaneser I. (about 1320) and his son Tukulti-Ninib had here a palace. Several of their successors were diligent builders. At the end of the reign of Shalmaneser II. (859–825), his son Asur-danin-apal revolted in Nineveh, but was overthrown by his brother Samsi-Adad IV., whose son Adad-nirari III. (811) built a temple of Nebo and Merodach, in the spot where the mound Nebi Yunus lies. With Sennacherib began Nineveh's period of highest prosperity, which lasted scarcely over a century.

Jerraiyah is a ruin-mound close to Nineveh, on the south, at a little distance from which irregular traces of walls are discernible, high over the Tigris, at Selamiye. Near here lies Calah (Kalhu), the modern Nimrud, at present at some distance from the river, but reached by it in floods. Northeast of Nimrud lies the ruin-mound of Balawat, and, somewhat farther off, Karâmlais. Also on the farther side of the Zab was Arbela (Arba-ilu, 'the city of four gods'), an important Assyrian city lying on an artificial terrace, with ruins of vaults and galleries. More to the south, and across the Lower Zab, lies Kerkuk, in the district of Garamaea, the ancient Mennis (where Curtius locates the naphtha-springs), the Karkha-de-Bet-Selukh of the Syrians. The most important place to the north of Nineveh is Khorsabad, east of which is Ba-azani. Towards the north is Sherif-khan (Assyrian, Tarbisi), with a group of lesser mounds of rubbish.

Everywhere, at the points mentioned, are to be found traces of Assyrian cities or of royal strongholds. Furthermore the whole

[1] The reading Adad-nirari, instead of Ramman-nirari, is now accepted by scholars, and therefore also Adad for the 'god of thunder and storms' (see Vol. II., p. 82), instead of Ramman.

country is strewn with ruin-mounds, easily recognizable by their Arabian and Turkish prefixes, Tel and Tepeh. Outside of Assyria proper we find of more important cities, first, on the Babylonian frontier, Opis (Assyrian, Upi), mentioned by Tiglath-Pileser I. (about 1200). Its ruins lie opposite the mouth of the Adhem (Physcus), and are now called Tel-Dhahab-Manjur. Formerly the Tigris flowed past the west of the city; and at this point of its old bed, now named Shat-Aidha, the remains of an ancient bridge are still extant. Westward of Nineveh, the Sinjar hills run transversely across Mesopotamia. West of Lake Khatuniyah, the range is broken through by the Chaboras (the Araxes of Xenophon), which, taking its rise in numerous springs in the neighborhood of Resaina (Ras-el-ain), and flowing past several small towns, falls into the Euphrates near Karkisiyah (Circesium). It receives numerous tributaries from Mt. Masius (Tur-Abdin). On the Jakhjakhah (Mygdonius) lies Nisibis (i.e., 'the stone columns,' from an early stone-cult), the most famed city in this region, which continued to be an important fortress till the times of the Parthians and the Sassanidae. Farther to the west lies Harran (Carrhae), with a shrine of Sin (the moon-god), on the Balikh (Belias), that falls into the Euphrates at Thapsacus. To the northeast lies Edessa; to the west, Serug (Batnae). Some four miles to the south were found two Assyrian lions of basalt.

The inscription found at Kalah Shergat by the German Expedition reveal as the earliest ruler of the city, Ushpia, who is called 'a priest of the god Ashur,' and was designated as the founder of Ashur's temple in that place. His date may be fixed at about 2200 B.C. Of other early rulers we also have short inscriptions mostly dealing with Ashur's temple, known as "The Mountain of the Lands," and with the help of a recently found inscription of Shalmaneser I., consisting of 168 lines, which gives dates for various of his predecessors, we are able to fix the time of Samsi-Adad I. at c. 1900 B.C. (580 years before Shalmaneser I.), and of Erishum at 159 years before Samsi-Adad—*i.e.*, c. 2060. Among other of the earlier rulers of Assyria, Adad-nirari I. (c. 1350) is represented by a detailed inscription furnishing his genealogy and telling of his work on the temple of Ashur at Kalah Shergat, while of his son, Shalmaneser I. (c. 1320), we know that he founded the city of Calah, where his successors long resided. We may well suppose that the conquest of Babylonia was not effected in one campaign. The kings say nothing of their defeats; but casual notices point to a long series of struggles, with varying success. Thus Sennacherib reports that the seal of Tukulti-Ninib I. of Assyria was found by him in Babel (Babylon) 600 years after it had been carried off. This presupposes a Babylonian advance on the Assyrian capital about 1300. Also in the reign of Bel-kudur-sur, who came to the throne c. 1250, the Babylonions revolted, their Assyrian governor at their head, and the king himself fell in the conflict. Not the less they were reduced to subjection by the son of the fallen monarch. Assyrian governors and native independent kings of Babylonia often endeavored to free themselves from Assyrian supremacy.

Of Tiglath-Pileser I. (Fig. 122), who reigned about 1200, we possess much information, derived partly from the bricks of the palace at Kalah Shergat, but especially from four octagonal clay prisms which were deposited at the corners of this edifice. Further details appear on a relief-sculpture at the sources of the Tigris, and on an obelisk from Kalah Shergat, found at Koyunjik. Sennacherib reports that the Babylonians —warring against Tiglath-Pileser—had taken the city Ekallat, and carried off two images of gods, which he himself brought back. These facts are not mentioned by Tiglath-Pileser, who was, however, more successful in a second campaign. He now captured the cities of Marduk-nadin-akhe, Dur-Kurigalzu (Akarkuf), Sippar, Babel, and Opis. Tiglath-Pileser extended his sway on the west and north, and the fact that he could undertake campaigns in these directions proves that he had subdued the Babylonians effectively. We have already become acquainted with the conflicts of the Egyptians with the Kheta (Hittites), and seen that the kingdom of the latter fell apart into various petty monarchies, which, however, combined with each other and with the cognate tribes of the Arme-

FIG. 122.—Tiglath-Pileser I.

nian highlands when it was necessary to make common cause against the grasping Assyrians. When Tiglath-Pileser carried his arms westward, some sixty years had elapsed since the time of Rameses III. (p. 281). He reports that the Moschi, who for fifty years had held the land Alzi and Puru-kuzzi (between the eastern Euphrates and the Tigris-sources, and tributary to the god Ashur), and who never before were subdued by any monarch, had descended 20,000 strong under five kings upon the land of Kummukh (Commagene). Without doubt this movement was connected with the invasion of Egypt of the Mediterranean races, which was repulsed by Rameses III. On the fall of the Hittites probably followed the advance of the Philistines into their later settlements; while the Hebrews took advantage of the commotion to press forward into the land west of the Jordan. Tiglath-Pileser collected his battle-chariots and warriors, marched through the mountain land Kashyara (northwest Sophene), and, descending like a thunder-storm, shattered the Moschi in Kummukh. Their heads he carried off as trophies, while their carcasses were cast into the ravines. He levelled their strong places, carried off captives with their goods and chattels, and made those who sued for peace subject to him. As they of Kummukh were friends of the Moschi, their land, too, was spoiled. They threw themselves into the strong city, Sirisi (Strabo's Sarisa, the city of the Gordyaeans), which lay on the east bank of the Tigris. This fortress must have lain somewhere between Diarbekir and Engil. The Assyrians took it, and, defeating the troops that had hurried from Kurkhi (western Kurdistan) to its relief, captured their king Kilite-hub. Among the spoils were found vessels of copper and iron, and gold and silver idols. The victors passed still farther on, and, entering Kurkhi, captured its chief city Urartinash, its prince, Shadite-hub, submitting himself.

Tiglath-Pileser boasts of having subjugated Kummukh; but, later, he himself gives the Euphrates as the boundary of his empire. Further, the inscription reports that he defeated a body of 4000 warriors, composed of Kaski (Colchians), then settled in Asia Minor between the upper Halys and the Euphrates, and of Urumaya, who, in the service of the Chatti (Hittites), were striving to defend Shubari, that part of western Mesopotamia inhabited by the

Aramaeans. He then turned once more against Kummukh, and, as he states, incorporated it with his empire. The campaign against Kurkhi also was renewed. The mountaints barred the advance of his war-chariots; but he overcame the difficulties, and after a bloody struggle took twenty-five places in the district of Kharia. An attempt on Milidia, in Khanigalmit (Malatia), miscarried. The city Carchemish, in the land of the Chatti, is first mentioned in the account of an expedition against the Aramaeans in Sukhi (in Job ii. 11, Bildad is a Shuhite); and in the report of a hunt of oxen, there occurs the name of Araziki, a city of the Hittites on the Euphrates, somewhat above Balis.

We find in Tiglath-Pileser's inscriptions reports of various other expeditions, or, rather, forays; as those into the land Murattash and Saradaush (probably the mountain region east of Kerkuk), and the land of the Nairi in Arzanibiu, between Diarbekir and Surt, where he triumphed over sixty chiefs of the Nairi with their allies from the Upper Sea, burned their towns, and carried off their goods and cattle. In an expedition to the land of Muzri, in the district of Khorsabad, he assailed the city Arini, at the foot of Mount Aisa, whither the Kumani had hastened in aid; but "they seized my feet; I spared the city, took hostages, and imposed tribute." Probably he was defeated; for shortly after he had to turn again against the Kumani, whom he conquered, burning their city Khunusa. A memorial of the king—his statue with inscriptions—was found at the sources of the Subnat (Sebeneth-su), a stream falling into the Tigris at a place named Karkar (Armenian, Anzit), near Egil. There his successors, Tukulti-Ninib I. and Shalmaneser I., caused stelae also to be set up. These sculptures are interesting as furnishing us the earliest likeness of an Assyrian king.

Under the successors of Tiglath-Pileser, the power of the empire seems to have waned. The mere absence of boastful inscriptions leads to this inference, while an inscription of Shalmaneser II. reports that he had taken Pethor (Pitru) on the Sagura (Sajur), on the far side the Euphrates, and recaptured Mutkinu, on the Assyrian side, after it had been surrendered by Asur-erbi (about 1000) to the king of Aram (Syria). Our knowledge of Assyrian history, however, for the two centuries after Tiglath-Pileser is as yet very meagre.

The first monarch who again made conquests was Asurnazirpal (884–860), son of Tukulti-Ninib II. (who reigned only six years), and grandson of Adad-nirari II. His inscriptions are extensive, and were found on his statue of limestone (Fig. 123), and in the temple at Calah. The statue represents him with a sickle, or crook, in his right hand as defender of the husbandman, and with a club in his left as crusher of his foes. His head is without a diadem; the right arm is bare, the left covered by the richly fringed mantle, which is thrown twice round the body. The great inscription, frequently translated, is engraved, in condensed form, on a tablet showing a likeness of him making a libation, and is repeated more than a hundred times on stones of his palace. Especially important are the wars against the northern mountain tribes, whose districts, however, can only rarely be determined. Thus, in the very beginning of the inscription, the mountain region Nummi (between Arzanias and Lake Van) is named, which no Assyrian had before entered. From Nummi he descended into the land of Kirruri, where he received tribute from Gilzan, on the north of Lake Urumiah, and from Khubushkia, in the upper region of the Zab, now inhabited by the Hekkari. He then marched by way of Kirkhi, and captured, among other mountain holds, a rock fortress, Nishtun, whose commandant was carried prisoner to Arbela, and there flayed alive, his skin being spread out on the city wall. From Nineveh, Asurnazirpal set out for Syria, passing through the cities at the foot of Mts. Nibar and Pasatu (Tur-Abdin), so as to cross the Tigris somewhere near Diarbekir, and fall upon Kummukh,—probably the first attempt on the Chatti (Hittites). But he had at once to turn back; for, behind him, the governor he had set over Suri, in the district of Bit-Khalupe on the Chaboras—a stranger from Hamath—had been slain, and, in place of him, a man from Bit-Adini (the region between the Euphrates and the Belikh, and hostile to Assyria) had been called to be king. In Kummukh he had attained no success: and this misadventure the rebels had to expiate. Many were seized, among them the new king, and carried off to Calah, along with a rich booty in silver, gold, copper, alabaster vases, iron utensils, women and maidens, war-chariots, horses, cattle, sheep, woollen and linen raiments, furniture of cedar-wood, and carpets. Here walls were

FIG. 123.—Statue of Asurnazirpal. From Nimrud. London, British Museum.

erected before the gate, in which some of the captives were immured alive; others were impaled on stakes set up on the walls; others, and among them the king, were flayed, and their skins spread on the walls. All this was done in the presence of the king. Further expeditions brought the Assyrians into the land of Nirbu, adjoining, on the one side, the district of the Nairi, between the Tigris, the Upper Euphrates, and Lake Van, and, on the other, Kashiyari, the southwestern Sophene. Here eight cities had combined, and fortified Ispilibria, an inaccessible height. The Assyrians seem to have effected nothing. They devastated, indeed, various parts of the country of the Nairi, and slew innumerable people: but new expeditions were ever necessary, for these brave mountain races remained unsubjugated. Only by the erection of fortresses were the latest kings enabled to keep them in check. As little was gained by the destruction of Pethor as had been by the flooding the land of Kummukh with war. Asurnazirpal marched also towards the southeast, and, crossing the Lower Zab and Radanu (Upper Adhem), pursued the Armenian, Ameka into the mountains in the direction of Suleimanieh. The Assyrian power came here nearly into collision with that of Babylon. The king advanced southwards by the Hirmas, which conducts the waters of the Tur-Abdin to the Chaboras, the cities on which, and among them Bit-Khalubie, purchased forbearance by tribute. Passing Khindani on the Euphrates, and Anat (Anatho), he reached Suri, where Shadudu, governor of Sukhi, stood in array against him. A two-days' fight ensued; the enemy fled over the Euphrates, and their city was taken. He conquered also a Babylonian host under Nabu-bal-iddin and his brother Sabdanu. Yet he did not venture to follow up his success on Babylonian soil, but returned to Calah. Scarce had he arrived when he received tidings that the hosts of Sukhi had recrossed the Euphrates. Once more the Assyrian conqueror set forth, but this time he did not march so far down the stream as formerly; but, destroying the cities as he ascended the river, he crossed the Euphrates at Kharidi, and defeated the armies of the Aramaeans, the Sukhi, and Lakai. Two cities were founded not far from Bit-Adini; viz., Kar-Asurnazirpal, on the north bank of the Euphrates, and Nibarti-Asur ('ford of Asur'), on the southern. Akhuni, ruler of Bit-Adini, was compelled to pay tribute; and the king boasts of having taken from Sangara, king of the Chatti, in Carchemish, 20 talents of silver, gold, bracelets, and sword-sheaths of gold (gilded bronze), 100 talents of copper, 250 talents of iron utensils, the inventory of the palace, elegant furniture, costly woods, many slaves (women), robes of woollen and linen, black woollen and purple cloths, precious stones, buffalo-horns, chariots ornamented with ivory, gold idols with their carpets, the chariots and war-engines of the captain of Carchemish. Hence the king set out for Labnana (Lebanon), passing through several districts and cities mentioned in his inscriptions, and reached the boundaries of the Lebanon at the city Aribua. On the seacoast of Amurri (the western part of Phoenicia) an offering was made to the gods. On his return, cedars and other woods were carried away from Amanus. The Hittite land, Patin, stretched hence from the Gulf of Alexandretta pretty far inland, having Phoenicia for its southern boundary. The prince of Kummukh at this time was named Katazili; he, too, is said to have sent tribute. This expedition, also, was more showy than successful or useful. Of actual conquests there is no mention.

These and similar expeditions extended undoubtedly the boundaries of the empire, and won respect for its power; but we turn with pleasure from the record of them — always monotonous, and often revolting by reason of the admixture of bigotry and horrible cruelty — to listen to the rough soldier when he tells of the buildings he erected. Yet even here he was actuated more by his thirst for glory than any true feeling for art. The walls of the palace served their highest purpose in affording room for pictures of his heroic deeds and inscriptions explaining them. Asurnazirpal built anew the city of Calah (Kalhu), founded by his forefather Shalmaneser I., and led a canal from the Zab, which he termed 'The Bearer of Fruitfulness,' and its banks he decorated with flowers and shrubs. "I founded a palace for my royal dwelling, and for an everlasting seat of my sovereignty. I decorated and beautified it, filled it with many bronzes (as lining for the walls and on the furniture). Great gates of sandal (?) wood I caused to be put together with bronze pins, and to be placed at the entrances. Thrones of cedar and other costly woods, cunningly carved ivory as ornaments, heaps of silver,

FIG. 124. Assyrian Battle-scene, from the Palace of Asurnazirpal at Calah (Nimrud). Marble relief. London, British Museum.

gold, lead, copper, and iron, the spoils of the peoples whom I subdued by my strength — all these treasures laid I therein." The inscription closes with a blessing for him who maintains the palace and the inscriptions, and a curse on him who shall be so godless as to efface the latter.

The structure here referred to lies on the northwest terrace of Nimrud, and is the oldest Assyrian palace whose plan we can follow in detail, and whose sculptures are preserved. The buildings in the royal city are so laid out — in conformity with the direction of the walls, in whose southwest corner they lie — that not their angles, but their sides, are directed towards the quarters of the heaven, while their façades must have looked out on the Tigris, which then flowed at the base of the terrace. In the distance the ruin-mound on the conical summit of the staged tower is to be recognized. The royal city contains the remains of the edifices erected by Asurnazirpal, Shalmaneser II. (859), Samsi-Adad IV. (824), Adad-nirari (811), Tiglath-Pileser III. (745), Esarhaddon (680), and Asur-etil-ili (625). The palace of Asurnazirpal consists of a suite of long, narrow apartments grouped around a court. The main façade is directed toward the ziggurat, or temple with platforms. There are two gates, which were decorated with cherubim in the form of winged lions with human fore-quarters. These figures strikingly resemble the Greek centaurs when the wings are wanting, as in a relief of this king. The gates, whose massive bronze hinges were still extant, led into a hall of great length, at whose eastern end traces of a dais for the throne are discernible. The walls were decorated with limestone tablets (now in the British Museum), showing relief-figures in greater than life-size, in which the king appears, surrounded by his court, as offering sacrifice, or in triumph (Fig. 124), or as a slayer of wild bisons.

The king has on his head the tiara—which reminds us of the Turkish fez—enwound by a broad band or shawl, and is bedecked with ear-rings, arm-rings, and bracelets (Fig. 125). He wears the woollen tunic, with an over-garment (*chlanidion*) of finest wool, resembling the cashmere shawl, bound round the waist with a richly fringed scarf, whose ends hang down at his side. The royal clothing is inwrought with manifold embroideries, that on the breast-piece

FIG. 125. — King Asurnazirpal. Relief from Nimrud. London, British Museum.

very especially rich. Here genii group themselves on both sides around a central figure, — often the sacred tree under the winged disk, — the whole being encircled by a round band of conventional plants, and fillets of mythological figures, — winged genii or animals, gazelles, winged horses, lions beside the sacred tree or beside the king, — which, following the direction of the arms and the lower part of the neck, are partially concealed by the beard. The sandals come high up behind around the heel; the short sword, with shoulderless hilt, is in a sheath covered and decorated with bronze or gold rosettes or other ornaments. Its extremity is generally tipped with a ferule in the form of a lion. The blade of the royal weapon was probably embellished. In possession of Colonel Hanbury is a sword with a curved bronze blade (an *acinaces*), on which, under the hilt, is a gazelle resting, and on the back an inscription picked out in gold. The inscription shows the name of Pudilu, son of Bel-nirari (towards the middle of the fourteenth century). Ornamentation also appears on two bronze cubes seemingly used as weights; the inlaid scarabaeus here points to an Egyptian origin. Behind the king stand his umbrella-bearer, fly-fanner, and other court officials. The vizier is apparelled like the king, his head being encircled by a diadem, instead of the tiara. The servants wear only the under-garment, with the scarf round the waist. All present who are not playing on instruments or bearing something stand with their hands folded over their breasts. The despot must feel secure that they bear nothing inferring danger to him. Pleasing friezes and wall-bands full of delicate designs—chamois standing on cliffs, winged bulls on rosettes, and the like—frequently alternate with warlike scenes. A gate decorated with bulls, between the middle of the throne-room and the east wall, leads into a second and shorter room. The reliefs here consist of winged genii with eagle's heads, who, on both sides of the tree of life, strew aromatic grains out of a basket upon its leaves. From this hall we pass into the court, and from that toward the left, into a suite of rooms stretching from north to south. Here we find sculptures that were never surpassed afterwards. Also on the south side the rooms are similarly distributed. The west side, destroyed by floods, was provided with stairs toward the stream, as Layard shows on his plan. This palace has, however, still numerous and highly elegant decorations. Part of these are painted on stucco-friezes, divided into several bands, and showing kneeling bulls, colored blue, between charming rosettes in blue, white, and red, on a white ground; under this, on a yellow ground, blue, white, and black ornaments of circles, chevroned leaves, and inward-cambered borders, also alternating with rosettes—both surmounted by crenated ornamentation. Another part consists of enamelled clay panelling, over which is a frieze of circles with entangled rims, bordered on both sides by rows of flower-cups, resembling the honeysuckle or carnation, pine-cones, and bell-flowers. The colors are mineral, the prevailing blue being prepared from lapis lazuli, procured commercially from Central Asia. Reliefs were painted with the same colors. In Khorsabad, Flandin found everywhere a coating of ochre. When the sculptures of Nimrud were exhumed, the hair, eyes, sandals, bows, the tongues of the eagle-headed genii, the diadems with their rosette ornaments, still retained their coloring. In Khorsabad the colors were best preserved on clothing, crowns, flowers, arms, chariots, and trees. The flames of burning houses and the torches of the warriors maintained their bright red hue. Under the palace, as well as in other places of the platform, Layard found vaulted outlets for the water. The upper part of the palace, as well as the structure generally, is destroyed; yet, from the arched fragments found amongst the rubbish, the exceeding narrowness of the apartments in proportion to their length, and the unwonted strength of their walls, it is not difficult to infer that many were closed in with vaulted roofs. The inscriptions make frequent mention of cedar-beams for carrying flat roofs, upon which were laid an arched covering of earth. Wood was used for other purposes in the interiors: for, as we see from the view of an Armenian city in one of the reliefs, low upper-chambers or attics used to be erected on the roofs.

The main gate of the palace, as well as the doors of the several rooms, were spanned by arches, the front archway being embellished with panels of enamelled clay. On each side of the entrance winged colossi in high relief stood extended along its walls, their fore-quarters projecting free, in the full round. The effect of such a portal was heightened by its contrast with the dead flatness [illegible] rest of the exterior: while the doors of cedar-wood, [illegible] bronze, and sometimes, at least, partially gilded, contributed to its brilliancy. Such bronzed doors were found by Hormuzd Rassam, in 1878, at Balawat, a square terrace on whose eastern side stood a temple of Asurnazirpal. At the entrance lay a chest of alabaster, wherein were three tablets bearing inscriptions giving in condensed form the great Nimrud inscription, with the additional information that the king had changed the name of the city to Imgur-Bel ('May Bel bless'), and had set up the image of the god Makhir in the temple; that he had caused the roof to be formed of cedar of Lebanon; the cedar doors to be mounted with copper, and that he had taken the bricks of the temple from the ruins of an older palace. On the west side of the mound lay the stone slabs which formed the threshold of the great bronze gates set up by Asurnazirpal's successor, Shalmaneser II. We may, however, infer that these doors are not the first work of the kind; for the technic of the plates, first hammered and punched out and then finished with the graving-tool, bespeaks an advanced mode of treatment. The wood was three inches thick, the height of the gates twenty-two feet, and the breadth of each leaf six. Both doors turned on round posts, a foot thick, fastened to the wall by a ring, and crowned with bronze balls. Their cone-shaped ends revolved in holes cut into the stone of the threshold. Bronze corner-pieces defended the doors where they closed on each other. The whole flat surface of the wood, as well as the round posts, had horizontal bronze bands attached with nails on which warlike subjects were delineated (PLATE XXIX.).[1] The figures are from two to three inches high, and between the

[1] DESCRIPTION OF PLATE XXIX.

In the upper band is represented a sacrifice made by Shalmaneser on the shore of Lake Van in Armenia. The relief does not contain the figure of the king himself. Beginning at the right, we see, first, a candelabra; next a tripodal altar; then two disks, erected on poles sustained on pedestals. Next follows a stele placed upon a rock, as was Shalmaneser's wont in all countries conquered by him. Farther to the left, two soldiers throw the limbs of the sacrificial animals into the lake, in order to propitiate its divinity. Among the inhabitants of the lake, who greedily snap up the fragments, we recognize a large fish, a tortoise, and a quadruped, perhaps an otter.

The lower band represents an Assyrian army on the march. The circle at the left is an encampment strengthened by towers. Within this is an arched bridge, over which a horse is passing with noticeable caution. Possibly the whole scene may represent a fortified bridge-head. To the right are two archers; beyond them, war-chariots, whose drivers keep a tight rein on the horses, which are also led by footmen, appear to be approaching a difficult and dangerous country. (After Perrot.)

panels run bronze bands with rosettes formed of the heads of the nails. Here we recognize the original of the rosette ornaments on the stone doors of the rock-graves and the borders of inscription tablets. A similar smaller door, as well as the larger one in the British Museum, show hunting-scenes. Besides bronze decorations, the palace had also ivory ornaments, like the houses of ivory of

FIG. 126.—Ivory carved work, found in Nimrud. London, British Museum.

Ahab (Amos iii. 15; 1 Kings xxii. 39), the ivory palaces of Psalms xlv. 8, and the Homeric hall of Menelaus, in which bronze, gold, silver, amber, and ivory adorned the walls (Odyssey iv. 73). The discoveries at Nimrud illustrate the employment of ivory as a decoration of walls; for instance, the front view of a female head seen over a balustrade, environed by a frame with many compartments (Fig. 126). From the repeated occurrence of this head, we conclude that a number of such were associated in a frieze. On the Assyrian sculptures we see elephants' tusks brought as tribute; and Layard found fragments of ivory. An ivory tablet from Nimrud appears to be an essay of an Assyrian artist; for the figure is habited as an Assyrian, although the attitude, as well as the lotus-stalk standing on the double volute, are Egyptian. Other pieces show good Assyrian work; still the wall-piece mentioned above, as well as the most of the ivory objects, bear the unmistakable stamp of Egyptian origin. Thus a well-known ivory tablet from Nimrud shows the cartouche of Aubenura, a Pharaoh of the Thirteenth Dynasty; so, if the work is not an imitation, it dates back to between 2000 and 3000 years B.C., and therefore was, in the time of the Assyrian monarch of whom we now write, quite a respectable relic of antiquity. We may, on the whole, conclude that there was a native art of working in ivory, the material being brought from India, while Egypto-Phoenician works were in addition imported. The Egyptians derived their ivory from Ethiopia, by way of the harbor Adulis; later by way of Ptolemais Theron, on the Red Sea. The Phoenicians were skilled workers in ivory. Tyrian artists incrusted the throne of Solomon with ivory and gold (1 Kings x. 18; 2 Chron. ix. 17); the 'white throne' is the seat of the Judge in the Apocalypse (Rev. xx. 11). The Phoenicians even laid the benches of their ships with ivory (Ezek. xxvii. 6); moreover, these docile pupils of the Egyptians brought ivory to Troy, where it appears in the First City. Layard found ivory ornaments, in conjunction with bronze plates, in the form of a lion, both derived from thrones, where they had been attached to the smaller surfaces between the incrustations of metal. If we might indulge in conjecture, we would suggest that the cornices had been utilized as shelves for metal utensils, — bronze plates, basins, etc., — beautiful specimens of which, with Egypto-Phoenician embossed figures, inscribed with Phoenician names, are preserved in the British Museum.

North of the palace of Nimrud lies the ziggurat, or stage-temple, cased to the height of some twenty-two feet from the ground with stone slabs. The upper stages or platforms, on which the sanctuary must have stood, are no longer extant. To this larger temple are annexed, on the east, two little temples, between which a stair led from the terrace to the plain. The apartments consist of a cella,

Fig. 127. Bel Marduk and the Dragon (Tiamat). Relief from Nimrud. London, British Museum.

incrusted with glazed tiles, and a little sanctuary. To one of the temples there was also annexed an anteroom, with a separate entrance. The sanctuary had, as its floor, a single slab of alabaster, twenty-one feet long, sixteen and a half feet broad, and a foot thick. This is covered with a great historical inscription of the same import on both upper and under sides. The one of the two gates on the east side of the great temple was ornamented with two winged lions with human heads, their height being sixteen and a half feet and their length fifteen feet. Each of its door-frames was decorated, in addition, with three winged genii, standing one over the other. On both sides stand stone pedestals, which undoubtedly carried free-standing columns. The threshold between the genii was covered with cuneiform writing. The second gate showed on the outer wall figures of priests; on the inner was Marduk, with the thunderbolt and sword, represented as driving the dragon — that is, chaos, or darkness, or the evil principle — out of the temple (Fig. 127). The dragon has open, wolf-like jaws, pointed ears, the body and haunches of a lion, and is winged. In the interior of the temple, the mythological figures repeat themselves; e.g., the fish-god, a human figure with the skin of a fish as an outer covering and head-dress (page 189). The roof of the temple was supported by cedar beams, as we learn from the inscription, and as the remains found by Layard show. In the ruins lay numerous cameo-like objects, including a relief miniature of Ishtar of blue enamelled clay; an eye of black marble, with ivory ball; and other objects probably derived from a wooden idol. Right before the portal was a triangular altar, with a round slab, hollowed out for the reception of the blood; behind this was a stele of limestone, on which a relief figure of the king was chiselled, for here offerings were made to him as to a god. The side surfaces and the back are covered with inscriptions. The portal of the lesser temple was flanked by lions entirely covered with inscriptions, one of the lions being in the British Museum (Fig. 129). In this temple, also, a monolith, covered on both sides with the inscription, constituted the flooring of the sanctuary; and in the rubbish lay the already mentioned statue of the king, three feet in height, with an inscription on the breast (see Fig. 128).

On the southeast of the platform lies the *débris* of a structure by Asur-etil-ili in the last years of the empire; and beside it are the relics of an older staged tower by Shalmaneser II. (859),

FIG. 128. — Portrait of a king. Relief from Nimrud. London, British Museum

along with a temple of Nebo by Adad-nirari III. (811–783), before whose portal two statues of the god were found, one of which is figured on p. 176 (Fig. 53).

Fig. 129. – Lion at the Portal of the Temple at Nimrud. London, British Museum.

Under the successor of Asurnazirpal, Assyria began to have relations with Palestine; and we now, therefore, take up again the history of this land.

ANALYTICAL CONTENTS.

(For General Index, see Volume XXIV.)

BOOK I.

EGYPT, FROM THE EARLIEST TIMES TO THE SHEPHERD KINGS (ABOUT 1800 B. C.).

INTRODUCTION.

PREHISTORIC EGYPT.

CHAPTER I.

EARLIEST EGYPTIAN HISTORY.

CHAPTER II.

ART IN THE ANCIENT EMPIRE.

CHAPTER III.

THE MIDDLE EMPIRE.

BOOK II.

ASIA: THE BEGINNINGS OF HISTORY IN WESTERN ASIA,—BABYLONIA, SYRIA, AND ASIA MINOR.

CHAPTER IV.

BABYLONIA.

CHAPTER V.

SYRIA AND ASIA MINOR.

BOOK III.

EGYPT AND WESTERN ASIA: THE NEW EMPIRE IN EGYPT AND THE RISE OF ASSYRIA.

CHAPTER VI.

THE RELATIONS OF THE NEW EMPIRE TO SYRIA.

CHAPTER VII.

ART UNDER THE NEW EMPIRE.

CHAPTER VIII.

THE EARLIEST ASSYRIAN KINGS.

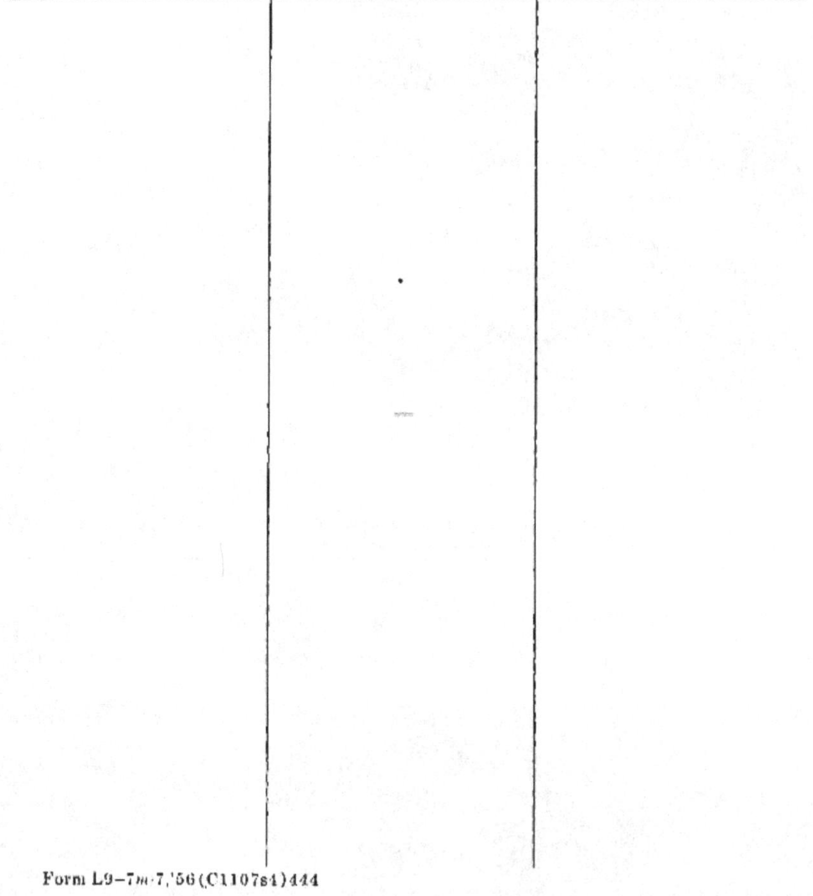

Zeitfracht Medien GmbH
Ferdinand-Jühlke-Straße 7
99095 Erfurt, Deutschland
produktsicherheit@kolibri360.de